WELSH FOLK CUSTOMS

NATIONAL MUSEUM OF WALES
WELSH FOLK MUSEUM

WELSH FOLK CUSTOMS

BY

TREFOR M. OWEN

1959
CARDIFF

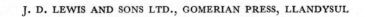
J. D. LEWIS AND SONS LTD., GOMERIAN PRESS, LLANDYSUL

CONTENTS

PREFACE

THE Welsh Folk Museum was established at St. Fagans in 1948. In its collections are included all the material relating to Welsh folk life accumulated in the National Museum of Wales in Cardiff since its incorporation in 1907. An important section of this collection was that relating to folk customs in Wales, some of which was acquired in the early days of the National Museum through the activities of the late T. H. Evans of Solfa, T. C. Evans (*Cadrawd*), T. H. Thomas and others.

It was felt that the time was now ripe to prepare an authoritative volume on Welsh folk customs, which would serve both as a handbook to the subject and as a catalogue of the national collection. This has been prepared by Mr. Trefor M. Owen, one of the Assistant Curators in the Welsh Folk Museum. The manuscript has been read by the Curator (Dr. Iorwerth C. Peate) and Professor G. J. Williams, and the former has written the Foreword.

The Museum's thanks are due to the family of the late Col. Frederick Evans (one of Cadrawd's sons) for permission to reproduce Plate 3.

National Museum of Wales　　　　D. DILWYN JOHN
Cardiff　　　　　　　　　　　　　*Director*
February 1959

FOREWORD

THE Welsh Folk Museum now (1959) exhibits a small cross-section of the national collection illustrating Welsh folk life. It is set up in a temporary gallery in the only part of the modern block of buildings so far erected. Included in it is a case devoted to folk customs and containing some two dozen specimens, whereas the number of specimens listed in this volume is 567. It is not until exhibition galleries are erected that an adequate display can be arranged. It was felt however, that a handbook dealing with the subject was badly needed now, for although much has been written in many journals on individual customs, no attempt has been made until now to bring all such studies together into one volume.

In the present study, the author has prepared a catalogue of the Folk Museum collection illustrating customs, each item being as descriptive as possible to enable the student to make full use of the material. In Chapters I—V the reader will find an integrated study of the subject based on the literature, on replies to questionnaires and on information collected in the field.

The Folk Museum staff hope to prepare a series of questionnaires on all aspects of Welsh folk life including a number on folk customs. Some have already been completed. The Curator will be glad to receive enquiries (see address below) concerning these questionnaires; answer-books will be provided for any person prepared to send replies to each, or any, questionnaire. It is proposed to establish at St. Fagans an Archive dealing with all aspects of Welsh folk life. The success of this venture will depend to a high degree upon the co-operation of helpers in all parts of Wales. Full details can be obtained from the Curator. Information concerning the existence of any custom dealt with in this volume will be welcomed.

This volume is intended to be the first of a series : others envisaged include studies of crafts, agricultural implements, furniture, costume, etc.

Welsh Folk Museum   IORWERTH C. PEATE
St. Fagans   *Curator*
Near Cardiff

INTRODUCTION

THE objects catalogued in this handbook are so different from each other that it may escape attention that they have at least one thing in common, namely a link with a folk custom found in Wales. Of these traditional customs some are associated with the various festivals and days of the calendar, while others commemorate the chief turning-points in the life of a human being ; there are several which defy neat classification and which we may conveniently term miscellaneous. Many customs which were colourful and interesting have ceased to exist and our life today is emptier and less varied for their passing. Often the material objects linked with them are all that remain to remind us of their former glory. The *dramatis personae* of each enactment of these customs are long since dead and forgotten, and we, in the middle of the twentieth century, are left with the mere gist of the play and a few odd, if significant, fragments of stage properties. In a museum gallery only the actual object can be displayed, and yet it is the vanished custom, the human action of which it once formed a part, that alone can give the object its full meaning. To understand its real significance we have to re-create the folk custom in our imagination and see it as the living whole it appeared to be to our forefathers. This is not done without some difficulty since we shall never fully recapture the feelings which were aroused by the preparations for these old customs and by their performance. The motives and expectations of the participants and their subsequent satisfaction are the ' vanished snows of yester-year ' which disappeared with the custom itself ; yet, more than in any other aspect of life portrayed by a folk museum, these qualities are the key to the significance of the material remains. The benefit men derived from the use of the objects included in this catalogue was neither the direct utilitarian satisfaction which can be had from tools and implements nor the bodily comfort provided by furniture and clothing. Since folk customs are associated less with material needs than with the intangible qualities of life, the objects used in connection with them do not of themselves tell us much

about their use and purpose. An oak dresser, a village con-
stable's truncheon, a peasant costume or a sickle each suggests
its particular function ; but who would guess from the white-
draped horse's skull what the custom of the *Mari Lwyd* was
like ? Similarly, the wren's house, the Easter-egg clappers, the
calennig orange and many other exhibits tell us nothing about
the traditional customs which they represent. It is important,
then, that a handbook cataloguing such diverse objects should
include also an account of the folk customs themselves as a help
to their understanding.

One peculiar difficulty which besets us as we try to look
objectively at discontinued folk customs and their paraphern-
alia is that we often have to make a conscious effort to see what
place they had in the life of our ancestors. We can envisage life
without them because they have no place in our own life today,
and, perhaps for this reason, when we conjure up a picture of
life in the not too distant past we do not immediately think
of these customs as being essentially a part of that life. Our
very remoteness places us at a disadvantage when we come to
interpret such customs. True, the lapse of a few generations
has given us a detachment and impartiality often missing in
people who lived nearer to the period when these customs
flourished, but nevertheless we are puzzled by the part which
they played, so archaic and irrational do they sometimes
appear, even in relation to contemporary life. We readily
assume that any attempt to interpret or ' explain ' them must
begin with a search for earlier, often conjectural, conditions
from which they can be both logically and historically derived.
The tendency is to overlook the fact that folk customs existed
side by side with less picturesque practices as part and parcel of
the same world.

A comprehensive study of folk customs would in fact take
account of both the historical and the sociological approach in
an attempt to understand why they exist and why they persist.
In this introduction a systematic treatment of the subject on
the lines of evolutionary ethnology is not attempted ; nor is an
exhaustive comparative study held to be within the scope of a
work of this character, although occasional reference is made
to the existence of like customs outside Wales. The aim, rather,

is to give a descriptive account of the customs illustrated by the collection, based on documentary evidence, and seen against their social background. In order to present as complete a picture as possible, certain traditional customs which are not represented in the Folk Museum's collection are discussed. It is hoped that an introductory account on these lines will both help the reader to understand the significance of the specimens catalogued and provide a general account of Welsh folk customs.

What do we mean by a folk custom? To answer this question it is necessary to think of this term rather more precisely than is usual among folklorists. We can begin by recognising that almost all our social life is based on habitual behaviour which is mostly inherited from the past. Now it would be absurd to hold that this constitutes a body of folk customs. Obviously in practice we distinguish between various kinds of customary behaviour. We think of certain kinds which we regard as commonplace daily or weekly occurrences deserving of no further consideration in this respect. These are customs, although we hardly ever think of them as such; to talk of going to work or catching a train or travelling by bus as customs strikes us as naïve even if logical. We reserve the term 'customs' for a different category of behaviour, and if we are further questioned on this matter we usually say that it is the picturesque or irrational or festive quality which sets them apart from the commonplace. To give an example : members of families eat several meals together every day, but we would not think in ordinary conversation of describing the practice as a folk custom. The fact that Christmas is marked by a special dinner with traditional dishes, however, distinguishes this meal from normal meals and we talk of it as an old custom, although in truth it is no older than the less picturesque routine meals. In fact, antiquity and repetition, in themselves, are not distinguishing marks of folk custom; it is rather the awareness on the part of the participants or observers that the behaviour involved in a folk custom is somewhat out of the ordinary and is called for by the singularity of the occasion. In other words, certain occasions call for certain special kinds of behaviour ; what kind of behaviour will depend on tradition and on the extent to which tradition is countered and modified by current influences. Looked at from this standpoint, folk customs appear as what may almost be called 'superfluous' behaviour, distinctively patterned on traditional lines, in which a society indulges on particular occasions. But while the behaviour is superfluous in the sense that it is over and above that required for the normal flow of everyday life, it would be unwise to over-emphasize this characteristic, for the fact that there is place for such apparently needless activity in social life in itself suggests that it is not without purpose. The superfluousness is probably more apparent than real, but nevertheless appears self-evident to an observer.

To the ethnologists and folklorists of the nineteenth century it was this 'superfluous' quality about folk customs which seemed significant. At that time the main emphasis in the study of man and his society was on an historical approach. Students aimed at reconstructing the evolution of religious ideas and forms, marriage, mythology, law, property and social institutions in general, through various stages of development from the apparently simple conditions of our primitive ancestors to the highly complicated conditions of Victorian society. To supply the details of this triumphant march of mankind, the contribution of the historian relying on written documents was supplemented by the work of scholars who were experimenting with new methods to throw light on an earlier unrecorded past. Geology and biology had both helped to show that the history of the earth and of living things was far older than had previously been realized, and even though Man had appeared rather late on the scene the new techniques of archaeology were already proving the high antiquity of the remains of his burial mounds and dwellings. Such a drastic revision of ideas about Man's ancestry coloured also the approach which ethnologists adopted in studying contemporary primitive peoples of which the western world was made increasingly aware during the colonial expansion of the nineteenth century. Here were living examples of the earlier stages of the growth of civilisation which could guide the archaeologists in their conjectural reconstruction of that side of life on which material remains were silent. Furthermore, even in civilised Western Europe, there appeared to be certain anachronisms which, like the customs of savage tribes, were obviously important evidence in the grand task of re-writing Man's history. Although folk customs and folk-lore, for the most part, were still flourishing in the middle of the nineteenth century, the emphasis in their study came to lie not on their relevance to their social setting but actually on their irrelevance. They were interesting as superfluous survivals of an earlier age, and, like geological fossils and archaeological remains, their chief importance was held to be that they could tell us about conditions of which we could otherwise hardly hope to learn anything. Of E. B. Tylor, the most important exponent of this approach, Margaret Hodgen has written ' When in him the archaeologist and folklorist combined, the mutilation of prehistoric artefact and the irrationality of rural rite were identified as imperfections of the same order, defects arising from the erosion of time ; and meaningless peasant practices were invested with the documentary significance already ascribed to ruined wall, burial urn and fossil. When again in him folklorist and ethnologist fused, village culture was accepted not only as ancestral to advanced civilisation, but, in its turn, as the legatee of savagery. . . . The assumption was suggested that folk culture fulfilled the function of a trans- mitting middle term, handing on to civilized culture traits like those of contemporary primitive people.'[1] It was because these traits were apparently misplaced in their contemporary setting that they could be identified as survivals. The question of how and why survivals survive was asked only when the underlying assumptions of Tylor and his contemporaries were re-examined in a later period and held in doubt.[2]

Even before the rise of evolutionary anthropology in the last century the peculiar character of these survivals had attracted attention. An earlier name for them, ' popular antiquities ' included, as we can see from the contents of Brand's bulky volume of that name, calendar customs, marriage, death and drinking customs, omens, charms, divination and ' vulgar

[1]M. Hodgen : *The Doctrine of Survivals*, 1936, pp. 52-3.
[2]cf. R. R. Marrett : ' Folklore and Psychology ' in *Folk-Lore*, XXV, 1914, pp. 12-33.

errors.'[1] A similar idea of the scope of this subject was held by
W. J. Thoms, the man who, in 1846, suggested the term ' folk-
lore' to replace the older 'popular antiquities.' Thoms defined
folk-lore as ' that department of the study of antiquities and
archaeology which embraces everything relating to ancient
observances and customs, to the notions, beliefs, traditions,
superstitions and prejudices of the common people.'   His
contribution in fact was not the creation of a new subject but
the giving of a new name to an old one.

Although over a century has elapsed since the term folk-lore
was suggested by W. J. Thoms, folklorists are unable to agree
on the precise delimitation of their field of study. There is no
difficulty about including tales, myths, beliefs, superstitions,
songs, riddles, proverbs and similar traditions which are handed
down by word of mouth and which live in an unwritten form in
the minds of ordinary people. The contention arises over what
else, if anything, should be included in addition to these oral
traditions. Are traditional customs, crafts, dances, ceremonies
and games also to be included as folk-lore ? A glance at the
twenty-one definitions of the term ' folk-lore ' in a recent
dictionary of the subject reveals a basic disagreement arising
from this question.[2] The argument for a wider conception of
the field of study under the alternative names of ' folk life ' or
' folk culture ' need not be pressed here, although the adoption
of a new approach on these lines would help to make things
clearer. It is necessary, however, to discuss briefly the relationship of folk-lore and folk custom at this point since the two are
patently closely connected.

The essential feature of folk-lore is that it is not only handed down by word of mouth but also that it exists in people's
minds or on their lips until it is finally written down by
collectors.   A narrow interpretation of the subject rightly
excludes traditional activities of all kinds which are not expressed solely by word of mouth, even though they may be,
like so much of our social heritage, handed down orally from
one generation to the next. Folk customs are among these

[1]John Brand : *Observations on Popular Antiquities*, Ellis's Edition 1841. The first
draft of this work was prepared for publication as early as 1795.
[2]Funk & Wagnall's *Standard Dictionary of Folk Lore*, 1949.

traditional activities which are excluded. They are essentially actions (of a particular kind) carried out by people, together or as individuals, and can be seen by an observer. They *contain* folk-lore in the form of set verses and music, but the custom consists of the singing of them rather than of what is sung. Often, too, folk-lore is the intangible background of folk customs and may help to explain the custom in terms of superstition, divination or propitiation etc.; but it is quite common for this background to be an historical rather than a contemporary one. The custom may exist for some time after the interpretative folk-lore which originally gave it meaning. Thus folk-lore can be of great help in understanding folk customs, but it includes a large body of beliefs, superstitions, sayings and similar material which is only indirectly connected with the customs practised. To understand the latter it is necessary to refer to material, economic and social conditions as well as to folk-lore. The point made here is merely that folk customs are comparable, on the one hand, to ordinary social behaviour based on custom but lacking folk-lore content, and, on the other, to folk-lore which is purely oral in expression and does not necessarily involve behaviour which can be observed. In the past, emphasis has lain almost entirely on this latter aspect. Folk customs, in brief, are closely related to folk-lore. They are often found side by side, and a knowledge of the one helps us to understand the other. Both, moreover, belong essentially to a particular way of life which was formerly prevalent in the Welsh countryside and in which forces were at work which made for their persistence.

The social setting within which both folk customs and folk-lore flourish is of a particular kind, and certain distinctive features are present which help us to understand how old customs are able to survive as living traditions. Up to the middle of the last century these conditions were present in the life of the Welsh countryside. Before the coming of the railway there had been no serious inroads on the almost self-contained life of country districts which was based on a high degree of economic subsistence. Country craftsmen made articles for local use, and most of the food eaten was produced locally, exports of surplus cattle and of certain other commodities balancing the limited imports of luxuries and goods otherwise unobtainable. Local communities did not need to open themselves up to outside influences on a large scale ; their way of life was one which turned inwards upon itself, relied on its own resources, and built up a highly integrated community which was isolated socially as well as geographically. To the countryman the most real social grouping apart from the family was his home district, a few square miles of land within which he knew intimately all the farms, houses, streams, hills and mountains, their names and the traditions and persons linked with them. This was the little world into which he was born and in which all his life would be spent. In it, too, would live nearly all the people he would ever know ; their influence on him would be more compelling than that of outsiders because it was so direct and personal, arising, as it did, from frequent contact in work, leisure and worship. Indeed, in nearly all spheres of life, the countryman would meet and mix with the same familiar persons. People living together in this intimate way in a moorland tract or a secluded valley shared the same interests and felt in a real sense that they ' belonged.' During the sheep-shearing or harvest and whenever normal family life was upset by death, confinement or illness, relations and neighbours were always at hand and ready to help. The social relationships of country folk, instead of being scattered haphazardly over a wide area and among a large number of persons, as in the industrial society of our day, were restricted to the small community within which they were repeated over and over again among the same people. The land and its way of life were a further unifying force, for although farming skills were many and varied, they were shared by most of the farmers and farm servants and even by the craftsmen and shop-keepers who were often either the sons of farmers or part-time smallholders themselves. Dividing interests based on greatly differing occupations were absent, and a common outlook on life was encouraged by the homogeneity of the local group. For although regional variations in dialect, customs, forms of recreation, foods and domestic architecture, as one would expect from the physical character of the country, were present in marked degree, there was homogeneity within the small local units. Only the landed gentry remained aloof and became increasingly estranged in both language and religion from the rest of rural society. With this important exception Welsh country life down to the middle of the 19th century, like that of other countries in western Europe was distinctly peasant-like in character.

In peasant life the factors favouring the preservation of traditional ways of doing things are interdependent and cumulative. The highly localized social life is given an intense quality by the repetitive and personal nature of the social relationships. For what is noteworthy about peasant society is the way in which a comparatively small number of people are all involved in a wide range of roles—economic, religious, recreational, administrative, ritual etc.—each of which has a better chance of bringing any two people into frequent personal contact with each other than in a complex urban community. Pressure making for conformity is so subtle and unobtrusive in such circumstances that to depart from conventional ways is inconceivable on the part of any individual. Ephemeral fashions and crazes belong to the society of the big city with its indirect and impersonal influences on individual lives. They are unthinkable in the stable peasant society where any innovation is undermined by the direct dependence of the peasant on his neighbours and relatives in so many ways. In the first instance, therefore, it is the inherent conservatism of the peasantry which keeps alive old customs ; for even though their original meaning may be lost they still have the sanction of established tradition.

There is, however, another more positive way in which the conditions of peasant life actively encourage the continuation of folk customs. As has already been suggested, peasant society in Wales was made up of numerous little communities each one enjoying a more autonomous and inward-turning social life than its ' descendant ' of today. In these circumstances, the compact little country community was not radically different from the smaller groups which sociologists have studied in detail in recent years ; indeed certain observations made in the course of this research appear to be equally applicable to peasant communities. The American sociologist G. C. Homans, in particular, has drawn attention to a tendency latent in all forms of group life which can help us to understand the recreational elements in culture. Any group of men, he points out, tends to complicate the conditions of its life and to make them more interesting. If they come together for a particular purpose, they will tend to build up their social life over and above that required by the original purpose.[1] For example, the party of farmers who meet on shearing day in the Welsh countryside is primarily a working group, but there is always an element of recreation provided at such gatherings by bantering, joking, discussion, story-telling and, formerly, ballad-singing. The day's meals are often festive, and the day itself an important social occasion. Furthermore, families which help each other in this way at shearing time often visit each other during the rest of the year, ostensibly in connection with their work but also for a chat on local events in general. What begins with an economic purpose turns out to have wider ramifications involving leisure activities also. This example refers, of course, to a particular group forming part of a community ; if we apply this approach to the whole of the little community characteristic of peasant society, we can see the folk customs which peasant conservatism maintains as providing a vehicle or outlet, sanctioned by tradition, for this elaboration upon the activities of daily life. In rather a different sense, therefore, from that meant by the evolutionary anthropologists of the nineteenth century, folk customs may be described as part of the 'superfluous' behaviour of the group-like peasant community, inherited from the past, it is true, but directly connected with the whole pattern of social life and arising naturally from it as an embroidering upon the personal, direct and frequent relationships represented by ordinary daily activities. Indeed, these same qualities of peasant society which help negatively to preserve folk customs by placing a premium on tradition also give rise to the 'superfluous' behaviour by which they find expression.

If we shift our ground slightly and look at folk customs such as the *Mari Lwyd*, the *gwylmabsant* (patronal festival), well

[1]G. C. Homans : *The Human Group*, 1951, pp. 109-10.

customs and many others, as practices which probably had a religious (if pre-Christian) origin, we can see how the change in their character was associated with two tendencies in peasant society. We have hitherto emphasised the near autonomy of the intimate little communities which made up the larger peasant society in contrast with the complexity and diffuseness of modern industrial society. This distinction is both valid and important, but if we turn to a comparison of peasant society and the isolated tribal group formerly typical of many non-European peoples, one of the significant differences now seems to be that whereas the little world of the primitive tribe is often an entity in itself, peasant society, in comparison with this antithesis of modern industrial civilization, is only a part-society.[1] True it preserves its identity and its folk-like quality in marked degree, but nevertheless it forms a part of a larger society which includes the town and trading centre, the court of a central ruling authority and its legal and administrative system, and also the creative religious, artistic and intellectual tradition of a civilization. In those respects in which little peasant communities are virtually independent we can see how folk customs are fostered, but in those respects in which they are not independent we can see the modification of the content of those customs from outside : how a primitive sacred origin of a custom is altered under the potent influence of civilized tradition disseminated by central institutions of religion, learning and political authority. Peasant tradition, in fact, was re-moulded in conformance with current notions about civilization, and what had originally been sacred became a mere diversion emptied of its religious content but perpetuated as a survival by the momentum of highly integrated peasant life.

The second tendency, closely related to the above, was the increasing assertion of what J. Huizinga has called the ' play-element ' over an original, and sometimes conjectural, religious purpose. To quote the comments of Huizinga on a period in which peasant society flourished in western Europe, ' Medieval life was brimful of play : the joyous and unbuttoned

[1]cf. R. Redfield : *The Primitive World and Its Transformations*, pp. 29-40, and A. Kroeber : *Anthropology*, 1948 edn., pp. 280-6.

play of the people, full of pagan elements that had lost their
sacred significance and been transformed into jesting and
buffoonery or the solemn and pompous play of chivalry, the
sophisticated play of courtly love. . . . In fine, the influence of
the play-spirit was extraordinarily great in the Middle Ages,
not on the inward structure of its institutions, which was
largely classical in origin, but on the ceremonial with which
that structure was expressed and embellished.'[1]

This then is the historical and sociological background of
most Welsh folk customs ; and given the continued play of
those social forces, outlined above, within the peasant community, the persistence—and modification—of these customs
is readily understandable.

Looking back from our own day at the period during which
folk customs flourished, how are we to account for their decay
and disappearance or, at best, the drastic change which has
overtaken them ? Why have folk customs which have had such
a long life finally vanished ? They were often archaic, even
when they were actively carried on, why then should they have
died ?

One explanation which has much to commend it is that
Welsh country life has become less and less peasant-like in those
characteristics which enabled old customs to linger on. No
longer are the countryside communities the intimate little
worlds they were in the last century. The railway, and later the
motor car, have broken down their comparative isolation.
Their near-subsistence has been replaced by a market economy
in which world affairs and trade conditions play a prominent
part. And people living in any rural area have more and more
relationships with people living outside their home districts
than ever before ; at the same time, local ties have been
loosened as it becomes less necessary to depend on one's
neighbours for help on the land. Local crafts are in general
decay and factory-made goods are brought in and paid for
from the sale of agricultural products. The material standard
of living has risen steadily as a result of the whole process, but
values have altered and the distinctively peasant character of

---

[1] J. Huizinga : *Homo Ludens : A Study of the Play Element in Culture*, 1949, pp. 179-80.

the countryman's life has vanished in the meantime. The vitality of peasant life, turning inwards upon itself and creating in the natural course of things a surplus of social life from its very intimacy and closeness, was sapped by the ever-widening mesh of social relationships. No longer would any custom which had lost its *rationale* continue to exist merely as a manifestation of the intimate and intense life of the peasantry : even the survival would cease to survive. At best it would only change in response to new social influences and be carried over, a shadow of a survival, into the new way of life. This seems to be why such familiar customs as, for example, those linked with Christmas time, have changed in character over the last hundred years, and why other customs, probably less amenable to adaptation, have withered away as the familiar peasant setting gives place to the more depersonalized and commercially-minded society of our day in both town and country.

Apart from this process of change in its very nature, Welsh rural society from the eighteenth century onward was being steadily influenced by the Methodist Movement. The religious reformers in their zeal attacked both harmful and harmless customs indiscriminately. Their attitude was that idle pastimes, however innocent they might appear, distracted men from their main task of searching their souls and cultivating their spiritual life in order to work out their salvation ; anything, however harmless it might seem on the surface, which stood in the way of this ideal was condemned as foolish and sinful. From the middle of the eighteenth century it was constantly impressed on the Welsh peasantry by the travelling preachers of Methodism that single-mindedness of purpose in religious matters was of paramount importance ; and apart from those old customs which were directly attacked as superstitions and ' popish,' many others were undermined by the transfer of interest to religion which led people's minds in other directions and involved them in other activities. Lady (Nesta) Evans in her study of mid eighteenth-century Anglesey has discerned a diminution of energy among the country people of the island at this time which resulted in a fading of ancient customs. ' The Methodist Revival,' she writes, ' saved Anglesey from evils other than those of which we hear from the itinerant preacher ; from lassitude and apathy in the ignorant, and a divided mind in the more thoughtful, rather than from the heedless pagan abandon of a healthy and full-blooded people.'[1] The exact relationship between the Revival and the traditional way of life in other parts of Wales, however, is a subject which has been neglected by historians ; it is possible that an analysis carried out on a broader scale would reveal subtle differences between various parts of the country according to the period during which the new religious ideas made their impact and to the character of those ideas at the time. It has been plausibly suggested that the earlier nonconformists were less antagonistic than the Methodists towards the traditional way of life of the countryside, and that this difference, in part at least, survived the process which infused the older nonconformists with the zeal of the Methodists.[2] No doubt old customs and observances for a time were to be found side by side with the newly-founded Methodist ' Societies ' and the reawakened nonconformist churches of older origin in communities torn between the attractions of two opposing worlds. Later, however, when nonconformity became a majority movement within the still largely peasant society, the ' surplus ' activity to which we referred earlier in this Introduction now arose out of the intense social life of the chapels rather than that of the community as a whole. Belonging to a chapel came to be an important factor in people's lives ; people came together more often as members of a local chapel than they did as members of the community and it was the developing secular life of the chapels that ousted the traditional customs which were alien to the Methodists' outlook on life. The social life of the chapels was not without its historical connections with the older order,[3] but it had developed out of the ideological upheaval which followed the Revival and imposed new social groupings and a new pattern of life on the Welsh peasant community.

[1]G. Nesta Evans : *Religion and Politics in Mid-Eighteenth Century Anglesey*, 1953. p. 63.
[2]R. T. Jenkins : *Bardd a'i Gefndir*, 1948, p. 7 and W. J. Gruffydd : *Owen Morgan Edwards*, 1937, p. 27.
[3]Alwyn D. Rees : *Life in a Welsh Countryside*, 1950, p. 129 and T. M. Owen : *Chapel and Community in Glan-llyn*, 1959.

The two conflicting attitudes to the place of folk customs and similar practices in the life of Wales during the first half of the nineteenth century are admirably revealed in two short comments by contemporary authors each of whom felt sincerely and passionately that his own standpoint was both right and best for the common good. The first is Edward Jones, *Bardd y Brenin* (1752—1824), a native of Merioneth who collected and published several volumes of the traditional music and poetry of Wales. To him, as we might expect, the changes which took place during his lifetime were a threat to all that he held dear. In a book published in 1802 he wrote :

> The sudden decline of the national Minstrelsy, and Customs of Wales, is in a great degree to be attributed to the fanatick impostors or illiterate plebeian preachers, who have too often been suffered to over-run the country, misleading the great part of the common people from their lawful Church ; and dissuading them from their innocent amusements, such as Singing, Dancing, and other rural Sports and Games, which heretofore they had been accustomed to delight in, from the earliest time. In the course of my excursions through the Principality, I have met with several Harpers and Songsters, who actually had been prevailed upon by those erratic strollers to relinquish their profession, from the idea that it was sinful. The consequence is, Wales, which was formerly one of the merriest and happiest countries in the World, is now become one of the dullest.[1]

Half a century later, a man of different interests and outlook wrote a book on the Religion of the Dark Ages and in it described the *Mari Lwyd* custom in order to discredit it by pointing out its origin. He was the Rev. William Roberts, *Nefydd* (1813-72) a native of Denbighshire who became a Baptist minister at Blaenau Gwent, Monmouthshire. After giving a valuable account of the custom as carried out in Monmouthshire and Glamorgan he wrote with great fervour about the need to supplant this and similar customs with more uplifting interests :

> Probably the *main*, if not the *only* cause of this adherence to these traditions is ignorance of their source. If this little essay proves the means of enlightening a few of these ignorant people the author will regard that sufficient reward for all his labour.

[1]Edward Jones : *The Bardic Museum*, 1802, p. xvi.

We must try and get the young people of our time to interest themselves more in intellectual and substantial things such as reading and composing poetry, essays, singing etc., as is encouraged and practised in our Eisteddfodau etc. I hope therefore that nobody will be so *foolish* and *ungodly* in Wales after understanding the origin and descent of these practices as to give the least support to a mixture of old Pagan and Popish ceremonies which have come down to us from the darkest ages in learning, behaviour and religion, and which have in all probability existed since Adam's day. I wish of this folly (*Mari Lwyd*), and all similar follies, that they find no place anywhere apart from the museum of the historian and antiquary.[1]

The Methodist Revival in Wales represented a force from within which worked to eliminate the less rational and useful of the traditional forms and to substitute new and acceptable forms in their place. Although these new forms were sometimes adaptations of earlier practices, as in the case of competitive meetings, choral singing, literary contests and the like, they are not true folk customs for they lack the essential antiquity of the latter. Like sports and games which were once closely linked with folk customs, they have been carried over from the old peasant society, elaborated and given a new orientation in the different conditions of our modern way of life. But a large body of folk customs has succumbed to the forces of change both sociological and religious, and the wish expressed by *Nefydd* that these ' follies ' cease to exist outside the museum has been largely fulfilled. It now remains to examine and describe the folk customs of Wales, living and extinct alike.

[1]W. Roberts, *Crefydd yr Oesoedd Tywyll neu Hynafiaethau Defodol, Chwareuol a Choelgrefyddol* . . . 1852.

CHAPTER I

THE CHRISTMAS SEASON

THE celebration of Christmastide, *Y Gwyliau*, has been observed throughout Europe from the earliest times. Primitive man had noticed that the lengthening of the days and the shorterning of the long winter nights began at this time after the winter solstice. This change in the skies was invested with a sacred significance probably associated with the worship of the sun. Each year after the winter solstice there was a heartening promise of the return of spring and summer, and of the rebirth of plant life ; the end of the critical winter season, though distant, was now certain. In ancient Rome the festival of Saturnalia was held at this time of the year and people gave presents, wore garlands of evergreen and waited upon their servants. It was also a festival of Light in which many candles were lighted and bonfires burnt. When pagan Rome took to Christianity the age-old festival was given a new meaning. It was held to commemorate the birth of Christ, the Light of the World, and ancient associations with the winter solstice were given a new symbolical significance by the Christian Church.

Christmas in Wales, as in Scotland, was at one time outshadowed by those festivities held to celebrate the New Year. In the middle of the nineteenth century, according to a north Pembrokeshire account, Christmas Day marked the beginning of a three-weeks period of holidays (*Y Gwyliau*) during which farm work was suspended. As a symbol of this the plough was carried into the home and placed under the table in the room where the meals were eaten (*rŵm ford*). Christmas Day itself was marked only by a sumptuous dinner of goose, beef and pudding etc. at the large farms in each neighbourhood to which all the other farmers and cottagers were invited. As for the rest of the holiday period till Epiphany, ' parties of men went about from house to house and were invited into the *rŵm ford*, where they sat around the table, regaling themselves with beer, which was always kept warm in small neat brass pans in every farm house ready for callers. But the peculiar custom which existed amongst these holiday-makers was that they always wetted the plough which lay dormant under the table with their beer before partaking of it themselves, thus indicating that though they had dispensed with its service for the time, they had not forgotten it, and that it would again, in due course, be brought out on the green sward and turn it.'[1]

In Cynwyl Elfed, Carmarthenshire, in the 1860's, Christmas did not mean much to the inhabitants. ' It was half Sunday and half work-day, a colourless day. People were afraid to work and avoided amusing themselves at all costs. . . . Its chief importance was that it was within a week of New Year's Day, the biggest day of the year for us children.'[2] The Christmas Season was more important than Christmas Day and the cessation of work made prolonged festivities possible.

In many parts of Wales, however, Christmas meant rising early (or staying up overnight) to attend the *plygain* service at the parish church.[3] This custom, formerly widely observed throughout Wales, has survived, in a modified form, in only a few districts.[4] From descriptions recorded by participants in the past at these services, and from the research of modern scholars such as Richards and Chancellor Fisher, it is possible to build up a fairly accurate picture of this traditional service and its setting.

The hour for the *plygain* appears to have varied between 3 a.m. and 6 a.m., the latter becoming more common as time went on. To await the service, young people, in particular, would pass away the time in one way or another. In some country districts young people would gather at certain farm-houses to make *cyflaith* (treacle toffee) and spend the night merrily, decorating the houses with holly and mistletoe, as at

---

[1]*Pembrokeshire Antiquities*, p. 47.

[2]Emlyn G. Jenkins : *Cofiant Elfed*, 1957, p. 46.

[3]*Plygain*, and its earlier forms *pylgain* and *pylgaint*, are derived from the Latin *pulli cantus*, ' cock's crow,' cf. Gwynfryn Richards, ' Y Plygain,' *Journal Historical Society Church in Wales*, I, p. 53.

[4]According to Richards, writing in 1947, the *plygain* service was still held at Llanllyfni, Caernarvonshire. It was discontinued in Llanfair Dyffryn Clwyd, Denbighshire, during the 1939-45 war because of the ' black-out,' and in Llansannan, Denbighshire, and Llancynfelyn, Cardiganshire, at the turn of the century. *ibid.*

Marford, Flintshire in the 1830's.[1] According to Mrs.
Thrale's journal of a tour in 1774 the inhabitants of Dyffryn
Clwyd kindled their lights at two in the morning and sang and
danced to the harp until the *plygain*.[2] In other districts,
especially country towns, the time was spent playing in the
streets. ' At midnight a number of boys and men on Christmas
Eve used to run up and down the street of Laugharne (Carmarthenshire) till the morning, carrying huge lighted torches,
enveloped in a covering of canvas pitched, bound firmly to a
staff, and fired. . . . They do always on Christmas Eve drive a
tar barrel with flaming torches up and down the principal
street as far as Milton Bank.'[3] Crowds behaved similarly in
Tenby, carrying torches, shouting verses and blowing cow-
horns, before finally forming a torch procession in which the
young men of the town escorted the rector from his house to
the church. The torches were extinguished in the porch and
re-lighted when the procession returned to the rectory after the
service.[4] A similar procession is recorded in Laugharne and
also in Llanfyllin, Montgomeryshire,[5] where candles were used
instead of torches.

In country districts the *plygain* at the parish church was
attended by people from even the remotest farmsteads. Often
each person brought his or her candle to help to light the church
since, until the nineteenth century, regular services were
rarely held at night-time and no provision for lighting was
usually made. The brilliant illumination from the candles of
the attenders was an important feature of the festival. In
Llanfyllin, special candles known as *canhwyllau plygain* were
made by local chandlers in the middle of the nineteenth
century. These were rather thick and had a large wick which
could withstand sudden gusts of wind during the procession to
church. They were sold in two sizes at twopence and fourpence
each.[6]

[1]*Bye-gones*, 24 December, 1901.
[2]*Bye-gones*, 12 January, 1910.
[3]Mary Curtis : *The Antiquities of Laugharne, Pendine, etc.*, 1880, p. 204.
[4]*Tales and Traditions of Tenby*, 1858, pp. 3-4.
[5]*Bye-gones*, 21 August, 1895.
[6]*Bye-gones*, 21 August, 1895.

During the service the church was decorated inside with chandeliers holding coloured candles and, in Dolgellau, for example, decked with holly.[1] In Maentwrog, Merioneth, candles were also ' fixed in sockets on the tops of slight standards or posts fastened to pews here and there in the building.'[2] In Llanfyllin ' the edifice was lighted with some hundreds of candles, placed a few inches apart from each other, around the walls inside which made the building look very brilliant.'[3] The accounts which have come down to us of *plygain* services make excessive generalisation dangerous. The detailed description of the service as held in Dolgellau[4] does not specifically mention that parishioners brought their own candles. In Maentwrog it was the ' carollers singing in the little gallery at the bell tower end of the church ' who brought their own candles for it was too dark in that part of the building to follow the service in the Common Prayer Book.[5] While no doubt the custom varied in detail from parish to parish, the brilliant illumination of the church appears to have made a lasting impression on the memories of those who have left us descriptions, and to have been a striking characteristic of the traditional *plygain*. The association between Christmas and lighted candles was to be seen in at least one Glamorgan village where no *plygain* service was held ; according to a correspondent writing in 1882, ' the village maidens as regular as Christmas came round decorated each a candle yearly and presented them to the bell-ringers, for we had no evening service. So on Christmas Eve there was quite a grand illumination in the belfry.'[6] As Richards has suggested, the spiritual significance of candle-lighting at Christmas as a symbol of the coming of the Light of the World, may be discerned in these practices. The Yule candle and Yule log in England probably have a similar significance, but it is interesting to note that in Derbyshire and Nottinghamshire at least,

---

[1]*Bye-gones*, 11 September, 1895.

[2]*Bye-gones*, 6 January, 1909.

[3]*Bye-gones*, 21 August, 1895.

[4]*Bye-gones*, 11 September, 1895.

[5]*Bye-gones*, 6 January, 1909.

[6]*Bye-gones*, 25 Jan., 1882.

the ' Yule candle is a house rather than a church decoration.'[1]

The *plygain* itself was an abbreviated form of morning service interspersed with and followed by carols sung by soloists and parties. William Payne described the *plygain* in Dolgellau as he knew it in the middle of the last century in the following words : ' Now the church is in a blaze, now crammed, body, aisles, gallery, now Shon Robert, the club-footed shoemaker, and his wife, descending from the singing seat to the lower and front part of the gallery, strike up alternately, and without artificial aid of pitch pipe, the long, long carol and old favourite describing the Worship of Kings and of the Wise Men, and the Flight into Egypt, and the terrible wickedness of Herod. The crowds are wholly silent and rapt in admiration. Then the good Rector, and his curate, David Pugh, stand up, and read the Morning Service abbreviated, finishing with the prayer for All Conditions of Men, and the benediction—restless and somewhat surging is the congregation during prayers—the Rector obliged sometimes to stop short in his office and look direct at some part or persons, but no verbal admonishment. Prayers over, the singers begin again more carols, new singers, old carols in solos, duets, trios, choruses, then silence in the audience, broken at appropriate pauses by the suppressed hum, of delight and approval, till between eight and nine, hunger telling on the singers, the Plygain is over and the Bells strike out a round peal.'[2] In Maentwrog a sermon was included in the *plygain* service, but the rector was careful to keep both sermon and service short, as he evidently felt that the chief attraction was not the service but the carolling that followed it.[3] In other places, such as Llanfair Dyffryn Clwyd, holy communion was administered during the *plygain*.[4]

The carols sung at the *plygain* were written in the traditional metres and set to old airs, including many of English origin, such as *Sweet Richard* and *Charity Mistress*, which had long been popular among Welsh ballad-singers. In preparation for the *plygain* local poets would write new carols, consisting of numer-

[1]Wright and Lones : *British Calendar Customs, England*, III, p. 217.
[2]*Bye-gones*, 11 September, 1895.
[3]*Bye-gones*, 6 January, 1909.
[4]Richards, *op. cit.*, p. 61.

ous verses on the traditional themes, which the carol-singers would memorize and sing unaccompanied in the church. In Llanllyfni as many as fifteen carols would be sung in the *plygain* at the beginning of this century.[1]

Seen against its historical background the *plygain* is a survival of a pre-reformation Christmas service modified to suit the new Protestant conditions. Richards points out that ' *plygain* ' in the sixteenth century denoted an ordinary morning service and only at a later date came to be restricted to the service held on Christmas morning. The *plygain*, he suggests, took the place of the midnight Christmas mass of the Catholic period and was originally associated with a communion service held later on Christmas morning. The practice of holding the communion service at eight o'clock ended the earlier association between the *plygain* (morning service) at six, seven or eight o'clock, and the High Mass at nine or ten o'clock. After the Reformation, carol-singing in the vernacular, which had hitherto been excluded from the Latin service of the church at Christmas, was incorporated in the early morning Christmas service, and, as nineteenth-century descriptions plainly show, had become the main attraction of the *plygain*. Chancellor Fisher has drawn attention to the similarity between the Manx festival of *Oiel Verrey*, held at midnight on Christmas Eve, and the Welsh *plygain*.[2] He points out that both became popular carol-singing festivals soon after the translation of the Bible into the respective vernacular tongues when the need arose for a hymnody in the language of everyday life.

Far from disappearing under the impact of nonconformity in the nineteenth century, the *plygain* was one of the few traditional church festivals not discarded by the chapels, at least in many parts of south Wales. Between two and three

---

[1]Richards : *op. cit.* The word *plygain* came to be so closely linked with carol-singing that it was used in some districts, such as Mallwyd and Llan-ym-mawddwy, Merioneth, to denote carolling in churches, chapels and even farmhouses on weeknights, some time after Christmas. (*Bye-gones*, 23 Feb., 1898). In a district referred to as ' in the highlands of Montgomeryshire ' a carol service held on a Sunday night after Christmas was called a *plygain*. This was at the end of the nineteenth century ; as many as thirty carols might be sung, some of them with twelve verses. (*Bye-gones*, 21 March, 1917).

[2]J. Fisher : ' Two Welsh-Manx Christmas Customs,' *Arch. Camb.* LXXXIV, 1929, pp. 308—316.

hundred candles, many of them coloured, placed on the communion table, pulpit rails, and window sills and pews would illuminate the chapels in some Glamorgan villages.[1] The women in the congregation would vie with each other to have the most ornate candle, the decorations themselves consisting of variously coloured paper strips. The candles were lit Sunday after Sunday for as long as they lasted. Indeed, the rational explanation of the *plygain* given in one of the chapels, near Wick, Glamorgan, was that it provided the chapel with cheap lighting for the evening services throughout the winter.[2] Evidence from Caernarvonshire, Merioneth and Montgomeryshire suggests that in these counties the parish church *plygain* attracted both church and chapel people, this being one of the few days when religious differences were laid aside. As a result the *plygain* was never introduced into the chapels although sometimes a simple commemorative service might be held at ten o'clock. Even where Welsh nonconformist churches did actually hold the *plygain* service, its character was changed by making it a variation of the ordinary week-night prayer-meeting.[3]

The *plygain* service, then, while having its origin in pre-reformation times, acquired its familiar character during the Protestant period when it became a kind of carol service. The rise of nonconformity led in some parts, notably Glamorgan, to the adoption of modified forms of *plygain*, but in many other parts the older non-sectarian nature of the service was maintained.

As a universal custom it ceased towards the end of the last century, although in some cases, as we have already seen, it survived to a later date. In some areas it was said that ' disorder on account of men under the influence of drink attending the Church after a night of revelry . . . put an end to the *plygain*,'[4] but it is likely that the development of a different way

[1] *Y Geninen* XXIV, 1906, p. 208.
[2] *Y Geninen*, XXIV, 1906, p. 144. The candles used in the *plygain* at the parish churches and some chapels were generally given to the parish clerks or caretakers, respectively.
[3] E. Isaac : *Coelion Cymru*, 1938, p. 179.
[4] J. C. Davies : *Folklore of West Wales*, 1911, p. 59. cf. W. Davies : ' Llên-gwerin Meirion' *National Eisteddfod Transactions*, 1898.

of celebrating Christmas was equally, if not more, responsible for the decline of this old custom.

After the *plygain*, the remainder of Christmas Day was given over to festivities. In Marford, Flintshire, the feasting began at 6 a.m. (the *plygain* there being held at 4 a.m.) and the fare consisted of hot ale and toasted bread and cheese. In this as in other districts, the yule log was burnt at Christmas, a custom which is also found in England.[1] In Dolgellau, Merioneth, guests and neighbours were invited to the Christmas breakfast after the *plygain*, the food being ' *brwes*,'[2] swig, strong ales, cakes and cold meats, goose being kept for the Christmas dinner.'[3] The topic of conversation at these small parties was the performance of the carollers and the new words written to the old carols by local poets. An elaborate Christmas pie was in some districts prepared for visitors during the Christmas celebrations. In Llansanffraid, Montgomeryshire, this consist-ed of a boned roast goose stuffed with a boiled tongue. The whole was encased in pastry lined with mincemeat and eaten cold. This dish, which was served in addition to mince pie, was intended to last the whole of the Christmas week.[4]

Apart from neighbourly visits Christmas Day was also spent in out-door activities. At Dolgellau and Maentwrog, rough-and-tumble football matches were played—one of the few occasions on which football was played—and the game lasted until dark.[5] The football-playing was less a matter of skill than of muscle, and little regard was given to the number of players on the field. Elsewhere, hunting was a popular way of spending the day. Glanffrwd relates how the youths of Llanwynno, having attended the *plygain* at the chapel, would decide to go squirrel-hunting after breakfast.[6] Dogs accompanied their masters in the chase, but the actual hunting consisted of hurling stones and sticks at the squirrel as it perched on a branch of a tree. The animal was followed from tree to tree

---

[1] *Bye-gones*, 24 December, 1901. cf. Wright and Lones : *British Calendar Customs, England*, iii, 234, 210-3.
[2] ' Oatcake steeped in broth, hot milk or water,' Geiriadur Prifysgol Cymru.
[3] *Bye-gones*, 11 September, 1895.
[4] *Bye-gones*, 31 December, 1873.
[5] *Bye-gones*, 11 September, 1895, and 6 January, 1909.
[6] Glanffrwd : *Llanwynno*, 1949 edn., p. 58-9.

and when it could no longer jump to another tree one of the
boys would climb after it taking a noose attached to a stick to
trap it. In the particular chase recorded by Glanffrwd the
poor squirrel leapt for his life and landed in the open jaws of a
waiting dog ' like a stone in a lake.' It is interesting to note that
squirrel-hunting at Christmas-time is also recorded in the New
Forest where weighted sticks were used as weapons.[1] In parts
of north Wales it was the rabbit which was hunted on Christmas
Day. In Llansilin, Denbighshire, the defendant in a case of
trespass in pursuit of game on Christmas Day maintained that
rabbit-shooting during the morning while the goose was cooking
was the custom of the country. He himself had done it regularly
for 45 years and had been under the impression that no licence
was needed for carrying a gun on that particular day only.[2]

The main features of Christmas in Wales in the first half of
the nineteenth century and earlier were, then, the early
morning *plygain*, preceded by the informal toffee-making
parties of the young folk and followed by the visits to the homes
of friends and relatives while the goose was cooking for dinner ;
the open-air sports of football and hunting added a little
diversity to a festival which was essentially sociable and
neighbourly. During the Victorian period, however, Christmas
changed gradually from an intensely social occasion in which
all the community took part to one of family celebration in the
seclusion of private houses. In the wake of this change came
many of the accoutrements of Christmas as we know it—the
Christmas card and the Christmas tree—while the earlier
observances slowly disappeared. The folk custom in the end
gave way to the commercialised holiday.

The increasing popularity of the Christmas card in the
second half of the nineteenth century, more than anything else,
reflects the changing character of Christmas celebration. From
a modest beginning in 1843 the manufacture and sale of
Christmas cards soon became an important trade. In 1880
more than $11\frac{1}{2}$ million letters over and above the ordinary
correspondence were posted during Christmas week and it is

[1]Wright and Lones, *British Calendar Customs, England*, III, 277.
[2]*Bye-gones*, 14 February, 1906.

likely that Christmas cards accounted for most of these.[1] Few
people could have anticipated the tremendous success of the
new custom and the rapid hold it gained on the public.
' Victorian cards were an integral part of the Victorian
Christmas ; they were in the focus of the most intimate annual
holiday for all ; they were carefully chosen and individually
considered by their senders and no less carefully studied in
every detail when received.'[2]

The first Christmas card, in the form we know it, was
produced in 1843 on the initiative of [Sir] Henry Cole. The
designer was John Calcott Horsley and the card was printed in
lithography and hand-coloured. Under a thousand copies
were sold at 1s. each.[3] The scene depicted in the main panel of
the card is of a family party the older members of which are
drinking a toast, presumably to the absent friend ; the side
panels show gifts of food and clothing being given to the poor.
Buday points out that it took a number of years after the first
card before the production of Christmas cards became a
profitable proposition. When this came about the cards resembled fashionable notepaper headings rather than the Cole-
Horsley card of 1843 or the later cards of the 1860's (SeePlate4),
They were ' considerably smaller in size and were in fact
"gentlemen's visiting cards" embossed and decorated with the
addition of a Christmas message, or direct descendants of the
popular valentines of the period. The function, however, was
the same : a convenient substitute for the older custom of the
Christmas letter or personal visit to convey the compliments of
the season.'[4] It must be remembered that in addition to this
desire to substitute something for the personal call there were
other contributory factors of a technical character which
popularized the Christmas card. Not only were the railways
facilitating travel over a wider area and enabling people to

[1]George Buday : *The History of the Christmas Card,* 1954, p. 6.
[2]Buday : *op. cit.,* p. 3.
[3]Buday : *op. cit.* discusses the conflicting claims to the honour of creating the
first card and concludes that that of Cole and Horsley is most credible. It is
interesting to note that a British Museum example of the 1843 Cole-Horsley card
illustrated in Buday's book is inscribed ' To his friends at Courtyrala ' and initialled
by Horsley. ' Courtyrala ' is the mansion of Cwrtyrala, Michaelston-le-pit, near
Cardiff.
[4]Buday : *op. cit.,* p. 16.

establish friendly contacts further afield than previously, but the introduction of the Penny Post in 1840 brought about a cheap and effective means of keeping in touch with distant friends and acquaintances. Not until a reliable postal system had been established could the production and sale of Christmas cards be undertaken on a large scale. The general introduction of the envelope coincided with the Penny Post, and Buday points out that previously envelopes would have been considered as enclosures or second sheets, and thus doubled the postal charges. The coming of the envelope encouraged printers to pay greater attention to the notepaper, decorating it with engraved illustrations of fashionable watering-places, resorts and similar views. Writing paper of this type may be regarded as the forerunner of the picture postcard as well as the Christmas card. In the 1830's, furthermore, the popular appeal of picture reproductions was greatly increased when George Baxter, a London wood-engraver, developed a method of colour printing suitable for the production of cheap illustrations. Buday shows how the ' colour-starved ' Victorian public which discovered a thousand and one uses for these gay or melancholy but always finely finished and brilliantly coloured trifles came to use them for Christmas greetings. ' It was only one step further from these popular usages to apply these little colour scraps and cutouts to visiting cards, either by the individual or by the manufacturer. It did not take long before the same and similar pretty colour prints, either pasted on to or printed directly on visiting cards, began to appear with the added brief greeting text, "A Merry Christmas" etc.'[1] These small cards soon acquired embossed, perforated or fringed edges and were sometimes decorated with die-stamped designs. Sometimes, too, Christmas motifs on coloured paper were mounted on embossed lace-paper which was equally suitable for valentine sheets. It must be borne in mind that valentines during the middle of the nineteenth century were far more popular and widely used than Christmas cards and that many of the printers and publishers of the latter were first and foremost producers of valentines.

[1]Buday, *op. cit.*, pp. 38-9.

In the 1870's a further fillip was given to the practice of sending Christmas cards when the half-penny postage was introduced for postcards and unsealed envelopes. By this time, too, the more personal messages had been discontinued in favour of a printed text on Christmas cards so that the lack of privacy which was a major criticism of the new postal rate for unsealed enveloped did not matter so much to either the sender or recipient. While the card became less personal in this respect the range of texts and illustrated subjects available was greatly increased by the expansion of the trade. The firm of Raphael Tuck and Son began to publish Christmas cards on a considerable scale in the early 1870's, and other firms which are known to have been producing cards in the 'sixties also expanded their trade.[1] In 1881 Tuck's Christmas-card production consisted of 180 sets representing 700 designs for that year alone.[2] In the 'seventies too, the trend was in favour of larger cards, but small folded cards were also becoming popular. The latter were often sold with decorated envelopes to match. Padded cushion or sachet cards, similar in appearance to the valentines of the period, were also in vogue and the firm of Rimmel, in particular, scented both valentines and Christmas cards of this kind with perfume. Various novelties were introduced to further the sale of cards and comic cards, often with mechanical devices, were widely bought.[3] Buday claims that from the 'seventies onwards it is possible to place in more or less accurate chronological order undated cards from the appearance, decorations and other features which varied from year to year.[4] These characteristics included multi-coloured silk fringes, ' jewelled ' embossments, cards and tassels, and silk ribbon bands tied in various ways. The designs also varied but several basic themes were apparent, often in numerous combinations. These included the Robin Redbreast, Holly and Ivy,

---

[1]These included Marcus Ward, De la Rue, and Goodall, firms which, unlike Tuck's, later abandoned the production of Christmas cards. Comprehensive lists of artists and designers, sentiment writers and publishers connected with the production of Christmas cards are given in Buday's standard *History of the Christmas Card*, pp. 213-282.

[2]Buday, *op. cit.*, p. 70.

[3]These had been produced at an earlier date, especially by the firm of Goodall, and were related to the comic valentines of the middle of the century.

[4]*op. cit.*, p. 95.

floral subjects, children, women, religious scenes and, latterly, snow landscapes with picturesque buildings or stage-coaches. These last motifs, indeed, have tended to create a particular kind of folklore of a white Christmas which is far removed from reality.

It is a far cry from the tinsel and sealing-wax Christmas of our own day to the festival of our ancestors known and enjoyed a mere century ago. Not that the celebrations entailed less activity in those seemingly distant days—quite the opposite in fact, since our forefathers sensibly spent their energy in the actual celebration rather than in the preparation. By comparison, our Christmas is a day of convalescence, well-earned, no doubt, but nevertheless something of an anticlimax after the last minute hunt for retaliatory Christmas cards and presents. In our atomized and secular culture of today we are incapable of celebrating any festival in a community fashion and our Christmas festivities have changed accordingly. Perhaps the most striking fact of all is that many people have so forgotten the old Christmas of the *plygain*, the squirrel-hunting, the toffee-making, the visiting and the local football match as to believe that the scenes depicted on our Christmas cards really represent an old-fashioned Christmas.

Boxing Day or St. Stephen's Day was in some areas commemorated by a custom which seemed cruel and barbarous to those nineteenth-century writers who recorded its existence in Wales. The custom was ' holly-beating,' that is a ' furious onslaught . . . made by men and boys, armed with large bushes of the prickly holly, on the naked and unprotected arms of female domestics and others of a like class ' until their arms bled.[1] In Tenby the ' terrors of the law ' had extinguished this custom by 1857, but it was still observed in 1879 in Llanmadog, Gower, where it was known as ' holming,' St. Stephen's Day being known as ' Holming Day.'[2] In both these places the victims were women and the perpetrators men or boys. A variation of this custom is recorded from Llansanffraid,

[1] *Tales and Traditions of Tenby*, 1858, p. 6.
[2] J. D. Davies : *Historical Notices of the Parishes of Llanmadoc and Cheriton in the Rural Deanery of West Gower Glamorganshire*, 1879, pt. II., p. 83. According to Davies, bundles of holly are called ' holms ' in Gower.

Montgomeryshire, where the last person to get up on St. Stephen's Day was whipped with a bunch of holly and nick-named ' tapster.' For the remainder of the year he was to do the behests, however menial, of all the family.[1]   Another con-tributor's evidence suggests that the custom of whipping one another's legs with holly on this day existed in Flint-shire in the early part of the nineteenth century.[2]   Two explanations of this custom have been suggested.   The first connects the bleeding with the death of St. Stephen, the first Christian martyr, which is commemorated on this day. Precisely how the link is established is not clear, and it is, as describers of the custom point out, ' no appropriate offering to the gentle Stephen.'[3]   An alternative explanation draws attention to the widespread practice of bleeding animals, especially horses, on this day and suggests that ' holming ' was associated with this.   Until 1885, at least, all animals in Llanasa, Flintshire, were bled on this day,[4] and the custom is also recorded in Herefordshire and Cheshire as well as other parts of England.[5]   An eighteenth-century note on this old practice reads as follows : ' About Christmas is a very proper time to bleed horses, for then they are commonly at house, then Spring comes on, the Sun being now coming back from the Winter Solstice, and there are three or four days of rest, and if it be upon St. Stephen's Day, it is not the worse, seeing there are with it three days' rest.'[6]   ' The periodical bleeding of livestock was believed to be good for the health and staying power of horses and other animals doing hard work '[7] and the choice of the Christmas Season was a natural one in view of the belief in the beneficial effect on health of the Sun after the winter solstice.   Apart from this consideration the symbolic significance of the first Christian martyrdom commemorated on this day was no doubt in men's minds when a rational explan-ation of an earlier custom was sought.   This would also give

[1]*Bye-gones*, 31 December, 1873.
[2]*Bye-gones*, 14 October, 1896.
[3]*Tales and Traditions of Tenby*, p. 6.
[4]*Bye-gones*, 14 October, 1896.
[5]Wright and Lones : *British Calendar Customs*, iii, 275.
[6]Brand : *Popular Antiquities*, I, 292.
[7]Wright and Lones : *loc. cit.*

some kind of ritual significance to the holming of persons, as opposed to horse-bleeding, although it does not help to account for the fact that women were always the object of the practice in Gower. It can be assumed that the notion of the beneficial effect of the sun at this time of the year was implicit in both the bleeding of horses and the holming of human beings. Indeed, it is likely that the bleeding resulting from the holming was thought to be beneficial in itself, its benefits made doubly certain by the position of the sun. Davies who records the practice of holming in Gower also refers to an old man who lived at Penmynydd in the early part of the last century who always holmed himself on this day until blood came.[1] In short, the evidence available points to a commemorative ritual supported by primitive medical and veterinary practice as a probable explanation of this custom.

With the coming of New Year's Eve and Day, the activities of the ' holidays ' reached a second climax, more important, in the past, than that of Christmas Day. An awareness of detaching one's self from the events of the immediate past and of embarking on an unforeseeable future gave the celebration of the New Year a sense of awe. Unlike the birthday anniversary of the individual it brought home to the whole community the transient nature of things and the irrevocable break with the past. Consequently the customs associated with this season of the year were those marking the completion of the activities and responsibilities of the previous year and the favourable start of the following year. Existing debts were to be repaid lest one spent the whole of the new year in debt ; and lending—even lending a light for a candle—was unlucky on New Year's Day. A man's behaviour at the beginning of the year was held to influence his behaviour throughout the succeeding twelve months ; hence to rise early on New Year's Day ensured that one would rise early throughout the whole year. Even inanimate objects and ostensibly chance occurrences were believed to be endowed with a significance on this solemn occasion in casting some light on the future. Divination and the interpretation of omens marked the Eve and the Day, just as they did

[1] W. Davies, loc. cit.

calangaeaf and *calanmai* ; people, pondering on what the future held in store for them, also became aware that the same uncertainty confronted others. But the solemnity of the occasion was also in part relieved by conviviality : concern for others was conveyed by the well-wishing and exchange of gifts which were a feature of the season. Both anxiety and relaxation found expression in the celebrations, and no doubt the intensity of the one contributed to the desirability and even the necessity of the other.

The custom of ' letting-in ' the New Year has been recorded in one form or other in many parts of the British Isles.[1] In Wales, in general, it was marked merely by the belief that good or bad luck was brought to the house by the first visitor of the new year according to his or her sex or certain personal characteristics. The details of this belief varied from district to district. In parts of Cardiganshire it was lucky for a woman to see a man first but unlucky for a man to see a woman first. In Carmarthenshire and Pembrokeshire it was unlucky for a woman to see a woman first, and in Pembrokeshire at least, for a man to see a man first. In Pen-coed, Glamorgan, it was unlucky to see a red-haired man first.[2] In Pendine, Carmarthenshire, the initial letter of the name of the first visitor was significant ; H, J and R were ' lucky letters because they denoted Happiness (or Health), Joy and Riches ; T, W and S foretold Trouble, Worry and Sorrow.[3] In south Cardiganshire and north Pembrokeshire it was the Christian names themselves that were important ; Dafydd, Ifan, Sion or Siencyn were ' lucky,' and ' if a man did not have these names the person seen first might as well be a woman if she bore one of the lucky names—Sian, Sioned, Mair and Margred.'[4] A correspondent from Montgomeryshire cited instances where little boys were paraded all through the house so as to ' break the witch ' should some girl or woman have been thoughtless enough to call.[5]

[1]Wright & Lones : *British Calendar Customs, England*, II, p. 2.
[2]*Bye-gones*, 29 September, 1897. Similar beliefs are recorded from Llandysilio, Montgomeryshire (*Bye-gones*, 17 Jan., 1900) Tenby (*Tales and Traditions of Tenby*, p. 8) and Llansawel (F. Price : *History of Llansawel*, 1898, p. 9).
[3]M. Curtis : *The Antiquites of Laugharne and Pendine*, 1880, p. 202.
[4]*Pembrokeshire Antiquities*, p. 41.
[5]*Bye-gones*, 17 January, 1900.

Related to this practice of 'letting-in' were two other customs which were concerned with the expression of good wishes for the forthcoming year. One, the collection of *calennig* (New Year's gift), is still widely observed in country areas ; the other, the 'New Year's water' custom appears to have disappeared about the turn of the century.[1]

The custom of New Year's water has been recorded principally in south Wales, especially Pembrokeshire. Early on New Year's morning, about three or four o'clock, crowds of boys visited the houses of the neighbourhood carrying with them a vessel of cold spring water, freshly drawn that morning and a twig of box, holly, myrtle or other evergreen (sometimes a branch of rosemary also). According to one account the vessel was kept out of sight. The hands and faces of every person whom they met on their rounds were sprinkled with water in return for a copper or two. In every house which they entered each room would be sprinkled with New Year's water and the inmates—who would often still be in bed—wished a Happy New Year. The doors of those houses which they were not allowed to enter were sprinkled. In Pendine, Carmarthenshire, where the custom was practised on Old New Year's Day, ' the best families would say to those they liked and respected "Bring us New Year's water". They always gave to the bringer five shillings or half a crown.'[2] While sprinkling the visitors sang (or recited) the following verse :

> Here we bring new water from the well so clear,
> For to worship God with, this Happy New Year ;
> Sing levy dew, sing levy dew, the water and the wine,
> With seven bright gold wires, the bugles that do shine ;
> Sing reign of fair maid, with gold upon her toe,
> Open you the west door, and turn the old year go ;
> Sing reign of fair maid, with gold upon her chin,
> Open you the east door, and let the new year in.[3]

[1] It is recorded as having ceased in 1873 in Pendine. cf. Curtis : *loc. cit.* But as late as 1913 in Kidwelly mothers used to sprinkle fresh water with a spray of boxwood on the faces of their sleeping children. cf. G. Evans : ' Carmarthenshire Gleanings (Kidwelly) ' *Y Cymmrodor*, Vol. **XXV**, p. 114.

[2] Curtis : *loc. cit.*

[3] Laws : *Little England*, 1888, p. 401. Among the variations are ' wives ' for ' wires ' in the fourth line and ' rain(s) ' for ' reign ' in the fifth and seventh lines, cf. Curtis : *op. cit.*, p. 203.

Mr. Francis Jones is probably correct in suggesting that the 'fair maid' represents the Virgin ; he also draws attention to the fact that the custom is practised on the Carmarthenshire—Pembrokeshire border at Llanfyrnach and Eglwys-Fair-a-Churig under the name of *dwr newy'* (lit. ' new water ').[1] The phrase ' levy dew ' has presented some difficulty to folklorists and attempted explanations have suggested that these words are corrupted from *llef i Dduw* (cry to God) or the French ' lever Dieu.'[2] One is inclined to agree with Mr. Francis Jones that ' without further forms, speculation as to the meaning of the phrase *levy dew* cannot be profitable.' The features of the custom point to a connection with an early well-cult made acceptable to medieval Christianity by its association with the Virgin and perpetuated both by the desire to wish one's neighbour well at the beginning of a new year and by the small monetary payment involved.

The giving of gifts on New Year's Day is an ancient custom once widely observed but more recently displaced by the growing importance of Christmas and Christmas presents. The collecting of *calennig* (New Year's gift) is a Welsh form of this custom. Though still extant, it is somewhat modified, having lost certain picturesque characteristics which marked it in the last century.

Like the New Year's Water custom, the collecting of *calennig* began early in the day and continued until noon. An account published in 1819 describes the custom in the following words : ' New Year is marked by all the children in the neighbourhood forming themselves in little groups and carrying from house to house their congratulations and good wishes for the health and prosperity during the ensuing year, which are symbolized by each bearing in his hand an apple stuck full of corn, variously coloured and decorated with a sprig of some evergreen, three short skewers serve as supports to the apple when not held in the hand, and a fourth serves to hold it by without destroying its many coloured honours.'[3] A later description states that the apple was studded with oats and raisins and well powdered

[1]Francis Jones : *The Holy Wells of Wales,* 1954, p. 91.
[2]*Bye-gones,* 20 January, 1892.
[3]Refers to west Glamorgan, *Gentleman's Magazine,* March 1819.

with wheaten flour, and that the prominent parts were touched
with gold leaf and sprigs of box and rosemary stuck on the top
of the apple. Half-cracked hazel nuts were attached to the ends
of the leaves so that the shells would clasp the foliage.[1] (See
Plate 6). In other districts the fruit used was an orange.[2]
Verses were sung at the door of the house and a trifling given to
the children. Sometimes the gift consisted of food which was
collected by the child in a bag carried for that purpose ; hence
the verse sung by Cardiganshire and Pembrokeshire children :

> Mi godais heddiw ma's o'm tŷ
> A'm cwd a'm pastwn gyda mi,
> A dyma'm neges ar eich traws,
> Sef llanw'm cwd â bara a chaws.[3]

Sometimes the song asked for money :

> Mi godais yn fore, mi gerddais yn ffyrnig,
> At dŷ Mr. ——— i 'mofyn am g'lennig,
> Os clywch ar eich calon roi swllt neu chwecheiniog,
> Blwyddyn newydd dda am ddimai neu geiniog.[4]

Latterly the carrying round of the apple has been discontinued and only the recitation of brief verses or greetings
and the collection of new pennies mark the custom in those
many districts where it has survived.

Literary references of seventeenth- and eighteenth-century
date show that the decorated orange stuck with cloves was often
given as a New Year's gift in England. Brand cites a remark in
the Christmas Masque of Ben Jonson, ' He has an Orange and
rosemary, but not a clove to stick in it ' ; and a later description
of New Year customs in England specially mentions decorated
apples : ' Children, to their inexpressible joy, will be drest in
their best bibs and aprons, and may be seen handed along
streets, some bearing Kentish pippins, others oranges stuck with

[1]*Bye-gones*, 28 February, 1894.
[2]*Bye-gones*, 29 September, 1897. Wirt Sykes : *British Goblins*, 1880, p. 252-5.
[3]' I came today out of my house with a bag and sticks, my errand here is to fill
my bag with bread and cheese.' *Pembrokeshire Antiquities*, p. 42 ; Ceredig Davies :
Folklore of W. Wales, p. 62.
[4]' I rose early and walked as fast as I could to ask for *calennig*, if you feel it in
your heart give a shilling or sixpence ; a happy new year for a halfpenny or a
penny.' North Cardiganshire : *Bye-gones*, 3 January, 1900.

cloves, in order to crave a blessing of their godfathers and god-mothers.'[1]   More recently the custom has been recorded in Gloucestershire, where ' the gift,' as it is called, is almost identical with the Welsh *calennig*, and in both Herefordshire and Worcestershire.[2] In Wales itself the decorated apple is not recorded as part of the *calennig* custom outside the counties of Monmouth, Glamorgan and Carmarthen.

Some of the festivities which marked New Year's Day were transferred to Old New Year's Day (*Dydd Calan Hen*), when the calendar was changed in 1752. In Carmarthenshire the practice among farmers of giving a feast to those who helped them at harvest-time was observed at the end of the last century, but this was done more often on Old New Year's Day than on the present New Year's Day (*Dydd Calan Newydd*). ' Those who had more than one place to visit would start early and go from one place to another and do justice as well as they could to the delicacies in each place. "Bread and drink" would be the first meal. They would be available as early as eleven in the morning. The geese and *poten* (pudding) would be ready by one or two o'clock, and even those who came late would not be turned away without a little *poten* and a drop of something to drink—a home-brewed drink as long as the law and its administrators allowed it. By nightfall everybody would be in a good mood, sitting together in the living-room, around the fire as far as was possible ; stories were told and verses sung, sometimes to the accompaniment of the harp, but I remember the pipe being in use in districts where the harp had left the Old New Year festival years ago.'[3]

Feasting of a similar kind took place on Old New Year's Day in the Gwaun Valley (Pembrokeshire) and was still kept up as recently as 1951.[4] In the Llandysul area, on the borders of Cardiganshire and Carmarthenshire, the day was formerly celebrated in a similar manner and with a riotous football match (*Y Bêl Ddu*). The two goals in this game were the parish

---

[1]Brand : *Popular Antiquities*, p. 9, where Brand cites ' a volume of Miscellanies in the British Museum, without title, printed in Queen Anne's time.'
[2]Wright and Lones : *British Calendar Customs, England*, II, p. 30-1.
[3]D. G. Williams : ' Casgliad o Lên Gwerin Sir Gaerfyrddin,' *Trans. Nat. Eisteddfod of Wales, Llanelly, 1895*, p. 296.
[4]*Tivyside Advertiser*, Jan. 1951.

churches of Llandysul and Llanwenog which are eight miles apart ; people on foot and on horseback took part in the play which continued until one side scored. ' They began early in the morning and by nightfall the lads were drunk and had given each other many clouts and nasty kicks. Many a lad came near to being killed too.'[1] The old custom of playing this match on Old New Year's Day was somewhat undermined when a Church Sunday School Festival was founded by the vicar of Llandysul, the Rev. Enoch James, in 1833 and held on the same date. Although opposed at first by many local people, the new festival (*Gŵyl 'Sgolion Calan Hen*) ousted the rough and tumble football game literally fought between the rival parties. The supremacy of the new religious observance was decided when one of the football players lost his life during a match. The festival in its present form consists of the catechising of thirteen Sunday schools each of which recites portions of the scriptures, and of anthems sung in turn by the thirteen choirs. The participants come from the neighbouring churches to Llandysul parish church to attend the festival. The custom is still widely supported and in 1958 celebrated its 125th anniversary.

In the ecclesiastical calendar the Feast of the Epiphany, 6th January, commemorates the manifestation of Christ to the Gentiles, and in the popular mind it has always been associated, in its religious aspect, with the Three Kings. Among the ordinary people of Wales in the last century the festival was important for two further reasons. In the first place it was commonly regarded as marking the end of the Christmas holidays—*distyll y gwyliau* (the ebb of the holidays)—although generally the festivities begun on Christmas Day lasted much longer than the nominal twelve days, sometimes indeed until Candlemas (2nd February). To mark the end of Christmastide, decorations put up at Christmas were taken down. An account of the festivals observed in Llansanffraid, Montgomeryshire, in the first half of the nineteenth century describes how the ' yule log ' was taken out and its ashes stored. ' On this day was removed from the fire place the *Cyff Nadolig*, or the yule log which

[1]W. J. Davies : *Hanes Plwyf Llandyssul*, 1896, p. 246.

had been placed with great ceremony on the fire on Christmas night, and being of large dimensions had continued burning for these twelve days. The ashes of this log were considered infallible in preventing evil, and a portion was carefully kept for the next "seedness," and was placed in the first hopper with the seed corn to act as a charm, and thus cause the corn to grow and become a fruitful crop. An old farmer living on the banks of the Verniew (i.e. Efyrnwy) went to the field forgetting to place the sacred ashes in his hopper, when the old woman, more mindful of this duty, ran shouting after her husband, "Sion, Sion, remember the *lludw cyff nos Nadolig*" (ashes of the yule log). "Ah ! Betty," said Sion, "How very fortunate for you to remember. Plague on my forgetfulness !" And having placed the ashes with the corn, Sion felt happy at the prospect of a good crop.'[1] This was not the only association, as we shall see, between Twelfth Day customs and the festivity of the crops during the coming year. The same writer also states that each of the twelve days after Christmas was thought to represent the corresponding month of the year : the first day, January, and so on. The old people carefully noted the weather on these days as a guide to the weather during the rest of the year.[2]

In another part of the country, the Vale of Glamorgan, the custom on Twelfth Night (the evening of 5th January), was to ' prepare a big loaf, or, rather a pile of cakes, in farm-houses against the Epiphany, and many harmless ceremonies were practised on the feast. The old people, who clung to ancient customs used to divide the cake, in a figurative sense, between Christ, the Virgin Mary, the Magi (or wise men) and the company.'[3] There, too, the yule log was intended to last for twelve nights. ' The King and Queen of Misrule were elected by concealing a ring in the cake, and whoever got the ring was chosen,'[4] a custom found also in England on this day.[5]

Apart from denoting the end of Christmastide in its narrower sense, 6th January was also Old Christmas Day following the introduction of the new calendar in 1752. In many districts,

---

[1]*Bye-gones*, 29 January, 1873.
[2]*op. cit.*
[3]*Bye-gones*, 26 August, 1896.
[4]*Ibid.*
[5]cf. Brand : *Popular Antiquities*, I, pp. 12-13.

such as Llansanffraid, the old festival date was tenaciously observed for over a century after the change. This association with both the beginning and the end of the Christmas holidays, while it emphasised the importance of Twelfth Day as a festival, also created no little confusion, and it is sometimes not easy to state with certainty that customs held on this date in the nineteenth century were not originally associated with Christmas itself rather than the Epiphany. Whatever the reason, there is no doubt that three of the most interesting of Welsh calendar customs were associated with Twelfth Night. These ancient customs, which flourished up till the end of the last century and which in many respects resembled each other, were the *Mari Lwyd*, wassailing, and the wren-customs.

The *Mari Lwyd* custom has been described as ' a pre-Christian horse ceremony which may be associated with similar customs spread over many parts of the world.'[1] Although it survives to our day in parts of Glamorgan and Carmarthenshire, there is evidence that it was formerly widely found throughout Wales, often in conjunction with wassail-singing.[2] It is known by other names besides *Mari Lwyd* (grey Mary) in different districts ; these include ' Horse's Head ' in Gower *Pen Ceffyl* (Horse's Head) and *Y Warsel* (' The Wassail ') in parts of Carmarthenshire, *Y March* (' The Horse ') or *Y Gynfas-farch* (' The Canvas Horse ') in Pembrokeshire. In addition the actual period during which the custom was carried on varied in different parts of the country. An account published in 1852 states that in Glamorgan and Monmouthshire the ceremony ' began on Christmas Night and was continued for a fortnight, three weeks or a month,' but in the same counties it was also specifically associated with the New Year and Twelfth Night. In Brecknock and Pembrokeshire it was associated with the New Year and in north Wales and Carmarthenshire with both Christmas and the New Year.[3] It is likely however that visits by the *Mari Lwyd* party were made over a period of several days in each case, and that the association with any

---

[1] I. C. Peate : ' Mari Lwyd : A suggested explanation,' *Man*, 43, 1943.

[2] I. C. Peate : *op. cit.* Welsh wassailing songs are discussed by Sir T. H. Parry-Williams in his introduction to *Llawysgrif Richard Morris o Gerddi* (1931).

[3] Fuller references to details are given in I. C. Peate : *op. cit.*

particular day during the Christmas Season had become exceedingly tenuous. By the nineteenth century the ritual significance of the *Mari Lwyd* had been almost completely forgotten and the religious custom had become a diversion which was felt in a vague way to be an essential part of the prolonged celebration of Christmastide. If the rival claims of Christmas and New Year's Day and the confusion brought about by the New Style of reckoning the days of the Calendar in the eighteenth century are borne in mind, the local differences in the dating of the *Mari Lwyd* and similar customs are readily understandable.

The *Mari Lwyd* itself consisted of a horse's skull which had been prepared by burying it in fresh lime[1] or which had been kept buried in the ground after the previous year's festivities.[2] Sometimes a wooden block was used instead of a horse's head.[3] The lower jaw was fixed with a spring which caused the mouth to shut with a loud snap when operated by the person carrying the *Mari*. A pole about five feet long was inserted into the horse's skull, and a white sheet draped over it. Coloured ribbons were used to decorate the skull, and bottle glass used to represent the eyes ; pieces of black cloth were sewn on to the sheet to serve as ears. The man carrying the *Mari* stood underneath the sheet, holding the pole and operating the lower jaw with a short wooden handle (Plate 2). Reins with bells attached were placed on the *Mari*'s head and held by the ' Leader ' who also carried a stick for knocking doors.

The decoration of the *Mari Lwyd* or *Cynfas-farch* as practised in the St. Davids district of Pembrokeshire was somewhat different (Plate 2). A canvas sheet a couple of yards square such as was ' used for carrying odds and ends of corn chaff etc. or the *brethyn rhawn* (horse-hair sheet) used over the kiln for drying corn . . . was sewn at one of the corners for about a yard to form a snout and head of an Ichthyosaurus or any other animal of such beauty ! The eyes were represented by large buttons and two brown harvest gloves tacked on for ears, the head tightly stuffed with straw. The man stood underneath the canvas and

[1]D. R. Phillips : *History of the Vale of Neath*, 1925, pp. 585-6.
[2]Davies : *West Gower*, II, p. 84.
[3]E. Powell : *History of Tredegar*, 1902, 118.

a long pitchfork stuck into the straw enabled him to turn the head about in every direction. It was then carried about and the first intimation often received was the sight of this prowling monster peeping around into the room, or sometimes shewing his head by pushing it through an upstairs window. One case was recorded, by my mother, of a sudden death through fright of this. It almost always created a collapse of some and the scamper of others.'[1]

No details are available of the composition of the party which accompanied the Pembrokeshire *Mari Lwyd*. In Glamorgan, however, the party was made up of the *Mari Lwyd*, the ' Leader,' ' Sergeant,' ' Merryman ' and ' Punch and Judy.' Merryman would sometimes play the fiddle, while Punch and Judy would be dressed in tattered clothes and had blackened faces. All the other members of the party (according to *Nefydd*), would be decorated with numerous ribbons and sometimes with a wide sash about their waists.[2] When the procession approached a house which it was intended to visit, the leader tapped the door while the party sang the traditional rhymes (See Plate 3). A number of different versions of the words and music sung by the *Mari Lwyd* party have been recorded ;[3] the version recorded by Nefydd[4] may be cited as an example. The party outside engaged in a battle of wits with the householders and sang *extempore* verses to which those indoors were obliged to reply in a similar manner.[5] Nefydd's example gives the verses in the form of questions and answers :—

Mari Lwyd	*People in the House*
1 Wel, dyma ni'n dwad	2 Rhowch glywed, wŷr doethion,
Gyfeillion diniwad	Pa faint ych o ddynion,
I 'mofyn am gennad—i	A pheth yn wych union—
ganu	yw'ch enwau ?

---

[1]Letter in W.F.M. from the late H. W. Evans, Solva, No. 36 in the Catalogue is a model made by Mr. Evans of the Pembrokeshire *Mari Lwyd* for the Museum.

[2]W. Roberts (*Nefydd*) : *Crefydd yr Oesoedd Tywyll*, 1852, p. 15.

[3]See the column ' Llên Gwerin Morgannwg,' in *Y Darian* (Aberdare) August, September and October, 1926. Also Maria J. Williams : *Ancient National Airs of Gwent and Morganwg*, 1844.

[4]*op. cit.*

[5]In the Nantgarw and Abercynon districts at the turn of the century the public houses used to engage a ' poet ' who would be clever enough to out-wit the *Mari Lwyd* party. If the procession entered the public house they were entitled to free drinks. Ex. inf. Mrs. Margaret Thomas, Nantgarw, and Mr. T. Evans, Abercynon. Mr. Evans adds that an hour might elapse before admission was obtained.

3 Chwech o wŷr hawddgar
Rhai gorau ar y ddaear,
I ganu mewn gwir-air—
am gwrw

4 Rhowch glywed, wŷr difrad
O ble r'ych chwi'n dwad
A pheth yw'ch gofyniad—
gaf enwi ?

5 Mae ffasiwn cwnsela
Er's mil o flynydda'
A hynny mewn ffurfia'—
gwna' brofi.

6 Mi gwnnais o'r gwely
Gan lwyr benderfynu
Y gwnawn i dy faeddu—di-ni
foddau.

7 Cenwch eich gorau
Felly gwnaf finnau
A'r sawl a fo orau—gaiff
gwrw.

8 'Dyw wiw i chwi'n scwto
A chwnnu'r *latch* heno,
Waith prydydd diguro—wyf,
gwiriaf.

9 Mae'm dawn i'n cynhyrfu
Wrth feddwl am ganu
Y nos yn y gwely—mi
goeliaf

10 I ffwrdd â chwi'r lladron
Ewch ymaith yn union,
Ni chewch chwi yn hylon—
fy ngweled.

11 Mi ganaf am wythnos
A hefyd bythefnos
A mis os bydd achos—
baidd i chwi

12 Mi ganaf am flwyddyn
Os caf Dduw i'm ca'lyn
Heb ofni un gelyn—y gwyl-
iau.

13 O tapwch y faril
Gollyngwch yn rhugil
Na fyddwch ry gynnil—i
ganwyr

14 Mae Jenkins y 'Ffeirad,
Yn dyfod, ar f'enad,
Gwna fe i chwi fynad—o
f'annedd.

15 Mae Mari Lwyd lawen
Am ddod i'ch tŷ'n rhon-
den,
A chanu yw ei diben—mi
dybiaf.

Translation :—

M.L.   1. Behold here we come, simple friends, to ask for permission to sing.

      2. Let us hear, wise men, how many of you there are, and
what exactly are your names ?

M.L.   3. Six fine men, the best in the world, to sing truly for
ale.

      4. Let us hear, honest men, where you come from and
what is your request, if I may ask ?

M.L.   5. The fashion of wassailing (has existed) for a thousand
years, and in (set) forms, as I shall prove.

      6. I rose from my bed having fully determined to win
against you.

M.L.   7. Sing your best, I shall do so too, and whoever is the best shall have ale.

       8. It is no use your pushing us or to lift the latch tonight, since I am an unbeatable rhymer.

M.L.   9. My talent is aroused as I think of singing at night in bed.

    10. Away with you, thieves, go away at once, you shall not cheerfully see me.

M.L. 11. I'll sing for a week, and a fortnight, even, or a month, if need be—there's a challenge to you.

    12. I'll sing for a year, if God is beside me, without fearing any evening during the Holidays.

M.L. 13. O tap the barrel, let it flow freely ; don't be too stingy with singers.

    14. Jenkins the parson is coming, upon my soul, he will make you leave my dwelling.

M.L. 15. Merry Mari Lwyd wants to come to your house, and to sing is her purpose, I believe.[1]

At this point, says *Nefydd*, the *Mari Lwyd* went forward, led by the reins, but before entering the house, the following verses were sung.

1 Y tylwyth teg o'r teulu
  A ddewch chwi i'r golau heb gelu,
  I weld y Wasael yn ddiaeth
  Nid oes eu bath hi'n Nghymru.

2 Mae'n berllan o lydan flodau
  O lwyrfryd hardd a lifrai
  Rhubanau gwychion brithion braf,
  A luniwyd yn ddolennau.

3 Mae'n gaseg lwysgedd wisgi
  Mae miloedd yn ei moli,
  Ei phen hi'n gnotog enwog iawn,
  O foddion llawn difaeddu.

4 Daw'r *Sergeant* gwych a'i gwmni,
  Yn wrol i'n blaenori,
  At y gwaith, mae eto i'w gael
  Wych wastad gorp'ral gwisgi.

5 Daw'r osler gyda'i gaseg
  A ledia hon yn landeg
  A'i ffrwyn a'i gyfrwy gydag 'e
  I rodio'r lle dan redeg

6 Daw hefyd Bwnsh a Shŵan
  Ar unwaith o'r un anian
  Dau filain draw'r un lliw a'r drwg
  Neu'r annedd fwg ei hunan.

[1] ' Cân cwnsela ' in the *Journal of Welsh Folk Song Soc.*, I, 30, is translated as ' Wassail Song,' but the University of Wales Dictionary omits this meaning of ' cwnsela ' and gives instead ' to take counsel together, conspire, . . . talk or converse in secrecy.'

> 7 Yn awr 'rwy'n darfod canu
> Rhowch i mi i ymborthi
> Blwyddyn newydd dda i
>   chwi i gyd
> A phawb o'r byd, serch
>   hynny.

Translation :—

1. The fair folk of the household,[1] come to the light without hiding, to see the wassail without pain, there's not one like it in Wales.
2. It is an orchard of broad flowers, beautiful indeed and liveried, marvellous speckled ribbons have been tied into bows.
3. It is a nimble comely mare ; thousands praise her ; her head is decorated with knotted strips.
4. Fine Sergeant and his company will boldly lead us ; there is also a sprightly Corporal for this work.
5. The ostler will lead his mare in, bringing his bridle and saddle with him to run about the place.
6. Punch and Judy who are kindred spirits will also come— two rogues as black as sin or hell itself.
7. Now I shall cease singing, give me something to eat. A Happy New Year to you all, and to everybody in the world for that matter.

Nefydd describes how the *Mari Lwyd* then entered the house and paid special attention to the womenfolk, nudging, blowing, neighing and biting them, besides talking. ' Merryman ' brought his fiddle in and performed all manner of tricks ; then, after him came Judy (*Siwan*) with the broom in her hand for cleaning the hearth. Punch then entered, threw Judy on to the floor and ran around kissing the women-folk while Judy chased him with her broom. Having sung, danced and played about, the party sat down to food and drink. Later, on their departure, the following verse was sung :

> Dymunwn ich lawenydd
> I gynnal blwyddyn newydd
> Tra paro'r gŵr i dincian cloch
> Well, well y boch chwi beunydd.

[We wish you joy to live a new year ; as long as the man tinkles his bell, may you improve daily.]

---

[1] *Tylwyth teg* also means ' fairies.'

Nefydd explains the reference to the bell by a footnote : ' as long as the church bell rings ' but is possible that Punch carried a small bell as part of his costume.

Several attempts have been made to explain the *Mari Lwyd* custom and its peculiar name. The question has been discussed in detail by Dr. Iorwerth C. Peate in an article to which reference has already been made.[1] The derivation from the English ' Merry Lude ' is rejected by Dr. Peate on linguistic grounds, and the connection with *Morris* dance and its hobby horse is held to be superficial. It is worthy of note, however, that in an account published in 1819 the local pronunciation of ' Morris dancers ' in west Glamorgan is given as ' Merry Dancers ' and that the dancing party, which proceeded from house to house dancing in each a sort of reel, frequently included a Punch and Judy, as in the *Mari Lwyd* party. In the same district, the article points out the name ' *Aderyn bee y llwyd* ' (' grey magpie,' translated by the writer as ' bird with the grey beak ') was given to the horse's head, and the custom is described as ' evidently the hobby-horse detached from the Morris Dance.'[2] It is clear that the writer of this account had no doubt that the horse's head custom was quite separate from the Morris dancing despite the similarity of the two practices and the fact that both were carried on in the same district. The name ' *aderyn bee y llwyd* ' for the horse's head custom may well be a mistake, for M. J. Williams of Aberpergwm in her *Ancient National Airs of Gwent and Morganwg* (1844) in a note on a wassail song describes the *Aderyn Pica Llwyd* as an artificial bird on a representation of a tree (from which hang apples and oranges) carried around by a member of the horse's head party. Another interesting point is that the contributor of the *Gentleman's Magazine* account describes the three members of the ' merry dancers ' as having short jackets which, as well as their hats, were decorated with a profusion of paper ornaments, while M. J. Williams states that the Twelfth Night wassailers, one of whom carried the horse's head, were ' fantastically dressed with ribbons of various colours.' It is evident that there were definite similarities between what were probably at first

[1] *Op. cit.*
[2] *Gentleman's Magazine*, March 1819.

distinct customs, but neither the name nor the practice of the *Mari Lwyd* can be safely attributed to the Morris dance.

The *mari* in *Mari Lwyd* is (Dr. Peate suggests) from the English ' mare ' which was, as in ' nightmare,' a female monster supposed to settle upon people to pound them to suffocation. As Dr. Peate points out, there is much to commend such an explanation, for the mediaeval pronunciation of the word ' mare ' in English was ' mari.' ' Lwyd ' would thus have its ordinary meaning of ' grey.' In yet another suggested explanation in which the word ' *mari* ' is equated with ' Mary,' *lwyd* is construed as ' holy ' by analogy with medieval expressions such as *Duw lwyd* [Holy God] which are, however, as far as is known, literary rather than spoken terms. Dr. Peate suggests after reviewing the evidence, that ' whether the name means "mare" or "Mary", the custom came to be associated with Mary-ritual.'[1] He substantiates this claim by citing evidence contained in some seventeenth-century wassail songs (*carolau gwirod*) which commemorate *Gŵyl Fair y Canhwyllau* (The Festival of St. Mary of the Candles, the 2nd February). One such wassail song, probably by Gruffydd Phylip, includes the following stanzas :

Roedd yn ddefod mynd a gwirod
Gŵyl fair forwyn ddechre gwanwyn

Pob dyn dedwydd, trwy lawenydd
A garo goffa Mair merch Anna . . .

Fe aned i hon fab Duw Cyfion
Ddydd Nadolig Gŵyl Barchedig.

Gŵyl fair hefyd sydd ŵyl hyfryd
Mair yn gymwys aeth i'r Eglwys.

A gwyryfon o'r cwmpason
Ai canhwylle i gyd yn ole.

Puredigaeth Mair yn odieth,
Pawb ai wirod iw chyfarfod.

Os rhydd Duw tad ini genad
Ni yfwn wirod hyd y gwaelod.

Ni yfwn Iechyd haelion hefyd
Heb fod mor sôn am gybyddion. . . .

[1] *op. cit.*

['It was a custom to bear drink at the Festival of the Virgin Mary at the beginning of Spring. Every happy man loves to remember with joy Mary the daughter of Anna. . . . To her was born the Son of the Just God on Christmas Day, revered festival. The Festival of Mary too is a delightful festival. Mary went meetly to the church, with virgins from the locality, their candles all alight. The purification of Mary, all with their drink meeting her. If God the Father gives us permission, we shall drink to the dregs. We shall drink the Health of the generous without any mention of the misers . . .']

Dr. Peate draws attention to the association of the 'bearing of drink' in this song with 'the beginning of Spring and to the commemoration of Mary's Purification' which is furthermore linked with the 'revered festival' of Christmas. The act of Purification, suggests Dr. Peate, may be associated with the idea behind 'wassailing' ('be whole, be healthy'). He concludes that the 'drinking to Mary' was customary during the period from Christmas Day to the 2nd February and correlates this with the evidence that the *Mari Lwyd* in Glamorgan 'began on Christmas night and was continued for . . . a month.' The similarity between the introductory phrases of the wassail songs commemorating Mary, and the *Mari Lwyd* verses is emphasized, and also the fact that some of the wassail songs contain the phrases 'open the windows,' and 'open the closed doors' which are reminiscent of the manner in which the *Mari Lwyd* party has to beg for admittance. The pre-Christian wassailing custom initiating the spring became the medieval custom of 'singing to Mary' with which an earlier horse-custom was also associated, and possibly some elements of medieval Miracle Plays such as Merryman and Sergeant.

While the age-old practice of wassailing was probably an early element in the development of the *Mari Lwyd* ceremony, as Dr. Peate suggests, it was not exclusively linked to the Mary-ritual. Christmas and the New Year were marked by wassailing in which neither the content of songs nor the form of the custom allude to the Virgin Mary. It may be that references to Mary were frowned upon after the Reformation and were eventually left out, but it is more likely that the Christmas and New Year wassailing were never closely associated with Mary. There are numerous wassail songs which contain no religious

references at all but merely describe the custom, the condition
of the singers and what they would like to have. A seventeenth
century wassail song quoted by Parry-Williams begins :

> Arfer y nydolig yw
> Rhodio/r/ nos lle bytho gwiw
> i edrych ple bo diod dda . . .

[The custom of Christmas is to wander during the night where it
is proper to find where there is good drink . . .][1]

Probably the custom meant no more to the wassailers than free
ale and hospitality preceded by the traditional verses seeking
admittance. The common practice of wishing the benefactor
fertile crops on his land and the increase of his livestock during
the coming year represents the true mark of the wassail
ceremony, the link with Mary in the *Mari Lwyd* would appear
to derive from a later, mediaeval, tradition.

As an example of a wassail ceremony in early nineteenth
century Wales, the account given by Hugh Hughes may be
quoted :[2]

> An old custom among the Welsh on Twelfth Night was the
> making of the wassail, namely, cakes and apples baked and set in
> rows on top of each other, with sugar between, in a kind of
> beautiful bowl which had been made for the purpose and which
> had twelve handles. Then warm beer, mixed with hot spices
> from India, was put in the wassail, and the friends sat around in a
> circle near the fire and passed the wassail bowl from hand to
> hand, each drinking in turn. Lastly the wassail (namely the cakes
> and apples after the beer covering them had been drunk) was
> shared among the whole company.
>
>   On Twelfth Night the wassail was taken to the house of a husband
> and wife who had recently married or a family which had moved
> from one house to another.[3] Several lads and lasses from the
> neighbourhood would bring the wassail to the door of the said
> house and begin to sing outside the closed door.

Hughes then quotes the twelve verses sung alternately by the
wassailers and the party indoors, and also the stanzas sung in

[1]T. H. Parry-Williams : *Llawysgrif Richard Morris o Gerddi*, 1931, p. lxxiii.
[2]H. Hughes : *Yr Hynafion Cymreig*, 1823, pp. 239—242. Hughes's book is a Welsh
translation of Peter Roberts, *The Cambrian Popular Antiquities*, 1815, but includes
additional material, including this description.
   [3]This latter point is also made by W. Howells : *Cambrian Superstitions*, 1831, p. 81,
where the custom is compared with house-warming.

the house on admittance and on leaving. The song is too long to print, but reference may be made to certain interesting features it contains which throw light on the custom.

One point of interest is the description, in verse, of the object or objects carried by the wassailers. Hughes himself does not allude to anything besides the wassail bowl with its looped handles. The song, however, includes the following couplet :

> Mae gennym elor hynod, a drywod dan y llen
> A pherllan wych o afalau yn gyplau uwch ei phen

[We have a remarkable bier, with wrens under the sheet, and a fine orchard of apples in couples above it.]

The significance of the reference to the wrens—especially in a Twelfth Night custom—will be apparent when the ritual of hunting the wren and the wren-house procession are discussed in the following pages. For the moment it is sufficient to draw attention to the *perllan* or orchard mentioned in the couplet which has its counterpart in a custom recorded in Kidwelly, Carmarthenshire, again as part of a wassail ceremony,[1] and in Llandybïe, in the same county, apparently as a custom on its own. This custom (or object) is also called by the name ' *perllan*.'

In the Kidwelly district the *perllan* was ' a small rectangular board with a circle marked in the centre and ribs of wood running from the centre to each of the four angles. At each corner of the board an apple was fixed, and within the circle a tree with a miniature bird thereon.'[2] An example of a *perllan* in its ' oldest and most correct form ' was made for the Museum in Llandybïe in 1914 and is described in the Catalogue (No. 28). While no description of the actual custom in the Llandybïe district has come down to us,[3] in Kidwelly the *perllan* was taken round one New Year's Day by a group of young men, one of

[1]The similarity to the *Aderyn Pica Llwyd*, referred to by Maria Jane Williams (cf. p. 55 supra) is also evident.

[2]This description was given in 1915 or earlier by a man who had carried the *perllan* in the Kidwelly district for many years. G. Evans : ' Carmarthenshire Gleanings (Kidwelly),' *Y Cymmrodor*, XXV, 1915, p. 114.

[3]The Rev. Gomer M. Roberts, M.A., the author of the parish history of Llandybïe informs me that he has no information about the existence of the *perllan* custom in Llandybïe. Letter dated 19.11.57.

whom carried the *perllan* itself while another bore ' a large cup full of beer,' in fact a wassail bowl. In the form recorded by Evans the verses do not form a poetic contest similar to that which accompanied the *Mari Lwyd* ceremony, and referred to in Hughes's account of wassailing. Moreover the *perllan* custom in Kidwelly existed alongside the *Mari Lwyd* which was ' exceedingly popular ' in the district, and, like the *perllan*, held on New Year's Day.

The song which accompanied the *perllan* ceremony included a similar reference to that noted in Hughes's account :

> A chyda ni mae perllan, a dryw bach ynddi'n hedfan
> Rheolwr pob adar yw hwnnw.

> [And with us we have a *perllan* with a little wren flying in it ; he is the ruler of all birds.]

It would appear that the verse quoted by Hughes referred to a *perllan* of the kind recorded in Kidwelly ; the references to wrens in both examples, and in particular the allusion to the wren as the ' ruler of all birds ' suggests an affinity also to the wren-cult here found in a modified and subdued form and subordinate to another custom.

Another possibility exists which, if true, helps to explain Hughes's omission of any reference to the *perllan* although the actual wassail bowl is included in his description. Three of the four examples of wassail bowls in the Welsh Folk Museum's collection have, in addition to the looped handles, decorated lids with motifs which include birds, berries, oak-leaves and other figures.[1] These examples are of Ewenny ware and possibly represent an attempt to reproduce in ceramic form the features of the *perllan*.[2] An earlier wassail bowl in the Museum's collection (No. 38) is made of *lignum vitae* and is much less elaborate in appearance. While any attempt to formulate a chronological sequence on the basis of such slender evidence is not justifiable, it is possible that this early eighteenth-century example

[1]Nos. 39, 40, 41 in the Catalogue (see Plate I).
[2]It is interesting to note that the *Mari Lwyd* verses as given by Nefydd and quoted on another page describe the wassail as being ' an orchard (*perllan*) of broad flowers with fine ribbons tied into bows.' Cf. p. 53 supra.

represents the traditional wooden vessel taken around during the wassailing season. A Gower wassail-song, for instance, mentions that the bowl carried is of 'elberry bough'[1] and even in the Vale of Glamorgan the wassail bowl of local Ewenny ware was by no means universal. A nineteenth-century observer writes : 'They (i.e. the wassailers) should by right have with them a wassail-bowl, or that which is, I believe, its proper Glamorganshire substitute, namely a feol (recte *ffiol*) made of Ewenni ware ; but the "survival" of these articles within the time to which my own memory extends was a common bucket, or even, it might be, a tin can ! '[2] It seems likely that the Ewenny wassail-bowls were a local form found in the Vale of Glamorgan and incorporating ornamental features which had earlier been separately displayed in the *perllan*.

Another feature of interest contained in the Wassail song recorded by Hughes, and found generally in singing of this kind, is the verse sung on departing, in which the visitors wish the benefactor and his family fertility and long life :

> Hir einioes a hir ddyddiau a hir flynyddau hardd
> A gaffoch i fyw'n ffrwythlon fel pur blanhigion gardd,
> Gael gweled plant ac wyrion yn llawnion yn un llu,
> A thyma ni'n ymadael, ffarwel yn iach i chwi.

[Long life, long days and long beautiful years may you have ; to live a fruitful life like pure garden plants, to see many children and grand—children, and now we leave you, farewell !]

Similar instances may be cited from Gower[3] where the wassailers drink the health of the farmer's cow and wish its owner ' a good crop of corn, both barley and oats and all sorts of grain ' as well as a long life. These elements are in keeping with the wassail tradition not only in Wales but in England also.[4]

---

[1] J. D. Davies : *Historical Notices of the Parishes of Llanmadoc and Cheriton in the Rural Deanery of West Gower, Glamorganshire*, 1879, pt. II, pp. 87f.
[2] David Jones (of Wallington) : ' The Mari Lwyd : a Twelfth Night Custom ' *Arch. Camb.*, 1888, pp. 389—394.
[3] J. D. Davies : *loc. cit.*
[4] The wassailing of apple trees was practised in the early nineteenth century in Cornwall and Sussex to induce bountiful crops. cf. Wright & Lones : *British Calendar Customs, England*, III, p. 235·7. A wassail song recorded in Wiltshire includes the line ' God send our master a good crop of corn,' *op. cit.*, p. 224, cf. also p. 59 (Herefordshire and Worcestershire).

Although wassailing and the *Mari Lwyd* are sometimes found together as a single composite custom, there is evidence which indicates that the two ancient ceremonies might exist, in the same district, as two distinct customs carried on during the Christmas season. We have already seen how the *perllan* custom, a form of wassailing, existed independently of the *Mari Lwyd* in Kidwelly. The same is true of the two rites in the Gower peninsula[1] and, if we accept the evidence of David Jones, in the Vale of Glamorgan. Jones distinguishes between ' singing *gwasseila* ' and the *Mari Lwyd* thus : ' But, while the *gwasseilwyr* proper needed not to trouble themselves with providing a *Mari Lwyd* those who went about with a *Mari Lwyd* were perforce obliged to sing *Gwasseila*.'[2] His description of the wassailers points to a similarity between the two varieties ; the wassailers who went around blackened their faces, wore rough masks, or disguised themselves in any way as best they could. One of them in women's clothes played ' Bessy ' and carried a besom ; the others carried staves and the party, once admitted, belaboured each other's sides and backs. They were, however, well protected by straw stuffed under their garments. In general the procedure agrees with that of the *Mari Lwyd* as described by Nefydd, with the exception, of course, of the horse's head.[3] Jones's categorical distinction between the two types of parties is interesting in view of a like difference in Gower and Carmarthenshire ; the way in which it is framed suggests that the *Mari Lwyd* was a variant of the wassail ceremony in which a horse-cult element was incorporated, possibly under the guise of Mary-ritual. Dr. Peate's point that ' surviving evidence proves this ' (i.e. the distinction between the wassailers and the *Mari Lwyd*) ' to have been the general rule ' and that all the traditional verses include requests for drink, does not preclude the possibility that the *Mari Lwyd* and wassailing were in certain districts quite separate, just as the English ' hobby horse,' an equally ancient custom, was distinct from wassailing in all known examples. The surviving evidence

---

[1] J. D. Davies : *op. cit.*, II, pp. 84ff.

[2] D. Jones : *Arch. Camb.*, 1888, pp. 389—394.

[3] Nefydd describes Judy, for example, as having a broom ; she was obviously the counterpart of ' Bessy.'

suggests that local variations were formerly numerous in Wales. The content of the custom, where it has been recorded, differed in different areas, and the date with which it was associated also varied. Moreover certain elements in wassailing which are found in the *Mari Lwyd* ceremony are also similar to those in the historically distinct wren-cult rites which are discussed in the next paragraphs.

Another ancient practice associated with Twelfth Night, which has puzzled the ethnologist, is that of hunting the wren and the related custom of carrying a wren from door to door in a ' wren-house.' Although certain sources of information about these customs in the nineteenth century suggest that two distinct practices are involved, it is more likely that the survivals which were recorded were formerly part of a single ceremony comprising both hunt and procession. Regional versions of the songs sung at wren processions (recorded as folk songs by members of the Welsh Folk Song Society) suggest that the practice was more widely spread throughout Wales than is usually realised. These local variations were recorded in Llanrhaeadr-ym-Mochnant (on the borders of Denbighshire and Montgomeryshire), Amlwch (Anglesey), Denbigh, Llwyngwril (Merioneth), Llŷn (Caernarvonshire) and in many parts of Pembrokeshire.[1] Furthermore, similar customs have been recorded outside Wales in places as far apart as southern France, Brittany, the Isle of Man, southern Ireland and Essex.[2]

An early description of the custom in Pembrokeshire is that given by Edward Lhuyd (1660—1709) in his *Parochialia*. He writes ' Arverant yn swydh Benfro &c. dhwyn driw mewn elor nos ystwylh ; odhiwrth gwr Ivank at i Gariad, sef day nae dri ai dygant mewn elor a ribane ; ag a ganant gorolion. Ant hevyd i day ereilh lhe ni bo kariadon a bydh kwrw v. &c. A elor o'r wlad ai galwant Kwlli (*sic*. Kwtti) wran.' [They are accustomed in Pembrokeshire etc. to carry a wren in a bier on Twelfth Night ; from a young man to his sweetheart, that is two or three bear it in a bier (covered) with ribbons, and sing carols.

[1]Llew Tegid : ' Hunting the Wren,' *JWFSS*, I, pp. 99—113.
[2]Brand : *Popular Antiquities*, iii, p. 103 ; Hone's *Year Book*, 1832, col. 1608 ; Wright and Lones : *British Calendar Customs, England*, III, p. 276, *Arch. Camb.*, 1859, p. 184.

They also go to other houses where there are no sweethearts and there will be beer etc. And a bier from the country they call Cutty Wran.][1] Some of the main features of the custom are referred to in this description : the link with Twelfth Night, the decorated bier carried by two or three bearers, carol-singing and the name ' Cutty Wren.'[2] These elements were still to be found in the Pembrokeshire countryside in the nine-teenth century, and the Folk Museum's collection includes a wren-house from Marloes in that county which was made in 1869[3] (No. 47, Plate 5). Like the elor or ' bier ' described by Lhuwyd it is decorated with ribbons and was carried in pro-cession on Twelfth Night, the wren having been caught and imprisoned beforehand. The song sung was as follows :—

> Joy, health, love and peace ; we're here in this place ;
> By your leave here we sing concerning our King.
> Our King is well drest in silks of the best
> And the ribbons so rare, no King can compare.
> Over hedges and stiles we have travelled many miles.
> We were four foot-men in taking this wren.
> We were four at watch and were nigh of a match
> Now Christmas is past, Twelfth Day is the last.
> To the old year adieu, great joy to the new.
> Please turn the King in.

In the same county the custom is also recorded in Tenby where the details were as follows : ' Having procured a wren, and placed it in a small ornamented box, or paper house, with a square of glass at either end, two or four men would carry it about, elevated on four poles fixed to the corners, singing the while a long ditty. . . . The four men would then enter the doorway, groaning under the weight of their burden, and looking as if they had just relieved Atlas of his shoulder-piece.' The song sung in Tenby included the following verses :

> 1. O ! where are you going ? says Milder to Melder,
>   O ! where are you going ? says the younger to the elder,
>   O ! I cannot tell you, says Festel to Fose,
>   We're going to the woods, says John the Red Nose.

[1] *Arch. Camb.*, 1910, p. 82, translated by Dr. I. C. Peate : ' The Wren in Welsh Folklore,' *Man* 1936.
[2] ' Cutty ' = little.
[3] No. 47 in the Catalogue.

2. O ! what will you do there ? . . . Shoot the Cutty Wren.
3. O ! what will you shoot her with ? . . . With bows and with arrows.
4. O ! that will not do. . . . With great guns and cannons.
5. O ! what will you bring her home in ? . . . On four strong men's shoulders.
6. O ! that will not do . . . On big carts and waggons.
7. What will you cut her up with? . . . With knives and with forks.
8. O ! that will not do . . . With hatchets and cleavers.
9. What will you boil her in ? . . . In pots and in kettles.
10. O ! that will not do . . . In brass pans and cauldrons.[1]

Versions of the wren-song which have been recorded in Welsh-speaking districts in Wales resemble the Tenby song rather than that noted in Marloes. The words as sung in Llanrhaeadr-ym-Mochnant may be quoted as an example of a Welsh wren-song :

1. Ddoi di i'r coed ? meddai Dibin wrth Dobin
Ddoi di i'r coed ? meddai Rhisiart wrth Robin,
A ddoi di i'r coed ? meddai Siôn wrth y tri,
A ddoi di i'r coed ? meddai'r cwbwl i gyd.

[Wilt thou come to the wood ? said Dibin to Dobin
Wilt thou come to the wood ? said Richard to Robin
Wilt thou come to the wood ? said John to the three ;
Wilt thou come to the wood ? said all of them.]

2. Beth wnawn ni yno ? etc. [What shall we do there ? etc.]
3. Hela'r Dryw bach etc. [Hunt the little wren, etc.]
4. Beth wnawn ni ag efo ? etc. [What shall we do with him ? etc.]
5. Ei werthu am swllt, etc. [Sell him for a shilling, etc.]
6. Beth wnawn ni â swllt ? etc. [What shall we do with a shilling ? etc.]
7. Ei wario am gwrw, etc. [Spend it on beer, etc.]
8. Beth 'tae'n ni'n meddwi ? etc. [What if we became drunk ? etc.]
9. [not recorded]
10. Beth 'tae'n ni'n marw ? etc. [What if we died ? etc.]
11. [Not recorded]
12. Ple caem ein claddu ? etc. [Where should we be buried ? etc.]
13. Ym mhwll y domen, etc. [In the dunghill pit, etc.][2]

[1] *Tales and Traditions of Tenby*, 1858, pp. 12-16.
[2] Translated by Dr. I. C. Peate from Llew Tegid's words in *JWFFS*, I, p. 107.

The other versions which have been recorded by the Welsh Folk-Song Society are basically similar to the Llanrhaeadr song. Unfortunately no feature of the custom other than the song has been recorded in Wales outside Pembrokeshire, but a note accompanying the above version states that it was taken down in 1876 (or earlier) from the lips of an illiterate farm labourer in the neighbourhood of Cwm-du, Llanrhaeadr-ym-Mochnant. 'He used to render it in a kind of chant exceedingly interesting to listen to, and often have I seen his fellow servants crowding to the stable-loft to hear him sing *and to see him act it.*[1] This suggests that some fragment of the action involved in the custom (besides the song) was still remembered in the district as late as 1876 but that it was by then a rarity unknown to many farm servants. We may assume that in the other parts of Wales where no details of the custom have survived, the song outlived the actual custom and testifies to its former existence.

Further details about the custom are known from Pembrokeshire. In the Solva district about 1890, when a house was not available, a lantern decked with ribbons was substituted. Sometimes too a sparrow would be used if a wren could not be obtained. The song recorded in this district was different and resembles the Marloes version rather than the versions recorded in Tenby (and other parts of Pembrokeshire) and other Welsh-speaking districts outside the county :[2]

1. Dryw bach ydyw'r gŵr, amdano mae stŵr,
   Mae cwest arno fe, nos heno 'mhob lle.

2. Fe ddaliwyd y gwalch, oedd neithiwr yn falch :
   Mewn stafell wen deg, a'i dri brawd ar ddeg.

3. Fe dorrwyd i'r tŵr a daliwyd y gŵr :
   Fe'i rhoddwyd dan len ar elor fraith wen.

4. Rhubanau bob lliw sy o gwmpas y Dryw,
   Rhubanau dri thro sy arno'n lle to.

5. Mae'r Drywod yn sgant, hedasant i bant
   Ond deuant yn ôl trwy lwybrau'r hen ddôl.

[1] *JWFSS, loc. cit.* (my italics).
[2] Ex. inf. H. W. Evans, Solva.

6. O, meistres fach fwyn, gwrandewch ar ein cŵyn :
   Plant ieuainc ym mi ; gollyngwch ni i'r tŷ.
   Agorwch yn glou, ynte dyma ni'n ffoi.

[1. A little wren is the fellow about whom there is commotion,
   There is an inquest on him tonight everywhere.

2. The rogue who was proud last night is now caught in a fair
   white room with his thirteen brothers.

3. The tower was broken into and the fellow caught :
   He was placed under a sheet on a white bier of many colours.

4. Ribbons of all colours encircle the wren, ribbons in
   three turns enclose him instead of a roof.

5. Wrens are scarce, they flew away, but they will return
   along the old meadow's paths.

6. O dear kind mistress, listen to our plea :
   We are young children, let us into the house.
   Open quickly or we flee.[1]]

Further knowledge about the custom is given by the Rev. D.
Silvan Evans (1818—1903)[2] in a general account which,
unfortunately, specifies no particular district in Wales. The
custom he tells us, was practised during the Christmas Holidays
ending with the Epiphany, ' distyll y gwyliau ' or the ebb of the
holidays. It was carried on by young men, not necessarily boys,
and it was strictly a nightly performance. The company
visited the abodes of such couples as had been married within
the year. As the verse sung indicates, a sparrow could be
substituted for a wren :

Dyma'r dryw, os yw e'n fyw
Neu dderyn to, i gael ei rostio.

[Here is a wren, if it is alive, or a sparrow to be roasted.]

' The husband, if agreeable, would admit the party and regale
them with plenty of Christmas ale.' If they were not admitted,
the following verse was sung :

[1]Recorded by H. W. Evans, cf. *Pembrokeshire Antiquities*, 1897, pp. 48-9, Translation by Dr. I. C. Peate, *loc. cit.*
[2]cf. *Bye-Gones*, 22 April, 1885. Evans, who was a well-known lexicographer, was
a native of Llanarth, in south Cardiganshire, and was educated at Neuadd-lwyd
School nearby. It is possible that his account describes the custom in his native
district, but there is no evidence to corroborate such a statement.

Gwynt ffralwm ddelo'n hwthwm,
I droi'r tŷ a'i wyneb fyny.

[May a raging wind come suddenly to turn the house upside
down.]

Evans's description throws some light on the obscure reference
to sweethearts which is contained in Edward Lhuyd's seventeenth-century reference.   However, why the wren-party
should not visit newly-weds of less than a year's standing, is not
at all clear. It is certain that this basis for choosing houses to
visit was not common to all Pembrokeshire, for another
account points out that ' those who took the little bird and
sang were invited by the farmer and especially their wives to
visit their homes on *Gŵyl Ystwyll*.'[1]

The reward in this case was money (' half a crown or more ')
and not drink, and the party came early, before the husband
and wife rose, and sprinkled water over them as they lay in bed.
While this particular variant is in one respect reminiscent of
the New Year's Water Sprinkling, it also tallies with the account
given by Silvan Evans (and Lhuyd's earlier description) in that
the wren-party's visit, it is hinted, is something which married
couples should welcome. This vague point, which may well be
related to fertility, is also suggested by the wassail song recorded
in Hughes's *Hynafion Cymreig*, in which, it will be recalled, it is
stated that the wassail party visited the house of a newly-wed
pair or a family which had moved house. As was previously
stated, the song recorded by Hughes, which is not ascribed to
any particular district, contains references to a bier, ' wrens '
and a *perllan* as part of the wassail ceremony.[2]

Here again one is reminded of the way in which these ancient
customs, whose origin and purpose were forgotten, were
confused with each other and their disparate elements mixed in
a number of picturesque customs which must have appeared
basically alike to those who practised them. The old rituals
had become what their detractors called excuses for collecting
money or drink ; whatever their origin, their purpose had
become the same.   The *Mari Lwyd* wassailing, the wren

[1]*Pembrokeshire Antiquities*, p. 45.
[2]cf. page 59 *supra*.

ceremonies and other customs carried on during the Christmas season, besides having many ancient traits in common, had a similar social function in recent times. As Mr. Alwyn Rees has pointed out in his social study of a Montgomeryshire parish, the ' back-end ' of the year, about Christmas time, was the season for relaxation when the work on the land made least demand on the countryman. The folk customs which we have been studying should be looked at against this background. Their attendant rituals, containing age-old features of forgotten significance, gave an approved means of entering the houses of neighbours in a culture in which there were few public assemblies—at least in the heart of winter—in which the convivial spirit of the season could be released. The poetic contest or singing of verses, in brief, institutionalized the house-visits and were no doubt kept up precisely for this reason after their religious import, if any, had been lost. The gifts of drink, food, or sometimes money, were made personally and no doubt helped to further the feeling of community among country folk while at the same time manifesting it. Conviviality was spun out and given a traditional and formal ' fore-play.' The new ways of celebrating Christmas, it has been suggested, reflect changing social conditions, and it is under the impact of these that the three ancient customs we have discussed have fallen into disuse. Our symbols of Christmastide are now Father Christmas, not the white-draped Mari Lwyd, the Christmas Tree and not the wassail bowl, the robin on the greeting card and not the wren on his bier.

CHAPTER II

CANDLEMAS AND THE MOVABLE FESTIVALS

THE lengthening days which follow the festivities of Christmas hold for the countryman the promise of spring and the re-birth of plant life. The yearly cycle of work on the land begins once again as the soil is prepared for the seed. In this gradual change from winter to spring the feast of Candlemas (2nd February) formerly held an important place. We have already seen how the seventeenth-century wassail song referred to this day as ' Gŵyl Fair forwyn ddechre gwanwyn ' (the Feast of the Virgin Mary at the beginning of spring)[1] partly, no doubt, to distinguish it from the other festivals of Mary, but also because of its special association with the impending approach of spring. Candlemas, *Gŵyl Fair y Canhwyllau* (Mary's Festival of the Candles), the popular names of the Feast of the Purification of the Virgin, were derived from the pre-Reformation ceremony of blessing the candles and distributing them amongst the people by whom they were afterwards carried lighted in solemn procession. After the Reformation the blessing was discontinued but the symbol of the lighted candles had too strong a hold on the popular imagination to be cast aside.

Some of the old practices carried on at Candlemas were still remembered in Kidwelly, Carmarthenshire, in 1915. The parents or grandparents of people then living always lit candles on *Gŵyl Fair y Canhwyllau* ; in one instance cited every pane in the small kitchen window was illuminated in this way, and the practice was probably widespread. In the same district ' some time in the autumn, the mistress of the farm ceremoniously gave *y forwyn fawr* [the head maid] a lighted candle for use in the outhouses. According to rule, the maid was bound to hand a candle back to her mistress on *Gŵyl Fair y Canhwyllau*. The older folk were positive about the date on which the candle had to be brought back. It was considered that on 2 February

[1] *Cân Gwirod neu Ŵyl Fair* by Gruffydd Phylip quoted by T. H. Parry-Williams, *op. cit.*, p. lxix, see p. 56 *supra*.

artificial light could be dispensed with.'[1] Henceforth the farm animals could be fed before dark.

Marie Trevelyan records that on Candlemas Day ' it was customary many years ago for people to light two candles, and place them on a table or high bench. Then each member of the family would in turn sit down on a chair between the candles. They then took a drink out of a horn goblet or beaker, and afterwards threw the vessel backwards over his head. If it fell in an upright position, the person who threw it would live to reach a very old age ; if it fell bottom upwards, the person would die early in life.'[2]

It is clear from the few Candlemas observances recorded in Wales that the lighted candle, divorced from church ritual and the cult of the Virgin, had become (or perhaps reverted to) a secular symbol associated with the coming of spring.

Easter, which commemorates the resurrection of Christ, is one of the three great religious festivals of the Christian year, the other two being Christmas and Whitsuntide. The Sunday on which it falls depends on the state of the moon ; according to the Prayer Book ' Easter-day is always the first Sunday after the full moon which happens upon or next after the twenty-first of March, and if the full moon happens upon a Sunday, Easter-day is the Sunday after.' In turn, Easter decides the dates of other movable feasts and fasts, including the nine preceding and eight following Sundays, Shrovetide, Lent, Ascension Day and Whitsun. The ancient customs observed on these days naturally changed their date from year to year in sympathy with Easter ; consequently unlike the Christmastide customs they were not confused with each other in the popular mind after the introduction of the New Style calendar in 1752.

The medieval church observed a period of fasting and solemnity during the forty days preceding Easter in commemoration of Christ's abstinence when under temptation. The period originally began on what is now the first Sunday in

[1]Gruffydd Evans : ' Carmarthenshire Gleanings (Kidwelly),' *Y Cymmrodor*, Vol. XXV, 1915, pp. 109-110. According to another Carmarthenshire source *amser gwylad*, or the period when working by candle-light was allowed, came to an end on St. David's Day. D. G. Williams : ' Casgliad o Lên-Gwerin Sir Gaerfyrddin,' 1895, p. 298.
[2]M. Trevelyan : *Folk-Lore and Folk-Stories of Wales*, 1909, p. 244.

Lent, Sundays being included in the reckoning. Later the Sundays were excluded as improper for fasting, and Lent began on Ash Wednesday (*Dydd Mercher y Lludw*). Shrovetide consisted of the last three days before Lent. Its Welsh name, *Ynyd*, is derived from the Latin *initium*, ' beginning' and refers to the approach of Lent. Fisher suggests that *Ynyd* proper refers to Ash Wednesday as the first day of Lent and points out in support of his argument that one of the Welsh names of Shrove Tuesday, *Nos Ynyd* [The Eve of *the Ynyd*]—which is as old as the fifteenth century—refers, like *Nos Nadolig* [Christmas Eve] and *Nos Galan* [New Year's Eve] to the eve before the festival.[1] In recent times, however, the popular name for Shrove Tuesday has been *Dydd Mawrth Ynyd*.

It was as the day preceding the beginning of Lent that Shrove Tuesday was important to our ancestors. The fasting had not yet begun and this was the last day on which any feasting could take place. It was natural therefore that foods prohibited during the coming fast should be eaten on this day. Ecclesiastically, Shrovetide, as its English name indicates, was the period during which sins could be confessed and souls prepared for the solemnity of Lent. In popular practice, however, it was interpreted, after the fashion of the carnival, as an opportunity to partake of foods and indulge in pastimes which would be forbidden during the fast. In parts of England ' Collop Monday,' the day before Shrove Tuesday, saw the last meat dish eaten from the flesh salted or otherwise reserved in readiness for the winter. Welsh records are silent on this point but illustrate the similar practice of eating the last supplies of butter and fat in the form of pancakes on Shrove Tuesday. Other related customs of shying at cocks and cock-fighting are also documented.

In numerous districts the couplet

Dydd Mawrth Ynyd
Crempog bob munud

[Shrove Tuesday, pancakes every miuute.]

was well-known and indeed aptly described the special activity of the day. An account of the festival in a Montgomeryshire

[1]John Fisher : ' The Welsh Calendar,' *Trans. Hon. Soc. Cymmr.* 1894-5, p. 112.

parish, Llansanffraid-ym-Mechain, may be quoted here to convey the atmosphere of the occasion. In almost every house in the neighbourhood, ' from early morn till rather late in the afternoon the pan was scarcely out of the cook's hand. It was considered a great feat to turn the pancake by throwing it up in the air, so as to fall flat on its face in the pan again ; and great disappointment ensued if it fell on the floor instead. Owing to the great demand for eggs on this day, woe be to the hen that did not lay before twelve o'clock ; for in such a case it became necessary, according to the old custom, to ' thrash the hen,' which was done in the following singular fashion : The hen was taken to the centre of a green meadow, where a turf was cut and a hole made, wherein the hen was buried under the turf, her head alone being out. Then any person who wished to try to strike her with a stick might do so—a bandage being first placed over his eyes—and this process was repeated until some one succeeded in striking her, when she became his property. The hen was kept until the following day, when she was killed, cooked and eaten with considerable ceremony. The poor go about collecting gifts of lard and flour this day, which is called *blawta a blonega*. This custom is in vogue to this day (1870).'[1]

The ways of celebrating Shrove Tuesday in Llansanffraid were also to be found, with local variations, in many other Welsh districts in the middle of the nineteenth century. In Worthenbury, Flintshire, the church bell was tolled at eleven o'clock on this day each year. Local tradition explained this as a signal for the pancakes to be put on the fire[2] ; but it is certain that Shrove Tuesday bell-ringing, in England as well as in Wales, had an older, religious, purpose of calling the parish to church for confession immediately before Lent.[3] The custom had outlived its original sacred significance and had been endowed by popular tradition with a purely secular purpose. At Rhydycroesau, on the borders of Denbighshire and Shropshire, it was customary to postpone taking down the Christmas decorations until Shrove Tuesday when they were burnt when

[1]T. G. Jones : ' A History of the Parish of Llansantffraid-ym-Mechain,' *Montgomeryshire Collections*, IV, pp. 135-6.

[2]*Bye-gones*, 30 August, 1893.

[3]Cf. Wright & Jones : *British Calendar Customs, England*, I, pp. 13-15.

frying pancakes.[1] No doubt this emphasized that the Christmas celebrations, in practice long since over, were giving way to the season of fasting and restraint.

Blawta a blonega, the collection of flour and fats on Shrove Tuesday for the making of pancakes was formerly carried on by the poor and by children in general. The verse customarily sung in Caernarvonshire, however, asks for pancakes rather than the ingredients :—

> Wraig y tŷ, a'r teulu da
> A welwch chwi'n dda roi crempog ?
> A lwmp o fenyn melyn mawr
> Fel 'r aiff i lawr yn llithrig ;
> Os ydych chwi yn wraig led fwyn,
> Rhowch arni lwyn o driog
> Os ydych chwi yn wraig led frwnt
> Rhowch arni lwmp o fenyn ;
> Mae rhan i'r gath, a chlwt i'r ci bach
> A'r badell yn grimpin grempog.[2]

[Lady of the house and good family, please give a pancake, with a large lump of yellow butter so that it will slip down easily. If you are a nice woman, put on it a mound of treacle. If you are a nasty woman, put on it a lump of butter. Some for the cat, a little for the dog, and in the pan a crimp pancake.]

Another verse sung in the slate-quarrying district of Carmel in the same county went as follows :

> Os gwelwch yn dda ga'i grempog,
> Os nad oes menyn yn y tŷ
> Ga'i lwyad fawr o driog.
> Mae Mam yn rhy dlawd i brynu blawd
> A'm tad yn rhy ddiog i weithio.

[Please give me a pancake, if there is not any butter in the house, may I have a large spoonful of treacle. My mother is too poor to buy flour and my father is too lazy to work.]

The custom was still alive in this district in the years immediately preceding the First World War, but a child was thought lucky if he was given more than half a dozen pancakes

---

[1]*Bye-gones*, 7 January, 1914 ; also noted in Lancashire.
[2]John Jones (*Myrddin Fardd*) : *Llên Gwerin Sir Gaernarfon*, [1909], p. 246.

on his round.[1] An observer writing of Anglesey twenty years earlier describes how the children there would often be seen returning to their homes their faces covered with fat and treacle from ear to ear.[2] Although the collecting of pancakes or ingredients has ceased in recent years the making of pancakes is still inseparably associated with Shrove Tuesday. It is now the only special distinction pertaining to that day.

As in Llansanffraid the barbarous custom of ' thrashing the hen ' or ' throwing at cocks ' was practised in many Welsh districts on Shrove Tuesday. Brand quotes a ' Mr. Jones ' as stating that the thrashing was carried out by means of a flail. ' If the man hit the hen and consequently killed her, he got her for his pains.'[3] Apart from this Welsh evidence the custom is recorded in England and was obviously well-known there.[4] The similar, but distinct, custom of holding a cock-fight on Shrove Tuesday was also formerly found in both countries, although the special connection between the day and this sport is obscure.[5]

In certain parts of South Wales the sport which was held on Shrove Tuesday was football rather than cock-fighting. Ashton names Pembrokeshire in particular as the scene of this custom and states that the players restored their strength from time to time during the course of the game by eating pancakes bought from women who carried them about in baskets. By 1890, Ashton writes, Shrove Tuesday football had been discontinued in most places, one exception being Narberth, and the eating of pancakes was less widely practised.[6] A somewhat more vivid account which conveys the enthusiasm aroused by the game

[1] ex. inf. Mr. John Parry, St. Fagans.

[2] C. Ashton : ' Bywyd Gwledig yng Nghymru,' *Eisteddfod Trans.* 1890, p. 68.

[3] Brand : *Popular Antiquities*, p. 49.

[4] cf. ' At Shroftide to shroving, go thresh the fat hen,
    If blindfold can kill her, then give it thy men.'
(Tusser's Five Hundred Points of Good Husbandry). The hen was hung on the back of a man who also carried some horse-bells. He was then chased by several men who were blindfolded and who carried bells. cf. Brand, *op. cit.*, p. 40.

[5] Cockfighting was once popular sport in Wales and contests were held during the wakes and frequently during the rest of the year. Possibly it was among the activities prohibited during Lent and therefore emphasized on the last day before the fast. For Cockfighting in general see G. R. Scott : *The History of Cockfighting*, London, n.d. [1957].

[6] Ashton, *op. cit.*, p. 68.

was given by a writer in 1842 who made the comparison between Shrove Tuesday football ' in certain towns in South Wales ' and the popular games of Ancient Greece. ' The balls consist of bulls' bladders protected by a thick covering of leather, and blown tight. Six or eight are made ready for the occasion. Every window in the town is shut by break of day, at which time all the youths of the neighbourhood assemble in the streets. The ball is then thrown up in front of the Town Hall, and the multitude, dividing into two parts, strive with incredible eagerness and enthusiasm to kick the football to the other extremity of the town. In the struggle several kicks and wounds are given, and many fierce battles take place. The ball sometimes ascends thirty or forty feet above the tops of the highest houses and falls far beyond, or goes right over into the gardens, whither it is immediately followed by a crowd of young men. The sport is kept up all day, the hungry combatants recruiting their strength from time to time by copious horns of ale and an abundant supply of the nice pancakes which the women sell in baskets at the corner of every street. To view this sport thousands of persons assemble from all the country round, so that to the secluded population of those districts it is in come sort what the battle in the Platanistas was to the Spartans or even what the Isthmian and Nemean games were to the whole of Greece.'[1] Football on Shrove Tuesday was apparently not unlike the game played on Old New Year's Day in Llandysul between rival parishes before the introduction of the Sunday School Festival ; or the Christmas Day football played at Maentwrog. As a means of recreation it could probably only be played on a large scale on those days which were observed as festivals and on which no work was done.

A semblance of the religious significance of Lent was preserved in a custom recorded in Kidwelly, Carmarthenshire. ' As soon as darkness set in, a number of youths would visit a house, generally a farm, in the locality ; secretly place on the kitchen window sill what was called a *Crochon Crewys* (Lenten

[1]Quoted in *Bye-gones*, 16 December, 1885. A similar account is given in *Tales and Traditions of Tenby*, 1858, p. 18, where the players are said to have numbered two or three hundred. In Laugharne, Carmarthenshire, the annual game was stopped by the local magistrates in 1838 because of the fighting which accompanied it. (Curtis : *The Antiquities of Laugharne*, etc. p. 204).

crock),—either an egg-shell, or a scooped-out turnip, containing little bits of bread, salt, leek, cabbage, or some other vegetable ; then shout rapidly and vociferously the following *rhigwm* (doggerel) or a variant of it :

> Crochon crewys ar ben ffenest,
> Bara, halen, cawl ceninen,
> Os na ddaw nol cyn Nos Lun Pasc,
> Can punt o *fine*.

[Lenten crock on the window-sill, bread, salt, leek broth, if it will not be back before Easter Monday, a fine of a hundred pounds.]

The kitchen door would open suddenly, and members of the household, intent upon capture, would rush after the youthful visitors. If one were caught, he was bound by the "rules of the game" to clean and shine all the "best boots" in the house. After the completion of this task he was rewarded with a generous feast of pancakes. The custom was exceedingly popular, and visits were not confined to the farms. One person remembered the *Crochon Crewys* placed on the window sill of his grandmother's house, the New Inn, Lady Street, in the town of Kidwelly.[1]

The Reverend Gruffydd Evans who recorded the custom interprets it as a reference to the hard fare of Lent. ' Some would pay scant heed to the rules of abstinence. If their neglect of duty became known, the *Crochon Crewys* would be set upon their window-sill by way of caution. That it was an offensive reminder is apparent from the running away of the youths to avoid capture. The crock would be placed in position on the eve of Ash Wednesday, but what the acted parable enjoined was to be observed, until the very end of the Fast, that is the Eve of Easter.' Evans reconstructs the third line of the verse to give this sense, and suggests that a variant with *cyn Nos cyn Pasg* (' before the night before Easter ') is probably the correct form. The last line of the verse he interprets as a reminder of the severity of the penance exacted for disobedience.[2] Another custom in Kidwelly, namely, the kicking of old

---

[1] G. Evans : ' Carmarthenshire Gleanings (Kidwelly),' *Y Cymmrodor*, **XXV**, 1915, p. 102-5, where variant forms of the verse are given.
[2] G. Evans : *op. cit.*

tin pans and other utensils along the streets by the youths of the
town on the eve of Shrove Tuesday, is interpreted in a similar
manner. The destruction of the pans, according to Evans,
emphasized the duty of putting away those working utensils
which were associated with the more cheerful fare not lawful
during the Fast.

Like the eating of pancakes, and indeed like all observances
of Shrove Tuesday, the local customs of *Crochon Crewys* and
kicking of old tin cans originated in the religious character of the
day preceding Lent as a preparation for the forthcoming fast.
Deprived of the religious impulse, however, they became
meaningless yet enjoyable activities maintained by the force of
tradition and the pleasure which was derived from them.

Shrovetide over, the solemnity of Lent began in earnest.
At one time, in the eighteenth century, it was the custom,
especially among old people, to wear black clothes during
Lent.[1] But on the whole, Protestant, and particularly nonconformist, Wales laid little emphasis on the observance of
self-denial and fastings. Nevertheless it was until recently held
to be unlucky to marry during Lent. The Lenten period
became more important as a framework for individual festivals
than as a time of fasting, and the correct sequence of Sundays
leading up to Easter was memorized in the following doggerel :

> Dydd Sul Ynyd, Dydd Sul hefyd,
> Dydd Sul a ddaw, Dydd Sul gerllaw ;
> Dydd Sul y Meibion, Dydd Sul y Gwrychon ;
> Dydd Sul y Blodau, Pasg a'i dyddiau.[2]

[Shrove Sunday, another Sunday, Sunday will come, Sunday
nearby, Mothering Sunday (lit. Sons' Sunday), Carling Sunday,
Flowering Sunday, Easter and its days].

The three Sundays which preceded Easter were each
observed with folk customs during the nineteenth century and
earlier. *Dydd Sul y Meibion* (Mothering Sunday), the fourth
Sunday in Lent was the occasion when servants or apprentices
took presents to their parents, especially to their mothers.
Although the name of the Sunday suggests that the custom was

[1]P. Roberts : *The Cambrian Popular Antiquities*, 1815, p. 112.
[2]Silvan Evans : *Ystên Sioned*, 1882, p. 96.

formerly widespread in Wales, there are few records of its existence. An eighteenth-century note relating to Chepstow, Monmouthshire, speaks of the custom, among servants and apprentices, of visiting their parents and taking them ' a present of money, a trinket or some nice eatable.' The custom is also recorded in the adjacent county of Gloucester.[1]

The various popular names for the Fifth Sunday in Lent in both Welsh and English refer to peas, probably an essential element in the diet during the Fast. Besides the straightforward *Sul y Pys* (Pea Sunday), the name *Dydd Sul y Gwrychon* was also given to the day and was included in the rhyme already quoted. Silvan Evans has shown that *gwrychon* were peas that had been steeped overnight in water, milk, wine, cider and the like, then put to dry, and afterwards boiled for eating.[2] The English name ' Carling Sunday ' (also Carline, Carlin, Carle, or Carl Sunday) probably derives from the word ' care ' in the sense of mourning and sorrow, and refers to the Passion of Christ.[3] But pea-eating was so widespread in parts of England, notably the North, that ' carlings ' was used to denote the fried peas eaten on this day.[4] The custom prevailed in Llansanffraid-ym-Mechain, Montgomeryshire, in the first half of the nineteenth century, of roasting peas or wheat grains and then taking them to the top of Y Foel, a hill in the district, to be eaten ' with very great ceremony ' on *Sul y Pys*. Water was also drunk on this occasion from a well on the hill. In the same district eating peas was so much a part of Lent fasting that ' the old people ' believed they would be choked if they ate peas before Lent.[5]

In the calendar of the church, the Sunday before Easter commemorated Christ's triumphal entry on an ass into Jerusalem, when palms were strewn on the road before him. In the mediaeval church the procession was re-enacted in a ceremony, and the blessed sacrament was 'reverently carried, as it were Christ upon the Ass, with strewing of bushes and flowers, bearing of palms, setting out boughs, spreading and

[1]*Gentleman's Magazine*, 1784, quoted by Brand, 1. p. 62.
[2]Silvan Evans : *op. cit.*, p. 96-7.
[3]Wright & Lones : *British Calendar Customs, England*, I, p. 51.
[4]*ibid.*
[5]T. G . Jones : ' A History of the Parish of Llansantffraid-ym-Mechain,' pp. 139 wh ere *Sul y Pys* is mistakenly described as the Fourth Sunday in Lent.

hanging up the richest clothes &c.'[1] A sixteenth-century reference cited by Brand mentions the custom of drawing a wooden ass with a rope on Palm Sunday,[2] and it is probable that traces of this ritual survived the onslaught of the Reformation. Marie Trevelyan records a similar custom in south Wales : ' The image of a donkey was made of wood. On this a stuffed effigy was placed, and these were glued fast to a platform, which was set upon wheels. The donkey and the effigy were decorated with flowers and bundles of evergreens. When brought to the church door by the procession, each member carried a sprig of evergreen, seasonable flowers, or herbs, box-wood predominating. The people were met by the clergyman, who blessed the procession and the evergreens and flowers. The sprigs were carefully preserved for the year as a charm to keep away evil spirits and witches, and a protection against mishaps.'[3]

The Welsh name for Palm Sunday is *Sul y Blodau* (the Sunday of the flowers, Flowering Sunday), a term which refers to the widespread custom of decking graves with flowers on this day. This practice is essentially a preparation for Easter, the festival of the Resurrection, and the time of the year when new clothes are worn after the drabness of winter and of Lent. Although the name *Sul y Blodau* occurs as early as the fifteenth century in Welsh literature,[4] many writers of the early nineteenth century who mention the decoration of graves in spring associate it with Easter or with both Easter and Flowering Sunday. Charles Redwood, in one of his tales set in the Vale of Glamorgan, gives an interesting account of the custom, linking it definitely with Easter Eve. ' On our return, I was surprised, as we came to the churchyard, to find it the scene of extra-

[1]Brand : *Popular Antiquities*, p. 68.

[2]Brand : *op. cit.*, p. 73.

[3]Marie Trevelyan, *Folk-Lore and Folk-stories of Wales*, 1909, pp. 245-6. Although the author gives no further details of where and when this custom was practised, the two sources of this account are given : (*a*) clergymen, ministers and others with an ' itinerary profession or trade ' who thus had opportunities of hearing folk-stories in north and south Wales ; (*b*) an old inhabitant who related stories well known in the first half of the nineteenth century. I know of no other Welsh reference to this custom.

[4]e.g. in a *cywydd* by Lewis Glyn Cothi (fl. 1447-86) ; see *Works* (1837), p. 135. cf. Fisher : ' The Welsh Calendar ', *Trans. Hon. Soc. Cymmr.*, 1894-5, p. 117.

ordinary employment, until I recollected that this was Easter Eve. All the village were there, engaged, after the old custom, in trimming and adorning the graves of their deceased relatives. Some were raising the sides with fresh turf, and putting fresh earth upon the surface ; and others whitewashed the stones at the ends ; while the women planted rosemary and rue, and the girls brought baskets of spring flowers, crocuses, daffodils, and primroses, which were placed in somewhat fantastic figures upon all the graves.'[1] A similar reference to the whitewashing and decorating of graves is given by a contemporary of Redwood's, William Howells, whose description suggests that there were regional differences in the details of the practice. ' On Palm Sunday, or Easter Day, in other parts of Wales, where no flowers are set, they proceed early in the morning to clean and whitewash the gravestones, take away weeds, and strew these simple tributes over the graves,—which is also done weekly by some affectionate individuals.'[2] As the closing words of this extract indicate, the practice was not restricted to Eastertide ; it was also connected with the two other important Christian festivals, Christmas and Whitsun. In a list of Glamorgan folk customs compiled by Edward Williams, *Iolo Morganwg* (1747—1826), the decorating of graves with flowers is described as taking place a month after the burial and every Christmas, Easter and Whitsun.[3] The evidence which has survived suggests that what was later exclusively regarded as a Palm Sunday custom was, until the middle of the nineteenth century, also a feature of the major religious festivals. Even as late as 1870 in Llansanffraid-ym-Mechain, Montgomeryshire, 'dressing the graves with flowers and evergreens ' was an Easter Sunday custom.[4]

By the late nineteenth century, however, the dressing of graves had become an exceedingly popular custom in south Wales on Palm Sunday. Newspaper accounts of the time describe the thousands of visitors who came to the cemeteries in

[1]Charles Redwood : *The Vale of Glamorgan : Scenes and Tales among the Welsh,* 1839, p. 305-6.
[2]W. Howells : *Cambrian Superstitions,* 1831, p. 171.
[3]G. J. Williams : *Iolo Morganwg,* 1956, p. 40.
[4]*Bye-gones,* 30 April, 1873.

Cardiff and Swansea to place flowers on the graves of friends and relatives.[1] The custom had undoubtedly been revived, especially in the rapidly growing industrial towns. In Carmarthenshire, ' the custom of strewing flowers on graves on Flowering Sunday is known in the county, but is not observed in the countryside as it is in the towns.'[2] Ceredig Davies describes how ' in West Wales, during the last sixty years, the practice to a very great extent has been discontinued, at least in rural districts. But it is reviving at the present day, and likely to grow as years go on.' He cites the evidence of an old man born in Llangwyryfon, Cardiganshire, in the eighteen-twenties, who ' well remembered the custom observed in his native parish ' many years ago, although it was rarely observed in 1910-11 when Davies wrote.[3] A correspondent replying to an enquiry in *Bye-gones*, 1906, on Palm Sunday in north Wales wrote that he believed its observance ceased there many years ago.[4] While negative evidence of this kind can hardly ever be conclusive, it is likely that the dressing of graves on Flowering Sunday had ceased in many parts of Wales and that the revival which was noted towards the end of the century was urban rather than rural in origin.[5] The custom is still popular in the well-populated areas of Glamorgan.

Good Friday was celebrated in a solemn manner with the holding of religious services in the parish churches, though even by the middle of the nineteenth century the strict observance of the day was becoming a thing of the past. A contemporary writer quoted an old Tenby woman who ' used to remark on the difference between the fashion of the present and her youthful days, when all business was suspended, no horse or cart to be seen in the town, and the people walked barefooted to church, that they might not "disturb the earth".'[6] In the

---

[1]' Over 25,000 ' visited Swansea cemetery in 1906, and ' at least 20,000 ' in 1909 to dress the graves. (*Bye-gones*, 18 April, 1906 and 8 September, 1909). In Cardiff, ' thousands wend their way to the Cemetry, the roads thereto presenting an appearance like unto a fair.' (*Bye-gones*, 9 September, 1896 ').

[2]D. G. Williams ' Casgliad o Lên-Gwerin Sir Gaerfyrddin,' p. 299.

[3]J. Ceredig Davies : *Folk-lore of West and Mid-Wales*, 1911, p. 54.

[4]*Bye-gones*, 9 June, 1906.

[5]The custom, described as ' essentially Welsh ' was recorded by Wright and Lones in St. Briavels, Gloucestershire and Albrighton, Salop, amongst other villages. Wright & Lones, *British Calendar Customs, England*, I, p. 56 Footnote.

[6]*Tales and Traditions of Tenby*, 1858, p. 19.

same town, the fare after the church service consisted of hot cross-buns. These were thought to have a curative power and a number of them were tied in a bag and hung up in the kitchen till the following Good Friday. It was believed that a portion of such a bun, when eaten, could cure any disease ; the buns were also given to domestic animals to cure diseases.[1] Both the eating of hot cross-buns and their use in folk medicine are well known in England,[2] but Williams's statement that the country people of Carmarthenshire knew very little about the existence of hot cross-buns suggests that the custom properly belonged to the English-speaking part of Pembrokeshire in which Tenby lies.[3] The symbolical significance of the cross marked on the buns eaten on Good Friday calls for no explanation, but it is interesting to find that two petrified loaves, five inches in diameter, were found at Herculaneum both marked with a cross. Disaster overtook Herculaneum in A.D. 79 and it is unlikely that the loaves were made for a Christian. It has been suggested that wheaten cakes marked with a cross may have been eaten at the Spring Festival in pre-Christian times before the Gospel suggested another meaning.[4]

Another custom which was formerly carried on in Tenby on or near Good Friday was that of ' making Christ's bed.' A number of young persons would gather a quantity of long reed leaves from the river and weave them into the shape of a man. The figure was then laid on a wooden cross in a retired part of a field or garden and left there.[5] It has been suggested that this custom originated in the pre-Reformation ceremony of burying the image of Christ on Good Friday.[6] In Barnabe Googe's translation of the German author Thomas Kirchmair (*Naogeorgus*), 1511-63, the following lines occur :

[1]*loc. cit.*
[2]cf. Wright & Lones, *British Calendar Customs, England*, I, pp. 71-73. In Dinas Mawddwy, Merioneth, a *loaf of bread* made on Good Friday of flour ground, kneaded & baked on that day, was thought to have curative properties & was kept indefinitely, *Bye-gones*, 15 June, 1904.
[3]D. G. Williams : *op. cit.*, p. 299.
[4]Laurence Whistler : *The English Festivals*, 1947, p. 114.
[5]*Tales & Traditions of Tenby*, p. 20.
[6]*loc. cit.*

An other Image doe they get, like one but newly deade,
With legges stretcht out at length, and hands upon his body
  spreade
And him, with pompe and sacred song, they beare unto his grave.'[1]

Nearly three centuries after the Reformation and the official discouragement of ' popish ' ceremonies, the ' making of Christ's bed ' preserved a vestige of the re-enactment of the burial of Christ, no longer as a ritual sanctioned and carried out by the parish priest but as a simple folk custom.

With Easter, the Feast of the Resurrection, the period of abstinence and self-denial is brought to an end. The interrupted pleasures of life are taken up once more, this time in the pleasant setting of spring. On Easter Day itself, the celebrations of the ordinary people began at (or before) sunrise, when in many districts crowds climbed to the summit of a nearby mountain to see the sun ' dancing ' in honour of the Re-surrection of Christ. The Rev. John Williams, *Glanmor* (1811-91) remembered the inhabitants of Llangollen, Denbighshire, ascending Dinas Brân on Easter Day to greet the rising sun with three somersaults, a peculiar variation on this custom.[2]   In other districts it was usual to take a basin of water in order to see the reflection of the sun dancing on the horizon.[3]   It is almost certain that behind this observance was the widespread belief that Christ rose from the dead at dawn on Easter Day ; while, further removed from medieval practice, there lurks the hint of an earlier, pagan rite. The custom is also recorded in many English counties and in the Isle of Man and Ireland.[4]   A more orthodox form of celebration on the same day was the Easter Communion Service attended by many who went to church but once a year. Even this had its gay side, for new clothes were often worn instead of the dark colours of Lent. ' It is thought (or was thought so) necessary to put on some new portion of dress at Easter, and unlucky to omit doing so were it but a new pair of gloves or a ribband.'[5]   So wrote Peter

[1]Brand : *Popular Antiquities*, i, p. 87.
[2]*Bye-gones*, 11 December, 1895.
[3]P. Roberts : *The Cambrian Popular Antiquities*, p. 124. In Anglesey it was customary to look at the dancing of the sun through wisps of straw. (cf. Hugh Owen : *The Life and Works of Lewis Morris (1701—1765)*, 1951, p. 141.
[4]Wright & Lones : *British Calendar Customs, England*, I. pp. 96-8.
[5]P. Roberts : *loc. cit.*

Roberts, about 1815, of a practice which continued long after his day. In his opinion the idea originated in the custom of baptizing at Easter when the new dress was a symbol of the new character assumed by baptism. Whether this be true or not, it is interesting in view of the associations with baptism, to note that in former times, many parents kept their children unbaptized till Easter Day.[1] The singing of Easter carols, which is mentioned in some churchwardens' accounts of the early nineteenth century was yet another indication of the special nature of the religious service on this day.[2] Whether merely as the end of fasting and self-denial or, on a higher religious plane, as the feast of the Resurrection, Easter undoubtedly made a particular appeal to the imagination of the countryman ; his observance of the occasion ranged from the superstitious belief in the dancing of the sun to the devout celebration of holy communion.

With the passing of Lent many forbidden acts, such as the eating of meat and eggs, and the playing of games, were permitted once more. Fresh meat, in particular, was a welcome change not only from the dull fare of the previous few weeks, but also from the salted meat eaten during the long winter. Peter Roberts noted that Easter ' is also marked by somewhat of better cheer, as a festival, of which lamb is considered as a proper constituent part.'[3] Similarly, more than half a century earlier, Lewis Morris emphasizes the 'decent celebrations of Easter ' among the peasantry of Anglesey, ' with dinner, eggs, Lamb or Kidd, even ye poorest family.'[4] No doubt the Easter dinner was as important to our forefathers as the Christmas dinner is to us. Lewis Morris's reference to eggs, which are given preference over lamb in his list, suggests their peculiar importance at the time of the Easter festival,[5] and it is interesting to note that it is in Morris's own county of Anglesey that one of the Easter-egg customs of Wales has survived to our own day.

[1] J. C. Davies : *Folk-lore of West and Mid-Wales*, p. 74.
[2] The Bryneglwys, Denbighshire, accounts, for example, record the payment of a shilling ' for singing an Easter carol ' in 1807 and 1808. (*Bye-gones*, 3 July, 1895).
[3] Peter Roberts, *loc. cit.*
[4] Hugh Owen. *The Life and Works of Lewis Morris (1701—1765)*, 1951, p. 147.
[5] cf. ' one of the [Welsh] border customs at Easter was that every dish prepared for Easter Sunday should have eggs as the principal ingredient. . . . Eggs were eaten at every meal,' *Bye-gones*, 31 March, 1897.

Just as it was the custom to collect *calennig* on New Year's Day
or pancakes on Shrove Tuesday, it was formerly the custom in
many parts of north Wales to ' clap for Easter eggs ' on the
Monday before Easter. This was known in Welsh as "*clepio*"
wyau'r pasg (Caernarvonshire) or *clepian wyau* (Anglesey).[1]
Some examples of the wooden clappers used in the latter
county are included in the Museum's collection (Nos. 48 to 50
in the Catalogue. See Plate 6). The Anglesey children used to
chant the words ' Clap, clap, gofyn ŵy, i hogia' bach ar y plwy '
[Clap, clap, ask for an egg for little boys on the parish] when
begging for eggs. Often the incantation was omitted, the noise of
the clappers being sufficient to indicate the nature of the errand.
Children might collect as many as forty eggs in this way in the
Amlwch district. Sometimes they would be given pennies
instead of eggs, and in certain houses they would be turned
away with such phrases as ' 'Dydi'r gath ddim wedi dodwy eto '
[The cat hasn't laid yet].[2] According to one writer the custom
was formerly to be found in west Denbighshire, and indeed
' was once general in North Wales.' The same writer points out
that in Denbighshire farm-servants had an egg for breakfast on
Easter Sunday and that in many districts the clergy formerly
received eggs as Easter presents from their parishioners.[3] Like
meat, eggs were among the prohibited foods of Lent, but unlike
meat, the egg had a symbolical significance which was peculiarly appropriate to Easter. From the earliest times the egg has
been the emblem of fertility and particularly of the regeneration

[1]An alternative form is *clapio*. The custom is recorded by Lewis Morris in the
18th century. cf. H. Owen : *op. cit.*

[2]ex. inf. Mr. David Hughes, Welsh Folk Museum. About 1890, according to a
correspondent to *Y Brython*, 1931, the children used to collect between 150 and
200 eggs during the week preceding Easter ; ' they used to take down the dishes
from the dresser, and put the eggs of the eldest child on the top shelf, those of the
second on the second shelf, and so on.'

[3]*Bye-gones*, 21 August, 1895. The giving of eggs as presents to friends still
survives in the countryside (e.g. Llŷn, Caernarvonshire). The contributor to
Bye-gones, E.O., notes that the gifts to the clergyman of two eggs for every cock
and one for every hen at Easter are mentioned in the terriers of Cerrigydrudion
(Denbighshire), 1749, and Llanycil (Merioneth), 1774. A seventy-four year old
farmer from Llanarmon Dyffryn Ceiriog (Denbighshire), giving evidence before
the Royal Commission on Land in Wales (1894), recalled that the same practice
existed in that district when he was a child ; the eggs were collected by the parish
clerk. (*Minutes of Evidence*, IV, Par. 55, 321 and 55, 426). See also W. Davies :
' Casgliad o Lên-Gwerin Meirion ', *Eisteddfod Transactions Blaenau Ffestiniog, 1898*,
p. 245.

of life. To the pagan the reawakening of plant and animal life in spring was epitomized by the egg, the lifeless shell which contained the germ of new life. To the Christian Church the same quality presented an analogy to the miracle of the Resurrection. Eggs, after consecration by the priest, were thought to be holy gifts when presented to any one. But after the Reformation, Easter eggs were used much less in church ceremonies and more in games played during Eastertide, especially in England, where hard-boiled eggs were dyed and rolled about upon the grass until they were broken whereupon they were eaten.[1]

Although games which were played with eggs have not been recorded in Wales[2] Eastertide, especially Easter Monday, saw a revival of interest in sports of all kinds which had been laid aside during Lent. In Tenby, Easter Monday ' was always devoted to merry-making ; the neighbouring villages (Gumfreston especially) were visited, when some amused themselves with the barbarous sport of cock-fighting, while others frequented the two tea parties, held annually at Tenby and Gumfreston, and known as the "Parish Clerks' Meeting".'[3] According to Peter Roberts, ' stool-ball,' a game ' resembling cricket, except that no bats are used, and that a stool is a substitute for the wicket,' and hand-ball (Fives) were popular on holidays. ' These amusements generally began on Easter-eve, and were resumed after Easter-day.'[4] In Bangor, Caernarvon and Conway, a certain amount of misbehaviour was tolerated on

[1]Wright & Lones : *British Calendar Customs, England*, I, p. 90-1.

[2]A custom recorded at Whitchurch, Cardiff, in the late eighteenth century is reminiscent of Easter-egg games although tennis balls were used. From time immemorial, ' it was usual for every married woman, who had never been blessed with issue, to repair to the church-yard on Easter Monday, being first provided with two dozen tennis balls, one dozen of which were covered with white, and the other dozen with black leather ; these were cast by the fair votaress over the church, from the back-ground, and scrambled for by the populace, who assembled for that purpose in front of the building. So imperative was this custom that neither rank nor age were excused, until they were relieved, by the birth of a child, from its annual performance.' (*Bye-gones*, 19 October, 1892). Possibly the tennis balls were a substitute for eggs, which are commonly used in fertility rites.

[3]*Tales and Traditions of Tenby*, p. 21. The tea party was possibly an innocent form of ' church ale ' held to raise money for church repairs, charity, etc. Wright & Lones, *op. cit.*, p. 94, point out that Easter was an important time for holding such gatherings.

[4]Peter Roberts : *The Cambrian Popular Antiquities*, p. 122-3.

Easter Monday. In the first two towns, according to an early eighteenth-century tourist, 'ye young fellows yt can get up soon in ye morning to come & pull y'ir comrades out of bed, put them in y' stocks & holding up one of y'ir legs, pour a pail of water down it.'[1] In Conway, the custom was called *stocsio* (stocksing) and has been described in greater detail. 'On Easter Sunday crowds of boys and men proceed with wands of gorse to proclaim on Pentwtil the laws and regulations which are to be observed on the following morning. The bridegroom who has been last married is always sought for to perform the office of crier; mounted on a heap of stones, he calls the attention of his audience, who listen respectfully with their hats off, and he proclaims notices to the following import :—
That all men under sixty years of age are to appear in the street before six o'clock on the following morning, and all under forty at four, and all under twenty not to go to bed at all under penalty of being put in the stocks. After proclaiming these and similar notices loud cheers are given, and the audience separate, the younger part to form plans for their amusements during the night, and those, who own any carts or other vehicles, to secure them with chains and locks, as they well know that they will be in requisition on the following day. At an early hour on the morrow the stocks are placed at the bottom of the street, and a party headed by a fife and drum proceed with a cart to convey delinquents to the place of punishment : when they come to a house where a proper object resides, the storming party try by all the means in their power to gain access into the house, and by climbing to the windows with ladders, or by forcing doors, they generally succeed. The culprit being arrested, and having time allowed him to dress, if caught in bed, is placed in the cart, and triumphantly hurried to the stocks where one of the party having secured his feet gives him a lecture upon the heinousness of idleness and breaking an old established custom ; then taking hold of his right hand, he asks him a few questions such as these : Whether he likes better the mistress or the maid, ale or butter milk ; whether he would go through the gate of a field if open, or over the stile, &c. If in his

[1]Loveday's *Diary of a Tour in 1732*, p. 25 quoted in *Bye-gones*, cf. November 1896.

answer he fixes upon what is obviously preferable, his hand is the more thickly covered with some dirty mud, and he is then released with cheers. This sport, which would be impracticable in a larger and less intimate community, is continued with the greatest good humour until eight, when the rest of the day is spent in playing ball in the castle.'[1] In Oswestry, the game of ' stubball ' (a variation of stool-ball) was played regularly at Easter by young people of both sexes. The contest was usually between two districts of the town, and took place in the streets.[2] It is described as being connected with another Easter custom, namely ' lifting,' or ' heaving ' which seems to have been as popular in the border districts of Denbighshire and Montgomeryshire as *stocsio* was in the towns of Caernarvonshire.

The custom of ' lifting ' or ' heaving ' took place on Easter Monday and Tuesday, and was kept up by ' the lower orders,' like so many folk customs. On Monday it was the men who ' lifted ' the women, and on Tuesday the women ' lifted ' the men. The ' lifters ' went around in parties of three or four—sometimes more—adorned with ribbon favours and carrying a chair similarly decorated. The men would go from house to house, sometimes preceded by a fiddler, calling at those places where they knew there were young women. These were seized and placed one by one in the chair which was then raised three times into the air, to the accompaniment of loud cheers. The victim was then kissed and obliged to give the men a small gift, called a ' reward,' for the favour. In Llanarmon, Dyffryn Ceiriog, according to the poet Ceiriog, the mothers of the girls gave presents of money, food and milk, so as to bribe the boys to go away quietly—they were afraid the girls would be injured in the ' lifting.' It was an occasion for much merry-making, and Ceiriog relates how, in one house, a corpulent old lady was persuaded to sit in the chair. She was so heavy that the chair could not be lifted ! The ' lifters ' usually pocketed about five shillings each in money, but the younger ones were often whipped with the birch rod and sent to bed supperless that

---

[1] Robert Williams : *History and Antiquities of the Town of Aberconwy*, 1835, pp. 108—110. See also the *Cambrian Quarterly Magazine*, III, p. 366, for another similar account dated 1831.

[2] *Bye-gones*, 10 May, 1876.

night.[1] The ' lifting ' ceased at noon on both days. ' Respectable young women would not be seen out of doors before twelve o'clock at noon, but kept within their houses with the doors locked—for nothing short of locks or bolts could keep out the lifters ; and great was their relief when afternoon came that day.'[2]

The explanation of the custom, it has been suggested, lies in the commemoration of the Resurrection on this day. In a degenerate form ' lifting ' represented the crucifixion of Christ —the dressing being intended to set forth the clothing of our Lord with the purple robe ; the lifting, the nailing upon the cross ; the kiss, the betrayal ; the reward, the thirty pieces of silver.[3] The re-enactment of events in the life of Christ is a common form of commemoration as in the Palm Sunday custom of drawing a wooden ass to mark the triumphant entry of Christ into Jerusalem. In our own day the nativity play is a well-known example of the same kind of sacred drama. The religious interpretation of the origin of ' lifting,' however, may well be a rationalization of an age-old custom associated with the rites of spring but brought into the framework of a Christian festival. There are indications that a form of ' lifting ' was practised on this day in a medieval record which describes how the ladies of the bed-chamber and maids of honour on Easter Monday, 1290, entered the room of Edward I, probably for this purpose, and received a payment of fourteen pounds.[4] It is certain that to the country folk of the Welsh border-counties in the first part of the last century the religious significance, if any, of this old custom had been completely forgotten. Easter Monday was for them a day of celebration and amusement, and ' lifting ' was probably no more than a particular kind of merry-making sanctioned by immemorial tradition on this day and expected of young people. In the closely-knit communities the custom was known to all ; nothing is more amusing than to read of the surprise shown by strangers obliged to take part in

[1]Quoted in *Bye-gones*, 17 May, 1893. See also P. Roberts, *The Cambrian Popular Antiquities*, p. 225. Pennant is the only writer to mention the fiddler who accompanied the lifters (cf. Brand, *Popular Antiquities*, i. p. 106).
[2]T. G. Jones : ' History of the parish of Llansantffraid-yn-Mechain.'
[3]*ibid.*
[4]Quoted by Brand : *Popular Antiquities*, i. p. 106.

this unfamiliar ceremony for the first time.[1] In England the custom was known in the counties of Cheshire, Derbyshire, Shropshire, Staffordshire and Worcestershire, in the last century, and seems to have died out in the eighteen-sixties.[2] As far as can be judged, the custom in Wales flourished in the counties adjoining these English shires. It was apparently not known in Merioneth, according to the local historian Charles Ashton,[3] and, as we have seen, a different kind of custom obtained in Caernarvonshire. ' Lifting ' appears to have been declining in popularity in the middle of the last century in Wales as in England. The Llansanffraid account quoted above relates to c. 1840, during which period the custom was also common in Oswestry.[4] The evidence in Ceiriog's account indicates that in Llanarmon Dyffryn Ceiriog the last ' heaving ' took place about 1844.[5] About the same time the custom was ' quite common ' in Newtown, Montgomeryshire, where it apparently took place in the public houses,[6] and it was known as late as the early eighteen-sixties in Welshpool in the same county.[7] It is interesting to note that ' heaving ' ceased in Shropshire after about 1868 ;[8] probably this marks the period of its disappearance in the Welsh border-counties of the north too.

The Sunday after Easter, Low Sunday, was called in Wales *Pasg bach* or *Pasg bychan*, a name which occurs in the Welsh Laws. The corresponding form ' Little Easter ' is also known in England. The adjectives ' low ' and ' little ' distinguish the Sunday from the *great* festival of Easter Day. In certain districts a fine distinction was made between Communion on Easter Day which was attended by the rich, and that on Low Sunday which was attended by the servants and the poor. This

---

[1]The narrow escape from this ordeal of a Wesleyan minister newly-arrived at Oswestry in 1842 is described in *Bye-gones*, 8 June, 1904. Brand quotes the account of a traveller who was ' lifted ' by the maidservants at the Shrewsbury hotel where he was staying in 1799 (Brand, i, p. 107).

[2]Wright & Lones, I, pp. 108—110.

[3]*Bye-gones*, 17 May, 1893.

[4]*Bye-gones*, 8 June, 1904.

[5]*Bye-gones*, 17 May, 1893.

[6]*Bye-gones*, 16 August, 1893.

[7]*Bye-gones*, 12 November, 1902.

[8]C. S. Burne, *Shropshire Folk-Lore*, 1883, p. 336.

practice obtained at Y Ferwig, Cardiganshire, in the middle of the last century.[1]

Many customs which were held at Easter were also practised at Whitsuntide. In Conway, Caernarvon and Bangor, the form of horseplay called *stocsio*, which has already been described, was carried on at Whitsun as well as Easter.[2] In Tenby, Pembrokeshire, as in many other places, the procession and annual dinner of the 'benefit clubs' took place on Whit-Monday.[3] Like the Parish Clerks' Meeting held in the same town on Easter Monday, the club dinner seems to have been a descendant of the church ales organised at Easter and Whitsun to raise money. The Tenby women's benefit club ' walked in procession to the church, with band and banners before them, and bunches of flowers in their hands. After the service they dined, and wound up the evening by dancing "Sir Roger de Coverley," "John Sanders" and executing various other Terpsichorean feats.' The day was also marked in the same town by rabbit and puffin-shooting on Caldy Island, followed by picnics and, apparently, intemperate drinking.[4]

Whitsun was also one of the occasions when the Morris dancers made their appearance. According to Peter Roberts, ' the dancers are all men ; their dress is ornamented with ribbands, and small bells are attached to the knees. The dance itself is somewhat like that of Country Bumpkin ; and in the course of it, some one of the more active exhibits a kind of somerset, with the aid of two others. They are attended by a Jack and Gill, or, as they are called in Wales, the Fool and Megen. The fool is the same as the clown of the old comedy ; the megen, a man dressed in women's clothes, and with the face smutted to represent a hag. Both entertain the mob by ridiculous tricks; and the megen generally solicits contributions from the spectators, and keeps off the crowd by the dread of blows of her ladle.'[5] Although this description probably refers to the Morris dance as practised in the northern counties,

[1]D. Bateman : ' The Churches of the Holy Cross, Mount, and St. Pedrog, Verwig'. *Ceredigion* II, 1955, p. 212.
[2]Williams : *Aberconwy*, pp. 108—110 and *Cambrian Quarterly Magazine*, III. p. 366.
[3]*Tales & Traditions of Tenby*, pp. 23-4.
[4]*ibid*.
[5]Peter Roberts : *The Cambrian Popular Antiquities*, pp. 126-7.

certain elements, especially the bells and the male and female clowns, are reminiscent of the Glamorgan *Mari Lwyd* of the Christmastide celebrations. As might be expected the tradition of morris-dancing as well-established in Glamorgan where the name *corelwi* was used for the dance. An eighteenth century poem by Wiliam Robert of Yr Ydwal, describes the Llancarfan Morris dancers.[1] The fine silk clothes of the dancers are referred to, and the eight members of the party and their harpist are named and praised in the course of the poem. Two of them, *Sion y Nêl* and *Mawd* (Maud) also referred to as Marian—correspond to the Fool and Megen in Peter Roberts's description, and it is probable that the *Mawd* in Glamorgan was impersonated by a man. A later account of the Morris dance in Glamorgan, however, differs from the above in certain respects : there are twenty-four dancers, twelve of each sex, the youths dressed in shirts of fine linen, with two knots of ribbons on each arm, and the young women's heads decorated with several such knots. This latter account relates to the part of the Vale of Glamorgan between Cowbridge and Llantrisant, scarcely a dozen miles from Llancarfan, and it was written down in 1842.[2] We can only conclude, if the evidence from both sources is correct, that there was no more uniformity in the precise details of the Morris dance than in the *Mari Lwyd* and wassailing party or the holiday football-games. A number of varieties of Morris dancing have been recorded in England and it has been suggested that the Welsh Morris ' approximates more to the Cheshire and Derbyshire type than the elaborate and difficult dances evolved by the Morris-men of Gloucestershire and Oxfordshire. It is quite possible that the latter are a comparatively modern development dating from the latter half of the 18th century, or even later, & that in the simpler Cheshire Morris we have, not a deterioration, but an approximation to the early form of the dance.'[3] It is equally possible that the disagreement between the two descriptions of the Morris in

[1] Transcribed by Professor G. J. Williams and printed in *Llên Cymru*, III, pp. 50-52.
[2] M. Rhys : ' Unpublished Traditions of Glamorganshire,' *Cambrian Journal*, II, 1855, p. 69.
[3] H. Mellor : *Welsh Folk Dances*, 1935, p. 21. See also I. A. Williams, *English Folk-Song and Dance*, 1935, ch. ix, and W. S. Gwynn Williams : *Welsh National Music and Dance* [1933], part II, Ch. 3.

Glamorgan may be explained in terms of this elaboration which seems to have occurred in the character of the dance about the end of the eighteenth century in the English counties bordering on south Wales.

As Laurence Whistler has pointed out, Whitsun, in comparison with the festivals of Christmas and Easter, was weak in emblematic customs of a popular sort : ' A birth in a stable can be imagined, and clothed from early childhood in all the warm and human symbolism of Christmas. Rebirth can be imagined too, less easily perhaps, though on it is pinned the most profound ambition of the human mind. But the gift of Imagination itself is less imaginable . . . Nothing but joy, it seems, and the accident of time, has brought into conjunction the Whitsun Morris and the feast of the tongues of fire.'[1]

[1]Laurence Whistler : *The English Festivals*, 1947, pp. 158-9.

CHAPTER III

MAY AND MIDSUMMER

A CCORDING to the old Celtic mode of reckoning, summer began in May when the yearly rebirth of plant life was well under way. The first day of May, *Calan Mai* was in former times also known by the name *Calan Haf*, the calend of summer, in the same way that the first of November, at the tail-end of autumn, was known as *Calan Gaeaf*, the winter calend. It was in this basic division of the year into the two dominant seasons of summer and winter that the significance of these ancient festivals lay. In a real sense they symbolized to our ancestors the whole character of the ensuing season. They became dates on which certain activities traditionally began or ceased ; it has been suggested that both the Welsh and Anglo-Saxon names for November, *mis Tachwedd* and *Slótmonath*, respectively, refer to a primitive custom of slaughtering animals for winter store.[1] Another writer has indicated how in many regions, such as Highland Scotland, where the seasonal movement of cattle took place, the advent of May-day was a sign for the exodus to the summer pastures.[2] Less remote from our own day is the practice common down to the late nineteenth century (and after) of hiring farm servants for yearly or six-monthly engagements beginning with May-day (or Old May Day) and the first or thirteenth of November.[3] Hiring fairs were held on or near these days, and in many parts of Wales May-day was also the termination of house and farm tenancies.[4]

In general those pastimes which were carried on during the long evenings of the summer also began in May. In eastern Montgomeryshire the *twmpath chwarae* (village green) was

[1]T. Gwynn Jones : *Welsh Folklore and Folk Custom*, 1930, p. 146.
[2]R. U. Sayce : . The Old Summer Pastures, I,' *Mont. Coll.*, LIV, 1956.
[3]*Royal Commission on Labour :* The Agricultural Labourer, II, Wales, 1893, p. 15.
[4]e.g. Llansanffraid-ym-Mechain (*Bye-gones*, 28 May, 1873), Anglesey, and parts of Caernarvonshire (*Royal Commission on Land in Wales, Report*, 1896, pp. 477-8). Lady Day, March 25th, was more common, but, in such cases, the out-going tenant retained the use of the house and buildings until May-day or Old May Day (*ibid*).

formerly opened with great ceremony on May-day.[1] The
historian of Llansanffraid has left us an interesting account of
the customs and sports of the *twmpath chwarae* which were still
remembered by the inhabitants in the middle of the last
century. ' Probably almost every village and hamlet on the
borders possessed a "green" (or *twmpath chwarae*), as numerous
localities still bear the name. Here the inhabitants assembled
together for the purpose of enjoying themselves with sports and
pastimes, but principally dancing. Their origin is unknown,
and now these customs have entirely fallen into disuse. The
scene, as it was wont to appear on summer evenings, is described as a very striking one—the soft and sweet tones of the
harp and the dancing of the country people in their holiday
attire in one place ; while in another tennis-playing, bowling,
throwing the stone or beam, or wrestling, went on (under the
supervision of some veteran as master of the ceremonies), all
observing strictly the rules of the green. The green was
generally situated on the top of a hill, on ground higher than
any which surrounded it. It was adapted for the purpose by
levelling the surface of the ground and raising a small mound
of earth in the centre where the harpist or fiddler sat. This
was called the Twmpath. Occasionally a large stone was made
use of instead of a mound, as at Cefn Lyfnog, in this parish.
Sometimes the mound was decked with branches of oak, and
those who joined in the play danced in a circle around the
musician, the mound, and the branch. A sort of fund belonging
to the mound was raised, out of which the musician was paid.
These games seem to have been kept up throughout the
summer,—farmers and others leaving their work generally at
4 p.m. for the purpose of attending. . . . There were in this
parish four mounds or village greens, . . . but the competitions
between the various parishes in dancing and other sports and
games were decided at the Golfa Mound near Llangedwyn.'[2]
In Glamorgan the name given to a similar recreational meeting
was *taplas haf*. Like the *twmpath chwarae* this was held regularly

[1] *Bye-gones*, 28 May, 1873.
[2] T. G. Jones : ' A History of the Parish of Llansaintffraid-ym-Mechain,'
pp. 138-9.

throughout the summer ; it began however on **Easter** Monday, and not on May-day.[1]

The festival of May-day began on the previous evening, and as on Hallowe'en and the Eve of St. John's—the two other ' spirit nights ' (*vsbrydnos*), May Eve had its own customs inspired by the belief that supernatural powers were unleashed and that the spirits of the dead roamed abroad that night. Bonfires were formerly lit on May Eve in many parts of Wales. The manner in which Lewis Morris cites this practice in his list of customs suggests that it was more widely known in south Wales than in the north.[2] According to Marie Trevelyan the last of these Beltane fires in the Vale of Glamorgan were kindled in the eighteen-thirties,[3] but details of the custom were still remembered at the turn of the century. ' The fire was done in this way : Nine men would turn their pockets inside out and see that every piece of money and all metals were off their persons. Then the men went into the nearest woods, and collected sticks of nine different kinds of trees. These were carried to the spot where the fire had to be built. There a circle was cut in the sod, and the sticks were set crosswise. All around the circle the people stood and watched the proceedings. One of the men would then take two bits of oak, and rub them together until a flame was kindled. This was applied to the sticks, and soon a large fire was made. Sometimes two fires were set up side by side. These fires, whether one or two, were called *coelcerth* or bonfire. Round cakes of oatmeal and brown meal were split in four, and placed in a small flour-bag, and everybody present had to pick out a portion. The last bit in the bag fell to the lot of the bag-holder. Each person who chanced to pick up a piece of brown-meal cake was compelled to leap three times over the flames, or to run thrice between the two fires, by which means the people thought they were sure of a

---

[1] ' Cwrdd cerdd pob nos Sadwrn o ddydd Llun Pasc hyd galan gauaf, a elwir hefyd taplas hâf.' [A musical meeting every Saturday from Easter Monday to *Calan Gaeaf*, also called *taplas haf*.] (G. J. Williams, *Iolo Morganwg*, I, p. 40. Cf. the Merioneth custom in the 18th century of holding a *noswaith ganu* [singing night] every Saturday night by young people who danced to the accompaniment of a harpist. (' Ymddiddan rhwng Scrutator a Senex,' *Y Drysorfa*, 1813).

[2] H. Owen : The *Life and Works of Lewis Morris*, p. 146.

[3] Newton Nottage (1828-30), Cowbridge (1833), Nash Manor (1835), Llanilltud Fawr (1837-40), Marie Trevelyan, *Folk Lore and Folk Stories of Wales*, 1909, p. 22.

plentiful harvest. Shouts and screams of those who had to face the ordeal could be heard ever so far, and those who chanced to pick the oatmeal portions sang and danced and clapped their hands in approval, as the holders of the brown bits leaped three times over the flames, or ran three times between the two fires. As a rule, no danger attended these curious celebrations, but occasionally somebody's clothes caught fire, which was quickly put out. . . . I have also heard my grandfather say that in times gone by the people would throw a calf in the fire when there was any disease among the herds. The same would be done with a sheep if there was anything the matter with a flock. I can remember myself seeing cattle being driven between the two fires to "stop the disease spreading." When in later times it was not considered humane to drive the cattle between the fires, the herdsmen were accustomed to force the animals over the wood ashes to protect them against various ailments. . . . People carried the ashes left after these fires to their homes, and a charred brand was not only effectual against pestilence, but magical in its use. A few of the ashes placed in a person's shoes protected the wearer from any great sorrow or woe.'[1] The Midsummer and Hallowe'en bonfires were similar, though on a smaller scale.[2]

Divination was also practised on May Eve. Lewis Morris names one Anglesey form in his list of eighteenth-century customs. ' Swper nos Glanmai ' (i.e. Supper on May Eve) ' Say ye meet on ye Table In ye night. The 4 women hideing themselves in ye corners of ye room. Their sweethearts will come in & eat, though a Hundred miles off.'[3] Morris also mentions *gware gŵr gwellt* (lit. playing straw man) without giving further details.[4] This custom which continued in Anglesey and Caernarvonshire until the middle of the nineteenth century was also associated with May Eve. It was the practice for a youth who had lost his sweetheart to another to make a straw effigy and to place it near the window of the unfaithful girl or in a

[1]Quoted in Marie Trevelyan : *op. cit.*, pp. 22-24.
[2]cf. ' Goddaith Gŵyl Ifan. hela'r da trwy'r Tân ' [St. John's Eve bonfire, sending the cattle through the fire]. G. J. Williams, *Iolo Morganwg*, I, p. 39.
[3]*op. cit.*, p. 144.
[4]*op. cit.*, p. 146.

prominent place near her house. The effigy was that of the successful lover for whom she had forsaken the youth. A letter was pinned to the effigy and the quarrel between the two men often ended in a fight at the May fair.[1]

In parts of England it was formerly the practice to express contempt in a similar manner by placing elder and nettles before people's doors, and to convey a compliment by laying hawthorn branches instead.[2] Lewis Morris's terse note ' Llysiau Haf, Nos Galanmai, i.e. maying ' (' Summer plants, May Eve i.e. maying ') probably refers to this more pleasant counterpart of the *gŵr gwellt*.[3] Unfortunately there is no local confirmation of later date of this conjecture, but it is interesting to note that the custom of ' maying ' similar to those known in England, was formerly practised in Tenby, Pembrokeshire. ' On May-eve the inhabitants would turn out in troops, bearing in their hands boughs of thorn in full blossom, which were bedecked with other flowers, and then stuck outside the windows of the houses.'[4] Thorn blossoms, in fact, featured generally in the folk-lore of the month of May ; it was unlucky to bring it into the house, even though it was used for out-door decoration. In the Pendine district of Carmarthenshire on Old May Eve, the 12th of May, it was usual to plant a white-thorn tree by the door of the house and procure it from a neighbouring parish.[5] As often happens the custom in this case had outlived any superstitious explanation which it might once have had. In parts of Montgomeryshire the custom was associated with the May-flower rather than the white thorn and was carried on early on the morning of May-day when people searched the fields and meadows for these flowers. ' Having found suitable ones, they returned home and adorned the house outside, the door, windows, and the little gate, and strewed the path leading to the house with these golden flowers.'[6] In Radnorshire it was mountain ash and birch twigs

---

[1] *Y Geninen*, vol. 6, 1888, p. 216 and vol. 7, 1889, p. 62.   The custom is in these sources called *crogi gŵr gwellt* [hanging a straw man].
[2] Wright & Lones : *British Calendar Customs : England*, II, p. 000.
[3] H. Owen: *Life and Works of Lewis Morris*, p. 145.
[4] *Tales and Traditions of Tenby*, 1858, p. 21.
[5] M. Curtis : *Antiquities of Laugharne and Pendine, etc.*, 1880, p. 296.
[6] T. G. Jones : 'A History of the Parish of Llansantffraid', 4, 1871, p. 137.

that were gathered, and, as we shall see it was the birch tree
that was often used in making a maypole.[1] The decoration of
house exteriors with greenery or flowers in readiness for the
first day of summer was undoubtedly intended to herald the
advent of the new season of plant growth and possibly originated in the worship of the pagan Goddess of the Earth, of
Nature and of fertility.

May-day itself began in most districts with the singing of
May carols. These were known as *carolau Mai, carolau haf*
['summer carols'], *canu haf* ['summer singing'], or by the
descriptive term *canu dan y pared* ['singing under the wall.'] 'The
singers on visiting a family early on May morning congratulated
them on the approach of summer, and the fruitful expectation
of the season, and thence called for their gratitude to the
bountiful giver of all good gifts.'[2] The custom was popular
during the seventeenth and early eighteenth centuries. One
poet in particular, namely Huw Morus (1622—1709) of
Llansilin, Denbighshire, wrote numerous May carols many of
which were handed down by word of mouth ;[3] it is interesting
to notice that the custom of *canu dan bared* seems to have
survived longest in the counties of Denbigh and Montgomery
with which Huw Morus was closely associated. Less well-known
poets also wrote carols to be sung on May morning and in
Llanbryn-Mair, Montgomeryshire, the Rhys family of Peny-
geulan was renowned for *canu dan bared* and was the last to
carry on the custom in the parish. The carols sung by this
family included a narrative of striking events which had taken
place during the past year, some pious reflections, and occasionally an appropriate couplet or two cleverly introduced, specially
applicable to each family whose house was visited.[4] The tone
of most May carols was usually serious and many were in fact
written by clergymen. From the carols themselves and from
the written instructions accompanying them an attempt has

[1]*Kilvert's Diary*, I, pp. 119—120. In Kidwelly it was mountain ash and, possibly,
holly which were placed over doors and windows until as late as 1845 (G. Evans,
' Carmarthenshire Gleanings (Kidwelly)', p. 116.
[2]From a MS. note by John Jenkins (*Ifor Ceri*) 1770—1829, cited in *Journal of the
Welsh Folk-Song Society*, III, p. 65.
[3]cf. D. Jenkins : ' Carolau Haf a Nadolig,' *Llên Cymru*, II, 1952-3, pp. 46-54.
[4]' History of the Parish of Llanbrynmair,' *Mont. Coll.*, XXII, 1888.

been made to form a clearer picture of the custom : ' A small party (e.g. "two men and two boys" generally accompanied by a harp or a fiddle or both), proceeded very early in May morning, before the servants were up . . . and sang their carol outside ("*tan bared*"). Sometimes the maids had decked and "perfumed" the windows with lavender, rose and lily. . . . Should the performance be approved of, the party would be invited into the house and regaled with food and drink— perhaps with money also—at least we know that money was often paid for Christmas carols, but that was in churches. The practice was not confined to *Calan Mai*, or the first of May, for some carols of the 17th century are described as suitable for singing *tan Barwydydd y boreuau yn Mis Mai, yn enwedig ar foreuddydd Calanmai*, i.e. during "Mornings in May".[1] It has been suggested that the May carols were more akin to the verses sung during the *canu yn drws* [' singing at the door '] at Christmastide in seventeenth- and eighteenth-century Wales than to the Christmas carol of the *plygain* service.[2] This is probably true, but there is also much truth in the suggestion that the singing of May carols, although not connected with a specifically Christian festival, was given a more religious slant and encouraged in order to counteract the demoralizing tendencies of the more frivolous May-day customs.[3]

May-pole customs in Wales, as far as can be judged from surviving literary evidence, were of two major varieties, one of them associated with the northern counties of Flint and Denbigh, in particular, the other with parts of south Wales. In Glamorgan, however, as far as can be ascertained, the May-day custom was secondary in importance and popularity to the 'summer birch' (*y fedwen haf*) which was raised on the feast of St. John at midsummer. One of the earliest references in Welsh literature to the may-pole occurs in the poetry of Gruffydd ab Adda ap Dafydd who died about 1344. In a *cywydd* to a birch tree cut down for transport to Llanidloes, he laments its fate and contrasts its new home near the pillory in the small Mont-

<hr>

[1] *Journal of Welsh Folk Song Society*, III, p. 68.
[2] D. Jenkins : *op. cit.*
[3] *Journal of Welsh Folk Song Society*. loc. cit.

gomeryshire borough with the wood where it grew.[1] Apart from the allusions in this well-known poem little is known of the may-pole custom until the seventeenth century when, according to Professor Dodd, ' maypole-dancing to the tune of the pipes, which was spreading across the border from Cheshire and Shropshire[2] ' was encroaching on Sundays and holy-days. Whether or not the popularity of may-dancing was the result of a revival originating across the border, it is in these districts of north-east Wales that the memory of the custom lingered longest. The staid William Roberts, *Nefydd*, who was born in 1813, confesses that he spent many a pleasant hour looking at the dancers when he was a child in Llannefydd, west Denbighshire ;[3] and even at the close of the century may-dancing had not completely died out in this part of Wales.

According to Nefydd the May-pole custom was called *Codi'r Fedwen*, [raising the birch], in south Wales, and *y gangen haf*, [the summer branch] in the north. He adds that *dawnsio haf*, [summer dancing]—often in conjunction with Morris-dancing or *dawns y fedwen*, [the dance of the birch] was at the time he wrote (1852) very well known throughout Wales. He describes the form which the custom took in south Wales as follows, 'The may-pole was prepared by painting it in different colours ; then the leader of the dance would come and place his circle of ribbon about the pole, and each in his turn after him, until the May-pole was all ribbons from one end to the other. Then was it raised into position and the dance begun ; each took his place in the dance according to the circle of ribbon which he had placed on the May-pole.'[4] A similar description with more details, is given of the custom in Tenby, Pembrokeshire. ' May-poles were reared up in different parts of the town, decorated with flowers, coloured papers, and bunches of variegated ribbon. On May-day the young men and maiden would, joining hand in hand, dance round the May-poles and "thread the needle," as it was termed. A group of from fifty to

[1]No. LXV in Ifor Williams a Thomas Roberts : *Dafydd ap Gwilym a'i Gyfoeswyr*, 1935. The poem is translated in full in *Trans. Hon. Soc. Cymmrod.*, 1940, pp. 226-9 by Sir Idris Bell.

[2]A. H. Dodd : *Studies in Stuart Wales*, 1952, p. 13.

[3]W. Roberts : *Crefydd yr Oesoedd Tywyll*, p. 95.

[4]*op. cit.*, p. 95.

100 persons would wend their way from one pole to another, till they had had thus traversed the town. Meeting on their way other groups, who were coming from an opposite direction, both parties would form a "lady's chain," and so pass on their respective ways. The may-poles belonged to the children of the several localities in which they were erected, and it was the custom for the possessors of a pole to endeavour to pull down those set up in other places. A watch was therefore left round each, and frequently the parents would mount guard to repel the daring invaders. If, however, a surprise was effected, and the assault proved successful, both parties joined in the joke, and everything proceeded amicably.[1] In Kidwelly, the May-pole was from twelve to fourteen feet in length, made gay with evergreens, flowers and ribbons. It was carried by the young people along the chief streets of the town with much singing and merriment. The procession ended with the fixing of the pole in the ground ; this was followed by dancing which was kept up till evening.[2] Apart from the small size of the may-pole used in Kidwelly—sixty feet was quite a common height for may-poles in England—the custom as practised in south Wales differed very little from the may-pole dancing found in many parts of England.[3]

The northern version of the may-pole custom was somewhat different. Nefydd, who has given us a brief summary of its characteristics compares it with the *Mari Lwyd* party at Christmas. ' Between 12 and 20 young men used to prepare to go may-dancing (*dawnsio haf*) like the youths of Gwent used to go around in the Christmas holidays to play *Mari Lwyd* ; they would dress in white clothes usually, decorated with ribbons of all colours, except two (members of the party) who were called Fool and *Cadi*. These two characters resembled *Pwnsh* and *Siwan* in the *Mari Lwyd* in respect of their clothes and appearance ; one was to carry the *cangen haf* [lit. summer branch] which was usually splendidly made. Quite often one might see about a dozen watches silver dishes etc. among other

---

[1] *Tales and Traditions of Tenby*, 1858, pp. 21-23. The stealing of the pole was also well-known in the *Gŵyl Ifan* birch custom in Glamorgan. See below p. 109.
[2] G. Evans : ' Carmarthenshire Gleanings (Kidwelly),' p. 116.
[3] Wright & Lones : *British Calendar Customs : England*, II, 217ff.

things, decorating the ' branch.' There were 12 dancers, sometimes more, sometimes fewer, and one man who played the *crwth* or harp ; or sometimes two, playing both *crwth* and harp. There was nothing particular, except the singing and the dancing—as well as the morris-dancing—in the whole observance, apart from the mirth of the Fool and the *Cadi*. Usually the best dancers available in the country districts were among the members of the party.'[1] Further light is thrown on this custom by an account written in 1825 by H.T.B., a correspondent of William Hone's *Every-Day Book*, who incidentally lamented the slow decline in the May-dancing, as he called it, during his day.

From H.T.B.'s lengthy account[2] we glean much interesting information about May-dancing, although, unfortunately, no reference is made to the district where the custom was found. It appears, however, from the details given—the use of the name *Cadi* and the popularity of the ' Cheshire Round ' as a dance— that the description relates to the Counties of Denbigh and Flint, i.e. the same region as that to which Nefydd refers. According to H.T.B. the May-dancing was carried on by the ' labouring classes ' who used to look forward eagerly to the annual performance. Even a fortnight before the day, there was much speculation as to who would be the *Cadi* and who would carry the garland. About a week before May-day, each youth borrowed the gayest ribbons possible and got his sweetheart to decorate his new white shirt of fine linen with bows and puffs of ribbons as she saw fit. Meanwhile the chosen garland-bearer and one of the more respectable dancers went from house to house to borrow watches, silver spoons etc. for the decoration of the garland, which consisted of a long staff or pole with a triangular or square frame attached to it. The frame was covered with strong white linen and the silver spoons were fixed on it in the shape of stars, squares, and circles. Between these were rows of watches ; and at the top of the frame opposite the pole in its centre, the collection was crowned by the largest of the ornaments borrowed—usually a silver cup or tankard. The

[1] W. Roberts, *op. cit.*, pp. 94-5.
[2] W. Hone : *The Every-Day Book*, Vol. I, 1825, cols. 562-5.

decorated garland was left over May-eve at the farmhouse from whence the most liberal loan of silver had been received, or with a farmer known to all as a good master and liberal to the poor ; its deposit was a token of respect.

According to H.T.B. the chief character in the May-dancing was the *Cadi* ; there is no mention of the Fool as a separate person, but the definition of the role of the *Cadi* as ' marshal, orator, buffoon and money collector,' and the description of his person make it clear that the *Cadi* was also the Fool in this case. His dress was partly male, partly female : a coat and waistcoat for the upper part of the body, and petti-coats for the lower part. He wore a hideous mask, or else his face was blackened and his lips, cheeks and the orbits of his eyes painted red.

We are also given some details of the dress worn by the rest of the party, which, including the garland-bearer, numbered thirteen. Their costume consisted of entirely new clothing from the hat to the shoes which were made neat and of light texture for dancing. The white plaited skirts (decorated in the manner also described) were worn over the rest of their clothing ; the black velveteen breeches had knee-ties half way down to the ankles, and the yarn hose was light grey in colour. In their hats were large rosettes of varied colours, with stream-ers ; and around the crown of each hat was placed a wreath of ribbon. Each dancer carried in his right hand a white pocket handkerchief.

From the place of assembly (usually a tavern), the procession set off on May morning to the sound of church bells. The dancers walked in single file or in pairs, headed by the *Cadi*, who was followed by the garland-bearer and the fiddler. As the procession moved slowly along the road, the *Cadi*, carrying a ladle, varied his station and sought a donation from every person encountered. When the party arrived at a farmhouse, the garland-bearer took his stand, and the violin struck up ' an old national tune ' traditionally used at this occasion.

The dances performed in front of each farmhouse are described by H.T.B. in a general way : ' the dancers move forward in a regular quick-step to the tune, in the order of procession ; and at each turn of the tune throw up their white handkerchiefs with a shout, and the whole facing quickly about, retrace their steps, repeating the same manoeuvre until the tune is once played. The music and dancing then vary into a reel, which is succeeded by another dance, to the old tune of "Cheshire Round".[1]

While the party dance their steps, the *Cadi* played the clown and sought money from the householders, thanking them with bows and curtsies. The whole procedure of dance and collection was repeated at each farmhouse visited. The dancers, we are told did not confine themselves to their own parish, but moved freely from one farm to another and to any nearby country town. In the evening they returned to their village to the accompaniment of church bells ; the money collected, after expenses had been duly met, was used in jovial festivity.

The descriptions given by Nefydd and H.T.B. agree on essentials, though certain minor points are different. H.T.B.'s garland-bearer seems to have been a different kind of character from Nefydd's Fool. John Jones (*Myrddin Fardd*) who is not always a reliable source, describes the Fool as a peculiarly dressed person who carried in one hand the 'secret banner of the order, covered with symbols of the summer ' and in the other a ' wooden cup with a long handle ' to take the collection. The *Cadi*, according to the same writer, was comically dressed in an old hag's clothes and carried a broom in her hand in order to keep the floor clean for the company to dance, to keep spectators away, and to induce people whom she met to part with some money.'[2] Another account, describing a party of boys who sang from door to door at Pen-y-ffordd, Mostyn, Flintshire, on May-day 1899, speaks of the blackened faces of the dancers, the branches which they carried, and the women's skirts worn by some of them.[3] Yet another account relating to the same district describes the colliers from Mostyn who danced in white skirts, tied up with red ribbon, and *white* trousers, and who jumped for the highest.[4] More recently, a brief description from

---

[1] *ibid.*
[2] John Jones (*Myrddin Fardd*) : *Llen Gwerin Sir Gaernarfon*, p. 255. It is recorded by *Llew Tegid* that May-dancers from Flintshire used to visit Bangor on May-day until about 1860. *JWFSS*, III, p. 73.
[3] *JWFSS*, III, p. 72.
[4] *JWFSS*, III, p. 69.

Llanasa, Flintshire, received in 1958 in reply to a questionnaire sent out by the Welsh Folk Museum, mentions the ' people dressed up in various costumes (who) danced and sang through the village carrying branches of trees as banners' about seventy years ago.[1] The tradition of May-dancing, in fact, died hard, and the memory of it has lingered down to the present day, as the foregoing extract indicates. Fortunately, the *Cadi ha'* dance was described in a fairly detailed manner ' some time before 1914 ' when a new interest was being taken in the traditional dances and folk songs of Wales.[2]

In contrast to the south-Wales may-pole dance, the *cadi ha'* was essentially a peripatetic custom in which the garland replaced the may-pole proper. Like most variations on the Morris dance, it was (unlike, for example, the Tenby may-pole dancing described above) danced exclusively by a party of males attended by humorous characters. Unlike the country dance, it was ' no dance to be indulged in carelessly by boys and girls upon any festive occasion.'[3] It was, rather, a dance for a team of experienced dancers who had rehearsed together and who were equipped with all the details of costume and adornments presented by tradition. Geographically, and probably historically, its connections were with the Morris tunes and dances of Lancashire and Cheshire. In fact one of the tunes recorded was identified as ' a somewhat garbled form of the well-known Lancashire professional Morris-tune connected with the Helston Furry Dance air ' on to which another old dance tune, the ' Liverpool hornpipe ' had been tacked.[4] The widespread use in the early eighteenth century of airs and dances having English names, and therefore probably an English provenance, has been noted in another connection by Dr. Thomas Parry in the county of Anglesey which, *a priori*, would have appeared far less open to English influence than the border counties of Flintshire and Denbigh.[5] Notwithstanding

[1]Welsh Folk Museum MS. 399.
[2]Several versions of the *Cadi ha'* songs are given in the *JWFSS*, III pp. 69-74. A description of the dance is given in Hugh Mellor : *Welsh Folk Dances*, 1935, pp. 19-20 and, in reconstructed form, on pp. 59-61.
[3]Iolo A. Williams : *English Folk-Song and Dance*, 1935, p. 145.
[4]*JWFSS*, III, 71.
[5]Thomas Parry : *Baledi'r Ddeunawfed Ganrif*, p. 81.

the possibility that May-dancing in the form recorded in the nineteenth century may have spread from over the border in the seventeenth century, as Professor Dodd has suggested, it clearly won a place in the affections of the Welsh-speaking ' labouring classes ' and had shed nearly all traces of its alien origin. On the other hand, it may be, as Cecil Sharp has suggested, ' obviously a Welsh form of the world-wide custom of celebrating, or worshipping the resurrection of the Nature Spirit at Spirit time . . .' with the man-woman character who possibly ' symbolizes the union between the father (i.e. the heavens and rain) and the mother (earth), resulting in the fertilization of the soil ; and the blossoming of vegetation.'[1] Its origin and early history may be obscure, but its popularity in those parts of Wales where it was recorded during the last century, cannot be gainsaid.

In Glamorgan the counterpart of the may-pole was the "summer birch" (*y fedwen haf*) which was placed in position on the eve of St. John at midsummer ; in fact the feast of St. John, and the preceding night, seem to have attracted this and other customs from the purely pagan festival of midsummer. In a poem, *Taplas Gwainfo*, by William Robert the blind poet of Yr Ydwal, Llancarfan, we have a contemporary description of the birch raised in Wenvoe in the Vale of Glamorgan on a St. John's Eve in the middle of the eighteenth century.[2] We are told that ' Sr Edmond Thomas ' had sent his carpenter to trim the pole until it was round in shape, and to decorate it with many-coloured pictures. The young women adorned it with gilded and ribboned wreaths ; and it was apparently surmounted by a weather-cock with gilded feathers and with ribbons fixed to its tail. Beneath the weather-cock a banner floated freely in the breeze. If anybody were to try to steal the pole, there would be enough hefty lads to prevent them. After calling on his listeners to come to see the fine dancing at Wenvoe, William Robert expresses the hope that the custom of ' raising the birch ' will be kept up each *Gŵyl Ifan*.

[1] *JWFSS*, III, pp. 73.

[2] G. J. Williams : ' William Robert o'r Ydwal,' *Llên Cymru*, III, 1954-5, p. 48-50. The erection of a pole on Midsummer day was also customary in Cornwall in early nineteenth century. See Wright and Lones ; *British Calendar Customs*, III, p. 21.

The details given by William Robert are confirmed and augmented by other accounts of the ' summer birch ' custom. The diary of William Thomas (1727-95), of Michaelston-super-Ely, near St. Fagans, contains, among other interesting material, a reference to the theft of the ' summer birch ' in June 1768.[1] The St. Fagans villagers that year were forced to guard their ' birch ' with guns against the attacks of about fifty persons from St. Nicholas and district. The ' painted wooden god ' was guarded all night ; and a day or two later the St. Nicholas inhabitants were to be joined by people from Penmark and Llancarfan, according to the reports received by the St. Fagans villagers. To prevent the theft of the ' birch ' the help of about a hundred persons from Llandaff and Cardiff was secured. As Professor G. J. Williams has pointed out,[2] another account written in 1842 by Morgan Rhys and dealing with the ' unpublished traditions ' of the Vale of Glamorgan indicates that ' it was considered a great disgrace for ages to the parish that lost its birch, whilst on the other hand, the parish that succeeded in stealing a decked bough, and preserving its own, was held up in great esteem. . . . According to usage, no parish that had once lost its birch could ever after hoist another, until it had succeeded in stealing one that belonged to some of the neighbouring parishes.'[3] This last description refers to the ' old mode of celebrating the Wakes ' and mentions specifically that the ' birch ' was hoisted on Easter Monday. Professor Williams states that the author was, in all probability, relying on what he had heard in his youth. If this is so, it is possible that the writer has confused the opening of the *taplas haf* on Easter Monday, to which Iolo Morganwg refers,[4] with the raising of the birch on St. John's Eve. Rhys's account emphasizes the special celebrations on Easter Saturday when the dancing began at two and continued until sunset ; he also comments that both old and young looked forward to the periodical return of ' this festive season.' These clearly refer to the *taplas*

[1]G. J. Williams : ' Dyddiadur William Thomas o Lanfihangel-ar-Elai,' *Morgannwg*, I, 1957, p. 21.

[2]G. J. Williams : Glamorgan Customs in the 18th century, *Gwerin*, I, 1957, p. 105.

[3]*The Cambrian Journal*, March 1853, pp. 68-9.

[4]See page 96 above.

which was held each Saturday from Easter to Hallowe'en, and
if Morgan Rhys was not guilty of confusion, it seems probable
that, in some parts at least, the ' birch,' which was the highlight
of the midsummer *taplas*, was also hoisted when the season was
inaugurated at Easter. Just as May-day celebrated the return
of summer, so did Easter Monday mark the passing of Lent and
its privations and the imminent approach of the benign spring
weather when out-of-door amusements could be revived once
more. What could have been more natural than for the
' summer birch ', the very symbol of summer, to have become
associated with the re-opening of the *Taplas haf*?

Evidence from other parts of Wales indicates that the
' summer birch ' custom was also known outside Glamorgan,
though not perhaps so popularly observed as in that county.
The bare reference, *Dydd gŵyl Ieuan Pawl Haf* [' St. John's Feast
Day, a summer pole '] which is given by Lewis Morris tells us
very little apart from the mere existence of a similar custom in
Anglesey.[1] Another tradition pertaining to the Capel Hendre
district of Llandybïe, Carmarthenshire, has been recorded
about 1863 by the writer of an essay on local history.

> Dances were held on Banc y Naw Carreg and in another place
> called Pant-teg. The dance was to begin on St. John's Day and
> to continue, if the weather were favourable, for nine days. There
> were one or two harpists, and the assembly, both males and
> females, used to dance. They used to set a birch tree in the earth
> and decorate its branches with wreaths of flowers. The prettiest
> wreaths were placed on the highest branches. This custom was
> kept up until 1725.[2]

If the account is accurate the birch was not trimmed as in
Glamorgan ; the branches instead of being lopped off were
used in the decoration of the tree. In the same county, at
Kidwelly, we have already noted that the may-pole custom
was practised on May-day.[3] By the latter part of the nineteenth
century the custom of hoisting a pole on May-day and on St.
John's Day had long been discontinued and even the memory
of it had virtually disappeared.[4]

[1]H. Owen : *The Life and Works of Lewis Morris* (1701-65), p. 145.
[2]Reproduced by the Rev. Gomer M. Roberts in the *Carmarthen Antiquary*, I, 59.
[3]See p. 103 above.
[4]D. G. Williams : ' Casgliad o Len-gwerin Sir Gaerfyrddin,' p. 298.

Like May Eve, St. John's Eve was celebrated by a bonfire ;[1] it was likewise an evening on which people peered into the future with the aid of various forms of divination. These generally took the form of finding out one's future partner in marriage. One method, which was prevalent in the border districts of Montgomeryshire, was *ffatio*, or washing an article of clothing in a well at midnight. ' This was done by beating the garment with a flattened instrument, called a Bat Staff, and whilst this operation was being carried on the following doggerel was repeated several times, *Sawl ddaw i gyd-fydio, doed i gyd-ffatio* [He who would my partner be, let him come and wash with me]. Many a tale is told of how the master met his servant at the well, and how that the maid in due course and in fulfilment of the ordeal of *ffatio* was advanced to the head of the table to *cyd-fydio* as lawful wife of her former master.'[1] Another method popular in the same district was to walk around the church nine times and a half ; ' when ending the circles at the church door, a knife which the diviner had in his hand was placed in the keyhole, and the following words were uttered at the same time with emphasis : *Dyma'r twca, lle mae'r wain ?* [Here is the knife, where is the sheath ?].'[2] Lewis Morris refers to similar forms of divination in Anglesey, a century earlier, and it is likely that they were widely known throughout Wales.[3]

Divination was popular at St. John's Eve probably because it was formerly believed that spirits went abroad, this eve being the second of *y tair ysbrydnos* [the three spirit-nights]. It was the custom in many parts of the country to place over the doors of houses sprigs of St. John's-wort or, if this were not available, the common mug-wort ; the intention was to purify the house from evil spirits.[4] St. John's-wort gathered at noon on St. John's Day was thought to be good for several complaints and if

[1]*Bye-gones* ; 25th June, 1873.
[2]*ibid.*
[3]' But ye most devilish of all is that of carrying a drawn sword in hand, laying ye scabbard under ye door of ye church and goeing 3 times round ye church & pointing the sword towards ye door each time, ye last time your true love or ye Devil will hold ye scabbard for you.' ' Golchi crys yn y ffynon, a'r cariad yn dyfod i'w droi ' [washing a shirt in the well, and the lover coming to turn it '] H. Owen : *op. cit.*, pp. 144 and 145.
[4]*Bye-gones*, 8 May, 1872.

dug at midnight on the Eve of St. John the roots were good for driving the devil and witches away. The plant could also be used to forecast the length of life ;[1] it was, in fact, at mid-summer, a charm and a means of divination, partly owing to its association with St. John, although the use of the plant may well be pre-Christian.[2]

In conclusion, two St. John's Eve customs, which appear to have little logical connection with the foregoing practices, may be mentioned. In the Gwendraeth Fawr Valley, Carmarthen-shire, it was the custom for the owners of the local lime-kilns to make merry with their men on St. John's Eve or, according to others, St. John's Day.[3] In the same county, at Pendine, it was customary on Midsummer Day for people to go from house to house to ask for milk wherewith to make the Midsummer pudding. We are told that it was given bountifully.[4] These are probably local customs peculiar to these particular districts ; for most of Wales, St. John's Eve and Day were the occasion for bonfires, divination and dancing around the summer birch.

[1]M. Trevelyan : *Folk-Lore and Folk-Stories of Wales*, p. 251.
[2]In *Iolo Morganwg's* list *Llysiau Gwyl Ieuan*, and *llysiau llwydion nos-wyl Ieuan*, in Lewis Morris's probably refer to the same plant.
[3]G. Evans : 'Carmarthenshire Gleanings (Kidwelly)', 1915, p. 110.
[4]M. Curtis : *The Antiquities of Laugharne, etc.*, p .205.

CHAPTER IV

HARVEST AND WINTER'S EVE

WITH the garnering of the harvest, the last of the major agricultural tasks of the year is at an end. The threshing, in the days when the flail was universally used, could be prolonged over the winter months to fill in time, but the harvest itself, in a country with a capricious climate, was always a matter for anxiety on the part of the countryman, and its end a subject for rejoicing. Since the early Victorian period it is in the harvest-thanksgiving service, in both church and chapel, that gratitude for a bountiful crop safely stored has found expression. Formerly, however, harvest-time was marked by customs which were probably pre-Christian in origin. In the course of many centuries these customs lost their ritual significance and had become merely an outlet for rejoicing and merriment natural to the occasion. They did not have to be understood to be enjoyed by those who took part in them ; and they were enjoyed all the more for the hard work and anxiety which had preceded them. They did not exist in a vacuum but were part of the economy and social organization which formerly prevailed in rural Wales. Some of them were, perhaps, no more than an adornment, but their survival depended in a real sense on the continuation of the farming system which they adorned.

The practice of *cymhortha* which was characteristic of Welsh medieval society had much to commend it to the peasants of Wales in more recent times, and co-operative work-groups on the pattern of the traditional *cymhorthau* were still characteristic of the farm economy of the *tyddyn* until the recent spread of mechanized agriculture. On a lesser scale the same principle is still evident at the present day in the shearing-parties where neighbouring sheep-farmers help each other in a task which would be impracticable if attempted individually. Dependence on one's neighbours for periodical help with the work is in fact one of the salient features of farming in a peasant society.[1]

[1]Cf. C. Arensberg : *The Irish Countryman*, 1937, pp. 62ff.

Although mutual aid involving twenty or more persons was formerly practised at other times during the farming season,[1] it was during the corn harvest that it was to be seen at its best and in conjunction with *y gaseg fedi* [the harvest mare] and other related customs. D. G. Williams, writing on Carmarthenshire, states that one of these customs, *y fedel wenith* [the wheat reaping-party] survived longer in the eastern and northern parts of that county than in the west. Basically, it was a working group consisting of farmers who arranged beforehand not to cut their wheat on the same day so as to be able to help each other. On an agreed date persons from each farm, together with any others who could work at the harvest, assembled on a particular farm in sufficient numbers to cut and bind the wheat crop of that farm in a single day. Both men and women participated in the work, and Williams gives details of the way in which the tasks were apportioned between the sexes. The day's work was rounded off with a special supper which included a dish, called *whipod*, consisting of rice, white bread, raisins, currants, treacle and other ingredients. Following this the whole party engaged in dancing and games including *Dai Siôn Goch* (a dance with a broom by two persons dressed in tattered clothes) and *Rhibo* which may originally have been a fertility rite. In this game six men stood in two rows facing each other, each holding the hands of the person opposite him. A man and a woman were laid side by side between the two rows and resting on the arms of the six men. The couple was thrown up several times into the air and caught by the arms of the throwers.[2]

A similar working party in the neighbouring county of Cardigan is described a century earlier by Lewis Morris. In a letter dated the 18th of August 1760 he wrote that he expected between forty and fifty neighbours to assist in reaping his rye. In the feast following the day's work, the fare consisted of

[1]Charles Ashton describes the co-operative manuring of land in Llanuwchllyn and Dinas Mawddwy in the 1850's when one or more persons from each farm would give a day's labour to a neighbour to help him complete the work in a single day. Each helper would be repaid in a similar manner and the work-party, its composition slightly different each time, would move from farm to farm in the district. During the period mentioned hand-barrows were used to carry the manure. ' Bywyd Gwledig yn Nghymru,' p. 58.

[2]D. G. Williams : ' Casgliad o Len-gwerin Sir Gaerfyrddin,' p. 302.

' the contents of a brewing pan of beef and mutton, with arage and potatoes and pottage, and pudding of wheaten flour, about twenty gallons of light ale and over twenty gallons of beer.' At this feast too, the supper was followed by dancing on the wooden floor of the barn to the music of the fiddle and with supplies of beer and tobacco to hand.[1] In replying to his brother's letter, Richard Morris refers to a similar practice in Anglesey where the food—potatoes, turnips, oatcakes and whey—was somewhat less remarkable.[2] It is interesting to note that although Lewis Morris was acquainted with the harvest-mare custom—it is mentioned as *torri pen y wrach* in his list of Anglesey customs—neither he nor his brother refers to its existence in this exchange of letters. D. G. Williams, further-more, discusses *y fedel wenith* and *y gaseg fedi* separately in such a way as to suggest that, despite a certain obvious overlap, the two customs existed independently in Carmarthenshire. The truth is probably that the harvest home could exist without the *caseg-fedi* custom, but that where the latter was kept up there was usually a festive harvest supper.

According to Williams,[3] the helpers who came to assist on the last day of the harvest on the larger farms were more numerous. They would include small-holders who gave so many days' help in the harvest in return for the loan of a horse and cart, for a row or two of potatoes in a field, or for a supply of farmyard manure. Although the helpers were in reality repaying a favour, it was customary for every man who took part to get some tobacco, and for every woman to receive a candle to take home with her each night. In north Cardiganshire it was formerly the practice to give each of the men and women a sheaf to take home in the evening.[4] The continual exchange of gifts and favours in this manner between dependent parties serves to build up a fund of good-will which in turn promotes active co-operation in work ; and it was in this atmosphere that the merry-making associated with the *caseg fedi* took place.

The *caseg fedi* or harvest-mare was an ornament made from

[1] J. H. Davies (ed.) : *The Morris Letters*, II, 1909, p. 241-2.
[2] *op. cit.*, p. 255.
[3] D. G. Williams : *op. cit.*, pp. 299—300.
[4] J. C. Davies : *Folk-lore of West and Mid-Wales*, 1911, p. 78.

the last tuft of corn to be harvested[1] (See Plates 7 and 8). The
excitement would begin to mount even before the last patch of
corn was ready for the reaping-hook. In the Llandysul district
of Cardiganshire, the whetstone was concealed when the reapers were preparing to sharpen their hooks for the last time.[2] We
are told that in Llansilin, Denbighshire, there was a special significance to the last rabbit captured from the shrinking area of
standing corn.[3] But in all areas where the custom has been recorded the ceremony began when the last tuft in the field was
reached. This was left standing, and the head-servant would
kneel and divide it into three parts, plaiting them skilfully together and securing them with straw below the ears. In some
parts there would be from eight to ten ears,[4] while in others it
was often the practice to prop up the plaited stems with a twig or
branch from the hedge, if it was too flimsy to stand alone.[5] The
reapers would stand a certain distance away from the ' mare '
and prepare to throw their reaping-hooks at it. Often the
distance would be disputed by some of the party, those with a
poor aim wanting to stand further away. Usually the distance
would be fifteen to twenty yards,[6] but sometimes as much as
forty yards.[7] Beginning with the head-servant the reapers would
hurl their reaping-hooks at the sheaf, the hooks being thrown to
travel horizontally just above the ground. Sometimes the worst
marksmen were allowed to throw first and if the sheaf were not
cut after each one had thrown his sickle, it was left to the head-
servant to cut it. The successful reaper would then cry out in
some such rhyme as :

> Bore y codais hi,
> Hwyr y dilynais hi,
> Mi ces hi, mi ces hi !

[Early in the morning I got on her track ; late in the evening I
followed her, I have had her, I have had her !].

[1]See also I. C. Peate : ' Corn-customs in Wales,' *Man*, 1930, No. 122.
[2]W. J. Davies : *Hanes Plwyf Llandyssul*, 1896, p. 233.
[3]*Bye-gones*, 31 October, 1928.
[4]*Bye-gones*, 18 December, 1872.
[5]D. G. Williams : *op. cit.*, p. 300.
[6]*ibid.*
[7]*South Wales Daily News*, 8 February, 1902.

He was then questioned by the rest :

Beth gest ti ? [What did you have ?]

and would answer, together with the others,

Gwrach, gwrach, gwrach ! [a hag, a hag, a hag !]

This was the doggerel used in Pembrokeshire where the term *gwrach* was applied to the last tuft. In parts of Carmarthenshire the last line of the reaper's rigmarole was *Pen medi bach mi ces !* [I got a little harvest-mare], the mare being also known by the name *y gaseg ben fedi* [the-end-of-the-reaping-mare]. In this version there was no questioning by the reapers, instead the whole party shouted in chorus, *Ar 'i gwar hi !* [On top of her !]

In parts of Pembrokeshire the successful competitor would be the master for the day, and we are told that the honour was much coveted. If it happened at ten o'clock in the morning or earlier, the remainder of the day would be spent in innocent games.[1] The most boisterous part of the custom, however, was the task of taking the ' mare ' into the farmhouse. The household was often warned of the cutting of the last tuft and the womenfolk probably augmented by helpers who had come to prepare the harvest feast, sought to make the entry of the ' mare ' difficult. For the reaper to succeed it was necessary for the plaited tuft to be kept wholly dry and to be hung in its proper place on a beam in the kitchen, or laid on the table. The womenfolk would fill buckets, pans and utensils of all sorts with water and other liquids and try to wet the ' mare.' As it was not known who the successful reaper was, a great deal of horse-play usually took place, and many attempts were made to deceive the womenfolk so that the bearer of the sheaf (who often hid it under his clothes) could complete his task.

If the sheaf was brought to the proper place dry, the bearer, by tradition, could command as much beer as he wanted. This was generally the practice in eastern Carmarthenshire ; to the west of the same county the prize in the nineteenth century was a shilling given by the master of the house.[2] In addition the winner was given the place of honour at the table during the feast. If he failed in his task he forfeited his beer and was made

[1]*South Wales Daily News*, 8 February, 1902.
[2]D. G. Williams : *op. cit.*, p. 301.

to sit at the foot of the table and be the object of derision. Whichever way the battle went, the special food and the evening's festivities were enjoyed by the reapers and the household alike. The ' mare ' would be kept in the house as a decoration and ' to show that all the corn had been reaped.' Often it would be replaced by a fresh one at the following harvest. In Llansilin, Denbighshire, corn from the dolly was sometimes used at sowing-time to mix with the seed corn, ' so as to teach it to grow.'[1] In the same district it was sometimes the custom for the last sheaf to be placed on the fork of a tree in the stack yard or on the cross beam of the barn.[2]

Besides making for the house with the ' mare ' concealed under his clothes, the reaper who succeeded in cutting the tuft could take it to the field of a neighbouring farm where the harvest had not been completed. He would pretend that he had come on an errand, and throw it in front of the head-servant as he reaped. Often this task was entrusted to the fastest runner ; and not without reason, for the reapers would hurl their hooks at him as he fled. If he were caught he would be bound hand and foot with straw and left on the field or thrown into a river. Sometimes the ' mare ' was taken surreptitiously into a neighbour's house, which had to be in a different parish. If this condition was fulfilled nobody would touch the bearer, but he could demand a prize of a shilling from the farmer if the ' mare ' were still dry. If he were caught he would be taken back to his own farm and made to clean all the clogs and old shoes within reach. But nobody, in Carmarthenshire, was allowed to take the ' mare ' to a neighbour's place nor shout at him over the hedgerow—a degeneration of the custom—after *Ffair Gŵyl Iwan Fychan*, a fair held on September 9th in Carmarthen.[3] In Pembrokeshire the custom was to send the ' mare ' to the farmer who was behind with his harvest only if his farm was between the sender's and the sea. This was a recognition of climatic influence and an imputation of dilatoriness on the part of the farmer who should already have finished reaping.[4]

[1]*Bye-gones*, 31 October, 1928.
[2]*ibid.*
[3]D. G. Williams : *op. cit.*, p. 301.
[4]*Bye-gones*, 25 December, 1895.

In the border districts of mid-Wales, there were certain variations in the custom. As will be seen from the descriptions in the catalogue, the corn ornaments from eastern Wales were more artistically made and were obviously made purely for decorative purposes. They were finely plaited and were hung not only in the farm-houses but also in the reapers' cottages. The example from Yockleton, Shropshire (No. 62, Plate 8), for instance, was made in 1928 by an 84-year old farm worker who brought one annually to his employer's house ' for luck ' ; his name for it was ' the little cage.'[1] In the same county the custom corresponding to the *caseg fedi* was known as ' crying the mare,' but in many districts the corn ornament had been completely divorced from the ceremony of completing the harvest. The custom was for the men of the farmer who was the first in the district to finish harvesting to assemble at the end of the task and proclaim their satisfaction and to taunt their less fortunate neighbours by offering to send an imaginary mare supposed to be in the possession of their master. In other parts of Shropshire a mare really was sent.[2]   In another border district, probably Montgomeryshire, the custom of ' sending the mare ' was said to be common about 1830. The mare in this case was a corn ornament and it was sent by the farm-workers, who had finished their harvest, to a less fortunate farmer, who similarly handed it on when he completed his harvest. The last farmer would have the disgrace of keeping the mare for twelve months.[3] Further north, in Denbighshire, the custom of the *caseg fedi* had deteriorated into hanging ' a tuft of wheat, neatly tied with a flattened straw ' from the ceiling, although better examples were formerly made.[4]

In the same border districts an ornament, similar to the Yockleton example, was put on corn-stacks as a decoration. In Llansilin, Denbighshire, the earlier stacks were always round, and a ' small sheaf of plaited ears and stalks ' was inserted, often with great ceremony, on the crown of the stacks after

[1]I. C. Peate : *op. cit.* See also L. F. Chitty : 'A Harvest Figure from Yockleton, Shropshire,' *Shropshire Archaeological Transactions :* XLVIII, i, 1935, pp. 61-3.
[2]*Bye-gones*, 13 May, 1896, and C. S. Burne : *Shropshire Folk Lore*, 1883, p. 373.
[3]*Bye-gones*, 18 December, 1872.
[4]T. Gwynn Jones : *Welsh Folklore and Folk Custom*, p. 157.

they had been thatched.[1] In the Tanat valley, east Mont-gomeryshire, where a similar practice has been recorded the name given to the plaited tuft was *twffyn*.[2] The custom was also found in Yockleton itself.[3]

In Wales, corn customs similar to the *caseg fedi* or its mid-Wales variant have been recorded in Anglesey,[4] Cardiganshire (Bow Street),[5] parts of Caernarvonshire,[6] and south Pem-brokeshire.[7] Dr. Peate has pointed out that the provenance of the customs, to the extent to which they have been recorded, coincides with some of the chief wheat-growing areas of Wales.[8] Similar ceremonies however, have been recorded in England, France, Greece, Germany, Scandinavia and Finland,[9] and it is possible that the widespread distribution of the custom reflects its great antiquity.

The most notable attempt to explain the content of these customs is that of Sir James Frazer in *The Golden Bough*.[10] After referring to the variations in different parts of northern Europe, he suggests that the corn-spirit is represented both by the last sheaf (which was sometimes anthropomorphic) and by the person who cuts or binds or threshes it ; the unseen power of vegetative growth still remains potent in the last tuft to be cut. Its fertilising influence is shown by the taking of some of the grain from the last sheaf to mix with the new corn, as in Llansilin. Frazer sees this characteristic of fertility in certain associated customs and beliefs as well as in the similarity of the corn ornament to a pregnant woman. Following this approach, the stripping off of some of the clothes of the bearer of the ' mare ' (which was sometimes done in Pembrokeshire in an attempt to discover the *caseg fedi*) might be interpreted as a fertility rite ; so also might the game of *rhibo* [? bewitching]

[1]*Bye-gones :* 31 October, 1928.
[2]I. C. Peate : *op. cit.*
[3]L. F. Chitty : *op. cit.*, p. 61.
[4]H. Owen : *Life and Works of Lewis Morris*, p. 145.
[5]local name *caseg fedi*.
[6]local name *gwrach*.
[7]local name ' the neck ' (also in Shropshire).
[8]I. C. Peate : *op. cit.*
[9]cf. Albert Eskeröd : *Årets Äring, etnologiska studier i skördens och julens tro och sed.* Stockholm 1947.
[10]esp. Chapter XLV, ' The Corn Mother and the Corn Maiden in Northern Europe ' (Abridged edition, 1929).

described earlier. The reference, in the description from Llansilin, to ' rolling the younger maid-servants (often helpers at harvest time) in the loose corn on the barn floor with attempts at kissing by the younger swains,'[1] could also be construed on similar lines. In fact there are few, even innocent, pastimes which do not lend themselves to interpretation as survivals of a fertility cult. It is probable, however, that Frazer, who could bring his intimate knowledge of classical mythology to bear in his study of folk customs on an European scale, has achieved more than any of his successors in an analysis of corn-customs from the folk-lorists' standpoint. Seen from another viewpoint the *caseg fedi* custom may be regarded as part of the body of degenerate ritual and ceremony which peasant society maintained for the mere fun of it. In a practical sense the custom was dependent on the continuation of a particular kind of husbandry ; and when the large parties of reapers with their reaping-hooks gave way to other forms of harvesting, the picturesque throwing at the last sheaf could not but be discontinued. In the days of the combine harvester even the harvest supper has diminished out of all recognition.

With the harvest the old Celtic year drew to a close and *Nos Galan gaeaf*, ' the eve of the winter kalend', marked the end of summer and the beginning of winter. A closer connection between the completed harvest and the departing season may formerly have existed. Iolo Morganwg notes that the harvest feast was held on Winter's Eve,[2] although other sources already quoted make it clear that the feast was normally held directly after the harvest was finished—a natural arrangement which made for spontaneous celebration. Iolo himself mentions the ' fiddle and harp with the reaping-party ',[3] which probably refers to some form of merry-making which followed the harvest. As was noted in another chapter it was formerly the

---

[1]*Bye-gones*, 31 October, 1928. A similar custom formerly existed in Tenby, Pembrokeshire, where, if anybody entered a field at hay-making time, ' he or she was immediately pounced upon by the haymakers of the opposite sex, tossed about on the hay-cocks, and bound with hay-bands, till a species of blackmail had been levied. . . . The ceremony when performed on females, was termed "giving them a green gown", and when on one of the other sex, "stretching their backs".' (*Tales and Traditions of Tenby*, pp. 24-25).

[2]G. J. Williams : *Iolo Morganwg*, p. 39.
[3]*ibid.*

practice for farmers in Carmarthenshire on New Year's Day (or Old New Year's Day) to invite all those who helped them in the harvest to a feast.[1] In Pembrokeshire this feast was called *cinio cynhaeaf* [harvest dinner] or *ffest y wrach* [the hag's feast],[2] surely an allusion to the corn-custom discussed above. The purpose of a festive occasion, such as this, held independently of the harvest-home, could only be to renew the ties of friendship, to look back on the harvest with gratitude, and forward to the coming year with confidence that the same help would again be forthcoming. It is conceivable that Iolo's harvest-feast held on Winter's Eve had a similar connection with the harvest, although assemblies of neighbours and friends for general festivities unrelated to the harvest were known in many parts of Wales.

It is more likely that *Calan gaeaf* was formerly more closely linked with the slaughter of farm animals for the winter than with the harvest. Professor T. Gwynn Jones has noted how the more prosperous farmers throughout the agricultural districts of north Wales until the eighteen-seventies were in the habit of slaughtering cattle and pigs about *Calan gaeaf*. 'What seems to have been a tradition of long standing is the habit prevailing in such districts until quite recently of inviting friends and dependents to partake of a kind of feast after the slaughtering of a bullock or a fattened cow at the farmhouses. In Merioneth, this practice was called *ciga* (meat-eating) and poor people were supplied with pailfuls of broth on those occasions. Neighbours would thus go to each other's houses in turn, as the opportunity arose.'[3] Professor Jones suggests that both the social character of the gathering and the distribution of part of the food to less favoured neighbours, point to a kind of sacramental feast as the origin of the custom.

Calan gaeaf, unlike the other pivot of the Celtic year—*Calan Mai*, was saddled with two important Christian festivals celebrated in early November. May-day remained a secular festival and, probably for this very reason, became the special day of the labour and socialist movements in many parts of

[1] D. G. Williams : *op. cit.*, p. 296.
[2] *South Wales Daily News*, 8 February, 1902.
[3] T. Gwynn Jones : *Welsh Folklore and Folk Custom*, pp. 146-7.

Europe in the late nineteenth century. Even Winter's Eve lost to the secular festival of Guy Fawkes' Day the bonfires which had formerly been one of its most distinctive features. The shifting of customs a few days before or after their traditional day is a common occurrence, as the confusion of customs at Christmastide indicates, but few important festivals in the calendar have suffered so much from this tendency as those held on or about Winter's Eve.

The festival of All Saints (1st November) originated in the seventh century with the conversion of the Pantheon at Rome into a Christian place of worship and its dedication to Mary and all the martyrs. At first the event was celebrated on the first of May but it was subsequently changed to its present date as the Feast of All Saints, and retained by the Protestant Church. The following day, 2nd November, All Souls Day, commemorated the faithful departed, namely those souls in purgatory for whose release prayers were offered and masses performed by the Church. Owing to its doctrinal implications the observance of this feast, which originated in the ninth century, was discontinued by the Protestant churches. In the calendar of the medieval church, these two festivals, so near each other in time and spirit, placed in a religious context remembrance of the dead which, at this season, was of much greater antiquity. As so often happened, popular belief and custom was given a new guise acceptable to the Church and made to serve a religious purpose. Although Protestantism undermined this position, many of the age-old associations of the season retained their vitality, and the least religious observances survived to within living memory.

Nos Galan gaeaf, All-Hallows Eve, was the weirdest of the three nights during the year ; on it spirits walked abroad. It was believed that on this eve the ghost of a dead person was to be seen at midnight on every stile ; and until quite recently country children would be afraid to go out of the house alone on this evening. In some parts of Wales the wandering ghosts took the form of a *ladi wen* [white lady], while in other parts, mainly in the north, it was the *hwch ddu gwta* [the tail-less black sow] which put terror into the hearts of men. The apparition of the black sow, in fact, was closely associated with one of the oldest *Calan gaeaf* customs, namely that of lighting bonfires after dark.

The bonfires were prepared in daylight ; there would be two or three within sight of each other on the more prominent hills in each district. Parties of young people, who were the most enthusiastic in the observance of this practice, used to compete with each other to see which bonfire would last longest.[1] To this end large quantities of fern, gorse, straw and thornbushes were carted to the hill-top site of the fire[2] and ordinary work would be set aside on the occasion.[3] When the bonfire was lit, often to the blowing of horns and other instruments,[4] potatoes and apples were placed in it to roast ; there would be dancing, shouting and leaping around the fire as it burned. The roasted apples and potatoes would be eaten by the light of the fire, and, according to some accounts the participants would run round or through the fire and smoke, casting a stone into the flames. As the fire died down all would run off to escape the *hwch ddu gwta* shouting rhymes such as :

Adref, adref am y cynta', Hwch Ddu Gwta a gipio'r ola'

[Home, home, let each try to be first, and may the Tail-less Black Sow take the hindmost]—a Denbighshire version.

An Anglesey version was longer :

> Hwch Ddu Gwta a Ladi Wen heb ddim pen
> Hwch Ddu Gwta a gipio'r ola'
> Hwch Ddu Gwta nos G'langaea
> Lladron yn dwad tan weu sana.

[A tail-less Black Sow and a White Lady without a head. May the tail-less Black Sow snatch the hindmost. A tail-less Black Sow on Winter's Eve, Thieves coming along knitting stockings.][5]

On the following morning the people who had thrown stones returned to the site of the bonfire and searched diligently for them. To find them indicated good luck during the next

[1]Gomer Roberts : *Atgofion Amaethwr*, p. 38.
[2]T. G. Jones : ' A History of the Parish of Llansantffraid,' p. 140.
[3]H. Hughes : *Yr Hynafion Cymreig*, 1823, p. 41.
[4]*Y Geninen*, VI, p. 215.
[5]T. Gwynn Jones : *Welsh Folklore and Folk Custom*, p. 146.

twelve months and the contrary was an omen of misfortune and even of death.[1]

In Merioneth there was usually a procession from the bonfire to the farmhouse where a party was held ; the meal would be followed by singing, story-telling and games of skill or of wit.[2] The traditional supper on All-Hallows Eve in Montgomeryshire always included ' the mash of nine sorts ' (*stwmp naw rhyw*) which, in common with the games played on that night, permitted a form of divination. The nine ingredients were potatoes, carrots, turnips, peas, parsnips, leeks, pepper, salt, and a sufficient quantity of new milk to make it of the proper consistency; a wedding ring was carefully concealed in the mash. ' The dish was surrounded by those who were anxious to know their fate, each with a spoon in his hand, who ate of the mash. Whoever was lucky enough to find the ring was the person, it was said, who would first be married, and considerable faith was placed in the omen. This dish of food was the common supper of most families in this parish at one time on Hallows Eve.'[3] In the Vale of Tywi, Carmarthenshire, in the eighteen-forties the wassail bowl was an essential part of the All-Hallows Eve party and the room was decked with evergreens as at Christmas ; the fire on the hearth, too, was exceptionally bright. Apples, dangling by twine from pot-hooks and hangers in the chimney corner were roasted in the heat of its flames, the cord being twisted from time to time to prevent the fruit burning. These were then added to boiling ale and ' water of life ' in the wassail bowl, together with biscuits, buns or raisins, spices and sugar.[4] Sometimes, in the same county, the puzzle jug was used to increase the hilarity, each person being compelled to drink out of it in turn. In design the puzzle jug (cf. Catalogue Nos. 42—46) was as follows : ' from the brim, extending about an inch below the surface, it has holes fantastically arranged, so as to appear like ornamental work, and which are not perceived, except by the perspicacious ; three projections of the size and shape of marbles are around

[1]*ibid.*
[2]Gomer Roberts : *loc. cit.*
[3]T. G. Jones : *loc. cit.*
[4]Anne Beale : *The Vale of Towey or Sketches in South Wales*, 1849, pp. 83-4.

the brim, having a hole of the size of a pea in each ; these communicate with the bottom of the jug through the handle which is hollow, and has a small hole at the top, which with two of the holes being stopped by the fingers, and the mouth applied to the one nearest the handle, enables one to suck the contents with ease ; but this trick is unknown to every one, and consequently a stranger generally makes some mistake, perhaps applying his mouth as he would to another jug, in which case the contents (generally ale) issue through the fissures on his person, to the no small diversion of the spectators.'[1] In Laugharne and district the ale or wassail was drunk to the accompaniment of small cakes similar to muffins specially made for All-Hallows Eve and called *pice rhana*.[2]

The *stwmp naw rhyw*, or the wassail bowl and puzzle jug, were only part of the merriment of the evening ; the games which were played were the main characteristics of the party and many of them were concerned with prying into the future, usually in order to discover future spouses. One of the most popular in most parts of Wales was catching apples with the teeth. In Merioneth this competition, which rounded off the evening's entertainment, took the following form. A large pan was filled with water to within an inch or two of the brim and placed in the middle of the floor. Then six or eight apples were placed in the water and allowed to float on the surface. Each competitor knelt on the floor and, after filling his lungs with air and opening his mouth wide, tried to bite an apple with his teeth. Care was taken to be sure that the apple was perfectly round and slightly larger than would go into a person's mouth. Often while the contestant was grappling with an apple he would forget that his nose was under water and would breathe in water, losing the apple at the same time.[3] In Montgomery-shire and in Carmarthenshire silver coins were also used in this game, and apples were suspended by cords from the ceiling for a similar competition.[4] Another variant of this

[1]W. Howells : *Cambrian Superstitions*, 1831, p. 175.

[2]M. Curtis : *Antiquities of Laugharne*, etc., p. 206. The *pice rhana* were probably a form of soul-cake originally associated with All Souls' Eve.

[3]Gomer Roberts : *loc. cit.*

[4]T. G. Jones : *loc. cit.* and Anne Beale : *op. cit.*, p. 80.

game was for a stick to be suspended from the ceiling by a string tied around the middle of it ; to one end of it was attached an apple, to the other a lighted candle. The feat was to catch the apple with the mouth, both hands being tied behind one's back. Often it was the candle and not the apple which was caught as the string revolved.[1]

Apples were also used in some of the games which were concerned with divination. The procedure was to peel the apples carefully without breaking or cracking the rind ; this was then thrown over the shoulder and it was thought that the letter of the alphabet which it most resembled would be the initial letter of one's future partner in marriage.[2] Possibly apples, like nuts and grains of wheat, which were also used in divination on All-Hallows Eve, had some symbolical association with the harvest which had just been garnered, although a more prosaic and utilitarian explanation would be that at this season they were the most easily-obtained fruit and that ways were found of trying to interpret their behaviour under certain conditions. Perhaps, too, there is a forgotten significance in the use of fire to induce nuts and wheat-grains to part with their secrets of the future ; both these fruit contains the germ of new life preserved under a hard outer-casing which reacts violently to the heat of a fire. In the Vale of Tywi, Carmarthenshire, every young man who attended a party on All-Hallows Eve brought a pocket full of nuts which he distributed to the women present. Each person in turn threw a nut into the fire ; if it burnt with a bright blaze it revealed that the thrower would still be alive twelve months hence ; if not, then death would come his way. In a similar way nuts could be thrown into the fire to see if wishes were to be fulfilled.[3] In the Llandysul district a brightly-burning nut indicated marriage during the next year.[4] Nuts for use in these divinations were sold in the fair held at *Calan gaeaf* at Laugharne in the middle of the last

[1]M. Curtis : *loc. cit.*

[2]Anne Beale : *op. cit.*, p. 86.

[3]Anne Beale : *op. cit.*, pp. 84-5 ; See also *The Life and Works of Lewis Morris* p. 144 and S. R. Meyrick : *History of Cardiganshire*, p. 56. The custom was also well-known in the north of England, where Hallowe'en was also called ' nut-crack night.'

[4]W. J. Davies : *Hanes Plwyf Llandyssul*, p. 253.

century.[1] In Glamorgan, according to Iolo Morganwg, nuts
were used in a game called *cnau mewn llaw* [nuts in hand] on All-
Hallows Eve.[2] The account which Iolo gives of the game is
somewhat confused, but according to Professor G. J. Williams,
it is unlikely that he is in this particular instance indulging
in his fond practice of proving by devious means the antiquity
of the game in his beloved Glamorgan.[3] The game is referred to
in *cywyddau* by the medieval poets, Dafydd ap Gwilym (fl. 1340-
70), Iolo Goch (c. 1320—c.1398) and Ieuan ap Rhydderch
(fl. 1430—70) and has been described by Dr. Thomas Parry as a
folk custom designed to discover whether a sweetheart was
faithful to one of the two who took part in the game. The name
of the game refers to the nuts which one of the players held in his
fist. If the nuts were an even number the sweetheart was held
to be faithful.[4] It is quite conceivable that a form of this game
had its place among *nos galan gaeaf* customs, although there is
nothing in Iolo Morganwg's description to suggest an association with divination.[5] In the Vale of Glamorgan, according to
another writer, grains of wheat were used to foretell the future
of lovers in a manner similar to the burning of nuts described
by Beale. ' A shovel was placed against the fire, and on it a boy
and a girl put each a grain of wheat, side by side. Presently,
these edged towards each other ; one grain would bob its head
forward, for a bow no doubt—and the other make an awkward
sort of a curtsy. Then, little by little, they would swell, and
look hot, until, anon. . . . they cleared the shovel at a bound.
If both grains went off together, it was a sign that the young
pair would jump together into matrimony ; but if they took
different directions, or went off at different times, the omen was
unhappy, and would often bring a sigh from the simple
creatures.'[6] A somewhat similar method is described by
Meyrick as being used in Cardiganshire, in addition to the more

---

[1]M. Curtis : *Antiquities of Laugharne*, etc., p. 207.

[2]G. J. Williams : *Iolo Morganwg*, p. 39.

[3]*op. cit.*, p. 52.

[4]Thomas Parry : *Gwaith Dafydd ap Gwilym*, 1952, pp. 485-6. See also Henry
Lewis, Thomas Roberts and Ifor Williams : *Iolo Goch ac Eraill*, 1937, pp. 62-3,
226-7.

[5]G. J. Williams : *op. cit.*, p. 52.

[6]Charles Redwood : *The Vale of Glamorgan*, 1839, p. 3.

common method involving nuts. ' Ivy leaves are gathered, those pointed are called males, and those rounded are females ; these are thrown into the fire, and should they jump towards each other, then the parties who had placed them in the fire, will be beloved by, and married to their sweethearts, but should they jump away from one another, then hatred will be the portion of the anxious person.'[1] Here again the reaction to fire is the basis on which divination is made, and it is likely that the especially bright fires which nineteenth-century writers make abundantly clear were prepared in the homes on All-Hallows Eve, were associated with the ancient tradition of the bonfire lit out of doors.

The fire itself, and the ashes from it, could also be used to discover one's future spouse. In Cardiganshire this method was carried out as follows : 'three furrows were made in the ashes which had fallen from the fire ; the person who wished to find out whom she would marry was to think of the names of three young men, one of which she gave to each furrow. Another person asks her three questions : 1. Whom will you love ? 2. Whom will you marry ? and 3. Who will throw you over the bed ? As each question is asked the questioner points to one of the three furrows in turn, beginning with any one of them. The set of questions is then repeated six times, in all, in the following order—123, 321, 231, 213, 312, 132. Whichever furrow is last but one touched is the person she is to have.'[2]

Yet another form of divination referring to matrimony was practised in the All-Hallows Eve parties with the aid of three bowls placed on the table. The contestant was blindfolded and asked to dip his hands into one of the bowls. It was on his choice that the prophecy was based. In the Llandysul area, one vessel would contain soil, another water containing sediment (*dwr trwbwl*), and the third clean water. The first signified death before marriage, the second marriage followed by much trouble, and the third success throughout one's life.[3] In a variation on this custom the three bowls contained clean water,

---

[1]S. R. Meyrick : *op. cit.*, p. 56. In Anglesey ivy leaves were placed in water for divination. (H. Owen : *Life and Works of Lewis Morris* : p. 144).

[2]S. R. Meyrick : *op. cit.*, pp. 56-7.

[3]W. J. Davies : *op. cit.*, p. 253.

dirty water and nothing, respectively. The first foretold widowhood, the second marriage, and the third bachelorhood or spinsterhood.[1]

The forms of prediction described in the preceding paragraphs have depended on the interpretation of natural phenomena or on unwitting choice. On a night associated above all with the roaming of supernatural spirits it was only natural that their aid should be invoked in revealing the future. Many of these supernatural methods of divination took place independently in the All-Hallows Eve party, sometimes out-of-doors (often in the church-yard), sometimes at midnight, the climax of the Eve, and sometimes in a dream for which one had duly prepared.

An intermediate form in which the help of spirits is sought at a party is described by Meyrick. A person leaves the house and walks round it nine times ; holding a glove in his hand he asks, *Dyma'r faneg, ble mae'r llaw ?* [Here's the glove where is the hand ?] ' He then meets the spirit of his sweetheart, who stretches forth her hand to obey his call, and the face he sees will certainly be the face of his wife.'[2] In central Cardiganshire one walked nine times round a dung heap singing *Dyma'r esgid, ble mae'r droed ?* [Here's the shoe, where's the foot ?], while in Carmarthenshire a leek bed was substituted for the dung heap and one carried seed in one's hand, invoking one's lover to appear to collect it. Generally, no response signified spinsterhood, while the appearance of a coffin implied death.[3] In these examples, and others, the number nine seems to have had a mystical significance. Probably the *stwmp naw rhyw* [dish of *nine* ingredients] reflects the same emphasis ; and in Carmarthenshire, where the *stwmp* was not known, at least by that name, it was recorded about 1895 that 'quite recently, *nine* girls used to meet to make a pancake with *nine* ingredients in it. This was divided among them and they retired to bed ; before morn they would see their future husbands.'[4]

As might be expected on a night when spirits roamed, the

[1]M. Trevelyan : *Folklore and Folk stories of Wales*, p. 255.
[2]S. R. Meyrick : *op. cit.*, p. 56.
[3]*Bye-gones*, 29 September, 1897.
[4]D. G. Williams : *op. cit.*, p. 354.

church and churchyard had a prominent place in prophetic rites concerning both matrimony and death. Redwood describes a form practised in the Vale of Glamorgan in the early nineteenth century. The suppliant went to the church-yard and turned his coat and waistcoat inside out ; he recited the Lord's prayer backwards and walked round the church an unspecified number of times. On the last round he entered the porch and put his finger through the key-hole.[1] We are not told how the future was revealed in Redwood's description (in which the divination relates to matrimony) but another account suggests that the apparitions of those who were to die would be seen through the key-hole.[2] Anne Beale cites a similar practice in the Vale of Tywi in which the people ' who would be called ' were named at midnight on All-Hallows Eve. Her account makes no mention of any preliminary encircling of the church.[3] Even in the divinatory games played indoors the special association of the church with the dead was sometimes noticeable. Lewis Morris records the belief in Anglesey that ' 3 Shell snails from church wall put under a Leeve on a Table *nos glangaia,* will write y[r] sweethearts name.'[4]

Another potent place on this Eve was any cross-roads where spirits were supposed to linger. In Tenby, Pembrokeshire, it was at a cross-roads that the custom of ' sowing hemp ' was carried out at midnight by women. Having raised a little of the ground the women would chant :

> Hemp seed I sow, hemp seed I'll mow ;
> Whoe'er my true love is to be
> Come rake this hemp seed after me.

The shape of the person sought would appear and rake the hemp seed.[5] This custom was widely known throughout Wales

---

[1] C. Redwood : *op. cit.,* pp. 6-7.

[2] *Y Geninen,* V, 1887, p. 144 ; M. Trevelyan : *op. cit.,* p. 254. A similar reference in Ellis Wynne : *Gweledigaethau'r Bardd Cwsg,* alludes to divination for matrimony; in some cases it was through a church window that the dead were to be seen (*Bye-gones,* 13 May, 1885).

[3] Anne Beale, *op. cit.,* pp. 93-5.

[4] H. Owen : *Life and Works of Lewis Morris,* p. 143.

[5] *Tales & Traditions of Tenby,* p. 27-8.

and in other parts of the British Isles ; often it took place in a churchyard.[1]

Several other methods of divination by womenfolk were practised indoors and resulted in the appearance of the future husband either at midnight or in a dream. One, which Redwood calls ' the Maid's Trick, which none but true maids were to try ' could be carried on on other ' spirit nights '—as indeed could hemp-sowing. It was done as follows : after the household had retired to bed, the fire was stacked, the table set, and among the foods laid on it was toasted cheese. The girl then stripped off her clothes one by one and washed her undergarment (' smock ') in a pail of clear spring water, afterwards spreading it carefully over the back of a chair in front of the fire. She then retired to bed to await the appearance of her future spouse.[2] Beale gives a similar account in which, however, three maids were involved. In this case the knives, forks and spoons were all placed upside down and everything else turned the wrong way. The girls remained dressed and waited until midnight when a spirit appeared and turned knife, fork, spoon and dish the right way. The apparation was seen only by the girl to whom the man concerned was later to be married.[3] The washing of the garment is missing from Beale's account but it was known in the same county though quite separate from the preparation of a meal for the expected lover. The apparition would instead come into the room and turn the shift.[4] In yet another example of a similar method the spirit would appear when a candle, stuck with pins along its length, eventually burned down to the lowest pin.[5]

To make the future partner appear in a dream on this evening several methods could be employed ; and because they were often more secret these beliefs and practices outlived the others. Sometimes they consisted of preparations which were made specially and placed under the pillows to dream on. In

---

[1]cf. Peter Roberts : *Cambrian Popular Antiquities*, p. 130 ; *Bye-gones*, 29 October, 1873. H. Owen : *Life and Works of Lewis Morris*, pp. 143-4.
[2]Redwood : *op. cit.*, pp. 16-21.
[3]Anne Beale : *op. cit.*, pp. 89—92.
[4]D. G. Williams : *op. cit.*, p. 354.
[5]*ibid.*

Tenby a blade bone of a shoulder of mutton was used in this way, but significantly it had to be bored with nine holes first. Another method was to place one's shoes in the shape of a T and to recite a rigmarole.[1] In Glamorgan a pair of garters obtained ' sure enough, with a great deal of trouble ' from one of the girls at the Hallowe'en party would suffice if they were woven into a true-lover's knot to the accompaniment of ' some fearful words ' and then placed under the skirt.[2] In Cardiganshire a similar method required that nine pieces of different kinds of wood be put in a stocking and tied with the garter of the right leg and then placed under one's head at night.[3] Another way, described by D. G. Williams, was for a girl, after walking around the leek patch in the garden, to lift a leek with her teeth and place it under the pillow. We are told that this was so effective that in at least one case the lover came in the flesh to visit the girl—probably a reference to the custom of ' courting on the bed ' (*caru yn y gwely*) which once flourished in rural Wales.[4] In other cases it often happened that country youths took advantage of these divination practices to make an appearance in person or to play practical jokes such as sending animals or other persons to the room where the spirit was expected. It was also not unknown for ardent but unwelcome suitors to seize the opportunity to identify themselves with the persons decided by Fate. Out-of-doors one of the most common ways of trying to frighten people was to hollow out a turnip and place it, with a lighted candle inside, on a tree by the side of a road or path.

All-Hallows Eve, like Christmastide and other seasons of the year, also had its groups who wandered from house to house at night. In Glamorgan boys dressed themselves in women's clothes and girls in men's clothing for these visits. The ritual practised on these occasions was far less picturesque than on May-day or Easter Monday. The verses sung had lost most of

[1] *Tales and Traditions of Tenby*, p. 29. Also known in Anglesey. cf. *Life & Works of Lewis Morris*, p. 144.

[2] C. Redwood : *op. cit.*, p. 9.

[3] *Bye-gones*, 29 September, 1897.

[4] D. G. Williams : *op. cit.*, p. 353.

their meaning, although certain cryptic references were included :[1]

> Nos g'langaea', twco 'fala',
> Pwy sy'n dod ma's i whara ?
> Ladi wen ar ben y pren
> Yn naddu croes ymbrelo ;
> Mae'n un o'r gloch, mae'n ddau o'r gloch,
> Mae'n bryd i'r moch gael cinio.

[Winter's Eve, baiting of apples, who is coming out to play ? A White Lady on the top of the tree, whittling an umbrella stick ; it's one o'clock, it's two o'clock, it's time for the pigs to have dinner.]

> O mae Jiwdi wedi marw
> A'i chorff hi yn y bedd
> A'i hysbryd yn y whilbar
> Yn mynd sha Castell Nedd.

[O, Judy is dead and her corpse is in the grave, and her soul in a wheelbarrow going towards Neath.]

A similar custom has been recorded in Montgomeryshire. In Llansanffraid 'men went about on this night assuming the dress and character of an old man and woman. These were called *gwrachod*, soliciting gifts from the affrighted and simple people. The young people still go about from house to house chanting quaint rhymes, and soliciting fruit in the following, which appears to be the only remnant of bygone rhymes left us that at one time were numerous—

> Apples or pears, a plum or a cherry
> Any good thing to make us merry,
> One for Peter, two for Paul,
> And one for Him who made us all
> Then up with the kettle, down with the pan,
> Give us an apple and then we'll be gone.'

In the same parish, ' the Welsh youths, being equally solicitous for good things, cry out from door to door, *Cnau ac afalau* and "apples and nuts" were provided especially for this night's enjoyment, and liberally distributed to all soliciting the same.'[2]

---

[1]T. Gwynn Jones : *Welsh Folklore and Folk Custom*, pp. 149-50.
[2]*Bye-gones*, 29 October, 1873.

An interesting variation of this custom was formerly found in the neighbouring towns of Llanfyllin ' among the lower order of the working men.' These used to ' dress themselves in sheep's skins and old ragged clothes and mask their faces, going about the houses and streets on Hallowe'en. They used to get coppers, apples, and nuts, and drink in public-houses. They were called *gwrachod*, that is, hags or witches, in allusion to the old traditions amongst the Celts that fiends, witches and fairies are thought to be all abroad on their baneful errands during this night. Children were often frightened by them, and they were sometimes bold and impertinent. This foolish custom was put down to a great extent by the police.'[1] It is interesting to note that Edward Jones, writing in 1794, refers to a similar custom in north Wales at *Christmas* when men and maids went about neighbours' houses disguised in each other's clothes and sometimes in masks. The name *gwrachod* was also used for these, and the members of the party danced, sang and performed ' antic diversions ' for which they received ' good cheer,' ale, apples or nuts.[2] The name *gwrachod* (hags) for these wandering groups seems to derive from the supernatural activity associated with All-Hallows Eve rather than from the *gwrach* of the corn-custom. Professor T. Gwynn Jones's suggestion that certain observances connected with New Year's Day ' point to non-Christian origins, and these were at first probably connected with the Winter Kalend '[3] seems apposite in a discussion of the example given by Edward Jones. The wassail ceremony of Epiphany, the New Year's apple-gift and certain forms of divination are other resemblances between the observances of these two seasons. Whether the similarities are significant and justify Professor Jones's contention is a difficult point to prove, in spite of the common tendency for folk customs to become attached to new days and seasons in the calendar.

An example of this confusion in the popular mind may be seen in the customs which were practised both on All-Hallows Eve and on All Souls' Eve ; both festivals had their associations with death and the departed and the transfer of a custom from

[1] *Bye-gones*, 6 May, 1891.
[2] Edward Jones : *Musical & Poetic Relicks of the Welsh Bards*, 1784, p. 108n.
[3] T. Gwynn Jones : *Welsh Folklore and Folk Custom*, p. 158.

the one day (or eve) to the other is quite understandable. Until the eighteenth century, for instance it was usual in many districts to burn candles in the parish church to ascertain the fortune of the inquirers during the year that was commencing. The candles brought by the parishioners were lighted at an appointed hour by the sexton and the manner in which the flame burned indicated what lay in store. A clear and bright flame signified prosperity and happiness ; slow and irregular burning forecast troubles and misfortunes ; and if the candle went out before it had burned to the socket, death would take the owner. The way in which different parts of the candle burned was also thought to indicate the prospects for different months of the year. When the last candle was burned out, all left the church, and, having walked two or three times round the church, they walked home in silence, so as to keep the spell which would allow them to see their future husbands.[1] The details of the first part of this description suggest that the practice was a survival in a secular form of a rite which was common to all medieval christendom at this festival, namely the commemoration of the faithful dead. The second part of this custom is hardly different from the Hallowe'en practices of divination already discussed. The reverse also happened and it is probable that the verses quoted earlier as being sung in Llansannffraid on All-Hallows Eve belonged originally to All Souls' Eve when the custom of ' souling ' was carried on. Correspondence on this subject in the columns of *Bye-gones*[2] makes it clear that ' souling,' like Christmas carol-singing in our own day, often began before the festival with which it was originally associated.

The custom of souling was known by several different names in Welsh. In north Wales *hel bwyd cennad y meirw* [collecting the food of the messenger of the dead][3] was the most common form, although *hel solod* [collecting souls or soul-cakes] was also known, as, for example in Corwen, Merioneth.[4] In another

[1] *Cambrian Journal*, 1860, pp. 68—70.
[2] *Bye-gones*, 11 December, 1872 and 29 January, 1873. Cf. also *Bye-gones*, 13 November, 1895.
[3] T. Gwynn Jones (*op. cit.*, p. 152) suggests ' more probably, the food of the letting loose of the dead.'
[4] *Bye-gones*, 25 March, 1891.

part of Merioneth, Dinas Mawddwy, the term *bara-a-chawsa* [bread-and-cheesing] was used.[1] The word ' sowling ' was used in south Pembrokeshire[2] but in Carmarthenshire the phrases *diwrnod rhanna* [doling day] *pice rhanna* [dole cakes] and *bara rhan* [dole bread] were found ;[3] the latter is also given by Iolo Morganwg in his list of Glamorgan customs.[4] The custom under one name or another, was widespread in Wales and was particularly popular in the English border counties of Cheshire and Shropshire.[5]

The one statement which can be made with certainty about soul-cakes is that their gift was in some way acceptable to the dead. Wright and Lones suggest that the giving of soul-cakes to relatives and acquaintances probably represents the custom in its older and purer form,[6] in which case it is presumably the dead kin of the giver who are concerned in some mysterious way. Another interpretation claims that the poor on All Soul's Day collected gifts for the priests, in pre-Reformation times, for them to pray for the release of their poor relatives from purgatory.[7] In view of the significance of the festival to the medieval church this explanation is quite plausible, but it is important to note that it is the dead relatives of the collector and not those of the giver who are concerned if this viewpoint is correct. A further complication is introduced by the association with the harvest which is implied by the form of the custom in certain districts. According to Pennant, the poor, on receiving the soul-cakes, prayed to God to bless the next crop of wheat,[8] while in Kidwelly, Carmarthenshire, only those who helped, or

---

[1]*Bye-gones*, 25 March, 1891.

[2]Wirt Sikes : *British Goblins*, 1880, p. 258.

[3]G. Evans : 'Carmarthenshire Gleanings (Kidwelly)', p. 112-3 ; M. Curtis : *Antiquities of Laugharne*, p. 206.

[4]G. J. Williams : *op. cit.*, p. 40. I am indebted to Professor Williams for the following reference which occurs in a letter written by William Aubrey (the brother of John Aubrey) to Edward Lhuyd, on the 19th November, 1703 : ' Doe you not take notice of an old Custome in Monmouthshire (& *p*haps in other *p*tes) on All Souls day Nov. 2nd, the poor people & children goes from house to house & sings Baracan Barracan [? *bara can* .. white bread] : God have mercy on all Xian Souls. for a soul cake.' (Bodleian MS. 25184, 124*a*).

[5]Wright & Lones : *British Calendar Customs, England*, III, p. 121.

[6]ibid.

[7]*Bye-gones*, 25 July, 1894.

[8]*Bye-gones*, 30 October, 1872.

the children of those who helped, at the harvest got the *pice rhanna*, the local name for the soul cakes.[1]

Details of the ingredients used in the preparation of soul-cakes have been recorded in different parts of Wales. In Cerrigydrudion, Denbighshire, about 1830, a small cake of barley meal was made, using so much salt that it was barely edible ; it was called *cacen gŵyl y meirw* [cake of the feast of the dead].[2] The symbolical significance of salt as a purifying and preserving agent is probably to be seen here as in the old practice of placing salt in or on a coffin. By 1893 the custom had altered somewhat, small coins, apples and pieces of bread and butter being given in Llangwm, and Llanfihangel Glyn Myfyr as well as Cerrigydrudion.[3] In the Edeirnion district of Merioneth small cakes were made for children, and larger ones for the old people who came round.[4] In Laugharne a large sack of flour was used on this occasion at each farm and the maids would be up all night making the barley bread which was given together with cheese to the poor.[5] In Cardiganshire the custom was to make big muffins and give them to one's friends and acquaintances,[6] a practice similar to that recorded by Wright & Lones.[7] The Kidwelly farmwife baked ' large flat cakes ' for the occasion,[8] while *bara can a miod* [white-bread and little cakes] have also been mentioned in a dictionary published in 1826.[9] In Corwen, Merioneth, ' the cake was generally made of barley-flour, without any addition of more appetising ingredients than salt and water ; it was about one inch thick and four inches in diameter.'[10] The fact that ' apples bread and cheese or any other article of diet were given at those houses where cake had not been prepared, or had been distributed ' suggests a degenerate form of the custom which had in fact become more usual than the earlier bread-gift in the

[1]G. Evans : *op. cit.*, p. 112-3.
[2]*Y Geninen*, VII, p. 200.
[3]*Bye-gones*, 24 May, 1893.
[4]Gomer Roberts : *Atgofion Amaethwr*, p. 38.
[5]M. Curtis : *op. cit.*, p. 207.
[6]*Bye-gones*, 29 September, 1897.
[7]*op. cit.*, p. 121.
[8]G. Evans : *op. cit.*, p. 112.
[9]ibid.
[10]*Bye-gones*, 25 March, 1891.

border areas. In those districts bordering on Cheshire and Shropshire, in particular, the verses sung[1] show how the influence of wassailing, the receipt of apples and nuts likewise show traces of a Winter's Eve custom of collecting fruit for use in divination and celebration rather than in commemoration of the dead.

As to the manner in which the custom was conducted, we are told that in Edeirnion the callers were labourers' children, poor women and occasionally old men. The door was knocked and whether there was an answer or not, the caller asked ' *Welwch chi'n dda gai damed o fwyd cennad y meirw ?* ' [Please may I have a little of the food of the messenger of the dead ?][2] In Corwen a similar request was made with the addition of an *Amen* at the end.[3] In Dinas Mawddwy the doggerel used was :

> Bara a chaws, bara a chaws
> Os ca'i beth, mi neidia',
> Os na cha'i ddim, mi beidia'.

[Bread and cheese, bread and cheese ; if I get some I'll jump ; If I don't I won't].[4]

Another piece of doggerel was used in Bryneglwys, Denbigh-shire in the late nineteenth century :

> Dega Dega, dowch i'r drws,
> A rhowch i gennad y meirw.

[*Dega, dega*, come to the door, and give to the messenger of the dead].

If the request was refused the following verse was repeated :

> Deca, deca (?*sic*) o dan y drws,
> A phen y wraig yn siwtrws

[*Deca, deca* under the door, and the wife's head in smithereens].[5]

The Carmarthenshire and Cardiganshire forms recorded were similar :

[1]In general the words were similar in character to those given earlier as being recited on Hallowe'en in Llansanffraid (See p. 134). Other examples are given in *Bye-gones*, 18 November, 1885 ; 13 November, 1895.
[2]Gomer Roberts : *op. cit.*, p. 38.
[3]*Bye-gones*, 25 March, 1891.
[4]ibid.
[5]*Bye-gones*, 25 July, 1894.

> Rhanna ! rhanna ! Dydd gwyl eneidie,
> Rhan i 'nhad am gywiro sgidie,
> Rhan i mam am gywiro sane,
> Rhan i'r plant sy'n aros gartre.

(Share ! Share ! All Souls' Day, a share to my father for mending the shoes, a share to my mother for mending stockings, a share to the children who stay at home.)

Dydd Gŵyl eneidiau had become *dwgwl aneidie*, a dialect pro‾nunciation which later gave the meaningless form *Dwbw^l dameidie* [double pieces].[1] Like collecting *calennig* (for which a similar type of the verse was used) or collecting *crempogau* [pancakes] the children gathered for their living relatives rather than for the dead, to such a degree had the custom lost its true purpose. In Merioneth the children carried a little bag or basket and began collecting at dawn continuing until noon, as in *calennig*-collecting, and in contradistinction to the evening visits of the border country souling parties who chanted ' wissel wassel ' and called for ' bread and possal, apple or a pear, plum or a cherry ' as well as a ' sol cake.'[2]

The other festival (if it merits the name), with which Winter's Eve practices became confused, was Guy Fawkes' Day. It is easy to see how the bonfires of the former gradually became linked with the fireworks and effigy-burning of the latter. The Guy Fawkes custom was popular in Corwen, Merioneth, in the 1870's and earlier, where the following macaronic verse was sung :

> Member, remember the fifth of November,
> Tipyn bach o lo ar ben bonifire ;
> Tresi, Tresi, come to the Tresi,
> Coal, coal, Queen's head for ever.[3]

In this form the custom is not far removed from that prevalent throughout most parts of England. An interesting point, however, is that in the detailed account of ' The High Days and Holidays of Llansanffraid ' no reference is made to Guy Fawkes bonfires although November 5th is discussed ; it was marked formerly by bell-ringing and the well-known rhyme

[1] G. Evans : *op. cit.*, p. 112, and *Bye-gones*, 29 September, 1897.
[2] *Bye-gones*, 13 November, 1895.
[3] *Bye-gones*, 5 November, 1873.

' Remember, Remember.' On the other hand the Winter's Eve bonfire is described by the author in detail ;[1] can we take this to imply that in the middle of the last century the bonfire had not shifted from the one festival to the other ? The introduction of the reformed calendar a century earlier had already necessitated one change and had probably paved the way. In some districts, such as Laugharne, the old style was retained and All-Hallows Eve was celebrated on November 11th although the bonfires seem to have been discontinued and even forgotten.[2] In Anglesey, on the other hand, we read in a letter by William Morris, dated 1758, that in that year, for the first time the bonfire and nut-burning had taken place on the *new* Winter's Eve instead of the old one displaced a few years earlier.[3] Even in 1741, before this change of date, we read of the custom in the same county : ' I saw but few *Coelcerths* or Bonefires this night, so it seems that old superstitious Pageantry is upon the decay.'[4] The custom, however, survived in Wales until within living memory and even today exists albeit as part of another, less ancient if no less blazing, festival of fire.

[1] *Mont. Coll.*, IV, p. 140.
[2] M. Curtis : *op. cit.*, p. 207.
[3] J. H. Davies (ed.) : *Morris Letters*, II, p. 94.
[4] G. Nesta Evans : *Religion and Politics in Mid-Eighteenth Century Anglesey*, p. 30 footnote.

CHAPTER V

BIRTH, MARRIAGE AND DEATH

THE customs which have been discussed hitherto have had in common a link with a particular day or season of the year ; their occurrence is an annual event which is ordained by tradition. Even if in certain customs the participants are few, the occasions during the yearly round which they celebrate did, in the past, concern the whole community. A folk custom often relies for its continuation not only on the section of the community which keeps it up but also on the tolerance or passive participation of the community as a whole. As was suggested in the Introduction, it was partly from this quarter—by the refusal of Methodist or ' enlightened ' opinion to condone customs which had often degenerated into undesirable practices —that the existence of many folk customs in eighteenth- and nineteenth-century Wales was threatened. From being a vital manifestation of community life these gradually became the attributes of *pobl yr ymylon*—the people whose place was on the fringe of ' respectable ' society—and the prerogative of children.

Another body of folk customs existed, however, which concerned the individual, his relatives and friends, and which pertained to those crises in life through which all persons pass. In the integrated peasant community where a real sense of interdependence was felt, the significance of the customs and the events they celebrated reached out from the individual and his closest relatived to embrace virtually the whole community. But as the isolation of the community gave way to a trend towards another kind of isolation—that of the individual within the community—the vitality of these customs too was sapped and their sociological driving force frittered away. Religion also added the weight of its sentiment to smother certain of these customs which could be said to foster intemperance and other forms of behaviour not in accord with strict religious principles. The christening became simply a part of a church or chapel service, no longer followed by a drinking bout. The funeral wake succumbed to temperance influences and

became a kind of prayer-meeting. Even weddings and 'recept-
ions', where a blind eye is turned to the presence of drink, are
tame and respectable—and less colourful—than those of the
early nineteenth century. There is hardly one of the customs
marking the important changes in a person's life which has not
been shorn of much of its traditional character in response to the
pervasive and persistent influence of social change.

The term which can best be used to denote the type of folk
custom to be discussed here is that coined by Arnold Van
Gennep nearly half a century ago, namely ' rite of passage.'[1]
The significant characteristic of these folk customs is that they
took place at a time when an individual passes from one state to
another in his relations with other people. The system of social
relationships, which the individual has come to regard as normal
is upset by a change in his status ; the transition from the old
to the new is made easier—both for the individual and his
circle of relatives and friends—by the existence of these
ceremonies and customs. In the case of marriage, which is one
of the most obvious of these occasions, the common use in Welsh
of such terms as *newid byd* (changing world) and *dechrau byw*
(beginning to live) indicates that the true significance of the
upheaval brought about in a person's life is commonly acknowledged. At birth and at death the social change is one which
primarily affects the group ; a new person enters into a system
of social relationships already in existence, or an old one temp-
orarily disrupts the system by leaving it. The meaning to
society of birth and death is vastly different from their significance to the individual, yet even the response of the social group
to such events is coloured by their universality : a personal feeling of involvement accompanies the sociological change and
adds to its human significance.

In addition to those customs which are directly related to
changes in the individual's status, there are others which are
more remotely connected. Thus customs during courtship—
the carving of love-spoons or the sending of valentines—which
relate to marriage have not the same significance as the
ceremonies at (and before and after) the wedding. Since they

[1]A. Van Gennep : *Les Rites de Passage*, 1909.

fit into the same general classification, however, they are discussed along with the ' rites of passage ' in this chapter.

BIRTH

Folklore contains numerous beliefs and instructions which formerly affected behaviour before and after birth. Natural phenomena are often thought of as revealing the number of births, an example being the Cardiganshire belief that if nuts were numerous, many children would be born.[1] This, of course, is found in many country districts in Britain. Often certain acts were forbidden to the expectant mother, in the belief that her behaviour influenced that of her unborn child. She might not step over a grave ; if she did her child would die. She might not dip her fingers in dirty water, otherwise her child would have coarse hands. If she tied a cord around her waist her child would be unlucky ; if she meddled much with flowers, her child would not have a keen sense of smell.[2] The occasion and circumstances of a child's birth were also thought to have influence on its life. Astrological beliefs are recorded in many countries, of course, and many examples are known in Wales. For example, children born when the moon was new would be eloquent ; those born during the last quarter would have excellent reasoning powers.[3] To be born at night made one open to see visions, ghosts and phantom funerals.[4] Each day in the week had its characteristics and a child acquired those of the one on which it was born. Folklore is also full of interpretations of the behaviour of the child during the period following its birth, and particularly of the way in which it does certain things—speaks or walks, for instance—for the first time.

These beliefs and practices do not constitute folk customs, but they are of interest in that they reveal both the assiduity with which the behaviour of persons and of natural phenomena was observed and interpreted, and also the anxiety for the future of the child which lay behind it. It was in the same state of feeling

[1] J. C. Davies : *Folk-lore of West and Mid-Wales*, 1911, p. 221.
[2] M. Trevelyan : *Folk-lore and Folk-stories of Wales*, 1909, p. 266.
[3] M. Trevelyan : *op. cit.*, p. 267.
[4] T. Gwynn Jones : *Welsh Folklore and Folk Custom*, p. 196.

on the part of parents and their friends that the christening ceremony had its significance, and many beliefs were formerly held which emphasized the beneficial effect of christening on the baby's health. The reaction of babies during the christening ceremony too was also studied carefully as being a portent. If a baby held its head up during the ceremony it would live to be very old ; if it allowed its head to turn aside or sink back on the arm of the person who held it, its early death was to be expected.[1] The fate of the baby could be influenced by the choice of its godparents ; if these came from three different parishes the child would live to an old age.[2] These beliefs arose understandably from the anxiety of the parents, but there was another side to the christening, namely the receiving of the child as a member of society by means of a ritual ; the child is given a name and its parents and god-parents reminded of their duties ; and finally the child is received into the church. The social aspect of the christening ceremony is in almost every culture less important than that of the wedding or the funeral mainly because it represents merely the introduction of a new person into a system of social relationships which he will only gradually influence. In certain countries with a patriarchal tendency only the birth of boys is attended by a ceremony ; and even in nineteenth-century Wales the birth of an heir to some of the landed families was followed by general celebration among the tenants, a fact which suggests that the social significance of the event—in this case the continuation of the family estate for another generation—enters into the picture. On a less spectacular scale the birth of a son or a daughter to a peasant family represented the survival and consolidation of the family, and their celebrations commemorated the same circumstance in a correspondingly modest manner.

One of the few descriptions we have of the ceremonies and celebrations following the birth of a child is that given by Lewis Morris, and even this is rather short. ' In Christenings [in eighteenth-century Anglesey], when the christening is over then the Father invites home his friends & yͤ Parson to drink yͤ health of yͤ woman in yͤ straw, and after dinner this they do for yᵉ first part so plentifully till they can drink no more for that day, money to yᵉ midwife, to yᵉ nurse and to the maid. Home stark drunk.'[1] It appears from this account that the christening party was confined to the family and to the persons directly involved in the birth and in the christening. The payment to the midwife, maid and nurse, was apparently made on the ceremonial occasion ; and the object of the toasts was the mother rather than the child. Drink, in intemperate quantities, was essential, at least to the eighteenth-century participants, and it is easy to understand how special christening glasses came to be made and to be cherished as family possessions. A pair belonging to ' an old Montgomeryshire family ' are described as being $18\frac{1}{2}$ inches long and resembling tall flower glasses. Their diameter at the top is 3 inches and $1\frac{1}{8}$ inches at the bottom ; their feet are $5\frac{1}{2}$ inches in diameter. ' At the christening meal the sponsors were supposed to drain at a gulp whatever was put into them. Each glass is capable of holding a pint easily—$17\frac{1}{2}$ ozs. to be correct—and the task must have been a difficult one for the sponsor, and a source of amusement to those present ; for after getting through half the contents, if he was not careful the remainder would be splashed over his face. This might easily happen if the sponsor, in his effort to carry out the task satisfactorily, tilted the glass too high, causing the liquid to rush out before he was aware of it.'[2] The conviviality of the christening party is amply reflected by this description ; the ritual was performed in the actual christening ceremony and the party was purely an occasion for merrymaking. In many parts of Wales gifts were made to the child at the party and also shortly after the day of his birth. In Glamorgan the giving of presents to newborn children in this manner was called *cyflwyno* or *cyflwyna*, and *mynd i weld* in Carmarthenshire, where a pound or two of sugar might be taken as a gift for the mother.[3]

Churching, namely the resuming of her normal life by the woman by means of a ritual purification, took place, according

[1]H. Owen : *Life and Works of Lewis Morris*, p. 142.
[2]*Bye-gones*, 19 June, 1901.
[3]G. J. Williams : *Iolo Morganwg*, p. 39 ; *Y Darian*, 4 October, 1928 and W· Roberts : *Crefydd yr Oesoedd Tywyll*, p. 52 ; D. G. Williams : ' Casgliad o Lengwerin Sir Gaerfyrddin,' p. 288.

to Lewis Morris, ' in a week or fortnight's time at most among yᵉ Poorer sort the mother walks to yᵉ parish church to be churchᵈ and takes along with her her midwife & offers a 12d. or 6d if poor.'[1]

COURTSHIP AND MARRIAGE

A common feature of courtship in nearly all countries is the giving of presents as tokens of love and affection. Sometimes it was the girl who presented a gift to her lover—we have seen how the men dancing on May-day in the border area of north Wales received ribbons from their sweethearts to use in decorating their costume. More often, however, it was the men who gave tokens of their feelings ; and in the course of time two kinds of gifts in particular came to be accepted as suitable for this purpose. The first was the love-spoon, made with care and skill by the suitor himself, and the second was the valentine, which in its earliest development was made by hand and inscribed with the sender's own composition. The one was an elaboration of an age-old domestic craft, and the other a special development of a calendar custom celebrating a day devoted to lovers. The first petered out towards the end of the nineteenth century : subsequently the making of love-spoons has been more often done with an eisteddfod competition in view than for its original purpose. The second became commercialized in character as factory-made valentines flooded the market ; the satirical or comic valentine was a light-hearted departure from the old custom which in its traditional personal form could only have expressed serious or at least sincere emotions. Unlike the giving of love-spoons, the sending of valentines has survived to our own day, but it is no longer a true folk custom.

There is hardly any other Welsh folk custom of which so little is really known as the giving of love-spoons (See Plate 9). In spite of the fact that numerous examples of love-spoons are to be found in museums or in private collections, there is little if any documentary evidence which throws any light on their making. It is clear that although the offer of a love-spoon by a

---

[1].H Owen : *op. cit.*, p. 142.

suitor and its acceptance or refusal by his lover could have developed into a ritual of betrothal or rejection amongst the Welsh peasantry, there is no evidence to support such a view. This lack of definition in the custom is perhaps to be ascribed to its very personal and intimate associations ; but of the popularity of the practice from the seventeenth to the nineteenth centuries there can be no doubt. Whether love-spoons were sent before the seventeenth century it is impossible to discover owing to the absence of dated examples and the complete lack of documentary evidence, but it can hardly be doubted that the making of ordinary wooden spoons was carried on in the home in medieval times. Spoon-making, whether for use in the home or in a special form as a love token, was a common pastime during the long winter evenings on the farm. It seems likely that the practice of sending love-spoons is older than the earliest surviving example in our collection (No. 99 dated 1667, Plate 10) ; what apparently did happen in the seventeenth century was the emergence of a specialized type of spoon having little or no utilitarian value but serving merely as a symbol of love and as a domestic ornament.

Some of the earlier examples of love-spoons show a distinct similarity to the metal spoons of the period, though it would be unwise to date love-spoons on the basis of their shape and design. The earliest dated specimen with its square, slotted handle and loose balls is typologically more advanced than other dated spoons made nearly a century later. Another warning against a hastily arrived-at evolutionary sequence is suggested by the continuing popularity in 1821 (Nos. 83 and 84) of a type of spoon found in the same part of Caernarvonshire nearly a century earlier in 1735 (Nos. 80 and 81). The difficulty of carrying out a systematic study of the history of the love-spoon is increased by the large number which are undated and often undatable. It is unfortunate too that the provenance of a large proportion of the specimens in the Museum's collection was not recorded by the original collector ; a study of the local forms of the love-spoon for this reason cannot be made with any exactitude. The only quality which is present in all the examples collected is their design, and the section dealing with love-spoons in the accompanying catalogue has been arranged so as to group together specimens of the same general appearance and (wherever possible) age, beginning with the simplest forms.

It can be argued that the first wooden spoons given as love tokens were also used by the recipient for eating—just as ' apostle ' spoons of metal and other engraved cutlery were used despite their special significance. However, once the utilitarian function of the love-spoon was discarded, there was no limit to the variations which could be introduced in size, shape and decoration.

Since the donor made the gift himself he sought to emphasize the feeling and care which had gone into its making by elaborating the technique and departing from the useful and functional original. The love-spoon in fact became an article of ' conspicuous waste,' its symbolical significance heightened by its complete break-away from the pattern of the spoon which could be used.

The elaboration of the love-spoon took place in several ways. The handle of the spoon was enlarged either by making it rectangular or by giving it the flat form of a panel. The bowl itself was rarely altered and was nearly always left undecorated ; the development here was the introduction of twin or even triple bowls usually with the accompaniment of a broad panel handle. The increased surface of the handle gave the carver further opportunity to reveal his skill to the best advantage. The forms of decoration commonly used were : piercing the thin panel and carving geometrical designs in fretwork ; chip-carving the panel with the knife-blade, sometimes in order to insert a red or black wax inlay, but often merely to incise a mass of geometrical (e.g. chevron) designs ; sinking a rect-angular or circular panel into the broad handle for mounting a picture or a glass-covered inscription ; carving in relief a vine-tree, bay-leaf or other motif ; escalloping the edges of the panel to give a serrated appearance ; and finally, poker-work. Often these methods were combined with each other to give a wide variety of techniques. The designs used in conjunction with these were usually geometrical, presumably because the carver was less likely to go astray ; circles, asteroids and segments, hearts, locks and keys, figures, initials, houses, anchors and ships were among the most popular. In certain specimens volutes have been added to the panel, and quite often the mode of hanging the spoon has been elaborated by making a swivel or chain link attachment. Most of the spoons of all types have provision for hanging, an indication of their ornamental function.

Some of the most attractive examples have rectangular or circular stems which have been hollowed out, leaving small wooden balls running freely in the slotted cavity. The aim, wherever possible, seems to have been to make out of one piece of wood a form which at first glance appears to have required several separate pieces, but which on closer inspection reveals the ingenuity of the carver. The use of slotted handles, swivels and chain-links afforded ample opportunity for the exhibition of skill in this manner on both panel and narrow handles. Sometimes a knife and fork were attached to the spoon handle by links, the whole being made out of one piece of wood. Another variation was to carve loose slotted cages within the slotted handle, a feat on the maker's part. Variations could be introduced, for example, by cutting several separate slots in the handle and separating them by horizontal ring incisions ; by chip-carving the edges or by giving the stem a twisted shaft between the handle proper and the bowl. In certain examples an intermediate form was achieved between the panel and the narrow-handle types ; most of these have relief carving of the bird-and-vine-tree kind, with supporting designs in open-work near the top of the handle, a motif which occurs in different parts of Wales.

Regional types, on the whole, are not easy to identify but would be a natural development in the evolution of the love-spoon. Reference has already been made to the plain spoon with a small glazed recess which seems to have been popular in Caernarvonshire. In the same county the type with a dolphin-shaped and ridged handle (e.g. Nos. 87 and 89) were also popular. In Pembrokeshire, while other forms were found, the large twin-panel type in which two clumsy panels are joined by a loop was formerly fairly common (e.g. Nos. 213 and 214). In general, however, the information is too scanty to justify postulating local forms.

Just as the making of love-spoons probably developed out of the earlier practice of carving wooden spoons for use in the homes, so did the valentine card originate in an older, but not utilitarian, practice. Since the seventeenth century the valentine too has developed on new lines ; indeed it was probably in this early period of the modern valentine that it resembled the love-spoon most in purpose. References in Pepys's diary show that in his day the valentine was a gift from the lover to his sweetheart—a gift costing a pound or two to ordinary men like Pepys himself but involving sums as large as £800 to people of the rank of the Duke of York.[1] During the same period, however, the valentine had an older significance which harked back to the days of the Roman Empire. In the state of flux in which valentine customs existed during the seventeenth century and even later, the ancient significance had not been lost nor had the more modern form of the valentine evolved.

The origin of valentine customs is disputed, but the most plausible explanation seems to be in the chance association between the feast of an obscure Christian martyr and the pre-Christian Roman festival of Lupercalia. The feature of the old pagan celebration which was rapidly disappearing in Pepys's time, but which establishes the provenance of the valentine custom, was the apportioning of girls among youths by lottery. In ancient Rome the result of the lottery decided who should be partners during the gaieties of Lupercalia. Tempered by the pervasive influence of the medieval church and made respectable by the patronage of a saint, the custom survived in a changed form. Bourne, writing in 1725, tells us that in the England of his day, ' It is a ceremony, never omitted among the Vulgar, to draw lots which they term Valentines. The names of a select number of one sex are by an equal number of the other put into some vessel ; and after that, everyone draws a name, which for the present is called their Valentine, and is also looked upon as a good omen of their being man and wife afterward.'[2] The element of chance was also to be seen in what was probably a new accretion to the

[1]cf. L. Whistler : *The English Festivals*, p. 92.
[2]*Antiquitates Vulgares* : chapter 20.

custom, namely the practice of regarding the first man to be
seen by a woman on St. Valentine's morning, 14th February,
as her valentine. This was the sense in which it was referred to
by Pepys. The important point is that the valentine in this
period was a person and not a letter or card. The first written
valentine message in England dates from 1684,[1] but the
valentine proper in the form that we know it only began to
gain in popularity—and at the expense of other aspects of the
custom—a hundred years later.

In Wales too, the valentine was known in this early form.
The earliest references known to me occur in the works of
Edward Morris, Perthi-llwydion (1633 ?—1689) and in a
poem by an anonymous author of the same period. The form
used by Morris, if we are to believe the orthography of his
editor, is the English word itself ; the anonymous poet has
disguised the word slightly as *falendein*. The contents of the two
poems are of interest also. Edward Morris thanks his sweetheart for the valentine gift she has sent him and the love she has
thus shown to him ; in order to remember her he will keep the
gift as long as it lasts.[2] The anonymous poem was written by, or
more likely for, a woman who asks for a valentine. The
initials of her lover's name, Lewis Jones, are woven into the
fabric of the verse. Even if she had the choice of all the men on
this island she would like above all to draw him as a valentine.[3]
These two sources suggest that valentine customs in Wales were
similar to those in contemporary England ; the reference to
ei dynnu'n falendein [to draw him as a valentine] makes it clear
that the custom described by Bourne had its counterpart in
Wales.[4] At the same time it must be remembered that neither
of these Welsh verses was itself a valentine, nor was either of
them sent accompanying a valentine. The custom had not
yet assumed the form which made it popular in the nineteenth
century.

There are several references to the sending of home-made

[1]Ruth Webb Lee : *A History of Valentines*, 1953, p. 7.
[2]H. Hughes : *Barddoniaeth Edward Morris, Perthi-llwydion*, 1902, pp. 49-50.
[3]*Beirdd y Berwyn*, 1902, p. 78.
[4]It is interesting to note that William Roberts, writing in 1852 refers to ' yr
hen ddefod a phoblogaidd, sef y "tynnu Valentine " ' [the old and popular custom,
namely ' drawing a valentine.'] *Crefydd yr Oesoedd Tywyll*, p. 62.

valentines in Wales during the last century. The oldest
example of this later form of the custom in England is dated
1750[1] and it is known that the practice of sending valentines
spread during the latter part of the eighteenth century ; the
earliest-known examples in Wales, however, belong to the
beginning of the nineteenth century. No. 250, if it is a genuine
valentine, represents an early form of hand-made token having
little reference to the subjects which were commonplace in
Victorian valentine-cards. Marie Trevelyan states that in
Glamorgan it was the custom to make true lovers' knots and to
distribute them like favours on St. Valentine's Day. ' These
were cometimes sent anonymously and great was the amusement, and sometimes the consternation, of the youths and
maidens when these favours appeared on the bodice or coat of
anybody present at the revels ' often held on this day.[2] The
lovers' knot was a common symbol of affection and devotion,
and had a place, as we have seen, in Winter's Eve divination ;
Williams tells us that young men during the long winter
evenings derived much amusement from the feat of tying a
lover's knot (clymu cwlwm cariad).[3] This would be an obvious
choice for a token to be sent on St. Valentine's Day ; it was in
fact later incorporated in many printed-valentine designs.

The Pembrokeshire example, No. 251 (Plate 11), is a better
example of the true valentine ; it is noteworthy that the verse
contains no reference to the practice of ' drawing valentines.'
The west Montgomeryshire specimen, No. 252 (Plate 12), of
which the Welsh text is given in the catalogue, reads as
follows in translation : ' Here is a letter sealed with a gold seal
with a kiss in it ; O that I could not put my heart in it too,
so great is my affliction. / I am not setting you any task apart
from asking you to remember me between now and Easter
—a complete silk kerchief, or a pair of gloves—whatever
you like. / It is easier to collect the sea into a spoon and to
place it all into an egg-shell than to turn my mind from you
my little darling. / Perhaps you will say of me that I send
saucy old verses, I can only truthfully say in reply that valen-

[1]In Hull Museum.
[2]M. Trevelyan : *Folk-lore and Folk-Stories of Wales*, p. 245.
[3]D. G. Williams : *op. cit.*, p. 357.

tines are an old custom. / O remember me, please ! To Mary.'
The allusion to a silk kerchief and gloves recalls an entry
in Pepys's diary which records the receipt by Mrs. Pepys
of ' half a dozen pairs of gloves and a pair of silk stockings and
garters ' from her valentine, Sir William Batten, in 1660, ' gifts
of a vaguely symbolic sort ' according to Whistler.[1] The custom
had changed so much that the Montgomeryshire suitor solicited
rather than gave presents. The third verse is similar in spirit
to many *penillion telyn* (verses sung to the accompaniment of the
harp) and may have been traditional ; this would explain an
allusion to *hen benillion* in the next verse, although the word *hen*
[old] may have here another, diffuse, meaning.

Quite often the poetry in the hand-made valentine was
written by a rhymester who undertook work of this kind. A
contributor to *Bye-gones* describes how two men in a district on
the border used to make and sell valentines for the then
considerable sum of half-a-crown each. The earliest examples of
the handiwork and poetic compositions of these particular
valentine makers were dated 1826, but an example by one of
the two men was dated 1885 and was probably made in
extreme old age. The technique used in their manufacture is
worth recording : ' They are made by folding a sheet of letter
paper about 15 ins. square in four, and then cutting a kind of
lace-work or "tracery" on a board with a pen-knife, so that
when unfolded, each corner is alike. The whole is surrounded
by a border of painted hearts, in various stages of inflamation.
In the corners are turtle doves of the same colour as parroquets
and yellow finches, eating cherries as big as their own heads ;
loving couples in various loving attitudes ; the swain in brown
beaver stove-pipe hat, sky-blue swallow-tail coat, with gilt
buttons, and yellow smalls ; the maiden in scanty skirt of
mousseline-de-laine, scarlet petisse, and antiquated bonnet of
straw, with a high crown and short poke—very convenient for
kissing.'[2]

More often it was the verses only which were composed by a
third party ; the stationery could be bought, sometimes already

[1]L. Whistler : *op. cit.*, p. 92 where the diary is quoted.
[2]*Bye-gones*, 26 December, 1894, some examples of the valentine verses are also
given here.

decorated, or perhaps used to convey the sender's own pictorial symbolism. ' Sentimental Valentine Writers,' books to help the uninitiated in the art of composing his own greetings, were on sale in England, but the Welsh-speaking countryman found it quite natural to turn to a local poet for a rhymed greeting just as he would ask him for elegiac verses or perhaps receive unsolicited verses commemorating a marriage or the birth of a child. The tradition of writing a form of social poetry was to hand, even though it often survived in a decayed condition, and several examples have been recorded of valentine verses written by nineteenth-century country poets. W. J. Davies states that, in the Llandysul area of Cardiganshire, young men and women used to go to Maeslan to Dafy' Ifans, whose bardic name was *Dewi Dyssul*, and that he used to compose the verses for them. He had written many in his time. Two examples of his work are printed in Davies's book, one of them for sending to a man, the other intended for a girl ; the latter is written to the metre of the old ballad tune *Gwêl yr Adeilad* [See the Building][1] which was also popular for Christmas carols. In the light of this fact it is possible that the verses were sung. Other examples from Llanwenog, Cardiganshire, are given by Cledlyn Davies, including a satirical one written in the local dialect. According to this writer the practice died out in this district between 1880 and 1890.[2]

The sending of ornate printed valentines, however, survived into the twentieth century in country areas. A recent writer refers in the following words to the practice in the Pren-gwyn district (between Llandysul and Llanwenog, the two parishes referred to in the preceding paragraph) : ' It was the practice too, about the beginning of the twentieth century to send valentines. The boys would be willing to pay about two shillings or half a crown for a valentine to send to their true loves. These were trimmed with a border of silk thread and ribbons, and flowers of all colours, and were packed in boxes. The girls used to keep these carefully and place them on the dresser after marrying and having a home of their own.'

---

[1] W. J. Davies : *Hanes Plwyf Llandyssul*, 1896, pp. 253-5.
[2] D. R. and Z. S. Cledlyn Davies : *Hanes Plwyf Llanwenog*, 1939, pp. 116-7.

Derogatory verses were often added to the comic valentines and the enveloped addressed in rhyme.[1]

One interesting feature about Welsh valentine custom is that while the near-English word *falendein* and the English ' valentine ' itself were used by the two seventeenth-century poets, a number of Welsh forms had evolved and were in common usage by the nineteenth century. These included *ffolant, ffalant* (Montgomeryshire), *folant lan* and *folant salw* (sentimental and comic valentines) (Llanwenog), *malant, malantau salw* and *molantau ysmala* (Pren-gwyn), *folant* (Llandyssul). It is tempting to conclude from this that the custom was new in the seventeenth century and that in the course of more than a hundred years it had become entrenched in the Welsh countryman's pattern of life and thus in his vocabulary. This however would be taking us beyond the evidence.

The machine-made valentines which took the place of the hand-made cards were manufactured in England, and the museum's collection includes many good examples of artistic work designed by Victorian craftsmen and sold by the large firms which specialized in this business. The history of the Valentine has been recorded in detail by the American writer, Ruth Webb Lee, whose book gives many excellent illustrations of the various types. The following remarks on the evolution of the printed valentine are based on Miss Lee's volume and are aimed more at illustrating the museum's collection than to provide a full historical account.

The transition from the hand-made to the factory-made valentine was gradual, and such intermediate forms as the hand-decorated type were popular for a number of years until the middle of the last century. The basic material and some of the embellishments were made by machine, but the final touches were added by hand. In the 'thirties an embossed (but unperforated) border of up to two inches width was often used as a frame to enclose a hand-coloured illustration in the central panel. This type was improved, mainly during the late 'thirties and 'forties, by the use of perforated borders and embossments, and paper lace work. Furthermore the latest

[1] Mrs. Kate Davies, in a MS. now in W.F.M. archives.

developments in methods of illustration were during this period incorporated in the making of valentines ; engravings, woodcuts and lithographs, all usually hand-coloured, also became common (See Plate 13). Often the centres of the valentine paper would be cut out and a panel of silk or satin inserted. An additional message could always be added by the sender, though the makers provided a suitable verse written in a neat copperplate hand. Mechanical devices of various kinds were also incorporated after about 1840 but these tended to be used more often in the comic valentines which began to be made about that time. The introduction of the Penny Post gave the valentine custom a tremendous fillip and also ensured the anonymity essential for the use of comic valentines. Like the Christmas-card industry, though probably on a smaller scale, because it was an older custom and because one sent fewer valentines than Christmas cards, the manufacture of valentines now attracted a number of talented artists and craftsmen whose skill was devoted to this medium. The period 1840-60 when the embossed and perforated lace valentine was in vogue has justly been called the golden age of valentines.

Early valentine patterns were often retained for many years and used in current production with a different type or style of decoration. But several new features were introduced during the eighteen-sixties which, in general, marked a decline in the artistic quality of the cards. The heavily-padded sachet, which was probably heavily scented too, became popular in the 'fifties and was incorporated in the increasingly ornate examples turned out to cater for the expanding Victorian market. Some indication of the scale on which the custom was carried on is given by Laurence Whistler who quotes the G.P.O. figures.[1] These show that about 800,000 valentines were posted in 1855, increasing (after a curious decline in the 1860's) to 1,634,000 in 1882. During the 'seventies elaborate two- or three-tiered valentines were introduced and sold in special boxes. By the 1890's valentines were all basically of the same style, consisting of a double sheet, the face or top of which was heavily or coarsely embossed in colour, with a verse printed on the middle

[1]L. Whistler : *op. cit.*, p. 96.

page. The more expensive ones would have two layers above
the face. In general the fussiness and pointless over-adornment
of these late Victorian specimens matches the trend in other
decorative work during this period of declining taste. The
Christmas card, which had become increasingly similar to the
valentine during the period 1850-1885—so much so that only
the pasted inscriptions were different—began to assume an
individuality of its own once more. The valentine, however,
had already reached the peak of its development and from
about 1900 declined in popularity, at the very time, in fact,
when the Christmas card was consolidating its position. The
grotesque and venomous humour of the comic valentine seems
to have had a longer lease of life, but its use was far removed
from the Victorian concept of romantic love which lay behind
the sentimental valentine. Notwithstanding this the comic
valentine served as a vehicle for anonymous social criticism as
the series of lithographed sheets attacking human foibles and
trade shortcomings in the catalogue suggests. The custom of
sending valentines has never completely died out—some would
argue that it is being revived—but it has long since ceased to be
a folk custom.

Reference must be made here to the custom of sending a
token in the form of a ' white stick ' (*ffon wen*) or a piece of
ginger to the rejected lover. The ' white stick ' was a hazel
wand of varying length and thickness freshly peeled of its bark
to expose the white stem. It was often trimmed with a black
crape bow or a ribbon, and was sometimes accompanied by
' a verse or so of homespun poetry setting forth the significance
of the article transmitted, with also sundry complimentary
references to the person addressed, on "being on the shelf", and
other pointed pin-pricks calculated to open old sores and to
wound the too susceptible feeling of a "good-old-has-been"[1].'
The stick was sent anonymously to the jilted person on or near
the wedding-day of his or her former lover. In Llansilin,
Denbighshire, and other parts of Wales in the late nineteenth
century, the *ffon wen* was often sent by post and could be easily
recognized by those who handled it in the post-office. In parts

[1]*Bye-gones* : 21 December, 1898.

of Merioneth the token sent to rejected suitors was a piece of ginger,[1] and in other districts both the ginger and the hazel wand were sent.[2] The custom of sending the *ffon wen* survived in western Montgomeryshire until the nineteen-twenties, and possibly later.

One of the aspects of Welsh folk life which appealed to the eighteenth- and nineteenth-century traveller was the body of picturesque customs associated with weddings and wedding-feasts. Those who were searching for material for their travel-books found the language less of a barrier in describing these customs than they did when they tried to understand some other sides of Welsh life. Consequently there are numerous references scattered among the literary output of these visitors and of local historians to the ' horse-wedding,' the race to the churchyard, the quintain, the ' bidding ' and other marriage customs.

It was necessary, before a wedding was held, for guests to be invited to the ceremony and to the feast afterwards. This was formerly done in two ways. Either a written notice—a ' bidding letter '—could be sent, or a *gwahoddwr* (bidder) was engaged to call at the houses of friends and acquaintances. The former predominated in the middle of the last century after the introduction of the penny post, but the latter, probably an older method, was not lightly discarded. The incentive to proclaim the date of the wedding and bidding by both methods was partly economic, for the invited guests brought with them presents and sums of money repaying earlier kindnesses or wedding gifts received from the family of the bride or bridegroom ; and the phrasing of the letter or the proclamation by the *gwahoddwr* followed more or less a set pattern delicately holding the balance between reminders of the hospitality offered and polite requests for the return of donations, to which the young couple were entitled.

Of the various accounts of the ' bidder ' at his work, one may be selected since it describes his costume and his lengthy speech. It relates to Laugharne, Carmarthenshire, where a man called John Williams was the bidder in the eighteen-

[1] *ibid.*
[2] *Bye-gones :* 8 April, 1899.

forties : ' He would be dressed in a white apron ; a white ribbon was tied in the button-hole of his coat, and the bidder's staff in his hand with which he knocked at the doors. No one now remembers any ribbons at the end of it. A bag was swung at his back, in which he put the bread and cheese the people at the farmhouses gave the bidder. His Rammas (the form in which he put the invitation rhymes) is described as most amusing. I have collected the substance of it, though by no means all—he varied it at different times ; nor have I succeeded in getting the rhyme in which he repeated it. It is as follows :—

"I was desired to call here as a messenger and a bidder. David J. and Ann W. in this parish of Laugharne, the hundred of Derllys, Co. Carmarthen, encouraged by their friends to make a bidding on Tuesday next ; the two young people made their residence in Gosport, No. 11, thence to St. Michael's church to be married. The two young people return back to the young woman's father and mother's house to dinner. They shall have good beef and cabbage, mutton and turnips, pork and potatoes, roast goose or gant, perhaps both if they are in season, a quart of drink for fourpence, a cake for a penny, clean chairs to sit down upon, clean pipes and tobacco, and attendance of the best ; a good song, but if no one will sing, then I'll sing as well as I can ; and if no one will attend, I'll attend as well as I can. As a usual custom with us, in Laugharne, is to hold a ' sending gloves ' before the wedding, if you'll please to come, or send a waggon or a cart, a horse and a colt, a heifer, a cow and calf, or an ox and a half, or pigs, cocks, hens, geese, goslings, ducks, turkeys, a saddle and bridle, or a child's cradle, or what the house can afford. A great many can help one, but one cannot help a great many, or send a waggon full of potatoes, a cartload of turnips, a hundred or two of cheeses, a cask of butter, a sack of flour, a winchester of barley, or what you please, for anything will be acceptable ; jugs, basins, saucepans, pots and pans, or what you can ; throw in £5 if you like ; gridirons, frying-pans, tea-kettles, plates and dishes, a lootch (a wooden spoon) and dish, spoons, knives and forks, pepper boxes, salt-cellars, mustard-pots, or even a penny whistle or a child's cradle. Ladies and gentlemen, I was desired to speak this way that all *pwython* (payments) due to the young woman's father and mother, grandfather and grandmother, aunts, brothers and sisters, and the same due to the young man's father and mother, &c., &c. must be returned to the young people on the above day. So no more at present. If you please to order your butler, or underservant, to give a quart of drink to the bidder"[1].'

A similar speech in Welsh was made in the Welsh-speaking districts of west Wales where the ' bidding ' appears to have flourished most. In parts of Carmarthenshire, the term *stori wawdd* [bidding story] was used as well as *rammas*, and many local variations on the general pattern existed. Sometimes a song and a dance would be given by the bidder ; in other places his entry into the house was more formalized : a bidder would walk into the house without greeting anybody, strike his staff three times on the floor, take off his hat and place it under his left armpit, cough and clear his mouth and begin his speech.[2]

Many of the characteristics of the speech, but little of its humour, were to be seen in the bidding letter which again followed a fairly set pattern. The earliest example of a bidding letter in the museum's collection is dated 1798 (No. 480, Plate 14), and the most recent 1901, when the custom had virtually died out, at least in the form which it took in its hey-day in the middle of the century.

An essential part of the ' bidding ' was the keeping of an account book in which all gifts were entered. The married couple looked on all the presents which they received as debts which they would in time have to repay in a similar manner. Some of the donations, of course, were repayments of debts to the young couple. The amount of money collected in biddings naturally varied, but often reached thirty or forty pounds—no small sum in the middle of the nineteenth century. Although a certain amount would inevitably have to be repaid over the years, the holding of the bidding enabled the couple to get married and to set up house. In effect it constituted a primitive form of hire-purchase or insurance in which payments were spread over a considerable period of time and the benefits

[1]M. Curtis : *Antiquities of Laugharne*, p. 210-11.
[2]D. G. Williams : *op. cit.*, p. 280.

enjoyed at a specific time. The gifts made were considered recoverable by law but prudence, as well as a desire to avoid expensive litigation, saw to it that the reciprocity was strictly observed.

The wedding itself, in south-west Wales, was either one in which the party rode on horseback (*priodas geffylau*) or, among poorer people, one in which the party walked to the church (*priodas dra'd*). All who could afford it (and many who could not) sought to have a 'horse-wedding', and animals were borrowed from neighbouring farmers on such occasions. One of the most picturesque features of this kind of wedding was the racing on horseback in which both the bridal party and the guests took part. Sometimes persons were injured or even killed in the course of the race. We are told, too, that well-to-do farmers were not always willing to lend their horses to labourers and others who indulged in such reckless behaviour.[1]

The pretext for the galloping to or from the church was the ancient custom of capturing or chasing the bride. The form which this custom took differed slightly in various districts, the feature common to them all being the horse-racing. In Llansawel, Carmarthenshire, ' it was the custom for the wedding parties to ride to and from the church. On the way thither they resorted to racing, and chasing each other over the country. For this purpose the bride was mounted on a pillion behind the person acting as her guardian, who, escorted by her friends, together with those of the bridegroom, sets off from the house to the church ; but when they arrived at a convenient spot, instead of proceeding to the church, the guardian would set spurs to his horse, and gallop off in a contrary direction, along some of the numerous cross lanes, apparently with every intention of carrying off the bride. Upon this, the bridegroom with his attendants, sets off in pursuit, while the other party are no less active in pressing forward to protect the fugitives and prevent their capture ; and for the more effective carrying on of this mystery of attack and defence, it is necessary that the whole country should be scoured in every direction, in order that the lanes and highways may be properly occupied by

[1]Amy [Lane] : *Sketches of Wales and the Welsh*, 1847, p. 66.

the pursuing party, to prevent the possibility of escape. It was a matter of principle with the guardian to be continually endeavouring to effect an escape with his ward. The appearance of such a number of men and women, all smartly dressed, and galloping about in every direction, gave the whole scene a most singular appearance, especially as the women were such bold and expert riders, kept up, and mingled with the foremost of the party, and entered into the spirit of the tumultuous procession in a most animated manner. It is scarcely possible to imagine anything more wild and irregular than the various movements of the whole party upon this occasion. When the bridegroom caught the bride, the whole party would gallop away to the church.'[1] We are told that the last *priodas geffylau* of this type in the parish of Llansawel was held in 1849.[2] But another writer states that he witnessed one near Abergwili, in the same county, in 1876—probably the last one held in this area.[3]

In many districts, especially in Cardiganshire, the ride to church was preceded by another ceremony, that of *pwnco* [question and answer in verse] at the door of the bride's home. The bridegroom's men, *gwŷr y shigowt* [the men of the ' seek out '] set out on horseback for the bride's home early in the morning on the wedding day to attempt to escort her to the church. Various obstructions are raised to prevent their acccess to the house—ropes of straw across the road, the barricading of the road with stones and, in many cases, the erection of a *cwinten* or *gwyntyn* [quintain]. This consisted of ' an upright post, on the top of which a spar turned freely. At one end of this spar hung a sand-bag, the other presented a flat side. The rider in passing struck the flat side, and if not dexterous in passing was overtaken, and perhaps dismounted by the sandbag, and became a fair object of laughter.'[4] The word *cwinten* in some parts of Wales came to be given to the rope held across the road before the bridal party, a custom which still flourishes in Cardiganshire and Carmarthenshire and elsewhere.

When these obstacles were passed the bridegroom's men—a

[1]F. S. Price : *History of Llansawel*, 1898, pp. 34-5.
[2]*ibid.*
[3]Herbert M. Vaughan in *Trans. Carm. Antiq. Soc.*, I, 1905, p. 45.
[4]P. Roberts : *Cambrian Popular Antiquities*, pp. 162-3.

party of from a dozen to a score in number—were prevented from entering the house by the secure barring of the door. To gain admittance they had to win a contest of wits carried on in verse between local rhymesters employed in the service of both parties. The contest might last for several hours and examples of the verses used have been recorded. The following were sung at Cardiganshire weddings and some of them, we are told, were used in the eighteen-nineties ;[1] the verses were sung (or sometimes recited) by the party in the house (A) and the bridegroom's men (B) alternately :

A. Dydd da ich, lân gwm-
    peini
  Pa beth yw'ch neges
    heddi' ?
  Ai hel eich bwyd y'ch chi
    ffor' hyn ?
  Mae bwyd yn brin eleni.

Good day to you fair company
What's your business to-day ?
Are you begging your way ?
Food is scarce this year.

B. Fy neges a fynegaf,
  Mewn 'madrodd gorau
    medraf ;
  Ond brysiais dipyn yn fy
    hynt
  Rhaid cael fy ngwynt yn
    gyntaf.

My business I will state
In terms as plain as I can,
But I have hastened on my
  journey
And must get my breath first.

A. Ai chwi yw teulu'r gorth-
    rwm
  Sy'n dod i werthu'r deg-
    wm ?
  A rhoddwch wybod a oes
    hedd,
  Gan fod eich gwedd mor
    bendrwm.

Are you the people of oppression
Who come to sell the tithe ?
Let me know if you come in
  peace,
As your countenances look so
  gloomy.

B. 'Rym ni yn dod ar neges
  Dros fab â chalon gynnes,
  I nôl eich Anni lygad lon
  Yn dirion hoff gymhares.

We are coming on an errand
From a warm-hearted young
  man,
To fetch your bright-eyed Annie
To be his loving partner.

[1] *Bye-gones* : 29 September, 1897.

A. Os soniwch am briodi,
   Yr ateb gewch gan Anni,
   Fod gofid mawr yn ddigon
       siwr,
   Ynglŷn â gŵr a theulu.

If you intend proposing marriage
You will get the answer from
    Annie
That there is certainly great
    trouble
In having a husband and
    family.

B. Taw sôn, yr ynfyd gwirion,
   Mae'r ferch yn barod
       ddigon ;
   A'r unig un mae e' yn nôl
   Yw Anni Dolebolion.

Quiet, you silly fool,
The young woman is willing
    enough
And the only one that he will
    have
Is Annie of Dolebolion.

A. A fuoch chwi'n awgrymu
   I'r bachgen bore heddi'
   Fod rhaid cael tipyn o
       'scylhaig,
   Cyn cadw gwraig a theulu.

Did you not suggest
To the young man this morning,
That a man ought to be a pretty
    good scholar
To keep a wife and family.

B. Mae'r mab yn hen ysgoler,
   Mae'n ennill arian lawer,
   Wrth dynnu glo o fol y
       graig
   All gadw gwraig yn glefer.

The young man is an old scholar
And makes heaps of money,
Drawing coal from the bowels of
    the earth,
He can easily keep a wife.

A. Ni chymer Ann mo'r colier
   Sy'n gweithio yn y
       dyfnder ;
   Mae'r rhai sydd yno,
       druain, gwael,
   Yn cael damweiniau lawer.

Ann will not have the collier
Who works in the depths ;
Those who work there, poor
    things,
Meet with many accidents.

At this point the door is
opened :

A. Wel, tewi rhaid yr awron,
   Os ynt yn caru'n ffyddlon,
   Mae'n well i chwi gael
       mynd â'r ferch,
   Na siomi serch eich calon.

Well, I had better say no more
    now
If they love one another faith-
    fully
It is better you should take her
Than disappoint the lover's
    heart.

On gaining entry the party had to find the bride, who had
meanwhile hidden or disguised herself. When she had been
discovered she was taken on horse-back by the groom's party in

the direction of the church with the bride's ' bodyguard ' in pursuit. According to certain writers the *pwnco* took place after the wedding ceremony and was followed by the feast.[1]

The bidding and the weddings described in the last few pages were most typical of south-west Wales, although they were to be found outside this region, as for example, in Defyn-nog, Brecknockshire.[2] In parts of north Wales, however, there were certain other features connected with the weddings. The best known of these was the wedding-cake which was the prize awarded to the fastest runner in a race which began at the church door the moment the bride had worn her ring, and ended in the house where the wedding feast was held. The custom was still kept up in Anglesey about 1890, though on a less spectacular scale.[3] Earlier in the century the race was quite impressive and we are told of one man from Llanllechid, Caernarvonshire, that he once ran four miles against thirty other young men and won the cake. Some indication of the importance of weddings in rural Caernarvonshire in this period is given by the remark that it was often at these social gatherings that young men met their future wives.[4] In Caernarvonshire and Anglesey, as in several districts in south Wales the bridal party and their guests often marched in procession to the church if no horses could be afforded. Lewis Morris mentions that the bridal party on their way to church danced Morris dances and were accompanied by the music of the fiddle or harp.[5] Another regional difference noted in Caernarvonshire and some other areas in north Wales was that the weddings were public ; friends and well-wishers attended of their own accord without being ' bidden.' A charge of one shilling was made for a dinner which often consisted of wheat bread and sweet milk.[6] Morris records the same practice in the eighteenth century : ' They come home from church, dinner custards & paying on a plate drinking woeing, dancing, *campio*, each paying

[1]P. Roberts : *op. cit.*, p. 162.

[2]D. C. Lewis : *Hanes Plwyf Defynog*, 1911, pp. 289-97.

[3]E. A. Williams : *Hanes Môn yn y 19eg ganrif*, 1927, t. 324.

[4]Elias Owen : ' On some customs still remaining in Wales,' *Y Cymmrodor*, II, 1878, p. 137.

[5]H. Owen : *Life and Works of Lewis Morris*, p. 142.

[6]*Bye-gones*, 17 November, 1875.

his shott, Fighting.'[1] 'Putting yᵉ young couple in bed,' another practice Morris refers to in the same context is also referred to by other writers, for example Pratt, who states that the men visitors put to bed the bridegroom, and the females the bride, 'after which the whole company remain in the chamber, drinking jocund health to the new-married couple, and their posterity, singing songs, dancing, and giving into other festivity, sometimes for two or three days together.'[2] A German traveller's version of a Caernarvonshire wedding in 1856 has recently been published in English.[3]

Many Welsh marriage-customs had their counterpart in other countries ; racing to church on horseback was well-known in parts of Scandinavia, as was the custom of accompanying the bridal couple to their chamber.[4] The quintain was known in England in Elizabethan times and later,[5] and so were a number of forms of the bidding, under the names of bride-ale (' bridal '), bride-wain (Cumberland), wedding-dinner (Essex)[6] In Scotland a similar custom was known as a ' penny-wedding.'[7] The *pwnco* or contest in verse at the door, as far as is known, was a purely Welsh form more akin to certain aspects of the Mari Lwyd and other similar customs. The setting for these marriage customs in whatever countries they were found was the closely knit peasant community where the setting up of a new household and the founding of a new family were matters of concern to everybody. In their economic aspect the underlying sentiment in the bidding and similar practices is well expressed by a phrase used in the bidder's ' rammas ' quoted on an earlier page, namely ' a great many can help one, but one cannot help a great many.' To this economic function had been added an element of merry-making and general social intercourse. It is difficult not to agree with the Rev. D. Parry Jones's

---

[1]H. Owen : *op. cit.*, p. 142.

[2]S. J. Pratt : *Gleanings through Wales, Holland and Westphalia*, I, 1797, p. 114-5.

[3]See *Gwerin*, II, 1958, pp. 38-43.

[4]Rigmor Frimannslund : ' Skikk og tro ved friing og Bryllup.' in K. Rob. V. Wikman : *Livets Högtider*, pp. 68, 75-6.

[5]It is named among the sports given to entertain Queen Elizabeth at Kenilworth Castle in 1573 ; the reference is to ' a solemn country bridal, with running at Quintin.' Brand : *Popular Antiquities* ii, p. 101.

[6]Brand : *op. cit.* ii, pp. 90-5.

[7]*ibid.*

comment that the disappearance of the pageantry of the Welsh wedding in its various forms ' did much to weaken the social ties that bound the rural community together,'[1] but the argument is also possible that the customs disappeared just because the social ties were being weakened and could no longer give rise to such vivid communal celebration.

The rural society which maintained these picturesque wedding customs was also concerned to ensure that the marriage vow was kept and that family life did not deviate too widely from the ideal pattern. Divorce did not have a place in the countryman's code, but there were several corrective devices which had become folk customs and through which any obvious breach of the ideal of married life could be rectified. These customs constituted an unofficial legal system (which often came into conflict with the law of the land) deriving its efficacy from the power of popular feeling in communities in which each man knew the business (and secrets) of his neighbour.

In south-west Wales the name given to a local form of penal custom was *y ceffyl pren* [the wooden horse]. The practice consisted of carrying a person, or his effigy, on a wooden pole in order to make him the laughing stock of the community.[2] In Tenby, Pembrokeshire, when domestic strife became too great—usually because the wife wanted to assume mastery of the home—' the neighbours step in with the *ceffyl pren* or wooden horse. An effigy of the offender is dressed up, seated on a chair, placed on a ladder, and carried on men's shoulders, a crowd in procession preceding and following the *ceffyl pren*, shouting, screaming, and beating tin saucepans &c. Halting at intervals, the nature of the offence is thus described by the spokesman :—

> Ran-dan-dan !
> Betty Morris has beat her man.
> What was it with ? '
> Twas not with a rake, nor yet with a reel,
> But 'twas with a poker, that made him feel.

[1]D. Parry Jones : *Welsh Country Up-bringing*, p. 97.

[2]Professor David Williams suggests that the custom may have been derived from the riding of the hobby horse in ancient revelry, and points out that the phallic significance of the posture may have retained for it a suggestion of obscenity which made it particularly appropriate as a punishment for mental infidelity. D. Williams : *The Rebecca Riots, A Study in Agrarian Discontent*, 1955, pp. 53-6.

At other times the neighbours are not contented with a mere effigy. When a man or woman are faithless to their marriage vows, the mob seize the offending parties, fasten them back to back, mount them on the wooden horse, parade them about, proclaiming their shame, and pelting them with rotten eggs and other offensive missiles. After continuing the exposure for some time the culprits are taken down, and followed with hootings and execrations to their respective dwellings, where they are left to digest the bitter reproaches of their injured partners.'[1]

According to D. G. Williams, the Carmarthenshire practice was to make a horse of straw and place a human effigy of straw on its back. These were carried as if on a bier by four men and joined by a crowd of masked people with blackened faces. Sometimes a gun was carried and the straw effigy shot. The processions were announced beforehand and would take place over a previously determined route for three weeks in succession. Finally the effigies of man and horse would be publicly burned.[2] At Cynwyl Elfed in the same county, until about 1865, a ' court ' was held in which a large effigy of the offender was tried by a ' judge ' in the presence of a large crowd. The punishment was invariably that of suspending the effigy by its arm or leg from the large oak tree growing where the villagers had assembled ; it was then burnt.[3] This seems to be a variation of the same custom. Professor Williams has shown how the *ceffyl pren* treatment was meted out to people who had given evidence in unpopular legal cases, and states that ' it can, indeed, be said with complete certainty that the Rebecca Riots were an extension of the practice of the *ceffyl pren*.'[4] The *ceffyl pren* was not, however, as Professor Williams supposes, confined to south-west Wales.

The terms ' coolstrin ' and ' skymmetry ' were used in Glamorgan to refer to a similar practice. The ' court ' has been described in detail by Charles Redwood in his book on the Vale

[1] *Tales and Traditions of Tenby*, pp. 95-6.
[2] D. G. Williams : *op. cit.*, p. 303.
[3] I. C. Peate : ' A People's Court,' *Folk-lore*, LVI, 1945, pp. 273-4.
[4] D. Williams : *op. cit.*, p. 56.

of Glamorgan.[1]   The ' judge,' who was an old man wore the triangular-shaped collar bone of a horse round the crown of his slouched hat ; his train was a coverlet which was fastened about his shoulders and borne by a youth who stalked solemnly behind him.   The ' court ' was held in the churchyard, the ' judge ' sitting on the churchyard wall and conducting the proceedings with great solemnity. His attendant officers carried long white wands and a ' posse of rustics ' armed with pitch-forks stood by to keep order.   The ' court ' was opened by a crier and the history of the case given.   The ' court ' was adjourned for a week and witnesses summoned to give evidence and the accused to defend herself.   The mock advocates argued the merits of the case in the subsequent meetings, and finally the judgement was delivered, to the accompaniment of a long speech on the dangers of the tyranny of women.   The verdict was that the inhabitants should ' hold a riding ' on the husband and wife. On the appointed day the procession was led by the judge in his ' hat ' and ' robes ' followed by the wand-bearers and by the ' musicians ' who used various household utensils to make an unearthly din.   Then came the two standard-bearers, one with a petticoat at the top of a pole, and the other carrying a breeches in the same manner, only reversed, with the upside down.   These preceded the two who impersonated the husband and wife, the former carrying a broom and the latter a ladle. Behind them followed the crowd who were delighted by their horse-play and who in turn made ' antic gestures and grim-aces.'   The procession was apparently made up of men only and when the party returned from a circuit through the villages of the vale, the women collected to scoff at them with hoots and yells. As the party passed the home of the husband and wife impersonated, the pole on which the petticoat flourished was fixed opposite the house and was pelted with mud, stones, addled eggs and dirt, until it dropped in tatters to the ground ; this occurred to the strain of the ' rough-music ' and the vociferous acclamations of the party.   The pole with the breeches was raised in place of that with the petticoat to

[1]C. Redwood : *The Vale of Glamorgan*, 1839, pp. 274ff. See also G. J. Williams : ' Glamorgan Customs in the Eighteenth Century,' *Gwerin*, I, p. 106-8. Cf, ' Skimmington ' (1609) *Oxford English Dictionary*.

conclude the proceedings. It will be noted that the horse does not figure in this Glamorgan form, unless symbolically in the collar bone of a horse worn by the judge, and that the miscreant was not represented in effigy.

Even in the parts of Wales where the *ceffyl pren* proper was known there were numerous variations in the custom. In Llanfyllin the wooden horse was mounted by a man (not the miscreant) and was carried about by four bearers ; verses were recited in the form of question and answer.[1] In Cardiganshire, only husbands who ill-treated their wives were coolstrined ; in Brecknockshire the wooden horse was only paraded in front of the house.[2] Degenerate forms of the custom were also found, such as the practice in Monmouthshire of tying straw round the gate of a married couple's house when the husband had been beating his wife, ' so that he might beat the straw instead of his wife'.[3] Burning in effigy, also called ' ran-tanning' (cf. Tenby), was formerly known in the Pant district near Oswestry where it was accompanied by ' rough-music.'[4] Farther north, in Wrexham the straw effigy was paraded past the two houses of the offending parties and then set on fire.[5] The custom has also been recorded in Conway where in 1882 a man and a woman were tied to a ladder and carried through the town to the singing of *Yr eneth ga'dd ei gwrthod* [The rejected maiden].[6] As late as the eighteen-nineties an example of a similar punishment took place in Amlwch, Anglesey ; the custom in that county was for persons found guilty of adultery to be carried naked on a ladder.[7]

Although the *ceffyl pren* custom in its various forms was found in many parts of Wales, it was in the south, and especially in the south-west of Wales that it appears to have been most frequently resorted to. Professor Williams quotes a government report of 1839, on the establishment of a police force, which draws attention to the increasing frequency of the outbreak of

[1]Owen Jones : *Cymru : yn hanesyddol, etc.*, II, 1875, p. 119.
[2]Wirt Sikes : *British Goblins*, 1880, p. 320.
[3]*Bye-gones*, 24 May, 1893.
[4]*Bye-gones*, 9 November, 1958.
[5]*Bye-gones*, 16 April, 1879.
[6]*Bye-gones*, 15 March, 1882.
[7]E. A. Williams : *op. cit.* p. 322.

disorders associated with the practice of employing the *ceffyl pren*.[1] With the introduction of an efficient constabulary the *ceffyl pren* and similar popular punishments became increasingly rare or more subversive. What must have been one of the last examples took place in the district around Tregaron in the early nineteen-twenties.

Like many of the marriage customs the *ceffyl pren* had its counterpart in England, where the term ' skimmington ' or ' skymmetry ' was often used. ' Riding the stang ' was a term which occurred in Shropshire where the effigy was called a ' mawkin.'[2] The custom itself has been recorded in Yorkshire, Cambridgeshire, Durham, London, Gloucestershire, Lothian and other districts.[3]

DEATH

The ceremonies which follow death are associated first with the preparation of the corpse for burial and with the burial itself, and secondly with the crisis in the family of the bereaved and among his friends. Death brings about the crisis ; the funeral brings it to a head, and displays both private and public grief in a solemn ritual.

The death of a person was formerly announced by the parish-bell, and the house where the corpse lies was called, in Caernarvonshire and Anglesey, *tŷ corff* [the corpse house].[4] No religious ceremony or rite took place immediately after death, although sometimes a person would be called in to pray *before* death.[5] Meanwhile the corpse had to be washed and prepared for the coffin. This was called *diweddu* [finishing] in Merioneth and Montgomeryshire, *rhoi allan* [laying out] in east Montgomeryshire, and *troi 'e heibio* [putting him by] in Glamorgan.[6] The carpenter meanwhile would have called at the house to measure the body before making the coffin. In Llanbryn-Mair, Montgomeryshire, it was the practice for all the shavings planed from the boards to be placed as ' bedding '

[1]D. Williams : *op. cit.*, p. 53.
[2]*Bye-gones*, 2 March, 1879.
[3]Brand : *op. cit.*, ii, pp. 118-20.
[4]W. Williams : *Observations on the Snowdon Mountains*, 1802, p. 13.
[5]*Bye-gones*, 14 October, 1891.
[6]*ibid*.

for the dead.[1] When the coffin had been made and the corpse laid in it certain steps were taken which were thought to preserve it both against decay and, possibly, against evil influence. A pewter plate, a quantity of salt on it, was placed on the breast of the dead person (see No. 566 in Catalogue) ; a piece of turf wrapped in paper was used in Shropshire,[2] and a green sod in the Betws-y-coed district of Denbighshire and Caernarvonshire. Probably the damp-absorbing qualities of salt and turf was responsible for this practice.[3] Between the time of death and the funeral neighbours volunteered to sit up each night in the room in which the body rested. This was called *gwylio'r corff* [watching the body] ; any supernatural significance, which it might once have had, no longer existed in the nineteenth century when it was regarded merely as a token of respect and sympathy on the part of the neighbours.[4]

On the night preceding the funeral the *gwylnos* [vigil, wake] was formerly held, and the term is still maintained in some districts. This at one time followed a pattern similar in many respects to the Irish and Scottish wakes, but like the Hebridean wake described by Vallee, the *gwylnos* had by the nineteenth century become an extremely respectable institution.[5] The form which it took in Anglesey in the middle of the eighteenth century still retained some traces of the light-hearted atmosphere which paradoxically were once associated with it. Lewis Morris writes of it thus : ' The night before y[e] Burying all the neighbours & Friends of y[e] Deceased come & watch his Body & to say their prayers, or Pater nosters as y[e] saying is, *padreua i'r wylnos* as they term it, and there sitt up all night a-drinking smoaking singing of carols or some ancient odes to y[e] purpose & playing all little mountebank tricks as they can think on to keep themselves awake. At their entrance into y[e] house they first go to y[e] room where (the) dead Body lies & say the

[1]ex. inf. Dr. Iorwerth C. Peate.

[2]*Bye-gones*, 20 April, 1910.

[3]It was formerly the practice to put a green sod on top of a beer barrel to absorb the damp.

[4]Like some other customs associated with death *gwylio'r corff* has its counterpart in other countries. In Barra, in the Outer Hebrides it was also called ' watching.' Cf. F. G. Vallee : 'Burial and Mourning Customs in a Hebridean Community', *Journal of Royal Anthropological Institute*, LXXXV, pp. 119—130.

[5]F. G. Vallee : *op. cit.*, p. 123.

Lord's prayer kneeling by ye dead body, and when they get up one of ye nearest relations or masters of ye ceremonies give each a cup of ale & they are ordered to sit down. At ye dusk of night an evening prayer is read by ye clergyman of ye parish or if not present by one of ye company. The neglect of which they think to be a great slur on ye family. The singing of psalms if they can, or else fall to singing of carols which are antient songs containing Reflections upon death &c. Immortality of ye Soul.'[1]   A later writer describing the neighbouring county of Caernarvon half a century or so later, gives a similar account but adds ' since Methodism is become so universal, some one stands up and delivers an oration on the melancholy subject, and then the company drop away by degrees.'[2] This marked the growing influence of Methodism on this ancient custom which was to turn it into a special form of prayer meeting called in parts of Denbighshire *cyfarfod galar* [meeting of lamentation].   The behaviour to which the Methodists objected was the light-hearted singing and bantering which were once typical of the *gwylnos*, although neither Morris nor Williams allude to the more extreme instances of what the Methodists thought of as unseemly behaviour. Robert Jones, Rhos-lan (1745—1829) describes a *gwylnos* during the course of which a youth carried the dead body in his arms from the room where the coffin stood to the room where the company sat ; after several attempts to frighten the neighbours, the youth fell with the corpse in his hands.[3] A Pembrokeshire writer states that until the middle of the eighteenth century it was a custom to draw the corpse up through the chimney of the house before replacing it in the coffin ;[4] whatever the original significance of this practice, there can be no doubt that, like other less objectionable customs, it was interpreted by the religious reformers of the nonconformist ascendancy as levity entirely unwarranted by the solemn occasion.   But many pre-Reformation details were retained in the nineteenth century ' wakes.' The room (usually

[1]H. Owen : *Life and Works of Lewis Morris*, p. 142.
[2]W. Williams : *op. cit.*, p. 14.
[3]R. Jones : *Drych yr Amseroedd*, 1898 edn., p. 39.
[4]*Man*, 1935, No. 33 and *Pembrokeshire Antiquities*, pp. 72-3.

the parlour) where the body lay was decorated for the *gwylnos*, the walls being covered over with linen sheets with laurel leaves pinned on to them in such a way that two leaves formed the letter ' T ' or a cross. Two lighted candles were placed at the head and feet of the body, respectively. Even until about 1850—1855 we are told that in a nonconformist neighbourhood on the borders of Pembrokeshire and Carmarthenshire a lighted candle on a plate was placed on the chest of the body during the *gwylnos*.[1] In the eighteenth century it is said that the custom was ' to invite some well-known singer to the *gwylnos* and it was expected he would come prepared with an elegy of his own composing, upon the deceased,'[2] surely a survival among the peasantry of a custom formerly common among the Welsh gentry and their family bards. The composition of elegiac verses which were later printed and distributed among friends was a practice which outlasted the *gwylnos* ; it was known even as late as the period of the Second World War. The *gwylnos*, in its later form, ceased in Anglesey in the eighteen-nineties, but continued in other districts, such as Glamorgan until recently.

The day after the *gwylnos*, all those who had been present would visit the *tŷ corff* again to take part in the funeral. In Anglesey in the eighteenth century they would be given ' a cup of drink, & if deceased be Rich servd with cakes, wine &c.'[3] In Llanfechain Montgomeryshire, one of the church communion vessels was used to distribute spiced ale on this occasion until the middle of the nineteenth century.[4] According to another writer, an elaborate meal was eaten before the funeral and three or even four hours spent smoking shag tobacco and drinking ale in the house before forming the cortege. Sometimes wine and finger biscuits were handed round after the guests had formed the funeral procession.[5] In Mallwyd and Llan-ym-mawddwy, Merioneth, the hot spiced ale (*diod boeth*)

[1]*Bye-gones*, 17 May, 1882.
[2]Elias Owen : ' On some Customs still remaining in Wales.' *Y Cymmrodor*, II, 1878, p. 134.
[3]H. Owen : *op. cit.*, p. 142.
[4]W. Maddock Williams : ' A slight Historical and Topographical Sketch of the Parish of Llanfechain,' *Mont. Coll.*, V., pp. 203-84.
[5]*Bye-gones*, 24 January, 1894.

consisted of ' beer diluted to the extent of one-half, sometimes two-thirds, of water ; and made strong again by adding spices, ginger &c. The drink was served from a table at the door, the usual quantity being about one-fourth of a pint to each man, with a small piece of cake.'[1] In Anglesey, when the jug of mulled ale and lemon peel appeared, all the males took off their hats and perfect silence was observed while the attendant presented the jug to each guest in turn, each of whom took a sip and handed it back. Alternatively, a set of small thin goblets, ' the size of a small wine-glass ' but different in shape and material were used specifically for this purpose. Only a few families possessed these, and they were borrowed by the poor families of the district for funerals.[2] In Ardd-lin, Montgomeryshire the currant cakes eaten before the funeral left are described as being ' about 2 inches square, with a kind of biscuit about 3 inches long by one inch broad placed across each.' These were handed out on trays just as the body was brought out of the house and placed on the bier.[3] In some parts of Denbighshire the familiar sponge cakes of the confectioner's shop were handed round, and it was considered an insult to the family to refuse to take one.[4] On the whole the custom was quite an expensive cost to the family and it is not surprising to read of the vestry meeting of a rural parish (Llanarmon Dyffryn Ceiriog, Denbighshire) in 1888 pledging those present to abandon the custom in their families and to use their influence with others. Besides being dear, it was stated to give much trouble to the family at a time of affliction and to cause the cortege to be late.[5] In some parts however, food and drink were left until after the funeral.

In certain districts a corpse-bell, or small hand-bell, was rung by the parish clerk who walked a short distance in advance of the funeral procession. The bell is referred to in a terrier of Llanfair Dyffryn Clwyd in 1729, and it is known that the custom continued there until the eighteen-sixties.[6] This pre-

[1]*Bye-gones*, 1 July, 1891.
[2]*Bye-gones*, 27 May, 1891.
[3]*Bye-gones*, 2 December, 1891.
[4]*Bye-gones*, 9 August, 1899.
[5]*Bye-gones*, 27 June, 1888.
[6]*Bye-gones*, 30 August, 1893, and 21 June, 1876.

Reformation custom was also recorded in the late nineteenth century in Caernarvon where a small hand-bell was rung to give notice of an approaching funeral.[1]   In Ysbyty Ifan, Denbighshire, the procession bringing the coffin to be interred in the parish church formerly had to wait at a certain place called Penrhiw'r Saint [the brow of the hill of the saints] until the church choir came to meet it. The choir, dressed in white surplices, used to sing before the bier all the way to the village.[2] In Llansanffraid, Montgomeryshire, it was the clergyman who came a short way to meet the cortege at the churchyard gate, where he would begin to read the service. In this village, as in many others in Wales, there was a traditional route which was invariably taken to the churchyard by funeral processions.[3] A similar traditional route was always followed in Dolgellau, Merioneth, despite the fact that the building of a new street offered a shorter one. In Llangattwg, Monmouthsire, in the middle of the last century it was thought that, by taking a corpse over a disused pathway which had been irregularly closed, the path would remain public.[4] At the higher end of the social scale, in a manner which the peasant did not emulate, the niceties of precedence were strictly observed in the arrangement of the funeral procession ; several lists have been preserved of the order followed in various funerals of the seventeenth century.[5] Apart from the procedure followed at these funerals little is known of their nature, but in the nineteenth century, among the peasantry, the procession often halted at cross-roads to change bearers and to sing a hymn ; usually the nearest male relatives carried the bier during the last part of the journey, and indeed, often lowered the coffin into the grave.

One of the most interesting group of customs practised in connection with funerals relates to the different kinds of offerings made on these occasions towards defraying the expenses involved. As in the wedding custom of holding a

[1]*Bye-gones*, 30 August, 1893.
[2]O. Gethin Jones : *Gweithiau Gethin*, 1884, p. 275.
[3]T. Griffith Jones : ' A History of the Parish of Llansantffraid,' pp. 132-3.
[4]*Bye-gones*, 23 October, 1895.
[5]e.g. the funerals of Sir Thomas Mostyn (d. 1644) and Sir Roger Mostyn (d. 1642) in Lord Mostyn and T. A. Glenn : *The Mostyns of Mostyn*, 1925, pp. 127-8, 134 ; cf. also the order at the funeral of Archbishop John Williams at Llandygai, 1650 (W. Williams : *op. cit.*, p. 67).

' bidding,' the co-operative tendency of the peasant community came to the fore and saw to it that the cost of the funeral meal and refreshments, as well as other necessary forms of expenditure, were defrayed, in part at least, by those who attended the funeral. Even the poor were not forgotten on this solemn occasion ; bequests were made by the gentry in parts of north Wales to reward them for attending. Sir Robert Williames Vaughan of Nannau who died in 1843 directed that 24 strong cloth hatbands be given to 24 of his poorest labourers or small tenants, ' the cloth to be enough to make them warm waistcoats,' and also the sum of 2/6 each for attending the funeral.[1] Lewis Morris records another simpler custom in Anglesey, ' But if poor or Rich when the deceased is carried out of ye house he is laid on ye Beer, before ye door where they bring Two wooden cups one they fill with milk & the other with ale, over ye Body. Some Loaves or Cakes of bread & a cheese, with a piece of money Stuck in ye cheese, and this they give to some poor object of charity, first tasting of ye milk & all, the poor tasting likewise, if deceased's name on ye cups.'[2] In Llansanffraid, Montgomeryshire, in the beginning of the last century the ceremony had degenerated to a distribution of alms (small silver), by one of the nearest relatives, to the poor in the yard of the house before the procession set off.[3]

In the church and churchyard two separate contributions were formerly made by the persons who attended the funeral service, the one to the clergyman, and the other to the parish clerk ; both these customs seem to have been confined to the northern counties. The offering (*offrwm*) to the clergyman was made during or at the end of the service ; in Llansilin, Denbighshire, a small board specially fixed to the altar rail was used for this purpose and the total was later announced by the clergyman.[4] In another parish nearby the service was interrupted in the middle when the clergyman left the reading desk, and, after a short prayer at the communion table, took his stand at a table or desk. At this point, the chief mourner left the pew in

---

[1]*Bye-gones :* 11 May, 1892.
[2]H. Owen : *loc. cit.* ; also recorded by Thomas Pennant : *Tours in Wales*, III, p. 160.
[3]*Bye-gones*, 11 August, 1909.
[4]*Bye-gones*, 17 October, 1877.

which he was sitting, went up to the table and placed a piece of money on it. The other mourners and friends present all followed his example.[1] According to Bingley, the offering was made as a mark of respect to the clergyman, and where the latter was not respected the offering would be made on the coffin at the door of the house and distributed amongst the poor relatives. The poorer mourners at the church gave sixpence or a shilling, the more opulent half a crown or a crown, or even as much as a guinea ; these were the contributions from relatives of the deceased. They were followed by the rest of the congregation who intended offering silver. After a short pause those who could not afford silver came forward to make their offering—usually a penny. Bingley adds that the collections sometimes amounted to £10 or £15, but where the relatives were indigent they did not exceed three or four shillings. Where families were left in distress the money was usually given to them by the clergyman. As much as £50 to £60 a year was collected at ' offerings ' of this kind in Llanbeblig, the parish church of Caernarvon at the end of the eighteenth century.[2] The origin of the custom, it has been suggested, lies in the pre-Reformation custom of paying the priest for saying masses for the deceased. After the Reformation the payment became a personal gift to the officiating clergyman, often used at his discretion to relieve any hardship in the bereaved family. Gradually the criterion used in giving changed from the status of the clergyman to the status of the deceased and his family.[3]

Outside the church, at the porch or at the graveside, a second contribution was made, this time to the parish clerk. This was commonly known as *arian rhaw* [spade money] because it was collected on a shovel held over the open grave by the clerk himself. The sum collected varied but was often about one-quarter of the amount given to the clergyman. Like the *offrwm* the spade money became a token of esteem for the deceased and varied accordingly. Only silver or gold was given in this collection in Llangurig, Montgomeryshire, in the

[1]*Bye-gones*, 24 February, 1875.
[2]W. Bingley : *North Wales*, 1804, ii, pp. 286-7.
[3]Elias Owen : *op. cit.*, p. 136.

middle of the last century.[1] In Merioneth, where a bowl was used for the collection instead of a shovel, the custom was open to abuse when a funeral went from one parish to another and a double offering collected by the parish clerks at the house and at the graveside respectively.[2]   At Llwydiarth, Mont-gomeryshire, the *offrwm* was a collection made in the church but given to the clerk and not to the vicar—an interesting variation on the custom. The funeral would be kept waiting while the clerk added up the sums given and announced the total.[3]   The *offrwm* and *arian rhaw* were probably similar in origin but came to be associated with the particular services rendered by the clergyman and his clerk.

Another form of contribution was found in some parts of north Wales until about 1830. In Mallwyd and Llan-ym-mawddwy, Merioneth, the ' shot ' as it was called was held at the nearest public house—usually near the church. ' All females, as well as males, were expected to go there and contribute towards the "shot", or, more plainly, for a supply of drink. Beer was brought on the tables in jugs, with small glasses, or earthenware vessels, for distribution. The male portion of the company would generally contribute sixpence, and in some cases, a shilling each ; and the females half of that sum. It would not be necessary for any one to stay there to get the value of his money ; he or she might take a drop and go. But any one who went home without going in and contributing to the "shot" was looked upon with suspicion. The names and addresses of all who contributed were written down, and the record would be handed over to the nearest relatives of the deceased, who, when an opportunity offered, would pay the same respect to the memory of their departed friends. After the first contribution was expended in drink, tobacco &c., the steward, or person in charge of the "shot" would cry out, *Y mae'r tŷ yn rhydd* ! [The house is free !] when those who wished

---

[1]E. Hamer : 'Parochial Account of Llangurig', *Mont. Coll.*, III, 272. An attempt to abolish this custom in Llangurig was made in 1894 (*Bye-gones*, 31 January, 1894). In Dolgellau, however, the custom still existed in 1917. (*Bye-gones*, 16 May, 1917).

[2]*Bye-gones* : 1 July, 1891.

[3]*Bye-gones* : 28 March, 1917. Lewis Morris states that a collection was made for the coffin-maker too. This was done outside the house when he was busy nailing the coffin ; the amounts varied from sixpence to a shilling. (H. Owen : *op. cit.*, p. 143).

to remain had to subscribe again, and so on.'[1] The ' shot '
according to another writer was held when the mourners were
too poor to bear the expenses of the funeral ; it consisted of a
collection made outside the house, a plate being placed over a
basin and the contribution being placed on the plate first and
' shot ' off the plate into the basin, ' so that the bereaved family
might know what each mourner gave.'[2]

Among the offerings made to near relatives of the dead person
Elias Owen mentions that neighbours, friends and relations
sent what was necessary for the meal given before the funeral
procession started ; the presents, often in kind, were taken
before the funeral.[3] In the slate-quarrying districts of north
Wales the usual gift was half a pound of tea or sugar ; this was
wrapped in plain paper so as not to give the name of the grocer
who supplied the commodity.[4] In some districts the gifts was
two shillings or half a crown or even more. The amount
received in one case about the beginning of this century was
£12/8/-. The custom was referred to as *danfon offrwm* [taking
one's offering] and the gifts were carefully recorded so that
they could be returned when a death occurred in the family of
any of the donors.[5] On the day of the funeral another offering
was made, everybody present placing a coin on the coffin as it
stood on the bier. This money went to the widow.[6] In the
quarrying districts of Caernarvonshire this second offering was
specifically towards the cost of the funeral and usually consisted
of sixpence or a shilling from each person. ' The house is so
arranged that if possible the neighbours come in through one
door and out through another ; on the way, a round table is
set, covered by a white cloth with a handkerchief laid cross-
ways over it. A deacon or elder of the chapel (usually the
senior deacon or elder) stands by the table as the mourners
pass by, placing their *offrwm* on the handkerchief. Those
neighbours who have not had an opportunity to *danfon offrwm*
previously may place on the handkerchief, in addition to their

[1]*Bye-gones*, 1 July, 1891.
[2]*Bye-gones*, 9 August, 1899.
[3]Elias Owen : *op. cit.*, p. 135.
[4]*Bye-gones*, 5 May, 1926.
[5]F. P. Jones : ' Danfon Offrwm,' *Gwerin*, I, pp. 91-2.
[6]Elias Owen : *loc. cit.*

sixpence or shilling an envelope containing their florin or half-crown, and bearing their name and address, so that it may be added to the list. When all the mourners have passed by, the deacon or elder takes up the handkerchief and hands over the *offrwm* to the head of the family.[1] Another account speaks of the handkerchief as being black-bordered.[2] Sometimes, when the offering was not made over the dead (i.e. on the coffin), it was given to the widow as she sat by the fireside, with her head covered with a shawl.[3] This was rather different from the ritual presided over by the elder and it is possible, as Mr. Frank Price Jones has suggested, that *danfon offrwm*, at least in the form described by him, was a usage which achieved importance in the remote and poverty-stricken villages and hamlets which sprang up around the nonconformist chapels in the late eighteenth and early nineteenth centuries.[4] The customary funeral was described by William Williams of Llandygai in 1802 but there is no mention of this practice ; instead the usual pattern of *gwylnos*, spiced ale at the house, offerings to the clergyman and clerk, and ' shot ' at the public house are mentioned.[5] Bingley, also writing about the same time, of Caernarvonshire refers to the same practices but makes no allusion to the custom of *danfon offrwm*.[6] Possibly the explanation is that the *gwylnos* which continued as a nonconformist prayer-meeting in south Wales and parts of north Wales, gave place, in the quarrying districts of Caernarvonshire, to the visit before the funeral during which the *offrwm* was given to the widow instead of to the clergyman or clerk. Bingley mentions that where the clergyman was not respected the offering was made on the coffin at the house and distributed among relatives.[7] In an increasingly nonconformist community

---

[1]F. P. Jones : *loc cit.*
[2]*Bye-gones*, 5 May, 1926.
[3]Elias Owen : *loc. cit.*
[4]F. P. Jones : *loc. cit.*
[5]W. Williams : *op. cit.*, pp. 14-15.
[6]W. Bingley : *loc. cit.*
[7]In Llanberis the practice of taking one's offering to the house of the bereaved family is said to have begun at the funeral of David Jones, Garreg-wen in 1821. The entry in the parish register states that an offering of £4/17/- was taken to the widow who was ill in bed at the time and adds '*Ar ol hyn y dechreuwyd offrymu wrth y tai yn y plwyf.*' [It was after this that offering at the houses began in the parish]. W. Williams : *Hynafiaethau a Thraddodiadau Plwyf Llanberis a'r Amgylchoedd*, n.d. (1892), pp. 79-80.

it would be natural for such a practice to become more wide-spread and for church offerings to decline. The presence of the chapel elder lends some strength to this view. It is likely that here again we have an example of the change of character in an ancient custom as it was adapted to meet new social conditions by merging it with another equally old custom and purging it of undesirable elements.

Mention must be made at this point of a custom whose very existence in Wales has been held in doubt, namely that of the ' sin-eater.' The first reference to the ' sin-eater ' anywhere to be found is in the manuscripts of the seventeenth-century writer John Aubrey who wrote of him thus : ' In the county of Hereford was an old custom at funerals to hire poor people, who were to take upon them the sins of the party deceased. . . . The manner was that when the corpse was brought out of the house and laid on the bier, a loaf of bread was brought out and delivered to the sin-eater, over the corpse, as also a mazard bowl of maple, full of beer (which he was to drink up), and sixpence in money, in consideration whereof he took upon him, *ipso facto*, all the sins of the defunct, and freed him or her from walking after they were dead.'[1] Aubrey adds that the custom existed in Llangors, Brecknockshire in 1640, and in 1686, he writes ' this custom is used to this day in north Wales.'[2] Apart from Aubrey, the custom is not mentioned by name by any other writer until 1852 when Mathew Moggridge of Swansea described the custom and added further details which he maintained were obtained from Llandybïe, Carmarthenshire, where the practice ' was said to have prevailed to a recent period.' The additional material comprised the following description. ' When a person died, his friends sent for the Sin-eater of the district, who on his arrival placed a plate of salt on the breast of the defunct, and upon the salt a piece of bread. He then muttered an incantation over the bread which he finally ate, thereby eating up all the sins of the deceased. This done he received the fee of 2s. 6d. and vanished as quickly as possible from the general gaze ; for as it was believed he really appropriated to his own use and behoof the sins of all

---

[1]Lansdowne MSS in B.M., cited by Wirt Sikes : *British Goblins*, p. 325.
[2]*ibid*.

those over whom he performed the above ceremony, he was utterly detested in the neighbourhood—regarded as a mere Pariah—as one inredeemably lost.'[1] The existence of the custom has been denied by Silvan Evans who described himself as not having been ' indifferent as to the customs and legends of the land of his birth ' and whose profession (clergyman), he added, often brought him to contact with funerals.[2] Moreover another writer who had lived at Llandybïe for many years and who claimed to be well acquainted with the history of the parish, its customs and traditions, had ' never heard of such a thing ' as a sin-eater.[3] The evidence of this writer is impressive because he had collected ' Welsh lore ' for Sir Thomas Phillips and claimed to be well-acquainted with ' Welsh lore ' in almost every parish in south Wales.[4] While Moggridge's claim may be open to doubt—he may well have been misled in his interpretation by the practice of placing salt on a plate on the body of the deceased—Aubrey's evidence may have been true of the seventeenth century. Even he may have been over-emphasizing a custom which Lewis Morris and Bingley describe as existing in Gwynedd, namely the eating of bread and ale over the coffin by a poor person. But neither of these writers, admittedly describing conditions in a later period, makes any allusion to a belief similar to that outlined by Aubrey, which accompanied this custom. The evidence as regards Aubrey's claim is not conclusive, but it appears that the nineteenth-century description of the custom is not well-founded.

The funeral is soon over and the memory of the dead, at least among distant relatives and acquaintances, soon weakens, and life resumes its normal course once again. It was probably the realisation of this fact which underlay the practice of giving memorial cards, printed elegies and mourning rings. Just as *memento mori* rings with their skull and cross-bone motifs

[1]*Arch. Camb.*, 1852, p. 330.
[2]*Bye-gones* : 24 November, 1875.
[3]*Western Mail*, 16 December, 1875.
[4]He was Mr. John Rowlands who had been a schoolmaster at Llandybïe for many years commencing 1850. He claimed that the custom had not existed within the memory of the oldest inhabitant, a view which was confirmed by the vicar of the parish at the time. (*Bye-gones* : 9 February, 1876). Cf. also Gomer M. Roberts, *Hanes Plwyf Llandybïe*, p. 271.

were worn by the living to remind themselves of the inescapable fact of death, so also were mourning or memorial rings worn to remind the living of their dead relatives or friends. Often the hair of the deceased person was woven into a neat pattern and incorporated into the bezel of the ring as a decorative feature, while his name, age and date of burial were engraved in the metal-work. Often provision was made in the dead person's will for a ring to be bought and paid for out of his estate. At the funeral of the Earl of Powis in 1801 gold memorial rings were presented to persons present at the funeral.[1] Often the rings were in black enamel with a miniature painted on ivory representing an urn with a figure. Small seed pearls were used as an enrichment especially for their value as symbols of tears.[2] The memorial card with verse, black bordering and sometimes a picture of the deceased, was a similar memento which was used by the families of the deceased for distribution among friends and relatives (See Nos. 501-521 in Catalogue and Plate 15). In an earlier age the payment of money to buy mourning clothes was provided for in the will of the cdead person. Madam Margaret Godolphin of Abertanat, Montgomeryshire, who died in 1766, herself prepared dresses to be in readiness for twelve poor widows of the parish on the occasion of her funeral ; similarly Sir Robert Howell Vaughan of Nannau, Dolgellau, who died in 1792 pirected that several poor persons be clothed to attend his funeral.[3]

It was formerly the custom for the funeral sermon to be delivered some time after the burial, usually on the first or second Sunday afterwards. On this occasion all who had attended the funeral came again to the church to hear the vicar preach the special sermon. All would wear their crape, silk and cloth emblems of mourning. In the Montgomeryshire and Denbighshire border districts this service was referred to as *yr ail gladdedigaeth* [the second burial] ; in the early nineteenth century it took place on the second Sunday but was later changed to the first Sunday after the funeral.[4] In Radnorshire

[1]*Bye-gones*, 10 December, 1876.
[2]Bertram S. Puckle : *Funeral Customs, their origin and Development*, 1926, p. 270.
[3]*Bye-gones* : 7 April, 1875. The same was done by Sir Robert's son, Sir Robert Williames Vaughan who died in 1843, see page 178 above.
[4]*Bye-gones*, 13 December, 1871, and 20 October, 1909.

the service was known as the 'Month's End', a corruption of the name 'Month's Mind' which was given to the pre-Reformation service held in commemoration of the dead person a month after his death. It was believed that it was unlucky to leave the house where the death had occurred before the 'Month's End'. In Radnorshire the custom which was general in Victorian times is still to be found, though not so often as in the last century.[1] Possibly traces of this custom survive in the nonconformist churches of Wales where a special *seiat* [society meeting] in which the elders and the minister testify to the character of the deceased member. This meeting is usually held after the evening service on the Sunday following the death or funeral.

[1]W. H. Howse : *Radnorshire*, 1949, p. 137.

THE CATALOGUE

CHRISTMAS AND THE NEW YEAR

1. Decorations for *plygain* candle : two examples of tissue paper (orange and white respectively) cut to give a loose bell-like decoration presumably for hanging from the candlestick ; a third example is differently cut. As formerly in use at Coelbren, Glamorgan. Donor : Edward Thomas, 10.1.

2. Christmas Greeting Notepaper : folded sheet of notepaper with a hand-coloured woodcut in place of letterhead. Illustration shows servant carrying in joint of meat decorated with a sprig of holly. With legend ' GOOD APPETITE TO YOU, SIRS ' and holly-leaf decoration. Early 1840's. 7.5″ x 4.6″. 14.159/326a.

3. Christmas Greeting Notepaper : folded sheet of notepaper with a hand-coloured woodcut in place of letterhead. Illustration shows a mother meeting her son at a railway station. With legend ' RETURNING FROM SCHOOL ' and holly decoration. Early 1840's. 7.5″ x 4.6″. 14.159/326b.

4. Christmas Greeting Notepaper : folded sheet of notepaper with a hand-coloured woodcut in place of letterhead. Illustration shows head and shoulders of a man(?) and is inscribed ' A MERRY CHRISTMAS TO YOU / AND MANY / RETURNS OF THE SEASON.' Early 1840's. 7.5″ x 4.6″. 14.159/326c. [Plate 4].

5. Christmas Card : with lithograph of robins in the snow and inscription ' With best / CHRISTMAS / wishes ' on front and the following verse on the back ' Such love be thine,—such / peace and joy, / as discord never can / destroy. / S. Herbert.' Second half 19th century. From Maesteg, Glamorgan. 4.2″ x 2.8″. Donor : Roderick G. Williams. 52.9/2.

6. Christmas Card : a padded sachet one side of which is decorated with silver paper lace and an oval satin medallion, centrally placed, on which is printed ' A / Merry / Xmas.' The other side consists of a satin cover with painted rose and violet flowers. Embossed ' E. RIMMEL / 96 / STRAND / LONDON.' c. 1875-80. From Glamorgan. 5.5″ x 3.8″. Donor : M. Thomas. 29.265/12.

7. Christmas Card : a padded sachet of embossed paper and paper lace. Decorated on the front with lithographed floral cut-outs and an oval medallion edged with silver paper. With verse entitled ' GOOD WISHES,' ' Oh ! smooth be thy path, / And unclouded thy sky, / And joy and prosperity / Ever be nigh ! / May Hope go before thee / And love walk beside, / And peace hover o'er thee / Whate'er may betide.' c. 1875-80. From Glamorgan. 3.9″ x 2.7″. Donor : M. Thomas. 29.265/13.

8. Christmas Card : embossed card decorated with cameo figures placed on either side of a central panel representing a stage with the curtains drawn. With the inscription ' A merry Christmas.' When two tabs, one on either side of the card, are pulled out the ' curtains ' open to reveal a coloured lithographed picture in three dimensions depicting a lake-side garden scene. Late 19th century. 4.6″ x 3.1″. Donor : Martin Phillips. 45.150/4.

9. Christmas Card : a stout card decorated in gold, green and yellow. A centre panel consists of four smaller hinged cards which unfold separately in four directions. These are decorated with lithographed flowers with Christmas and New Year greetings. Published by Marcus Ward & Co. Late 19th century. From the Vale of Neath, Glamorgan. 4.7″ x 3.6″. Donor : Miss E. M. Thomas. 49.207/6.

10. Christmas Card : yellow background with gold margin. To a lithographed and embossed posy of coloured flowers is attached a label bearing a Christmas greeting. Late 19th century. From Barry, Glamorgan. 3.6″ x 2.25″. Donor : Miss M. C. Cooke. 47.342/18.

11. Christmas Card : mounted in a box, edged with paper lace. It consists of a folded card fringed and heavily padded on the outside where a fringed satin panel with printed flower decoration is mounted on the satin cover. Inside the card are two coloured lithographs of roses, with biblical text, religious verse (by Cecilia Havergal) and greeting for New Year and Christmas respectively. Late 19th century. From south Wales. 7″ x 7″. Donor : D. J. Davies. 42.73/10.

12. Christmas Card : decorated with gilt scalloped and embossed edge. ' A / Merry Xmas / to / you ' inscribed on central oval medallion. Last quarter 19th century. 3.5″ x 2.1″. Donor : Anonymous. 54.166/89.

13. Christmas Card : a padded sachet with a cover of embossed white and silver paper decorated with a floral cut-out on one side and a lithograph panel with representations of flowers and the inscription ' Accept my best / wishes for a / Happy Christmas ' on the other side. Last quarter 19th century. 4.8″ x 3.1″. Donor : Anonymous. 54.166/90.

14. Christmas Card : with serrated edges, projecting corners. Gilt decorations on a light blue background. The book-cover-like rectangular medallion is black with an embossed lithographed bouquet of coloured flowers and has gilt decorations around the edges. It opens to reveal a posy of lithographed flowers and a small envelope inside which when unfolded has the inscription ' A / Merry Christmas / to you.' Last quarter 19th century. From Glamorgan. 4.5″ x 3.0″. Donor : Miss Penelopen Price. 50.63/31. [Plate 4].

15. Christmas Card : mounted in a box. It consists of a folded card fringed and heavily padded on the outside where the satin cover is decorated with a printed posy of flowers. The card opens to reveal two embossed lithographs of cherubs, the one playing a trumpet and the other studying a sheet of music. The clothes of the cherubs are of velvet and satin embossed to reproduce the contours of the body. With Xmas and New Year greetings. c. 1895-6. Box bears a Carmarthen address. 7.0″ x 5.5″. Donor : D. J.Davies. 42.73/9.

16. Christmas Card : postcard with lithograph of three cherubs on front, with scroll inscribed ' Glory to God in the Highest.' On the back is the inscription : ' A joyful Christmas to you ' and the verse : ' My joys I bring to Thee, / The joys Thy love hath given, / That each may be a wing / To lift me nearer Heaven. / I bring them, Saviour all to Thee, / For Thou hast purchased all for me.' (Frances Ridley Havergal). Published by Raphael Tuck & Sons, London. Dated 1899. From Rumney, Monmouthshire. 5.7″ x 3.9″. Donor : Miss Mavis Cooke. 55.236/13.

17. Christmas Card : small folded sheet with scalloped edges. Monogram ' L' and address printed on cover. Greetings and name of sender printed inside. Envelope to match, with Caerleon, Monmouthshire, address and Paignton postmark dated 1901. 5.0″ x 1.75″. Donor : Miss Mavis Cooke. 55.236/11.

18. Christmas Card : folder with printed greetings on cover and, inside, a photograph of waterfalls in the Vale of Neath, Glamorgan, mounted in an embossed paper frame. Dated 1902. From Rumney, Monmouthshire. 5.0″ x 4.0″. Donor : Miss Mavis Cooke. 55.236/14.

19. Christmas Card : with embossed decoration. Inscribed '70, Connaught Road, / Cardiff. / Accept Shapland Dobbs ' / Best Wishes for a Happy Festival. / Eve of Christ's Mass, 1902.' 8.5″ x 5.5″. Donor : Miss Mavis Cooke. 55.236/18.

20. Christmas Card : postcard with a photograph of a house on front. Greetings and Caerleon, Monmouthshire, address on back. Postmarked Tintern, Monmouthshire, 1905. 5.5″ x 3.5″. Donor : Miss Mavis Cooke. 55.236/15.

21. Christmas card : folder ; hand-coloured decoration with birds and flowers in medallion on cover and inscription in embossed gilded lettering. Inside are printed the greetings, name and address of sender. Dated 1906. From Taffs Well, Glamorgan. 3.7″ x 3.7″. Donor : Miss Mavis Cooke. 55.236/17.

22. Christmas Card : picture postcard of Tintern Village (Monmouthshire) with ' A merry / Christmas ' superimposed on picture in gilt. Greeting on back. Early 20th century. 5.35″ x 3.4″. Donor : Miss Mavis Cooke. 55.236/16.

23. Christmas Card : small folded card with embossed oval panel on cover. Decorated on cover and inside with hand-painted flowers. In envelope postmarked Cardiff 1910, and bearing a Rumney, Monmouthshire, address. 3.0″ x 2·25″. Donor : Miss Mavis Cooke. 55.236/12.

24. Christmas-tree figure : a doll with straw body, wooden hands and legs, and the head (in wax) of a bearded white-haired old man. The clothing consists of knee length trousers, tunic, short cloak, and phrygian type cap, all of woollen canvas. A pair of spectacles is painted on the doll's face. L. 1′ 3″. Used on a Christmas tree at Abertillery, Monmouthshire, about 1855. Donors : Miss H. Cole, J. Cole, Mrs. M. J. C. Massey. 46.329/10.

25. *Calennig* : skewered oranges (in wax) studded with oats and surmounted with sprigs of holly. Donor Dr. C. T. Vachell. Pro. 97. [cf. Plate 6].

26. *Calennig* : skewered orange (in wax) with oats and holly decoration. From Llandaff, Glamorgan, 1909. Donor : Mrs. Halliday. 08.78. [cf. Plate 6].

27. *Calennig* : skewered orange with oats and holly decoration [incomplete]. Used in the Llandaff district, Glamorgan, on New Year's Day, 1939. Donnor : Miss Maud David. 39.5. [cf. Plate 6].

28. *Perllan* : numerous twigs, leaves and fruit (including berries and oranges) are fixed in holes bored in a semicircular wooden board which is mounted on a slightly larger cardboard base having three cork studs underneath. A small panel centrally placed in the semicircular side of the board is decorated with a little wool. L. 15.5″, B. 9″. Made near Llandybïe, Carmarthenshire, 1914. Donor : T. Matthews. 14.13.

29. New Year Card : with gilt border and coloured lithographs of flowers. Inscribed ' *With Best Wishes* ' and with a verse entitled ' The / Secret of a Glad New Year ' : ' He is thy Lord ! oh, I am glad / of this / So glad that Thou art Master, Sovereign, King ! / So glad,—because it is such rest to know / That Thou hast ordered and appointed all, / And wilt yet order and appoint my lot. / For though so much I cannot understand, / And would not choose, has been, / and yet may be, / Thou choosest and Thou rulest, / Thou my Lord ! / And this is peace. / F. R. Havergal.' Printed by C. Caswell. c.1880. From Maes-teg, Glamorgan. 4.3″ x 3.0″. Donor : Roderick G. Williams, 52.9/3.

30. New Year Card : with narrow gilded border and embossed posy of flowers. The inscription ' May the New Year / be a Prosperous one ! ' is embossed in gilt. Inscription in handwriting on the back. c.1880. From Maes-teg, Glamorgan. 4.4″ x 2.3″. Donor : Roderick G. Williams. 52.9/4.

31. New Year Card : two flaps of gilded embossed paper fold over a card of padded silk similarly decorated. On both sides of the card and flaps are coloured lithographs of flowers, a robin, a sailing ship at sea and Santa Claus. On the back of the card a cut-out consisting of a coloured lithograph of a posy of forget-me-nots lifts to show the following verse entitled ' A NEW YEAR'S / Wish. / May this year the happiest / be / of all you have passed below— / May you peace and prosperity see, / Such as none but a God can / bestow ; / May all possible blessings / attend you ; / May heavenly enjoyment be / yours ; / And may Jesus protect and / befriend you, / Till you reach those / Elysian / shores.' c. 1880 ; from Glamorgan. 5.3″ x 3.8″ (folded). Donor : Miss E. M. Thomas. 49.104/5.

32. New Year Card : a folded red card with a coloured representation of St. George and the Dragon embossed on the cover. Inside the cover a red ribbon holds in place a plain folded card on which New Year greetings are printed. c. 1900 ; from Rumney, Monmouthshire. 4.7″ x 3.5″. Donor : Miss Mavis Cooke. 55.236/19.

33. New Year Card : a folded red card with a photographic print of Builth, Brecknockshire, on the inside of the back. The cover, which has a small calendar, is inscribed ' Times / change, / and we with Time, / but not in ways of Friendship.' c. 1900 ; from Rumney, Monmouthshire. 4.5″ x 3.5″. Donor : Miss Mavis Cooke. 55.236/20.

34. *Mari Lwyd* : horse's skull, draped with white cloth and decorated with rosettes and coloured tapes, and with eyes of bottle-glass. Made at Llangynwyd, Glamorgan, in 1888. Donor : T. C. Evans. Pro. 92 [cf. Plate 3].

35. *Mari Lwyd* : horse's skull with bottle-glass eyes. Used by the late John John of Cowbridge, Glamorgan. (d. 1937 aged 91). Donor : Harry Thomas. 49.347.

36. *Mari Lwyd* : horse's skull draped with white cloth and decorated with rosettes and coloured tapes, and with eyes of bottle glass. Made and used in 1932 in Pen-tyrch and Whitchurch, Glamorgan. A *Mari Lwyd* of this type had been in donor's family for over 60 years previously, and the donor had taken it round each Christmas since 1897. Also the stick carried by the man who led the *Mari Lwyd*. Donor : Thomas Davies. 33.4/1-2. [Plate 2].

37. *Mari Lwyd* (model) ; a rectangular piece of white cloth is folded along one of the diagonals and the outer edges sewn together in one corner. Stuffed with cotton wool and with pieces of coloured material attached to represent ears, the corner which comprises the head is shark-like in shape. A mouth and eyes are inked on the cloth. L. 18″. Made |for N.M.W. by donor to depict the type of *Mari Lwyd* in use in Solva, Pembrokeshire, in the 19th century. Donor : H. W. Evans. 19.329. [Plate 2].

38 Wassail-bowl : *lignum vitae*, turned, with cordons. Early 18th century. Ht. 8.8″. Diam. 8″. 11.32/1.

39. Wassail-bowl and cover : of reddish-brown earthenware covered with white slip and glazed. The slip forms a ground for incised decoration consisting of zig-zags, geometrical figures and crude tree and plant patterns. The bowl is encircled with looped handles, the cover appears to be a replacement. It is ornamented with loops and moulded figures of animals and birds. Around the edge of the bowl is the inscription : ' dated in the Year of our Lord 18 x 27 1827.' Formerly used at Llangynwyd, Glamorgan. Made at Ewenny, Glamorgan. Ht. 13″. Diam. 11.5″. Base 7.25″. A 1318.

40. Wassail-bowl and cover : of red earthenware coated with white slip and glazed. The slip forms a ground for incised decoration consisting of zig-zags, geometrical figures and crude tree and plant patterns. The bowl is encircled with looped handles. The cover is ornamented with loops and moulded figures of animals and birds. Inscribed ' Thomas ArthyrDeber 30 Maker 1834.' On the cover ' Langan ' and ' Spring,' and on the lower part of the bowl is the following imperfect attempt at an *englyn* : ' Diai nid oes bai yn bod / Ar lester wna I mi wylisdod / O waith Arthir weithiwr hynod / Y gora iw y chwi fe garia'r clod.' Ht. 16.25″. Diam. 14″. Base 6.5″. Donors : Mr. & Mrs. Knapton. 23.394/1. [Plate 1].

41. Wassail-bowl and cover : of reddish-brown earthenware covered with white slip and glazed. The slip forms a ground for incised decoration consisting of zig-zags, geometrical figures, and crude tree and plant patterns. The bowl is encircled with looped handles ; the cover ornamented with loops and moulded figures of animals and birds, and inscribed ' Gift to Mr. William Cox House of Correction Swansea from Mr. Morgan Morgans Road Surveyor Bridgend Decr. 23, 1836. Made at Clay Pits.' (i.e. Ewenny, Glamorgan). Ht. 15.5″. Diam. 13.5″. Base 6.75″. Donor : F. E. Andrews. 24.276. [Plate 1].

42. Puzzle-jug, earthenware, glazed, decorated with incised tulip and other plant designs. With inscription ' MD/17011 ' (*sic*). Said to have been made at Ewenny, Glamorgan. Ht. 6.7″. Diam. 4.2″. Base 2.5″. 54.340.

43. Puzzle-jug, earthenware covered with white slip and glazed. The slip forms a ground for incised decorations consisting of crude plant and leaf designs. The jug inscribed ' GE '. About 1750. Made at Ewenny, Glamorgan. Ht. 8.1″, Diam. 4.8″, Base 3″. Donors : Mr. & Mrs. Knapton. 23.394/2.

44. Puzzle-jug, red earthenware, partly covered with white slip and glazed. Inscribed ' August 16 in the year of our Lord 1822.' Made at Ewenny, Glamorgan. Ht. 7″. Diam. 4.8″. Base 3.6″. Donor : Dr. L. Cobbett. 32.522.

45. Puzzle-jug, of red earthenware coated with white slip and glazed. Decorated with incised designs depicting cockerel, tulips and stylized floral motifs. Inscribed ' G + G 1834.' Made at Pen-coed, Glamorgan. Ht. 5.5". Base 2.75". Diam. 4.5". Donor : C. F. Fox, F.S.A. 38.10.

46. Puzzle-jug, earthenware, glazed, with rural scene. Ht. 7", Base 5", Diam. 5.7". 49.502/1.

47. Wren-house, of wood, decorated with coloured ribbons. Made in 1869 by Richard Cobb, sexton, Marloes, Pembrokeshire like those he made sixty years earlier. L. 14". B. 7½". H. 9". Donor : T. H. Thomas. 98.333. [Plate 5].

EASTER

48. Egg-clapper : two small oblong wooden boards are loosely strung at one end to a third piece with a handle, which lies between them. L. 8". B. 2½". Used in collecting eggs at Easter-time by donor when a boy at Amlwch, Anglesey. Donor : David Hughes. 50.6.

49. Egg-clapper : similar to No. 48. L. 9". B. 2½". 31.206/1. [Plate 6].

50. Egg-clapper : an oblong board 7" long and 3" wide is pierced in the centre by a cylindrical piece of wood, one end of which acts as a handle. A small hammer, with a head 2½" long is hinged to the other end. When shaken the hammer swings and knocks the board at both ends. 31.206/2. [Plate 6].

51. Easter Card : consisting of a small booklet of 6 leaves with embossed and lithographed rose sprig on cover. The Title ' The / Flow-rets Easter / Admonition ' is embossed on the cover. The pages are decorated with coloured lithographs of flowers and sea-side scene and contain verses by Isa. J. Postgate. Dated Easter 1898. From Rumney, Monmouthshire. 4.5" x 4.0". Donor : Miss Mavis Cooke. 55.236/21.

HARVEST

52. Corn maiden : in wheat ; consisting of the upper sections of nine straws with ears bound with string (replacing earlier straw binding). L. 7". From a cottage at Newton, Porthcawl, Glamorgan. Donor : A. H. Lee, M.C., M.A. 15.130.

53. Corn maiden : three strands, each consisting of 15 stems, are entwined and tied with string at the head and at the ears. Made in 1929 for the National Museum of Wales ; of the kind known at Llangoedmor, Cardiganshire. L. 18". Donor : Ff. G. Payne. 29.672.

54. Corn maiden : of plaited oats, each of three strands consisting of approximately ten straws. The upper parts of the stems bearing the ears are left unplaited. L. 32" ; plaited section 2" wide and 1" deep. Made at Troedrhiw-fer, Pencader, Carmarthenshire by the donor. Donor : David Jones. 30.69.

55. Corn maiden ; of flat-plaited wheat with ears protruding at half-inch intervals giving the appearance of a fern. The plaited portion is between 1" and 1¼" wide and tapers towards the top. L. 31". B. 7½". Made in Llangynllo, Radnorshire by the donor. Donor : David Evans. 36.224. [Plate 7].

56. Corn-maiden : of flat-plaited barley and similar to No. 55 in design and construction. The plaited portion varies between .7″ and 1.1″ in width. L. 32½″. B. 10″. Made in Llangynllo, Radnorshire by the donor. Donor : David Evans. 35.258/2. [Plate 7].

57. Corn maiden : of flat-plaited oats and similar to No. 55 in design and construction. The plaited portion varies between .6″ and 1.2″ in width. L. 32″. B. 9″. Made in Llangynllo, Radnorshire, by the donor. Donor : David Evans. 35.258/1. [Plate 7].

58-60. Corn maidens : in wheat ; plaited with five straws to give a stem heptagonal in section. L. 10″. Average width ¼″. Made in 1936 by the donor, at Pen-rhiw, Tŷ-coch, Ciliau Aeron, Cardiganshire. Donor : T. Davies. 36.526/1-3. [Plate 8].

61. Corn maiden : in oats ; the straw is plaited to give a hollow spiral stem about 2″ thick, the base of which consists of a bunch of ears. From the top of the stem spring two similar loops which return to the stem near its centre and terminate in two bunches of ears tied with red ribbons. There is a short loop for hanging ; both this and the heads of the other loops are bound with red ribbon. L. 29″. Made in 1948 in Llan-non, Cardiganshire by the donor. Donor : W. D. Williams. 48.269. [Plate 8].

[NON-WELSH]

62. Corn maiden : a plaited stem (¾″ thick) of oats with bunched ears at the head is decorated with eight loops of plaited straws springing from top and centre. At the centre also are bunched ears. With a loop for hanging the ornament. Made in 1928 by Edward Minton, aged 84, of Ford's Heath, Yockleton, Salop. L. 13½″. Donor : Miss S. F. E. Bromley. 29.532. [Plate 8].

63. Corn maiden : about 50 straws of oats are bound tightly with straw and string, giving a stem 1½″ thick from which the ears hang in a tight bunch. The stem is decorated with plaited straw in the form of two loops passing through the centre of the stem, and with ears protruding at the base of the loops. A smaller loop is used for hanging the ornament. L. 13″. From Mordiford, Herefordshire. Donor : Miss M. Wight. 36.92.

64. Corn dolly : a thick circular stem of plaited straw is surmounted by the loose heads bearing the ears of oats ; thinner plaited stems springing from the base form loops with others springing from the top. L. 17″. B. 4½″. Made at Rockford, Tenbury, Worcestershire. Donor : Mrs. Bishop. 43.322/1.

65. Corn dolly : similar to No. 64 but in wheat. Made at Rockford, Tenbury, Worcestershire. Donor : Mrs. Bishop. 43.322/2.

66. Corn dolly : in wheat ; the straw is worked to give a hollow pyramid form, the edges of which are formed through plaiting. At the apex of the pyramid is a bunch of ears while through the pyramid passes a straw which is looped at its extremity for hanging. L. 13″. Width 4″. Hung up in Winford Church, Bristol. September 1943. Donor : The Rev. A. J. H. Hobbs. 44.101.

67. Corn maiden : in wheat, barley and oats. The straw is worked to give a large conch-like form with spiral edges made by plaiting. This hangs from the square open base of a much smaller conch similarly constructed. From each corner of the square base of the lage conch hang four other

conchs with ears of wheat, barley and oats. The square opening in the base of the large conch is formed by straw work receding in a pyramid shape into the body of the conch. It is decorated by ears of wheat, barley and oats. L. 29″. B. 7″. Depth 7″. Made at Conderton, Tewkesbury, Gloucestershire. 1941. 48.151.

68. St. Brigid's Cross : each of the four arms of the cross is made up of six rush stems bent in half and interlocked with those of the other three arms. Copy of a cross made in 1907 in Co. Antrim, Ireland. 10″ x 10″. Donor : T. H. Thomas. 10.5.

69. St. Brigid's Cross : similar to No. 68 but made of larger stems. From Glencolumbkille, Co. Donegal, Ireland. 14.5″ x 14.5″. Donor : A. C. Haddon. 10.6.

70. St. Brigid's Crosses : one is similar to No. 68 with the arms of the cross bound together with woollen thread, the other is a three-armed cross. From Co. Donegal, Ireland. 12″ x 12″. Donor : T. W. Proger. 32.379/1-2.

BIRTH

71. Birthday Card : paper lace and embossed paper with elaborate design depicting harvest scene with houses and train crossing a viaduct in the background. With centre oval medallion of satin on which verses entitled ' TO A FRIEND / ON HER BIRTHDAY ' have been printed : ' Again appears thy natal day, / Again with blessing be it crown'd / In feeling fresh, and wisely gay, / May'st thou on each return be found. / Health and peace, and plenty smiling, / Blessings more than earth can tell, / Life's tempestuous hours beguiling, / Gild thy pathway—Fare thee well.' With manuscript greeting on back. Mid 19th century. 3.8″ x 2.8″. Donor : Mrs. D. Middlehurst. 51.47/8.

72. Birthday Card : paper lace and embossed paper with representation of birds and flowers etc. Circular centre medallion consists of a verse entitled ' A BIRTHDAY ' printed on satin : ' Dear friend, on this thy / natal day, / Accept my fond and ardent / Wish, / That many many more you'll see / And each one happier than this. / And that each year that circles / past, / May with earth's sweetest joys / be crowned ; / And ever find thee on this / day, / In health and wealth / and friends around.' Embossed ' WOOD.' Mid 19th century. 3.7″ x 2.6″. Donor : Mrs. D. Middlehurst. 51.47/9.

73. Birthday Card : embossed in gold and silver and having a scalloped edge, with an oval central medallion depicting a wreath of flowers around the inscription : ' Wishing you / MANY HAPPY RETURNS / of the Day.' On the back in hand-writing is the inscription : ' Nov. 17th / 1863 / from your affectionate / Papa / the last Birthday / at School.' From Cardiff. 3.9″ x 2.4″. Donor : Mrs. M. Baker. 55.566.

74. Birthday Card : a booklet of lithographs and verses entitled ' God's best for thee ' published by Castell Brothers, London, and printed in Bavaria. Early 20th century. From Rumney, Monmouthshire. 4.7″ x 4.4″. Donor : Miss Mavis Cooke. 55.236/22.

75. Birthday Card : an envelope of paper lace padded with paper. With verse entitled ' Birthday ' and floral decoration : ' Many happy returns / of the day, my friend,— / Many happy returns to thee,— / and when Heaven to earth its / blessings send,—May yours a / large share be ;—May many a day of pleasure come,—and thy life be devoid of care,—and wherever / you may chance to roam,—May / you still find happiness there. / Again

and again I wish thee / Well,—With more of truth / than this can tell.'
Embossed ' MEEK.' c. 1870—1880. From the Vale of Neath, Glamorgan.
3.1″ x 2.3″. Donor : Miss E. M. Thomas. 49.207/9.

76. Birthday Card : a padded envelope of embossed paper. A flap of paper lace
with coloured representation of forget-me-nots as centre medallion lifts to
reveal verse entitled ' The Birthday ' : ' All hail to / the day of your /
birth on this morn ! / —For your health and / prosperity always I pray. /
May your life be all roses, / and free from a thorn ! And / may you have
many happy returns / of the day,—And though years roll / by with
unvarying round,—And old / age creeps on as we travel our / way—Yet
still, with a love / that life only can bound, / I'll wish you "A happy
return of / the day".' c. 1875-80. From Glamorgan. 4.2″ x 3.2″. Donor :
M. Thomas. 29.265/11.

77. Birthday Card : embossed card with perforated border. A flap consisting
of an embossed card in the form of a bouquet lifts to reveal centre medallion with floral decoration and inscription ' Wishing you / Many Happy
Returns of the Day.' Late 19th century. From the Vale of Neath,
Glamorgan. 4.0″ x 2.7″. Donor : Miss E. M. Thomas. 49.207/8.

78. Birthday Card : embossed card with perforated border. A flap consisting
of an embossed card in the form of a bouquet of roses lifts to reveal centre
medallion with floral decoration and inscription ' Wishing you / Many
Happy Returns of the Day.' Late 19th century. From the Vale of Neath,
Glamorgan. 4.0″ x 2.7″. Donor : Miss E. M. Thomas. 49.207/7.

COURTSHIP

79. Spoon, handle decorated with chip-carving and inscribed 'MI 1721.' The
top terminates in a rectangular head with a notched geometric design.
With a small hole for suspension. From Tonyrefail, Glamorgan. L. 9.2″.
Donor : Mrs. Mary Coxe. 41.240.

80. Spoon, Caernarvonshire-type stem, on which is a shield-shaped panel
containing glazed inscription on paper ' O. Daws / Ty Hen / Clynnog /
1735.' The head has a heart-shaped hole for suspension. L. 8.4″. From
Clynnog, Caernarvonshire. 11.121/90. [Plate 9].

81. Spoon, similar to No. 80 with the glazed inscription on paper ' M. Daws /
Faeday / Clynog / 1735.' L. 8.4″. From Clynnog, Caernarvonshire.
11.121/91.

82. Spoon, handle adorned with chip carving, heart device and date ' 1767,'
pierced end, with loose wooden ring, small cruciform device on bowl.
L. 8.4″. From Colwyn Bay, Denbighshire. 00.106/1.

83. Spoon, similar to No. 80 with the glazed inscription on paper ' M. Jones /
Cyrnant / lodge / Waenfawr / 1821.' L. 8.1″. From Waun-fawr, Caernarvonshire. Donor : Alan O. Whitehead. 37.259/1.

84. Spoon, similar to No. 80 with the glazed inscription on paper ' C. Jones /
Cyrnant / lodge / Waenfawr / 1821.' L. 8.3″. From Waun-fawr, Caernarvonshire. Donor : Alan O. Whitehead. 37.259/2.

85. Spoon, delicate tapering handle with representations of plants and geometrical designs in chip-carving. Parallel grooves on stem and back of
handle. L. 10.5″. Loan : Alan O. Whitehead. 53.101/1.

86. Spoon, handle has heart-shaped opening above which is a hole for suspension. The top edge of the handle is decorated with notching. From Coed-coch, Abergele, Denbighshire. L. 6.9″. Donor : Miss Margaret Brodrick. 46.407/4.

87. Spoon, with dolphin-shaped handle and pierced hole for suspension. From Caernarvonshire. L. 6.9″. Donor : S. E. Pascoe Williams. 54.197/3.

88. Spoon, with large boat-shaped bowl decorated on back with incised leaf design. Small loop-handle. Possibly from Caernarvonshire. L. 6.3″. Donor : S. E. Pascoe Williams. 54.197/5.

89. Spoon, with ridged stem and curved disc terminal. From Bangor, Caern-arvonshire. L. 7.6″. Donor : Dr. G. Evans. 23.356/1.

90. Spoon, with ridged stem and curved disc terminal. L. 8.2″. Loan : Alan O. Whitehead. 53.101/2.

91. Spoon, with ridged stem and curved terminal. On the stem the outline of a heart and arrow(?) has been cut in relief and delineated with studded pins. L. 7.7″. 58.254/1.

92. Spoon, with narrow ridged stem. The curved disc terminal is asymmetrical in shape, and the bowl is attached at right-angles to the stem. L. 7″. Loan : Alan O. Whitehead. 53.101/3.

93. Spoon, with ridged stem expanding towards the head where it consists of the shape of a heart outlined with chip-carving. L. 5.3″. Loan : Alan O. Whitehead. 53.101/4.

94. Spoon, with flat narrow handle widening towards the head which is decor-ated with the outline of a heart in relief. L. 13.4″. 58.254/2.

95. Spoon, with handle of a non-geometrical outline ending in a curved disc terminal. With a heart, inscription ' M.J.' and ' 19 ' inlaid with red sealing wax, much of which has disappeared. L. 7.9″. Loan : Alan O. Whitehead. 53.101/5.

96. Spoon, handle of irregular outline decorated with chip-carving and a fretted heart design. L. 8.2″. Loan : Alan O. Whitehead. 53.101/6.

97. Spoon, decorated with chip carving and simple fretted design. Thick stem. From Pencarreg, Carmarthenshire. L. 10.4″. Donor : Mrs. D. R. Davies. 55.123/2.

98. Spoon, with handle formed into an irregular-shaped pair of spectacles, with angular loop for suspension. L. 10.1″. From south-west Wales. 25.235/7.

99. Spoon, handle square in section, with two slots, one above the other, formed by four pillars containing loose balls. The head of the spoon consists of a circular panel chip-carved with a heart and geometrical designs. The inscription ' L.R.' is found on the back of this panel, and the date ' 1667 ' on the handle. The letters ' IW ' have been roughly incised on the back of the stem. L. 8.6″. Loan : A. J. Irving. 35.62. [Plate 10].

100. Spoon, with handle square in section, chip-carved, hollowed and containing a ball, with a seven-linked chain for suspension. L. 24″. c. 1750. From Llanrwst, Denbighshire. 03.198. [Plate 9].

101. Spoon, with box-like handle cut out of the solid, showing a cross on pierced base in front, flanked by slots containing balls. With a loose ring for suspension. Inscribed ' M. Powell. Com-nant-moch 1779.' L. 10.5". 04.169. [Plate 9].

102. Spoon, with octagonal-shape handle hollowed out to form a slotted chamber in which two balls run freely. An octagonal ring encircles the handle below the slotted chamber, and a similar one (or swivel) probably formed the head of the spoon. (It is now missing). The inscription ' M. POWELL 1781 ' is carved on the handle. From Brecknockshire. L. 8". 58.111/2.

103. Spoon, handle consists of two short chambers alongside each other, each containing two free-running balls. At the top of the handle is a swivel attached by three double links (one pair of which has been replaced by wire) to a small panel pierced with a hole for hanging and inscribed ' E/W/1831 ' in poker-work. With circular designs in poker work. L. 12.3". Loan : Alan O. Whitehead. 53.101/23.

104. Spoon, with glazed recess in handle, containing the inscription ' Mary Phillips / Sept. 28 / 1844.' The stem has four wooden balls running in an elongated slot. With loop for suspension. Painted black. From Carmarthenshire. L. 10". 04.226.

105. Spoon, stem square in section slotted to hold two running balls and expanding to give a fan-shaped head with beaded outline. Decorated with two interlinked hearts and initials ' M ' and ' S.' L. 9.3". Loan : Alan O. Whitehead. 53.101/11.

106. Spoon, with handle square in section, hollowed, with two loose balls. Head has a sunk rectangle (now empty). With chip-carving. Behind the head and of the same dimensions, is a fixed loop (for suspension) springing from the same base. L. 6.9". Loan : Alan O. Whitehead. 53.101/13.

107. Spoon, handle square in section with hollowed chamber containing three loose balls. With two sunken recesses one containing the inscription ' E.I.' on paper covered with glass and the other containing a piece of glass. Decorated with zig-zag chip-carving and fretted heart, diamond and other designs. L. 8.2". Loan : Alan O. Whitehead. 53.101/14.

108. Spoon, plain handle square in section with hollowed chamber containing three loose balls. The curved terminal is pierced with five holes and bears the date '1884'. Handle and terminal decorated with zig-zag chip-carving on front and back. L. 7.4". 58.254/3.

109. Spoon, handle square in section in lower part with a hollowed chamber containing four loose balls. A plain panel is mounted at the head of the handle. L. 7.1". Loan : Alan O. Whitehead. 53.101/16.

110. Spoon, handle square in section in lower part, with hollowed chamber containing two loose balls. The head of the handle consists of an inverted pear-shaped panel with a fretted heart device. Decorated in chip-carving. L. 7.9". Loan : Alan O. Whitehead. 53.101/17.

111. Spoon, lower part of handle carved and fretted in the form of a shield, being outlined in relief on the inner side and having debased volutes on the outer side. The upper part of the handle consists of four pillars containing a loose ball. With loop and chain of eight links for suspension. Delicately carved. L. 15.7". Loan : Alan O. Whitehead. 53.101/18.

112. Spoon, with handle square in outline hollowed into two chambers of different sizes. The lower chamber contains five balls, the upper none. Decorated with criss-cross chip-carving. The head of the handle is outlined in the shape of a ball. L. 10.4″. Loan : Alan O. Whitehead. 53.101/19.

113. Spoon, handle rectangular in outline, hollowed into two chambers running alongside each other containing two loose balls each. Below the chambers is an inverted heart device in fretwork. The head of the handle has debased volutes. Decorated with chip-carving and grooving on back and front. Stem consists of a twisted shaft. L. 7″. Loan : Alan O. Whitehead. 53.101/20.

114. Spoon, handle square in section hollowed out into a chamber containing three free-running balls. The head of the handle consists of a narrow panel with a cross in relief and a fretted heart device. L. 15.2″. Loan : Alan O. Whitehead. 53.101/21.

115. Spoon, from a small two-looped panel two heavy spoons hang by means of two links. The handles are thick and square in section and each contains a single slot with four loose balls. Handles and stems are decorated with chip-carving. The bowls are almost triangular in shape, with the apex towards the stem. L. 16″. Loan : Alan O. Whitehead. 53.101/51.

116. Spoon, with handle square in section, hollowed, with three loose balls. Curved disc terminal on the back of which is inscribed ' C. Owens. / A.D. 1871.' L. 7.0″. Loan : Alan O. Whitehead. 53.101/12.

117. Spoon, with handle oval in section and divided into four separate openings surmounted by a swivel ring, the ball of which works in the topmost opening. Each of the other openings has a free-moving ball. Decorated with chip-carving, incised floral designs and inscribed ' A.PHs.'. L. 10.2″. From south Wales. Bequest of the late Miss A. G. Evans. 39.593/2.

118. Spoon, handle rectangular in section, with two parallel openings each containing a wooden ball. Heart and diamond-shaped openings above. The face has simple wavy-line-and-dot carving and the initials *WB* are inscribed on the back. Bowl ladle-shaped. L. 10.9″. From Narberth, Pembrokeshire. Donor : John Harris. 34.74/2.

119. Spoon, handle square in section, with two wooden balls playing in a four-pillared opening ; heart-shaped loop (imperfect) above for suspension. Chip-carved. No details. L. 7.9″. 31.496.

120. Spoon, handle square in section, with two slots, one above the other, formed by four thin pillars and enclosing loose balls. Decorated with chip-carving. To the head of the spoon, which is decorated with a heart, a knife and fork are attached by means of a loop and link. An anchor is attached to the head by means of a nine-link chain, and a whistle by a three-link chain to the anchor. L. 26.5″. Said to have been made on a farm at Bridgend or Caerphilly, Glamorgan. 29.369.

121. Spoon, handle square in section, with wooden ball playing in elongated slot. Incised surface decoration (heart and x's). Looped, with loose ring for suspension. L. 8.3″. From south-west Wales. 25.235/6.

122. Spoon, handle square in section, with a four-cornered opening containing a loose ball. Below it is another opening, the front face of which is solid and is chip-carved with a geometrical design. There is also chip-carving at the head. The stem is octagonal and fitted with a movable collar. There are two links for suspension attached to the spoon by a swivel fitting. The bowl is heart-shaped. L. 14.5″. 18.116.

123. Spoon, handle square in section and hollowed out, with bevelled angles, imperfect heart design at the head. Interior contains two cages, one within the other, a loose ball within the innermost ; the outer cage inscribed ' A. J. Plain.' L. 9.8″. 13.49.

124. Spoon, with handle rectangular in section, forming a four-windowed opening, surmounted by a rectangular loop. The bowl imperfect. Roughly made. L. 8.3″. 04.288.

125. Spoon, handle square in section with hollowed chamber (balls missing). Stem of bowl ridged. With loop for hanging. L. 6″. 58.254/4.

126. Spoon, handle formed of four thin pillars enclosing loose ball. A chain of four links is attached by a swivel working in a heart-shaped opening. L. 15.2″. From Beaumaris, Anglesey. 02.82/2.

127. Spoon, handle square in section, with broken swivel ring for suspension, the lower end of which is visible in a hollowed slot ; another elongated slot contains three balls. Incised decoration. L. 10.1″. From Colwyn Bay, Denbighshire. 01.374/4.

128. Spoon, with handle square in section, chip-carved hollowed and containing two balls in separate slots.   With a five-linked chain for suspension. L. 19″. From north Wales. 01.374/5.

129. Spoon, with handle square in section, chip-carved and hollowed, containing three balls in two slots, with a nine-linked chain for suspension.   Inscription ' R/O & J/M ' on head, and date ' 1894 ' on stem both inlaid with red wax. L. 22.6″. From Llysfaen, Denbighshire. 04.104.

130. Spoon, the handle combines two types usually found separately.   Near the bowl it is square in section and has a slotted chamber with nine free-running balls. About 5½ ins. from the bowl the handle assumes the shape of a narrow panel 6 ins. long, decorated with fretted heart and diamond devices and a swivelled loop.   The initials ' AD ' and two concentric circles, in red sealing wax, decorate the panel. L. 16.5″. 58.254/8.

131. Spoon, like No. 130, this combines both panel shaped and slotted rectangular types, but the proportions are different ; whereas the panel is about 6 ins. long, the slotted rectangular section is only 2 ins. long. Decorated with chip-carving, fretted geometrical and horse-shoe devices, and a few red sealing wax designs. Balls missing from slotted chamber. L. 11.1″. 58.254/9.

132. Spoon, like Nos. 129 and 130 this combines two forms which are normally distinct. The slotted chamber, which is rather short in length (1.6 ins.), contains five balls. The panel section is thicker than usual and is flanked by a pillar on each side. Decorations consist of a geometrical design in fretwork and some sealing-wax work. Swivel missing. L. 10.8″. 58.244/11.

133. Spoon, narrow panel fretted with heart and geometrical designs. Decorated in parts with chip-carving filled with red sealing wax (unfinished) with initials ' T.J.P.' L. 10.2″. 58.254/10.

134. Spoon, with tapering handle bearing vine leaf decoration. L. 10.5". From Colwyn Bay, Denbighshire. 01.374/6.

135. Spoon, with tapering handle carved in bas relief to show a vine branch springing from a conventionalized vase, and bird. With a small hole for suspension. L. 10.8". From north Wales. 00.106/4.

136. Spoon, tapering handle carved with bird and vine branch springing from vase ; chip-carving on stem. L. 11.9". From north Wales. 00.106/5.

137. Spoon and fork, with identical handles. The tapering panel is carved in bas relief below a vine branch springing from a conventionalized vase and bird. L. (of each) 10.2". From the Pumpsaint district, Carmarthenshire. Donor : H. Lloyd-Johnes. 30.311/23.

138, 139. Spoon and fork, narrow panel handles with chip-carving (leaf motif) and criss-cross decoration. Spoon has vase and plant motif at head of panel while fork has bird and rabbit. Apart from this difference they are identical. The following inscription, in relief, occurs on both : ' MADAM : SYBIL : MARGARET : THOMAS / BORN : FEBRUARY : THE 25TH 1857 / MARRIED : 27TH OF : JUNE : 1882.' L. 11.7" (fork) 11.2" (spoon). Spoon 58.254/12. Fork 58.254/13.

140. Spoon, with tapering handle carved in bas relief to show a vine branch springing from a conventionalized vase, and bird. L. 11". From Caernarvonshire. 18.7/40.

141. Spoon, with tapering handle carved in bas relief to show a vine branch springing from a conventionalized vase, and bird. L. 10". Probably north Wales. Pro. 100.

142. Spoon, with panel handle 2.9" broad, carved with birds on vine branch springing from a vase ; chip-carving decoration. Debased volutes at junction of panel and stem (one volute missing). Stem inscribed ' 1879.' L. 12.2". From Llysfaen, Denbighshire. 04.105. [Plate 9].

143. Spoon, tapering handle carved with vine branch springing from vase and fretted heart and key-hole designs above. Chip-carving on stem. L. 12". From Llysfaen, Denbighshire. 04.103.

144. Spoon (part of handle only) : small flat panel, with undulating sides, one face with leaf and flower motif carved in bas relief, the other with vine leaf decoration treated similarly. The edges chip-carved. Fine and delicate workmanship. Length of fragment 4.1". 00.107.

145. Spoon, handle swings on a pivot, and is heavily decorated with chip-carved bird, geometrical and other designs which are inlaid with red sealing-wax, curved disc terminal. On the back are carved the inscription ' LOUISAR / FLECHER ' and the date ' 1825.' L. 7.2". Loan : Alan O. Whitehead. 53.101/9.

146. Spoon, handle decorated with criss-cross incisions and chip-carving and inscribed ' M. L/1829 ' in inlaid red sealing-wax. With a pierced hole for suspension. From the Bridgend district, Glamorgan. L. 9.7". 42.33.

147. Spoon, panel handle decorated with fretted geometrical, heart, and shield devices outlined with chip-carving. A lozenge-shaped sunken recess is now empty. L. 8.3". Loan : Alan O. Whitehead. 53.101/27.

148. Spoon, narrow panel handle with the name ' JOHN ' in large letters cut out in fretwork. L. 9.5″. 58.254/5.

149—154. Six identical spoons, narrow panel handle decorated with chip-carving and inscribed ' M + N / 1836 ' in red sealing wax. MN for Mary Nichols, Golden Grove, Carmarthenshire ; the spoons were probably made in the Llandeilo district, Carmarthenshire. L. 9.5″. 58.223/1-6. Donor : S.A.T. Bullock.

155. Spoon, with tapering handle, square-ended, chip-carved and fretted with heart-shaped and rectangular openings. L. 9″. 11.121/92.

156. Spoon, tapering handle (looped at end) with two glazed diamond-shaped recesses (glass missing in lower recess) and two fretted hearts. The stem has two wooden balls running in an elongated slot. From Pembroke-shire. L. 12.3″. 08.69.

157. Spoon, handle broad and chip-carved, with heart-shaped opening. From Solva, Pembrokeshire. L. 9″. 05.127/1.

158. Spoon, narrow panel handle fretted and carved to depict serpent with coiled body, and bird preying on it. L. 8.5″. 58.254/7.

159. Spoon, with handle tapering into a narrow panel. With a fretted heart design and hole for suspension. Rudely executed. L. 7.2″. Loan : Alan O. Whitehead. 53.101/7.

160. Spoon, with narrow panel handle 1.4″ broad decorated with simple fretwork and chip-carving. Fluted stem to bowl. From Aberdare, Glamorgan. L. 7.5″. Donor : Miss E. Jones. 56.334/23.

161. Spoon, with ridged stem and panel handle 1.5″ wide fretted with key and other designs outlined with chip-carving. L. 7.1″. Loan : Alan O. Whitehead. 53.101/15.

162. Spoon, slightly tapering panel handle decorated with fretwork designs (hearts and other devices) and zig-zag chip-carving. Debased volutes at base of panel. With initials ' JJ ' and date ' 1858 ' in red and black sealing wax respectively. L. 9.2″. 58.254/6.

163. Spoon, with tapering handle decorated with chip-carving and fretted heart and rectangular designs. Varnished. Inscribed ' W W ' on back. L. 9.9″. Loan : Alan O. Whitehead. 53.101/10.

164. Spoon, panel handle decorated with chip-carving and inscribed ' AW.' There is a shield-shaped opening at the head. From a collection at Ruthin, Denbighshire. L. 9.6″. Donor : Alan O. Whitehead. 37.259/4.

165. Spoon, similar to No. 164 in shape and form, though with slightly different dimensions and detail of design. Inscribed ' JW.' Panel head imperfect. L. 8.6″. From a collection at Ruthin, Denbighshire. Donor : Alan O. Whitehead. 37.259/3.

166. Spoon, panel handle covered with chip-carving on a zig-zag pattern. With fretted heart design. From Merioneth. L. 9.8″. Loan : Alan O. White-head. 53.101/32.

167. Spoon, with slim undecorated handle square in section and a ladle-shaped bowl. Handle broadens near the top where there is a hole for suspension. L. 10.5″. From Rhiwbeina, Cardiff. Made by donor, Rev. S. W. E. Williams. 47.255/5.

168. Spoon, similar to No. 141 but with slimmer handle. L. 11.4″. From Rhiwbeina, Cardiff. Made by donor, Rev. S. W. E. Williams. 47.255/6.

169. Spoon, handle consists of narrow panel with wavy outline and openings in the form of hearts, circles and a horseshoe (with incisions representing nail-holes). Small loops for suspension. L. 11.6″. From Rhiwbeina, Cardiff. Made by donor, Rev. S. W. E. Williams. 47.255/7.

170. Spoon, with narrow panel handle decorated with several sets of geometric designs, mainly circles and diamonds. The topmost stage consists of a semi-circular opening for suspension. L. 14.3″. From Upper Porthkerry, near Barry, Glamorgan. Donor : Mrs. I. Lewis. 51.103/1.

171. Spoon, panel handle carved with geometrical designs (square-with-diagonal motif) and a little fretwork. From Brecknockshire. L. 9.8″. 58.111/1.

172. Spoon, panel handle fretted with heart, geometrical and other designs and decorated with chip-carving. With inscription ' JW ' inlaid with black wax. In the stem a pear-shaped opening is inlaid with a different wood which is held in position by metal pins driven in through the side of the stem. L. 9.75″. Loan : Alan O. Whitehead. 53.101/31.

173. Spoon, panel handle fretted with three horizontal rows of vertical slots and a segment of a circle at the top for hanging. L. 8.3″. Loan : Alan O. Whitehead. 53.101/28.

174. Spoon, with panel handle decorated with fretted designs outlined by grooves. One of the fretted sections contains a twisted shaft. L. 9.2″. Loan : Alan O. Whitehead. 53.101/25.

175. Spoon, with handle of irregular outline decorated with chip-carving and fretwork. L. 7.8″. Loan : Alan O. Whitehead. 53.101/24.

176. Spoon, with handle of irregular outline. With heart designs carved in relief and decorated with chip-carving and geometrical fretwork designs. Inscribed ' E + J.' L. 8″. Loan : Alan O. Whitehead. 53.101/8.

177. Spoon, with head of wavy outline decorated with chip-carving, joined to bowl by two twisted shafts. L. 10.2″. 04.99.

178. Spoon, with panel handle, 2.6″ broad, with fretted heart and other designs. L. 13.5″. From Rhyl, Denbighshire. 04.108.

179. Spoon, with panel handle 2.2″ broad, chip-carved, fretted with heart and other designs. L. 8″. 04.410.

180. Spoon, panel handle with fretted heart and geometrical designs and chip-carving. The initials ' M.E.' occur twice being both fretted and pricked. L. 8.8″. Loan : Alan O. Whitehead. 53.101/33.

181. Spoon, with tapering panel handle fretted with geometrical heart and other designs and decorated with grooving and chip-carving. A wooden ring for hanging the spoon is looped through the fretwork. L. 9.4″. Loan : Alan O. Whitehead. 53.101/30.

182. Spoon, with panel handle fretted with geometrical and heart devices and covered with chip-carving. L. 8.3″. Loan : Alan O. Whitehead. 53.101/29.

183. Spoon, panel handle decorated with a conventionalized representation of a house and a bowl of flowers. Inscribed ' H W ' on panel and ' 1822 ' on horse-shoe-shaped head of handle which is pierced with a hole for hanging. Decorations and inscriptions formerly inlaid with red sealing wax of which traces remain. L. 9.7″. Loan : Alan O. Whitehead. 53.101/26.

184. Spoon, narrow panel handle decorated with chip-carving around the edges, geometrical and maze motifs in red sealing wax in lower part, and fretted heart and other devices near head. With hole for hanging. Inscribed ' PRESENT I CHWI ' in red sealing-wax. L. 11.5″. 58.254/14.

185. Spoon, bent into the shape of a pair of tongs. The two bowls are attached to short handle, square in section, which is slotted with free-running balls ; the panel, which is bent to provide a spring, is ornamented with heart and other devices in fretwork. L. 7.9″ (closed). 58.254/18.

186. Spoon, with panel handle, fretted with heart and other designs. A delicate leaf pattern and the date ' 1813 ' are inlaid in red sealing wax. L. 11.2″. From north Wales. 00.106/2.

187. Spoon, fretted panel handle ending in a heart-shaped device, the whole being elaborately carved. Inscribed ' IC 18 22.' L. 9.3″. 06.393.

188. Spoon, originally consisting of one large and two small linked panel-handle spoons (one of the small spoons is missing). The panel of the large spoon has a sunken square recess with a representation of a clock face covered with glass. This is surmounted by a coach and horses inlaid with black and red sealing wax. Below the recess is a sailing vessel also in black and red sealing wax. Decorated with chip-carving inlaid with wax. The stem is inscribed ' BD(?) / RICHARD / GRIFFITH / RHAGF. 26 / 1823 ' and is decorated with the outline of a human face at the point where it meets the bowl. The smaller spoon is joined to the larger by means of a link and swivel and has decorated carving inlaid with black and red wax. It is inscribed ' R.G. / 1823.' Suspension is by means of a loop attached to a swivel. L. large spoon 13″, small spoon 7.5″ ; made by donor's grandfather, Rhoshirwaun, Caernarvonshire. Donor : Mrs. Lydia Jones. 49.356.

189. Spoon, roughly carved with intersecting circles. A hand forms the head and the regularity of the designs is modified at the attachment of the bowl, roughly made. L. 19.5″. Pro. 28.

190. Spoon, with panel handle, fretted with geometrical and heart designs some of which are outlined with zig-zag chip-carving. The panel is decorated on the front with a border of zig-zag chip-carving down both sides, and with a geometrical representation of a plant stylistically executed in inlaid red sealing wax. L. 14.2″. 18.87.

191. Spoon, panel handle fretted with geometrical heart and other designs, and chip-carved. Inscribed '1843 ' and ' I + L.' The letter ' S ' is carved in each bottom corner of the panel on the front and back. L. 9.6″. Loan : Alan O. Whitehead. 53.101/36.

192. Spoon, square-shaped panel handle decorated with heart and geometric designs in fretwork. L. 7.9″. 58.254/17.

193. Spoon, with rectangular panel 7.1″ broad, with inlaid red wax ornament-
      ation, and the date ' 1856,' also inlaid in red wax. Fretted with heart,
      bird and other devices, and the letters ' MD.' A knife, fork, four spoons
      and anchor are attached by strings to the panel. Shallow bowl. L. 12.1″.
      From Beaumaris, Anglesey. 02.89/3. [Plate 9].

194. Spoon, panel handle 5.3″ broad, fretted with geometrical and heart designs,
      and decorated with painted circular and heart designs. The top of the
      panel is fretted to give a circular opening occupied by a loop for hanging.
      Three bowls. From Penrhyn-coch, Cardiganshire. L. 17.7″. Donor :
      Miss A. Jones. 56.333/7.

195. Spoon, panel handle 4.5″ broad, fretted with heart, key-hole and geometric
      designs ; and decorated with painted circular and heart designs. Two
      bowls. From Penrhyn-coch, Cardiganshire. L. 15.3″. Donor : Miss A.
      Jones. 56.333/6.

196. Spoon, with panel handle, rectangular with wavy top ; with fretted heart
      circle and keyhole devices and chip-carving decoration. Inscribed ' A.T.'
      Possibly from Caernarvonshire. L. 8.1″. Donor : S. E. Pascoe Williams.
      54.197/1.

197. Spoon, with panel handle fretted with heart and keyhole designs and con-
      taining, in a sunken rectangular recess covered by glass, the inscription
      ' The Owner of / this spoon was / Ellis Wynn / of Wyrfai.' (Ellis Roberts,
      1827-95, Llandwrog, Caernarvonshire). The stem is square in section
      with five wooden balls playing in a four-pillared opening. L. 8.9″.
      54.197/2.

198. Spoon, panel handle, fretted with heart and other devices, inscribed ' E T.'
      Broad stem. From south-west Wales. L. 10″. 25.235/5.

199. Spoon, with panel handle, rectangular, with fretted wheel and geometrical
      designs and chip-carving filled with red sealing-wax, and a hole for
      suspension. The panel handle is broken. Cardiff, ' formerly owned by
      donor's grandmother.' L. 8.5″. Donor : Mrs. Eleanor Davies. 27.376.

200. Spoon, with panel handle divided into four sets of geometric designs princi-
      pally circular and in part fretted. The topmost stage has a sunken circular
      recess for a photograph and is surmounted by a horse-and-coach design
      (imperfect). The spoon has four small bowls. L. 23″. Carmarthenshire.
      Donor : Alan O. Whitehead. 37.259/5.

201. Spoon, curved panel handle with elaborate chip-carving and fretwork
      embodying heart and geometrical designs embellished with chip-carving.
      With cruciform incisions in the four corners and on the stem. L. 10.2″.
      From Llandovery, Carmarthenshire. Donor : H. Lloyd Johnes. 30.311
      /99.

202. Spoon, panel handle decorated with chip-carving, inlaid wood and fretted
      heart and geometrical designs. Inscribed ' J H ' in inlaid red sealing-wax.
      Lower section of panel of irregular outline. L. 11.3″. From Llandovery,
      Carmarthenshire. Donor : H. Lloyd Johnes. 30.311/100.

203. Spoon, rectangular panel handle 2.8″ broad, with fretted designs embodying
      horses and initials ' M J J.' L. 8″. From south-west Wales. 25.235/1.

204. Spoon, with broad tapering panel, fretted with heart, key-hole and other designs in a fine geometrical pattern. The frets are outlined with chip-carving. L. 14.5″. From south-west Wales. 25.235/2.

205. Spoon, with panel handle chip-carved and fretted with heart and other designs, connected with bowl by rounded stem having criss-cross decoration. Bowl ladle-shaped. From south-west Wales. L. 14.3″. 25.235/3.

206. Spoon, flat tapering handle, finely shaped, fretted with heart patterns and chip-carved. From south-west Wales. L. 12.6″. 25.235/4.

207. Spoon, with panel handle containing a sunken rectangular recess for a photograph surrounded by circular geometric designs in open-work and notching, and surmounted by a conventionalized representation of a house (or chapel). There are three bowls. From Cardiganshire. L. 17.5″. 25.136.

208. Spoon, with panel handle containing two elongated slots with two balls running in each, a fretted heart and another device, and incised ornament. Two bowls joined together are linked to the handle by twisted shafts. Inscribed ' 1872.' L. 6.75″. 13.91.

209. Spoon, with panel handle of irregular outline, roughly made. Decorated with fretted heart and geometrical designs. With two bowls and pierced with a hole for suspension. From Carmarthenshire. L. 8.2″. Donor : Alan O. Whitehead. 37.259/6.

210. Spoon, with panel handle fretted in geometrical and heart designs, and curving up at the head. Debased volutes at base of panel. L. 8.5″. 13.146/3.

211. Spoon, with panel handle containing a sunken rectangular recess for a photograph, surmounted by a circular geometric design in open-work which, in its turn, is surmounted by a figure of a horse ridden by a cockerel. The spoon has two bowls, the stems of which, together with the recess-frame and other parts, have notched decoration. The whole painted black. L. 23″. 11.56/1.

212. Spoon, with panel handle, having sunk recess containing faded photograph, with geometrical designs, in part fretted, ending in a hand holding the bowl. Carmarthenshire. L. 18.9″. 11.56/2.

213. Spoon, with broad tapering handle in two panels joined by two wooden links. Fretted with keyhole and other devices ; very large and coarse. L. 29.5″. From Pembrokeshire. 08.66.

214. Spoon, with broad tapering handle in two panels joined by a wooden link ; fretted with heart and other designs ; the frets are outlined with chip carving. From Pembrokeshire. L. 15.8″. 08.67.

215. Spoon, with panel handle fretted with linked hearts and decorated with asteroid incisions. With an inverted heart forming a loop for suspension. From Pembrokeshire. L. 11″. 08.68.

216. Spoon, with panel handle having serrated edges and decorated with criss-cross chip-carving and heart designs. Inscribed ' T R.' The head of the panel is of an irregular design and has a pierced hole for suspension. There are two bowls attached to the panel by means of long stems between which the design of a cross has been fretted. From Solva, Pembrokeshire. L. 11.7″. 05.127/2.

217. Spoon, with panel handle fretted with heart and geometrical designs. With two bowls, pierced for suspension. From Colwyn Bay, Denbighshire. L. 15.5″.   04.100.

218. Spoon, with tapering panel handle, fretted with heart and other designs ; bordered with chip-carving. Ring and swivel (now attached with a string) for suspension. Two bowls. From Colwyn Bay, Denbighshire. L. 23.5″. 04.101. [Plate 9].

219. Spoon, with panel handle, 5″ broad, rounded shoulders, with central cresting and with volutes at lower corners. Fretted with bay-leaf and angular designs and with letters ' JRR.' Chip-carving on stem. From Llysfaen, Denbighshire. L. 14.5″. 04.102.

220. Spoon, with panel handle (imperfect), rectangular (slightly tapered) with rounded shoulders ; with fretted heart and geometrical designs and chip-carving. Two bowls. From Conway, Caernarvonshire. L. 8.2″. 04.107.

221. Spoon, with rectangular panel handle, 3.8″ broad, fretted with heart and other designs in upper half ; lower half plain. Thin stem. From Beaumaris, Anglesey. L. 10.6″. 02.89/4.

222. Spoon, with slightly tapering rectangular panel decorated with fretted geometric designs (mainly circular, two inverted heart-devices and chip-carving in places filled with red sealing-wax). Two anchors and the name(s) ' Edw. . . Hugh . . .' have been faintly inscribed on the panel. Near the top of the panel is a sunken rectangular recess for a photograph. The panel has a large bowl at the top, with three short wooden blades on either side, and also two smaller bowls at the bottom. None of the bowls is hollowed out. From north Wales. L. 16″. 01.374/2.

223. Spoon, with panel handle, decorated with chip-carving and fretted with hearts and key-holes ; bowl imperfect. From Beaumaris, Anglesey. L. 7.75″. 02.89/1.

224. Spoon, with panel handle 4.7″ broad in three sections. Decorated with elaborate chip-carving inlaid with red and black sealing-wax and fretted heart and geometrical designs. From north Wales. 01.374/1. L. 17.5″.

225. Spoon, with square panel handle, 2.3″ wide, fretted with hearts, keys and key-holes ; joined to bowl by two shafts. Decorated with chip-carving. L. 8″. From north Wales. 01.374/3.

226. Spoon, panel handle 5.75″ broad, fretted with heart and other designs. From the bottom of the panel a knife, spoon and fork hang independently by means of three separate links. A fretted handle with a loop for suspension is attached to the head of the panel by means of two nine-linked chains. From Dolgellau, Merioneth. L. 33.7″. Donor : Mrs. G. Mills. 56.14.

227. Spoon, with panel handle (imperfect) 2.7″ broad, fretted with heart and other designs. From north Wales. L. 11.5″. 00.106/3.

228. Spoon, handle consists of a short rectangular chamber, with a single loose ball, and a small panel fretted with heart, lozenge and semi-circular devices. Head of handle imperfect. L. 7″. Loan : Alan O. Whitehead. 53.101/22.

229. Spoon, panel handle with fretted geometrical and heart designs outlined with chip-carving. L. 8.5″. Loan : Alan O. Whitehead. 53.101/34.

230. Spoon, panel handle fretted with geometrical, heart and keyhole devices. Curved terminal. L. 8.7″. Loan : Alan O. Whitehead. 53.101/35.

231. Spoon, panel handle fretted with letters ' L ' and ' N,' key and key-hole, heart and other devices. Crudely made. Painted black. L. 9.5″. Loan : Alan O. Whitehead. 53.101/37.

232. Spoon, panel handle fretted with heart, geometrical and other devices, and decorated with chip-carving. There is a rectangular sunken recess which is now empty. L. 9.4″. Loan : Alan O. Whitehead. 53.101/38.

233. Spoon, tapering panel handle fretted with geometrical designs and chip-carved. L. 9.3″. Loan : Alan O. Whitehead. 53.101/39.

234. Spoon, panel handle with fretted edges giving a series of debased volutes and curved surfaces. With fretted heart devices and chip-carving. L. 9.8″. Loan : Alan O. Whitehead. 53.101/40.

235. Spoon, similar to No. 234 but with slightly different details. L. 9.6″. Loan : Alan O. Whitehead. 53.101/41.

236. Spoon, panel handle with geometrical designs in relief partly inlaid with black wax. Two bowls. L. 12.1″. Loan : Alan O. Whitehead. 53.101/42.

237. Spoon, similar to No. 236. L. 12.1″. Loan : Alan O. Whitehead. 53.101/43,

238. Spoon, panel handle fretted with hearts and other devices. With inscription ' A J ' on front and ' B J ' on back. Chip-carving decoration. Two bowls. L. 10.2″. Loan : Alan O. Whitehead. 53.101/44.

239. Spoon, panel handle with geometrical and heart devices in fretwork. The inscription ' MAI 7/1812 ' (or ?1819) is also fretted. The edges of the panel are irregularly shaped and consist of debased volutes. Two bowls. L. 9.1″. Loan : Alan O. Whitehead. 53.101/45.

240. Spoon, panel handle with heart and geometrical devices in fretwork. The edges of the panel are irregularly shaped and consist, in the lower part, of debased volutes. Chip-carving begun but not finished. Bowl not hollowed out. L. 12.3″. 58.254/15.

241. Spoon, panel handle with irregular outline, decorated with chip-carving and criss-cross incisions. L. 11.0″. 58.254/16.

242. Spoon, panel handle with fretted geometrical heart, plant and bird devices. The panel is bordered by a series of fretted crescents and chip carving. L. 9.8″. Loan : Alan O. Whitehead. 53.101/46.

243. Spoon, panel handle fretted with heart and geometrical devices ; varnished. Two bowls. L. 11.5″. Loan : Alan O. Whitehead. 53.101/47.

244. Spoon, simple panel with geometrical decorations and a bowl at each end. L. 10.7″. Loan : Alan O. Whitehead. 53.101/48.

245. Spoon, panel handle decorated with criss-cross chip-carving. Of the three bowls one is mounted on a long stem and somewhat larger than the others. L. 8.2″. Loan : Alan O. Whitehead. 53.101/49.

246. Spoon, panel handle with fretted geometrical devices outlined with chip-carving. Notched and chip-carving decoration. Inscribed ' D W.' Two bowls. L. 14.7″. Loan : Alan O. Whitehead. 53.101/50.

247. Spoon, with handle consisting of five loops, the topmost and bottom-most loops being much smaller than the others. Small hole for suspension. L. 13.2″. From Rhiwbeina, Cardiff. Made by donor, Rev. S. W. E. Williams. 47.255/8.

248. Spoon, with panel handle fretted with geometric designs. With small loop for suspension. L. 10.7″. From Rhiwbeina, Cardiff. Made by donor, Rev. S. W. E. Williams. 47.255/9.

249. Spoons, two identical, with edges toothed and hearts, crosses and ' 1937 ' carved in bas relief on handle. Loops for suspension on a heart-shaped stand fitted with two wooden hooks and surmounted with a ring. In the centre of the stand is carved in bas relief within a toothed circle a heart and ' 1937.' The stand is fitted at the back with a movable foot. L. (of spoons) 6″. Made by D. Lewis, Ffostrasol, Cardiganshire, for the Llangeitho (Cardiganshire) Eisteddfod, 1937, at which he won first prize. Donor : Miss M. Wight. 37.682/1-3.

250. ? Valentine : sheet of paper with pin- and knife-work and floral decoration. Centre medallion depicts woman, with halo, carrying a branch in one hand and an instrument resembling tongs in the other. With inscription ' S / Apolonia ' (? Appolonia). Said to have been used as a Valentine. About 1800. From Llanfair Caereinion, Montgomeryshire. 7.3″ x 5.2″. Donor : Mrs. E. Paull-James. 32.570/2.

251. Valentine : of cut paper-work with heart, bird and tulip motifs. The following manuscript inscription is written round the edges of the valentine and in towards the centre : ' A friend of Mine I chuse you for my Valintine I hope you not take it a [miss] Because I have sent you this the Ring is Round and as no Eand I Chouse you for my Loving friend if you this Paper Do Refuse Burn it Penn ink and Paper and me Excuse. The Roses Read the Grass is Green the Days are Pass that me are seen some draw Valentines by [lot] and some draw them as they love not But Ive drawed to my harts contents the fire frese if I Repent Sleep seet [? sweet] Creater and take you Rest while my Poor hart lies Bleeding in your Brest When you Bright from Sleep Doth a Weake Remember me that Die for you sake While my Poor dear Bleading head in chains you my hart to take it for you Pains and if you think that Recompense to small take hand take hart take my Life an all.' Early 19th century. From Narberth, Pembrokeshire. 13.5″ x 12.5″. Donor : Miss S. A. Evans. 28.360/1. [Plate 11].

252. Valentine : home-made ; decorated on one side with sampler-like patterns in ink and colours. On the other side the following Welsh verses are written :

> Dyma lythyr gwedi ei selio
>   A sel air a chisan ynddo
> O na allwn gan fy ngofid
>   rhoi fy nghalon ynddo hefid
>
> nid wyf yn rhoddi arnoch Dasg
>   ond i chwi ngofio o hyn i'r pasg
> a macin sidan cyfan coch
>   nei Bar o fenig yr in y fynoch

haws iw hela y mor ar lwi
  ai ddodi oll mewn plisgin wi
nag iw troi fy meddwl i
  fy anwilid fach oddi wrthi chwi

fallai Dywedwch chwi am Danaf
  mai hen Benillion sosi yrraf
Dyweid yn wir a allaf finai
  mai hen ffasiwn iw ffalantai
      O Cofiwch fi
        Da chwi
        I Mary.

Made and sent by donor's father. First half of 19th century. From Llanbryn-Mair, Montgomeryshire. 13.8″ x 8.6″. Donor : G. H. Peate. 33.335/1. [Plate 12].

253. Valentine : lithographed and hand coloured ; showing roses arranged in the shape of a heart enclosing the portrait of a man. Floral margin. With the following printed verse : ' An emblem this of happy life, / Unknown to care—devoid of strife / Where Beauty's self reposes ; / May it prove so with you and I, / If Wedlock's Sweets we chance to try, / With Love among the roses.' With the following verses in handwriting : ' February 14 1845 / My dearest Sarah / please to accept of this / pair of gloves from / your true lover / The ring is round and with no end / so is my love to you my friend X / The blackest crow that ever flew / shall turn its feathers wite / before I prove fals to you my love / the day shall turn to night X / Green was the laurel and green was the rue / sory was I love when I parted from you / but when I return youre alays (?) I renew / and turn the green laurel to orange and blue / Excuse me dear for being so bold, / as not to wright your name in gold / the gold was scarce as you may think / that made me wright your name with ink / From your well wisher.' Originally folded and sealed for posting. Bridgend, Glamorgan, address and postmark (dated 1845). 9.2″ x 6.9″. Donor : Miss C. M. Llewellyn. 46.132/2. [Plate 13].

254. Valentine : woodcut, hand coloured. With central medallion carried on Cupid's shoulders showing a man proposing to a woman on a sofa and offering her a ring. With the printed verses : ' *This little Ring I offer you / Conveys to you my Heart / 'Tis wounded—but I know my dear / You soon can heal the smart. / Before I part with gifts so fair, / The Hostage I shall want / Are Truth and Love—as pledges [illegible] / Your hand you soon will grant / Then lets to Church without delay, / No longer let us linger / That I may place this sacred Tie / Upon your pretty finger.*' Also with the following verses in handwriting : ' My Dearest Dear / Tis very clear / that you my heart has won / i hope you will some favour show / orelse i ham undone / By this you know / my Sarah dear / That i do love you so sincere / Therefore to church let haste a way / and Join in wedlock all our days / no more to part my dearest dove / But to remain in silent love / The ring his Bought / Tis verry plain, tis your hand i want to gain / therefore to church let haste a way for that i will go astray / My Love my dove / my Dearest Jewel / if you wont have me / you are very cruel for tho you / allow that I can love so / fare well my dearest / Dove / Adue my Love / Fare well a duei / my heart i his Beatin / now for you / my Love/.' Originally folded and sealed for posting. With Bridgend, Glamorgan, address and postmark (dated 1846). 9.8″ x 7.9″. Donor : Miss C. M. Llewellyn. 46.132/3.

255. Valentine : woodcut with hand-coloured medallion showing woman on balcony and suitor below. With floral decoration and verses : ' *With you enraptured I should share | The pleasures and the ills of life | And make it my continual care, | To render you the happiest wife. | On you depends my future peace | One kindest look, one tender sign. | Shall bid my every trouble cease. | Come then and be my Valentine.*' Mid 19th century. From Llandysul, Cardiganshire. 7.5″ x 4.7″. Donor : Miss Katie Jones. 46.227/5.

256. Valentine : card decorated with drawings of leaves, flowers and butterflies in scarlet, green and white on gold background. Flag with lithograph of girl and flowers lifts to reveal verses entitled ' VALENTINE by Lord Haughton : I would be calm—I would be free | From thoughts and images of thee ; | But Nature and thy will conspire | To bar me from my fair desire. | The trees are moving with thy grace ; | The waters will reflect thy face ; | The very flowers are plotting deep, | And in thy breath their odours steep. | The breezes, when mine eyes I close, | With sighs, just like mine own, impose ; | The nightingale then takes her part, | and plays thy voice against my heart. | If thou then in one golden chain | canst bind the world I strive in vain ; | Perchance thy wisest scheme would be | To join this great conspiracy.' Printed ' MARCUS WARD & CO.' Late 19th century. 4.2″ x 3.0″. Donor : Martin Phillips. 45.150/9.

257. Valentine : hand-coloured showing hand and ring in mirror. Mirror lifts to show a swan and a woman's head, with inscription : ' *What the magic mirror shows | Tells me I must make no vows.*' With embossed border and scalloped edge. Mid 19th century. 7.0″ x 4.5″. 14.159/268.

258. Valentine : in a hand-coloured posy of forget-me-nots labelled ' FLOWER OF LOVELINESS ' the flap on which the flowers are printed unfolds to show caricature of woman with exaggerated hair-bun. With couplet : ' Unfold this little flower Blue | And there behold your image true.' Scalloped and embossed border. Mid 19th century. 7.0″ x 4.5″. 14.159/269.

259. Valentine : paper lace with hand-painted oval medallion centre showing man in top-hat reading at roadside. Tab operates man's head and brings womans head into sight behind a fence. With verse : ' *There is a wreath dear maid entwined | By Love and Hymen's mutual powers, | Which two fond hearts in one will bind, | Say shall that wreath, sweet girl be ours ?*' Embossed ' KERSHAW '. Mid 19th century. 4.7″ x 6.9″. 14.159/272.

260. Valentine : paper lace with hand-painted oval medallion centre showing man with raised hand about to step out of boat. Tab causes the man to rise and embrace a woman waiting on the bank. With verse : ' *A Victim to love's fatal dart | Your pity, fain would move | Then kindly ease his aching heart | And bless him with your love.*' Embossed ' KERSHAW.' Mid 19th century. 6.9″ x 4.7″. 14.159/273.

261. Valentine : paper lace with hand-painted oval medallion centre showing dove on woman's shoulder delivering a letter from man behind bush in background. Tab raised woman's hand to shoulder and moves her head. With verse : ' *Let love soft beaming from thine eyes | To me its bliss impart. | Like summer sun in orient skies, | Speaks solace to my heart.*' Embossed ' KERSHAW. Mid 19th century. 6.9″ x 4.7″. 14.159/274.

262. Valentine : paper lace with hand-painted oval medallion centre showing woman seated by window with letter in hand. Tab raises her hand and also opens window to reveal top-hatted lover outside. With verse :

'*Earth's proudest diadem | with pleasure I'd resign, | For the dear hope of one | day being thine.*' Embossed ' KERSHAW.' Mid-19th century. 6.9″ x 4.7″. 14.159/275.

263. Valentine : paper lace border with scalloped edge. Centre shows flower· Tab slides to remove petals and reveal head and shoulders of a man. With couplet : ' In budding flowers a type we see | Of loveliness resembling thee.' Mid 19th century. 6.8″ x 4.7″. Donor : Mrs. R. E. Edmund Jones. 30.607/2.

264. Valentine : with embossed border. A hand-coloured lithograph has been pasted on the card ; on it is shown a rural scene with the figures of a boy and girl mounted on two flaps which open to reveal a river. With inscription : ' OH LET YOUR EVERY ACTION PROVE | THE JOYOUS TRUTH OF | YOUTHFUL LOVE.' Mid 19th century. 6.5″ x 4.1″. Donor : Martin Phillips. 45.150/2.

265. Valentine : embossed and paper lace. Large central panel with oval medallion decorated with cut-outs of flowers lifts to reveal hand-coloured lithograph of garden scene. With verse : ' Oh could I hear thee once declare | That fond affection lives for me ; | Oh could I once delighted share | The sweet return of love from thee." Manuscript inscription : 'Ann Williams | From Ebenezer Williams | 1849' on the back. Given to donor's mother by her uncle in 1849. From St. Davids, Pembrokeshire. 9.7″ x 7.8″. Donor : Harry W. Evans. 27.611.

266. Valentine : paper lace with flower and leaf motif. Central circular medallion consists of gauze over hand-painted floral decorations. With inscription ' *Love | me or I | die.*' In original embossed envelope bearing Aberdare, Glamorgan, address and postmarked Swansea, 1857. 6.8″ x 4.6″. Donor : Miss E. M. Griffith. 40.410/1.

267. Valentine : paper lace pasted on plain paper. Centre medallion consists of hand-coloured woodcut of a kneeling couple and a verse : ' Many are lost in the noonday of pride | That shines forth to dazzle, but seldom | to guide, | Oh, blest is the fate of the one who has | found | some loved star to guide through the | wilderness round, | And such have I found, my beloved one/ in thee, | For thou art the star that shines upon me.' Mid 19th century. From Llandysul, Cardiganshire. 3.7″ x 2.5″. Donor : Miss Katie Jones. 46.227/2.

268. Valentine : Hand-coloured lithograph with embossed border depicting man and woman seated in a garden. With verses and floral decoration : ' *After long hours of anxious hopes and fears | That always fill the ardent Lover's breast, | How sweet the knowledge that dispels our fears | And sets at once all further doubts at rest, | 'Tis then the heart feels the full bliss of Love | And sweet content its rosy pinion spreads ; | While joys as pure as those the Angel's prove,| Dream-like descend upon true Lovers' heads.*' Mid 19th century. From Llandysul, Cardiganshire. 9.1″ x 7.4″. Donor : Miss Katie Jones. 46.227/6.

269. Valentine : hand-coloured lithograph by ' B. F. Lloyd & Co., Edinburgh ' with embossed border. Shows man carving on a tree trunk while Cupid hides in the branches. With verse : ' *Love, on this tree I fain would tell | The feelings thou canst guess too well, | This tree from all memorial free | Reserved to plead my love to thee | But could I thus to thy fond heart | My own poor image thus impart | Where no impression yet has been | Where no memorial yet has been | O ! it should be my anxious care | To keep that image ever there.*' Mid 19th century. From Llandysul, Cardiganshire. 9.8″ x 7.9″. Donor : Miss Katie Jones. 46.227/7.

270. Valentine : embossed silver paper. Centre medallion represents arch with steps leading up to it ; it is covered with silk on which coloured paper cut-outs of a church, a bouquet of flowers, and a tricolor (another flag having been lost). With verses printed on silk inside the folded sheet : ' *I'll sing a wee song | It will not keep you long | You'll see by my style I'm not prosy, | I'll tell a wee tale, | Like a wee drop of ale, | It may cheer you, but not make you dozy. | I want a wee wife, | That I'll love as my life, | I want a wee fireside so cosy ; | I want a wee friend, | Who will love to the end, | And that is the end of my story.*' With manuscript inscription : ' To Miss Stead / from the composer / EE.' Embossed ' WINDSOR.' Mid 19th century. From Abergavenny, Monmouthshire. 7.0″ x 4.8″. Donor : Mrs. D. R. Paterson. 41.275/2.

271. Valentine : paper lace border around a large oblong medallion on which floral decorations have been painted and pasted. With manuscript verses : ' I would that these flowers / had lips to talk / That I do *love thee | passing well* / All charms of loveliness / and grace are in these / flowers and in thy *face*.' Embossed ' ADDENBROOKE.' Mid 19th century. From Abergavenny, Monmouthshire. Donor : Mrs. D. R. Paterson. 41.275/3.

272. Valentine : silver paper lace decorated with cherubs and with a heart-shaped medallion containing a paper cut-out vase and flowers, mounted on gauze. With manuscript verse on inside of folded sheet : ' These beauteous flowers to thee I bring / Treasures of the opening spring / Their blended fragrance speaks to me / of Thy sweet Love and Charity / dedicated to Mrs. Stead / by the composer.' Embossed ' WINDSOR.' Mid 19th century. From Abergavenny, Monmouthshire. 5.5″ x 3.2″. Donor : Mrs. D. R. Paterson. 41.275/4.

273. Valentine : paper lace backed with tissue paper and decorated with cut-outs of flowers and leaves. A small coloured lithograph of a girl's head and shoulders is framed by gilded paper lace separately mounted. Dated ' 1860 ' in sender's handwriting. 6.9″ x 4.7″. Donor : Martin Phillips. 45.150/3.

274. Valentine : paper lace with oval centre medallion consisting of a coloured lithograph of a bird framed by gilt embossed paper. With inscription ' TO / My Dear Young Friend.' Embossed ' KERSHAW & SON.' Dated 1860 in sender's handwriting. 5.5″ x 3.8″. Donor : Martin Phillips. 45.150/5.

275. Valentine : embossed paper with scalloped edge, decorated with embossed figures of cherubs etc. and gilded paper lace. Inscribed ' *To my Favorite* ' and embossed ' WINDSOR.' Dated 1862 in sender's handwriting. 4.3″ x 2.9″. Donor : Martin Phillips. 45.150/7.

276. Valentine : paper lace with scalloped edge. An elaborate central oval medallion with gilt embossed fringe depicts a fountain and monument and is mounted on a flap with lithographed decorative designs. Over this is a separately mounted gilded paper lace frame. With verse : ' Oh may thy heart / Responsive be, / To mine in love / And constancy.' In original embossed envelope with Cardiff address and postmarked ' Cardiff / Fe 13 / [18]66.' Card : 7.0″ x 4.5″ ; envelope : 7.9″ x 5.0″. Donor : Miss Olwen Burt. 33.473.

277. Valentine : in embossed envelope. On embossed paper a scalloped frame also of embossed paper is mounted. With verse entitled ' HOPE : There is a smile for / every sigh, / For every wound a balm ; | A joy for every

mostened eye, / For every storm a calm, / Each smile is sent a sigh to / light, / Each would in mercy given, / Each tear-filled eye will yet / be bright, / Each storm subside in heaven.' Separately mounted within the frame is an oval card with a coloured representation of two children feeding birds. Third quarter 19th century. Card 3.7″ x 5.5″. Envelope 5″ x 7.75″. 14.159/282.

278. Valentine : in embossed envelope. On embossed paper a scalloped frame, also of embossed paper is mounted. It is decorated by coloured represent- ation of a child's head and garland of flowers. Within the frame on an oval centre is a verse entitled ' Let me / Love Thee : Round thy path be sunshine, / every happy hour, / Gilding all life's desert / Into fairy bower./ Never fail thy courage, / And lest earth should cloy / Let me love thee, dearest, / Doubling every joy.' Third quarter of 19th century. Card 5.5″ x 3.7″. Envelope 5″ x 7.75″. 14.159/283.

279. Valentine : mounted in contemporary wooden frame. Paper lace with scalloped edge. Central medallion consists of water-colour painting and cut-outs of flowers framed by a margin of embossed paper. With couplet : ' Constant and true till death I'll prove / No one but you shall have my love.' Embossed ' KERSHAW.' Third quarter 19th century. Frame 11.5″ x 9″. Valentine 7.0″ x 4.5″. Donor : Miss G. Morgan. 34.293/1.

280. Valentine : mounted in contemporary wooden frame. On a base of em- bossed paper with scalloped edge is mounted a frame of silver paper lace with leaf decorations. This surrounds a medallion of embossed silver paper fringed with satin and with verses entitled ' *May Heaven / Guard Thee* ' printed on satin in the centre : ' Though set with snares the desert be / And many a fiendish throng ; / Oh, may His watchful Providence, / Convey thee safe along. / May hopes of Heaven be to thee / A day-star from on high ; And sweet / smile thro' ev'ry cloud / Of life that passes by.' Third quarter 19th century. Frame 13.5″ x 9.5″. Valentine 7.6″ x 4.8″. Donor : Miss G. Morgan. 34.293/2.

281. Valentine : embossed paper with scalloped edge. Central oval medallion consists of lithograph of a fountain in a garden. This is encircled by a frame of paper lace separately mounted on tabs and decorated with cut- outs of posies. With inscription : ' Yours for ever.' Inside is written by hand ' With kind love.' Third quarter of 19th century ; from Monmouth- shire. 5.5″ x 3.5″. Donor : Miss Edith Jones. 37.469/1.

282. Valentine : embossed paper with medallion consisting of lithograph showing sailing vessel and coastline. This is framed by a separately mounted sheet of silver paper lace with floral decorations. With inscription ' AFFECT- ION.' Third quarter of the 19th century. From Monmouthshire. 7.0″ x 4.6″. Donor : Miss Edith Jones. 37.469/2.

283. Valentine : mounted in contemporary wooden frame. On a plain sheet with scalloped edge is mounted a lithograph showing man, woman and child. This is surrounded by a coloured garland and gilded embossed paper. A separately mounted frame consists of elaborate paper lace and satin decorations with coloured paper flowers. With inscriptions ' CON- STANCY,' ' TRUTH,' ' FIRST LOVE ' and ' DEVOTION.' Third quarter of 19th century. From Ynys-ddu, Monmouthshire. Frame 11.4″ x 10.6″. Valentine 6.8″ x 4.8″. Donor : Mrs. Ivor Evans. 38.793.

284. Valentine : padded, with paper lace edge, of irregular outline. Circular central medallion consists of verse entitled ' MEMENTOS / OF THE PAST : The little violet in our / path / May give us days of sorrow, / 'Tis such a fondness memory / hath, / of youthful years to borrow ! / Whole volumes, at such times / are read / Within the humblest flower, / As we the paths of child- / hood tread— / If but for one brief / hour ! ' Sender's inscription in handwriting in a heart-shaped medallion on the back. Embossed ' WOOD.' Third quarter of 19th century. 3.6″ x 2.7″. Donor : Martin Phillips. 45.150/8.

285. Valentine : paper lace design pasted on plain paper. Centre medallion consists of verse entitled ' CAN I FORGET THEE ? : Forget thee ! No, not while heaven / spans its starred vault across the sky ; / Oh, may I never be forgiven, / If I cause thine heart a sigh ! / Sooner shall the forget-me-not / Shun the fringed brook by which it grows, / And pine for some sequestered spot, / Where not a silver ripple flows, / By the blue sky that bends above me, / Dearly and fondly do I love thee.' Embossed ' MEEK.' Third quarter of 19th century. From Llandysul, Cardiganshire. 5.4″ x 3.4″. Donor : Miss Katie Jones. 46.227/3.

286. Valentine : floral pattern paper lace with oval centre medallion consisting of verses entitled ' A WISH ' printed on satin and framed by gilded embossed paper : ' My friend, I'd breathe a wish that thou / Might'st spend thy life in love and / peace ; / May care's chill hand ne'er touch thy / brow, / But age shed joys as years increase. / And I would wish that visions fair / might ever gild thy thoughts of me, / That there may'st sometimes breathe a / prayer / For ONE who ever thinks of thee.' Embossed ' MEEK ' Third quarter 19th century. From Llandysul, Cardiganshire. 6.9″ x 4.6″. Donor : Miss Katie Jones. 46.227/4.

287. Valentine : fine gauze with scalloped paper-lace border. Centre medallion consists of coloured paper cut-out of rose and butterfly pasted on the gauze and framed with a paper cut-out garland of coloured flowers pasted on paper lace. With inscriptions ' I LIVE / in HOPE,' ' HOPE,' ' CONFIDENCE,' ' LOVE,' ' FORGET ME NOT.' Third quarter 19th century. From Glamorgan. 7.1″ x 4.7″. Donor : Miss E. M. Thomas. 49.104/4.

288. Valentine : silver paper lace with irregular outline. Flap of coloured flower cut-outs lifts to reveal centre medallion consisting of picture of flowers and fruit with scroll inscribed ' A Tribute for my best / Beloved.' Embossed ' MULLORD.' In embossed envelope. Third quarter 19th century. From Glamorgan. 3.7″ x 2.5″. Donor : Miss E. M. Thomas. 49.104/6.

289. Valentine : gilded paper lace, padded. Two flaps of paper lace lift to reveal coloured paper cut-out of roses which in turn lifts to reveal a medallion with inscription entitled ' A BLESSING : May the blessing of God await / thee ; may the sun of glory shine / around thy bed ; and may the gates / of plenty, honour, and happiness, be / ever open to thee ; may no sorrow dis- / tress thy days ; may no grief distrub thy / nights ; may the pillow of peace kiss thy / cheek, and the pleasures of imagination / attend thy dreams ; and when length of / years make thee tired of earthly joys, / and the curtains of death gently / close around thy last sleep, / may the angel of God take care, that the ex- / piring lamp of life shall not / receive one rude blast to has- / ten on its extinction.' Oval centre medallion on back consists of coloured paper cut-out of posy of flowers. Third quarter 19th century. From Glamorgan. Donor : Miss E. M. Thomas. 3.8″ x 2.6″. 49.104/7.

290. Valentine : in the form of a padded sachet of embossed paper, silver on the outside. Oval centre medallion on outside consists of coloured lithograph of posy. On the inside the oval medallion consists of a verse entitled ' REMEMBER ME,' printed on satin : ' *One little thought | In absent hour, | Do thou in friendship | Turn to me ; | And I while life | Shall grant me power, | Will never cease | To think of thee.*' Third quarter of 19th century. From Glamorgan. 4.2″ x 2.8″. Donor : Miss M. E. Thomas. 49.104/8.

291. Valentine : paper mount for making a. Embossed with woodland scene and figures. Oval centre medallion space is empty. Embossed ' MANSELL.' Third quarter of 19th century. From Llwyngwril, Merioneth. 7.0″ x 4.6″. Donor : Anonymous. 54.166/91.

292. Valentine : paper lace with fine gauze centre on which are mounted an interweaving garland of cut-out flowers and a number of smaller cut-outs depicting a winged hour-glass, Cupid, a lyre etc. The following hand-written couplets are visible through the gauze : ' Oh I have met with many friends / and parted with regret, / The smiles, the favours of the fair / I never can forget ; / But oh, would one give me her heart / and make my heart her own / 'T would please me more, "It is not good / For man to be alone". The valentine is signed ' E.' Third quarter of 19th century. From Chepstow, Monmoutshire. 9.9″ x 7.9″. Donor : Mrs. Amy Hartland. 33.77/1.

293. Valentine : embossed paper with a central oval medallion depicting a bouquet of flowers (with a gilded ' S ') and Cupid in paper cut-outs. The medallion is framed by paper lace with floral decorations. Third quarter of 19th century. From Chepstow, Monmouthshire. 7.1″ x 4.8″. Donor : Mrs. Amy Hartland. 33.77/3.

294. Valentine : paper lace backed with satin. Oval centre with cut-out of Cupid is surrounded by a separately mounted and elaborate frame of gilded paper, gauze material, paper lace with pearls attached, and silk (or satin) tabs. Third quarter of 19th century. From Chepstow, Monmouthshire. 7.7″ x 4.8″. Donor : Mrs. Amy Hartland. 33.77/4.

295. Valentine : paper lace with scalloped edge. Central medallion of gilded and embossed paper with figure and bouquet of cut-out flowers and ins-cription ' *I am alone in the | world without you.*' Medallion is mounted on gauze and framed by embossed paper with leaf design coloured gold and blue. Third quarter of 19th century. From Chepstow, Monmouthshire. 7.8″ x 5.1″. Donor : Mrs. Amy Hartland. 33.77/5.

296. Valentine : paper lace with scalloped edge. Central medallion consists of silver embossed cut-out of girl with garland of flowers. With inscriptions ' Constant to Thee ' and ' *Be thou so to me.*' Embossed ' MANSELL '. Third quarter of 19th century. From Chepstow, Monmouthshire. 5.4″ x 3.6″. Donor : Mrs. Amy Hartland. 33.77/7.

297. Valentine : paper lace with scalloped edge. Central medallion consists o paper cut-out bouquet which lifts to reveal manuscript inscription. With inscription ' REMEMBER ME.' Embossed ' MULLORD.' Third quarter of 19th century. From Chepstow, Monmouthshire. 5.4″ x 3.7″. Donor : Mrs. Amy Hartland. 33.77/8.

298. Valentine : scalloped paper-lace edging around central medallion on which are pasted paper cut-outs of forget-me-nots. With inscription : ' *Affection's Offering | to thee sweet Valentine.*' Embossed ' MANSELL.' Third quarter of 19th century. From Chepstow, Monmouthshire. 4.3″ x 3.7″. Donor : Mrs. Amy Hartland. 33.77/9.

299. Valentine : paper lace with scalloped edge and central oval medallion on
which are pasted a vase of embossed silver paper with a large leaf of linen
and paper cut-outs of flowers and leaves. With inscription : ' *Oh ! pity a
desponding heart.*' Third quarter of 19th century. From Chepstow, Monmouthshire. 5.3″ x 3.5″. Donor : Mrs. Amy Hartland. 33.77/10.

300. Valentine : scalloped paper lace edging around central medallion on which
are pasted paper cut-outs of a rose draped with cloth and gilded fringes
and cords inscribed ' *Hope* ! ' With manuscript inscription : ' Thou art all
to me.' Card folds into an envelope with paper-lace front inscribed
' *From your Valentine* ' in sender's handwriting. Card and envelope embossed ' MANSELL.' Third quarter of 19th century. From Chepstow,
Monmouthshire. Card 5.3″ x 3.5″, envelope 3.8″ x 2.1″. Donor : Mrs.
Amy Hartland. 33.77/11.

301. Valentine : in the form of a padded envelope gilded and embossed. Oval
medallion on cover consists of embroidered inscription ' *Remember | Me* '
embellished with leaf decoration. Third quarter of 19th century. From
Chepstow, Monmouthshire. 4.0″ x 2.7″. Donor : Mrs. Amy Hartland.
33.77/12.

302. Valentine : scalloped paper-lace edging surrounds central medallion which
is decorated with water-colour flowers. With manuscript verse. Embossed ' MANSELL.' Third quarter of 19th century. From Chepstow,
Monmouthshire. 5.3″ x 3.5″. Donor : Mrs. Amy Hartland. 33.77/13.

303. Valentine : embossed paper lace with scalloped edge has central oval
medallion of pink satin with paper cut-outs of flowers, a flaming torch
and a quiver ; with inscription ' *Forget-me-not.*' On this base and around
the medallion a frame of gilded paper lace of similar outline is mounted
on hinged tabs. Third quarter of 19th century. From Chepstow, Monmouthshire. 5.3″ x 3.6″. Donor : Mrs. Amy Hartland. 33.77/14.

304. Valentine : embossed silver paper lace with scalloped edge. In the centre
is mounted representation of a bird on its nest. This is framed by silver
paper lace separately mounted on paper hinges and decorated with
white leaves and artificial pearls. With inscription : ' Attachment.'
Embossed ' C. RIMMEL / PERFUMERS / LONDON & PARIS', and
' MEEK.' Received by a member of donor's family c. 1890-80, from
Glamorgan. 6.7″ x 4.9″. Donor : T. W. Proger. 26.115.

305. Valentine : paper lace with scalloped edge. Oval centre medallion carries
the inscription ' *As over the Pages | your Eyes | you pass look out for | your
own name | Ass.*" A flap consisting of a cut-out paper lithograph of an ass
in man's clothing lifts to reveal manuscript inscription ' you will do / for
me.' Embossed ' MULLORD 417.' In original envelope bearing London
address and postmark, and dated 1874. 5.4″ x 3.7″. Donor : Anonymous.
54.166/86-87.

306. Valentine : embossed paper with scalloped edge. Central medallion
consisting of lithograph of flowers with fringe of paper lace is separately
mounted as is also a frame of paper lace with floral decoration. With
inscription ' A TRIBUTE / OF PURE / AFFECTION.' Embossed
' MEEK.' In original envelope bearing Clydach, Swansea, address and
postmarked Pontypool, 1875. 5.6″ x 3.4″. Donor : The family of the late
Mrs. F. M. Edmunds. 37.37/65.

307. Valentine : embossed paper with scalloped edge. At the base of a central medallion consisting of a small embossed figure of a girl is attached a posy of artificial flowers in linen. A frame of silver paper-lace with heart motif and, originally, four artificial pearls is separately mounted on hinged tabs. With inscription ' To my darling.' c. 1875-80, from Glamorgan. 7.1″ x 4.5″. Donor : M. Thomas. 29.265/1.

308. Valentine : in the form of a wallet, consisting of silver paper lace on scarlet paper background. Front has coloured lithograph of man and woman in garden as central oval medallion. Inside cover has oval medallion flap which lifts to reveal verse entitled ' TO / A FRIEND : Whate'er my lot on / earth may be, / My friend, I must re- / member thee, / And know that thou the / same will feel / In my prosperity and weal, / We met as friends as / friends we parted, / From both our eyes the / tear drop started, / But angel Hope doth / ease our pain, / And whisper, Ye / shall meet again.' Embossed ' WOOD.' c. 1875-80 ; from Glamorgan. 4.0″ x 3.0″ (folded). Donor : M. Thomas. 28.265/2.

309. Valentine : embossed and gilded paper lace in the form of an arch, with scalloped edge, with cut-out flower decorations inscribed ' SINCERITY.' Centre medallion represents two gates which open to reveal bunch of artificial flowers in linen. Card embossed ' WOOD.' c. 1875—80 ; from Glamorgan. 3.8″ x 2.7″. Donor : M. Thomas. 29.265/3.

310. Valentine : paper lace with separately mounted frame of gilded paper lace round the circular central medallion of embossed paper and artificial flowers of linen and feather. With inscription : ' BELIEVE / ME YOURS / DEAR / VALENTINE.' c. 1875-80 ; from Glamorgan. 3.0″ x 2.1″. Donor : M. Thomas. 29.265/4.

311. Valentine : paper-lace base of irregular outline overlaid with similarly shaped embossed and gilded paper decorated with cut-outs of garlands and a cherub. Inscribed ' I AM FONDLY THINE OWN ' and em- bossed ' WOOD.' With manuscript inscription : ' For little Margaret Ann with Cassie's fond love.' c. 1875-80 ; from Glamorgan. 3.6″ x 2.6″. Donor : M. Thomas. 29.265/5.

312. Valentine : in the form of a padded envelope gilded and embossed. Embossed paper cut-out of flowers on cover lifts to reveal central oval medallion of satin with verse entitled ' I Wish : I wish I / could look / in thy heart, dear, — If only a moment to see / how large and / how faithful a / part dear, Is / the corner / kept sacred / to me./ (Copyright).' c. 1875-80 ; from Glamorgan. 4.8″ x 3.1″. Donor : M. Thomas. 29.265/6.

313. Valentine : in the form of a padded envelope of embossed paper. Oval medallion on cover shows lithograph of two children in a garden. On the back of the envelope is another oval medallion of satin edged with em- bossed silver paper with verse entitled ' Forget-Me-Not : Amidst the world's gay revelry, / Or in its troubled stream, / Forget me not, let not the past / Be as a fleeting dream. / Let not the happy hours be shared, / Be past as nothing by, / Forget me not, e'en if you must, / Remember with a sigh.' c. 1875-80, from Glamorgan. 4.2″ x 2.8″. Donor : M. Thomas. 29.265/7.

314. Valentine : embossed paper with scalloped edge. Central oval medallion with lithograph of swan is surrounded by frame of paper lace decorated with floral cut-outs and separately mounted on hinged tabs. With inscription ' SOUVENIR ' ; embossed ' MULLORD BROS ' ; c. 1875-80, from Glamorgan. 6.9″ x 4.5″. Donor : M. Thomas. 29.265/8.

315. Valentine : padded and of irregular shape. Silver paper lace with oval central medallion on either side, the one depicting bunch of roses and leaves, the other a verse entitled ' TO / A FRIEND : Whate'er my lot on / earth may be, / My friend, I must re- / member thee, / And know that thou the / same will feel / In my prosperity and weal, / We met as friends as / friends we parted. / From both our eyes the / tear drop started, / But angel Hope doth / ease our pain, / And whisper, Ye / shall meet again.' Embossed ' WOOD.' *c.* 1875-80 ; from Glamorgan. 4″ x 2.8″. Donor : M. Thomas. 29.265/9.

316. Valentine : gilded and embossed paper with fringe of silver paper lace. Cut-out of bird and flowers on embossed paper lifts to reveal verse entitled ' UNCHANGING / LOVE ' printed on oval medallion of satin : ' Though absence parts us for / a while, / And distance rolls between, / Believe, whoever may revile, / I am still what I have been. / For to my dying day, my heart, / Through every fate will be, / If doom'd till then to mourn / apart, / Unchanging still / to thee.' Embossed ' MOSSMAN.' *c.* 1875-80. From Glamorgan. 6.8″ x 4.7″. Donor : M. Thomas. 29.265/10.

317. Valentine : Two sheets of silver paper lace, one of which is padded, are held together by ribbons and tied together with ribbons when folded. The central medallions on the four sides consist of a verse entitled : ' FORGET ME NOT ' printed on satin and framed by floral paper cut-outs ; a paper cut-out of a plant in a vase ; a lithograph of a girl with a garland of forget-me-nots, and a lithograph of a girl with a garland of violets, respectively. Verse reads : ' OH LET THIS LITTLE TITLE / OFT BRING ME TO THY / VIEW, / AND WALKS WE'VE HAD TO- / GETHER, / AND WORDS OF KINDNESS / TOO ; / AND WHEN YOU TREAD EACH / FAVOURITE SPOT / ALONE I ASK— FORGET ME / NOT.' *c.* 1878—81. From Portmadoc, Caernarvonshire. 5.4″ x 3.5″. Donor : Mrs. E. M. Owen. 35.126/3.

318. Valentine : paper lace with scalloped edge and central medallion consisting of satin background on which flowers are pasted. Over and around this a frame of silver paper lace with leaf decoration and satin fringe is mounted on hinged tabs. With inscription ' Love's Garland to thee.' *c.* 1878—81. From Portmadoc, Caernarvonshire. 5.3″ x 3.6″. Donor : Mrs. E. M. Owen. 35.126/4.

319. Valentine : paper lace overlaid by silver paper lace frame around a bouquet of artificial flowers. With inscription : ' True to thee.' Embossed ' MEEK ' and dated ' 1881 ' (in ink). From Cardiff. 6.7″ x 4.6″. Donor : Mrs. E. Briard. 44.321/6.

320. Valentine : embossed paper with scalloped edge. A paper garland of coloured flowers encircling two clasped hands is pasted on a separately mounted oval central medallion of silver paper lace. A frame of silver paper lace with floral decoration is mounted separately. With inscription : ' In fond / remembrance.' In original embossed envelope bearing Cardiff address and postmark dated 1882. 7.7″ x 4.8″. Donor : Mrs. E. Briard. 44.321/5.

321. Valentine : embossed paper with scalloped edge. A basket of artificial flowers is mounted on a thickly-padded centre medallion encircled by a garland of artificial leaves and fringed with silk. With a coloured paper representation of a hand holding a posy labelled ' True.' Dated 1884 (in ink). From Cardiff. 7.0″ x 4.8″. Donor : Mrs. E. Briard. 44.321/10.

322. Valentine : paper lace base with silver paper lace sheet of similar size superimposed and attached by means of hinged tabs. Padded oval medallion of satin with printed verse entitled ' I Think of Thee: To me, through every season dearest, / In every scene by day or night, / Thou present to my mind appearest, / A quenchless star, for ever bright.' With floral decoration. Inscription and Verse in sender's hand-writing. ' I have told thee I love thee / How often I told thee many times over / I have told thee I love thee / What can I say more— / I crave not for wealth, / For riches, or fame / I love thee and your love is all I / claim. / Then look not thus doubting nor turn thee away / And cease your reproaches day after day / I tell thee this once as I have told thee before / I love thee until I can love thee no more /. From yours most affectionate / Lover / Dan Davies.' ' From your dearest / Dan.' About 1885. From south Wales. 6.7″ x 4.7″. Donor : D. J. Davies. 42.73/1.

323. Valentine : in the form of a padded folder of silver paper lace with a silk fringe. Centre medallions decorated with coloured cut-out of flowers and with verse entitled ' BE MINE ' printed on satin : ' Wilt thou be / mine love, mine / evermore—Darling ! / I'll cherish thee, love, / and adore.— Summer, / Winter, Autumn and / Spring ;—Each sea- / son recurring, fresh / gladness shall bring. / Answer me quick- / ly, do not delay ; / Answer me / kindly do not / say nay.' About 1885. From south Wales. 5.3″ x 3.6″ (folded). Donor : D. J. Davies. 42.73/2.

324. Valentine : paper lace with scalloped edge. Centre medallion of coloured paper cut-outs framed in a garland of white leaves. About 1885. From south Wales. 6.3″ x 4.1″. Donor : D. J. Davies. 42.73/3.

325. Valentine : silver paper lace attached by hinged tabs to embossed paper. Centre medallion consists of coloured lithograph showing boy and girl with deer. With artificial flowers and leaves and inscription ' ACCEPT THIS / *LOVING HEART* / OF *MINE*.' With verse and inscription in sender's handwriting on the back : ' best wishes from / D. Davies ' ' There's Love / For you and Me / There is dew for the flow'ret / And honey for the bee / And flowers for the wild bird / And love for you and me / There are tears for the many / And pleasures for the few / But let the the (*sic*) world pass on / *dear* / There's love for me and You.' About 1885. From south Wales. 7.2″. x 4.7″. Donor : D. J. Davies. 42.73/4.

326. Valentine : silver paper lace, padded, with scalloped edge. Centre medallion on front consists of coloured lithograph of flowers and berries, with inscription ' This Valentine accept my Love / For true to thee, I ever will be.' Oval centre medallion on back consists of verse entitled ' I'VE TOLD THEE / I LOVE THEE ' printed on satin : ' To me, through every season dearest, / In every scene by day or night, / Though present to my mind appearest, / A quenchless star, for ever bright.' ' I have told thee I love thee / How often I told thee many times over / I have told thee I love thee / What can I say more— / I crave not for wealth, / For riches, or fame / I love thee and your love is all I / claim. / Then look not thus doubting nor turn thee away / And cease your reproaches day after day / I tell thee this once as I have told thee before / I love thee until I can love thee no more. / From yours most affectionate / Lover / Dan Davies.' ' From your dearest / Dan.' About 1885. From south Wales. 6.8″ x 4.4″. Donor : D. J. Davies. 42.73/5.

327. Valentine : embossed paper with scalloped edge and with central medallion consisting of verse entitled ' Love's Smile ' printed on satin : ' The smiling / mouth of her I / love ; Is like the / rose that decks the / Spring :—

Yet while its / fragrance I approve, / my bosom feels / the rose's sting / '
An elaborate frame of paper lace with coloured floral decoration is
separately mounted over and round the medallion. About 1885. From
south Wales. 5.3″ x 3.7″. Donor : D. J. Davies. 42.73/6.

328. Valentine : in the form of a folder consisting of four rectangular panels
decorated with silver paper lace. The centre medallions on both sides of
each panel consist of coloured paper cut-outs of flowers, lithographs of
flowers, and verses entitled ' O Think of Me ' printed on satin : ' Oh,
think of me when far away, / Along life's stormy path I stray ; / When
laughing with the gay, the free, / Oh tell me, wilt thou think of me ? /
When all thou lovest shall deceive, / And those thou trustest most betray ; /
Oh then remember, and believe, / One heart is true, and will not stray. /
Oh, think of me in every hour, / In every place, where'er thou art ; /
And be thou sure that nought has / power, / to chase thy image from my /
heart'. About 1885. From south Wales. 4.8″ x 3.5 (folded). Donor :
D. J. Davies. 42.73/7.

329. Valentine : embossed paper with scalloped edge. On this a silk-fringed
sheet of silver paper lace has been mounted. The centre medallion on this
sheet consists of a coloured paper cut-out of a cherub pasted on a crescent-
shaped silver paper background. This is framed by a separately mounted
border of silver paper lace fringed with silk. With inscription ' For ever /
Thine.' About 1885. From south Wales. 7.6″ x 4.8″. Donor : D. J.
Davies. 42.73/8.

330. Valentine : embossed paper with scalloped edge. A flap of coloured cut-outs
of flowers lifts to reveal verse entitled ' Don't say / nay but yea. Oh,
dearest, but / one wee word say, / And let that little / word be yea ! /
And I will hail the / happy day / That makes thee / mine for / ever.' Late
19th century. From Dyffryn Uchaf, Margam, Glamorgan. 3.9″ x 2.7″.
Donor : Mrs. A. Williams. 35.466/5.

331. Valentine : embossed paper with scalloped edge. On the oval centre
medallion is pasted a coloured paper representation of a hand writing and
a verse : ' Accept my note / of hand / For the love I owe thee / As long as
life shall stand / Faithfulness I'll show thee.' The frame around the
medallion consists of paper lace decorated with coloured forget-me-nots on
paper and is fringed with silk. Embossed ' MANSELL.' Late 19th
century. From Cardiff. 6.9″ x 4.4″. Donor : Mrs. E. Briard. 44.321/7.

332. Valentine : paper lace with coloured floral decorations attached. Centre
medallion consists of coloured representation of posy with scroll inscribed
' Forget me not.' Late 19th century. From Cardiff. 4.6″ x 3.3″. Donor :
Mrs. E. Briard. 44.321/8.

333. Valentine : a basket of artificial flowers inscribed ' *Truly* / *thine* ' mounted on
corrugated blue paper forms the centre medallion. It is framed with
embossed silver paper decorated with linen flowers. Late 19th century.
From Cardiff. 5.3″ x 3.7″. Donor : Mrs. E. Briard. 44.321/11.

334. Valentine : embossed paper, oval centre medallion consists of coloured cut-
outs of birds and rose with artificial floral and leaf decoration. A frame of
embossed silver and white paper which encircles the medallion is separately mounted. Late 19th century. 7.0″ x 4.8″. Donor : Martin Phillips.
45.150/1.

335. Valentine : in the form of a padded envelope. Front decorated with panel of coloured flowers against a gilt background. Oval centre medallion consists of verse entitled ' Love Token ' printed on satin : ' All things in vain look bright and / gay. / If those we love are far away. / Their smiles alone can joy impart / And like a sunbeam cheer the heart.' Late 19th century. 3.9″ x 2.4″. Donor : Martin Phillips. 45.150/6.

336. Valentine : a folded card which opens like a book. Embossed silver paper with coloured floral decorations in the medallions on the cover. The medallions on the inside consist of rose painted on silk and verse printed on satin respectively : ' If deepest, / truest LOVE / Responsive love can / gain, / Then, DEAREST, thou / wilt prove / I have not LOVED / in vain.' Embossed ' MULLORD ' and ' 413.' Late 19th century. From St. George's-super-Ely, Glamorgan. 4.4″ x 3.0″ (folded). Donor : Mrs. A. Bennet. 49.87/3.

337. Valentine : a folder of embossed paper decorated on the outside with two oval centre medallions of lithographed flowers and opening to reveal, on one side, a padded panel of silver paper lace with an oval centre medallion of embroidered flowers and, on the other, a similar (but unpadded) panel with a centre medallion consisting of a verse entitled ' Lasting Friendship ' printed on satin and framed in a garland of coloured paper cut-out flowers. ' Thy love so faithful, calm, / serene, / I liken to the ivy leaf, dear / friend, / which often emblematical / hath been, / Of friendship changeless / to the end, / when all around is faded, This still is green.' In original embossed envelope, unstamped but with Pontypridd, Glamorgan, address. Late 19th century. 4.9″ x 3.2″ (folded). Donor : Miss Penelopen E. Price. 50.63/30.

338. Valentine : paper lace border around large medallion of satin on which a coloured paper cut-out depicting a vase of flowers has been pasted. A separately mounted frame of silver paper lace with lace fringe encircles the medallion. Late 19th century. From Cardiff. 7.6″ x 5.0″. Donor : S. C. Churchill. 50.116.

339. Valentine : in the form of a padded sachet of embossed paper, the folding flaps of which are decorated on the outside with coloured paper floral cut-outs pasted on satin and on the inside with two coloured lithographs of flowers. The padded section consists of silver paper lace pasted over a centre medallion of satin on which a verse entitled ' SINCEREST / LOVE ' has been printed : ' I offer to thee, my dearest, / The love of an earnest heart ; / I offer with truth sincerest / Affection could e'er impart. / The life that thy love can / bless, / Or thy scorn submerge in / woe, / I dare to hope for a little / "yes" ; / Oh dearest, say not "no" ! ' Late 19th century. 5.0″ x 3.4″ (folded). Donor : Mrs. Dorothy Middlehurst. 50.442/6.

340. Valentine : consisting of a posy of artificial flowers and leaves attached by pins to a sheet of paper lace of irregular outline. With inscription printed in a miniature valentine at the foot of the posy : ' Dearest Love / Believe Me / I never will deceive / THEE.' Late 19th century. 7.0″ x 3.8″. Donor : Mrs. Dorothy Middlehurst. 50.442/7.

341. Valentine : embossed paper with scalloped edge. Centre medallion consists of coloured lithograph showing Christmas party scene. Around this is a frame of paper lace backed with satin. With inscription ' I cling / to thee ' on coloured paper cut-out of garland and bow, arrow and quiver. Late 19th century. 5.9″ x 3.9″. Donor : Mrs. Dorothy Middlehurst. 50.442/8.

342. Valentine : embossed and gilded paper with fringe of gilded paper lace.
     Centre medallion inscribed ' Souvenir ' and ' The Lover's Oracle.' On
     each of the four sides of the card is a tab which, when pulled, reveals a
     panel containing a coloured picture of a bouquet of flowers and a verse :
     ' 1. This simple flower betrays my heart / And breathes for me the wish I
     wot : / It bids my thoughts to language start / And asks thee to "Forget me
     not." 2. Once when my heart was sad and sore / I thought a fair hand
     to me bore / A bunch of flowers such as these / I'd bid my heart no more
     repine, / Did I but know that hand were thine.' 3. This old world is
     scarce worth seeing / Till Love wave his purple wing / And we guage (*sic*)
     the bliss of being / Thro' a golden wedding ring. 4. Would you draw
     fair Eden nearer / And to Earth the angels bring / You must seek the
     magic Mirror / Of a golden wedding ring.' In an embossed envelope.
     Late 19th century. From Llwyngwril, Merioneth. 4.3″ x 2.9″. Donor :
     Anonymous. 54.166/88.

343. Valentine : mounted in box. Within a frame of paper lace with artificial
     flower decoration is depicted a garden scene with gilded cameo embossing.
     The whole valentine lifts up to reveal manuscript verse at bottom of box :
     ' i send you a word / as soft as sweet as breathing from the / south a kiss
     but / no when next / we meet a kiss by / word of mouth / My Dear John.'
     Embossed ' WINDSOR'. Of mid 19th century date. Box has St. George's-
     super-Ely, address ; it is unstamped but marked ' Paid.'   Formerly
     belonging to John John, Ty-fry Farm, St. George's-super-Ely, Glamorgan,
     who died about 1900 aged 84.   7.2″ x 5″.   Donor : Mrs. A. Bennett.
     49.87/2.

344. Valentine : of boxed type but original box missing. An outer frame of lace
     and silver paper lace has a scalloped edge. Within this is a separately
     mounted inner frame of silver paper lace with a garland of flowers and
     fine lace. This encloses an arch of silver paper lace and an embossed cut-
     out of a woman carrying garlands of flowers. Inscribed ' I LOVE BUT
     THEE ' and embossed ' Mossman.'   Sent in 1869 by John Perkins,
     Porthcawl, Glamorgan. 7.7″ x 5.1″. Donor : C. Lewis. 38.146.

345. Valentine : mounted in box. A rectangular frame of gilded paper lace
     decorated with four small embossed cut-out flowers encloses a garland of
     embossed cut-out flowers. Within this is an oval medallion with a verse
     ' LOVE TO THEE ' : ' I LOVE THEE STILL / I LOVE THEE
     STILL / THY CHANGELESS / CONSTANCY AND TRUTH / THY
     NAME YET / WAKENS / PLEASURE'S THRILL / STAR OF
     MY BRIGHT / AND JOYOUS / YOUTH.' Box edged with paper lace.
     Second half 19th century. From Cardiff. 7.1″ x 4.6″ x 5″. Donor : Mrs. E.
     Briard. 44.321/9.

346. Valentine : mounted in box. A satin pad with an edging of silver paper lace.
     On the pad is mounted a posy of linen artificial flowers and a bow. The
     words ' Love / PURE LOVE ' are inscribed on a paper cut-out posy
     pasted on to the silver paper lace. On the inside of the lid is a card
     depicting a flower, the petals lift to reveal a lithograph of a cherub (or
     ? cupid). It is inscribed ' THINK SOMETIMES OF THE SENDER.'
     c. 1878-81. From Portmadoc, Caernarvonshire. 7.7″ x 5.0″ x 1.25″.
     Donor : Mrs. E. M. Owen. 35.126/1.

347. Valentine : mounted in box. On a base of embossed paper is mounted a
     frame of silver paper lace with a pad of satin to which are attached
     artificial flowers. With inscription : ' With best Love.' Box edged with
     paper lace. Attached to the lid is a smaller valentine of embossed paper

overlaid by a silver paper lace frame around a lithographed oval medallion showing cherub with lyre. With inscription ' Guess who sends this.' c. 1878-81. From Portmadoc, Caernarvonshire. 7.4″ x 4.8″ x 1.25″. Donor : Mrs. E. M. Owen. 35.126/2.

348. Valentine : mounted in box ; card decorated with bouquet of roses and inscribed with verse entitled ' FORGET ME NOT ' : ' Oh ! could I but count on / the gift of thy love / My life's lamp would / glow like the bright / stars above.' It is secured to a sheet of embossed paper by hinged tabs. Box fringed with paper lace. Late 19th century. 4.25″ x 3.25″ x 5″. 14.159/238.

349. Valentine : mounted in box. To a sheet of paper embossed in floral design with coloured rose bouquets in each corner is attached by hinged tabs a raised oval perforated band enclosing a bouquet of flowers inscribed ' Thine in love.' Box fringed with paper lace. Late 19th century. 4.25″ x 3.25″ x .5″. 14.159/239.

350. Valentine : mounted in box. Through a frame of two mounted sheets of embossed paper is seen a separately-mounted oval centre inscribed ' GOD / ABOVE / INCREASE / OUR / LOVE.' Box edged with paper lace. Late 19th century. 4.75″ x 3.25″ x .5″. 14.159/240.

351. Valentine : mounted in box ; an embossed rectangular sheet with lace edging and four posies of roses is mounted on double-hinged tabs. The oval centre inscribed ' WITH / BEST / WISHES ' is similarly mounted. Box edge with paper lace. Late 19th century. 4.25″ x 3.25″ x .5″. 14.159/241.

352. Valentine : mounted in box. Coloured flower bouquet in the form of a flap conceals a verse entitled ' LOVES DREAM ' : ' Last / night I dreamt / a tender dream, / 'twas of thy sun- / bright face—Ah ! / could it ever on / me beam, Earth / were a perfect place.' Box fringed with paper lace. 4.25″ x 2.8″ x .5″. 14.159/242.

353. Valentine : Mounted in box. An oval central medallion with inscription ' WITH / BEST / WISHES ' with a separately mounted frame of gilded and embossed paper with scalloped edge attached to lace paper of rectangular shape. Box edged with paper lace. 4.6″ x 3.1″. Late 19th century. 14.159/243.

354. Valentine : mounted in box. A rectangular sheet of fringed silver paper is mounted on hinged tabs. On it is a card embossed with roses and forget-me-nots and the inscription : ' To / one I love.' Box edged with paper lace. Late 19th century. 5″ x 3.75″ x .5″. 14.159/244. Duplicate 14.159/245.

355. Valentine : mounted in box. A frame of paper lace encloses a bouquet of forget-me-nots which lifts to reveal oval medallion with the inscription : ' A WISH ' and a verse : ' This little tribute / which I send,—I / hope you will receive / And keep it for the / sake of one, who / never will de- / ceive.' Box edged with paper lace. Late 19th century. 5.1″ x 3.6″ x .5″. 14.159/246.

356. Valentine : mounted in box. A rectangular sheet of embossed paper with fringe is mounted on hinged tabs. On it is a representation of a hand holding a bouquet of flowers. This lifts to reveal a verse ' The faithful / Heart. Dearest love, believe / me / Through all else de- / part, / Nought shall e'er de- / ceive thee / In this faithful heart.' Box edged with paper lace. Late 19th century. 5.2″ x 3.6″ x .5″. 14.159/247.

357. Valentine : mounted in box. An oval medallion showing flowers is surrounded by a frame of paper lace separately mounted. With the inscription ' Remember me.' Box edged with paper lace and lid inscribed with trade mark and ' THOMAS STEVENS COVENTRY & LONDON.' Late 19th century. 5.7″ x 3.7″ x .5″. 14.159/248.

358. Valentine : mounted in box. Two large flaps covered with red material form a rectangle which is fringed and has a leaf on it. By lifting the leaf the flaps open revealing flowers and leaves inscribed ' *My heart is wholly thine.*' Box edged with paper lace. Late 19th century. 6″ x 5″ x .5″. 14.159/249.

359. Valentine : mounted in box. A rectangular centre covered with a pink material. On it is a paper cut-out of a woman's hand holding a rose. The centre is fringed and opens like a book, to reveal prints of flowers with inscriptions ' TO MY LOVE / WITH MY FOND LOVE.' Box edged with paper lace. Late 19th century. 6.0″ x 5.0″ x .5″. 14.159/250.

360. Valentine : mounted in box. The square centre with fringe is covered with light blue material and has on it a paper cut-out of two hands holding each other surrounded by flowers. It opens like a book to show two prints of flowers with couplets : ' Dear, / with these flowers / accept mine heart / And take with me in life a part. / May / these sweet / flowers / convey to you / My fond affection, / deep and true.' Box edged with paper lace. Late 19th century. 6.0″ x 5.0″ x .5″. 14.159/251.

361. Valentine : mounted in box. An oblong velvet pad edged with lace has on it a folded card in a frame of woollen cord. With inscription ' *I Love thee well* ! / *Wilt thou Love me ?* ' and verse : ' *Something is prompting me today / These simple words to thee to say, / Oh may these flowers I send to thee, / Make love bloom in thine heart for me* ! / *A.H.B.*' Card opens to reveal inscription ' *Sweet / Love / forget me not* ' and a further verse : ' *I'll think of thee, dear, on this day / Although thy face I cannot see, / and wheresoe'er thou art, I pray / That thou wilt cast a thought on me. / A.M.B.*' Box edged with paper lace. Late 19th century. 6.0″ x 5.0″ x .5″. 14.159/252.

362. Valentine : mounted in box. Central oval medallion with verse entitled ' I will think of / Thee ' framed by garland of artificial flowers and leaves and embossed paper with lace edging : ' Yes, I will think of thee / when stars are bright, / And day is mingling with / the shades of night ; / When nature in her ebon / locks is seen, / Spreading her mantle o'er the / leafless green. / My heart shall worship at / thy lovely shrine, / Sacred to love, imma- / culate divine.' At the bottom of the box, which is edged with paper lace, as a number of pressed leaves and flowers ; also two manuscript verses from the ' Bells of Aberdovey ' in English and Welsh respectively. Sent by donor's father to donor's mother, the box bearing a Lampeter, Cardiganshire, address and post-mark of the 1880's. 7.7″ x 4.9″ x 1.75″. Donor : Mrs. Ella Thomas. 45.294/1.

363. Valentine : mounted in contemporary cork-work frame. A sash with tassels decorated with gold tinsel paper is attached to the centre of a padded velvet base. In one corner is an artificial flower. A border of fluff and of paper lace lines the sides of the box. With inscription ' Ever the Same.' Newspaper backing of frame is dated 10th March 1886. From Llanbleddian, Glamorgan. Frame 9.25″ x 6.5″. Donor : Mrs. Arthur John. 55.206/3.

364. Valentine : mounted in contemporary cork-work frame. A posy of paper roses is mounted on a plain ground and the sides of the box are lined with paper lace. c. 1886. From Llanbleddian, Glamorgan. Frame 9.25″ x 6.7″. Donor : Mrs. Arthur John. 55.206/4.

365. Valentine : mounted in box with sloping sides. Central medallion shows bouquet of flowers framed by separately-mounted paper lace. The following verses entitled ' MY LOVE ' are printed on satin and framed with silver paper lace inside the lid : ' Timid gentle as the dove, / in each glance of thine, I see, / And each action, tender love, / Treasure dear art thou to me. / Joyous the moments that I spend, / My dearest one with thee ; / O ! may they never to life's end, / Lose their sweet charm for me.' Late 19th century. From Merthyr Tydfil, Glamorgan. Base 6.7″ x 4.8″. Donor : Miss M. E. Lee. 43.53/2.

366. Valentine : in box. On a frame of blue-and-white embossed paper with scalloped edge and paper leaves in each corner is mounted on oblong paper lace medallion. To this is attached a small garland of artificial flowers and leaves surrounding a paper cut-out of bird carrying a note inscribed ' Absent but / dear.' Verse entitled ' Love ' by ' M.Y.W.' on inside of decorated lid : ' If hearts be true, and hearts be fond, / No earthly power can break their / bond, / Or turn awry love's wilful course, / Or war for long against its force. / Then keep you to me strong and / true ; / My love returned, you ne'er will / rue, / For all my aim, and all my thought / Will be to keep the heart I've sought.' Late 19th century. 5.7″ x 3.9″. Donor : Mrs. Margaret Jones. 46.332/4.

367. Valentine : in box ; in the form of an irregularly-shaped book of twelve pages of verses by Frank Ferndale with the title ' Chimings.' The front cover has embossed floral decorations and figures of cherubs arranged around three panels which have been cut out of the cardboard and covered with gauze. Published by The Art Lithographic Publishing Co., New York and The Artistic Lithographic Company, London ; ' Printed at the works in Munich.' Late 19th century. From Moylgrove, Pembrokeshire. Box 9″ x 7″. Donor : Clifford Davies. 55.211/2.

368. Valentine : showing hand-coloured caricature of a woman's face. A tab operates the lower jaw which when open reveals a row of teeth and the inscription ' AM I NOT A / CHARMING MAID.' At the bottom of the card are the words ' And this is what the men all say.' Scalloped and embossed border. Mid 19th century. 7.0″ x 4.6″. 14.159/267.

369. Valentine : showing hand-coloured masked face, the expression on which changes when a tab is pulled. With couplet : ' CAN YOU BY ANY SCIENTIFIC RULE TELL, ARE YOU A MAN OR A FOOL ? ' Scalloped and embossed border. Mid 19th century. 7.0″ x 4.5″. 14.159/270.

370. Valentine : hand-painted picture of woman with parasol. A gauze skirt lifts to reveal hooped frame and under-clothes. With verse : ' *Ears like Donkey, Eyes like cat / To be genteel, you are too fat / While there's another in the land / I'll never claim your mutton hand*.' Inscribed and embossed ' WOOD.' Mid 19th century. 5.4″ x 3.7″. 14.159/271.

371. Valentine : hand-painted picture of woman. Flap on face lifts up to reveal angry expression. With couplet entitled ' LOVES CHANGES ' : ' Grant her wishes, she's an Angel / Thwart her she's a very - - -.' Scalloped and embossed border. Mid 19th century. 7.3″ x 4.7″. 14.159/276.

372. Valentine : hand-painted picture of sash window. Tab slides to open window showing cat inside. With verse entitled ' *I'll open the Casement to thee*. / Oh ! Romeo, Sweet Romeo, I am waiting for thee, / The Casement is shut, but it opens quite free, / In the dusk of the evening I hope you won't see, / What is plain to the World as well as to me.' Scalloped and embossed border. Mid 19th century. 7.3″ x 4.7″. 14.159/277.

373. Valentine : hand-painted picture of a closed door. Flap raises to open door and to show dog dressed as man. With verse entitled ' PUPPY DOGS NOT ADMITTED ' which reads : ' Puppy Dogs are not admitted here, / So you had better quickly hook it, / Put on the muzzle my ugly dear / For if you're not a Cur you look it.' Scalloped and embossed border. Mid 19th century. 7.3″ x 4.7″. 14.159/278.

374. Valentine : hand-painted picture of housetop and chimneys. Tab slides to show cat on roof. A verse entitled ' Meet me by Moonlight ' reads : ' Meet me by Moonlight above, / And then I will list to thy love tale, / And we'll wander on house tops alone / Till morning breaks softly and pale.' Scalloped and embossed border. Mid 19th century. 7.3″ x 4.7″. 14.159/279.

375. Valentine : hand-painted picture of garden arch and trees. Flap in the archway opens to show an ass. A verse entitled ' Come to my Bower ' reads : ' Oh ! Come to the Bower I have shaded for you, / Your food shall be Thistles bespangled with dew, / To vary it dear you shall graze on the grass, / My own one, my Neddy, my bonny Jack-ass.' Scalloped and embossed border. Mid 19th century. 7.3″ x 4.7″. 14.159/281.

376. Valentine : showing woman entering horse-drawn bus from behind. The crinoline skirt which is of floral pattern material lifts to reveal hooped frame and underclothes. With verse : ' No doubt you think when out you walk, / And 'long the pavement daily stalk, / You in the fashion shine, / But mounting in the "Bus," I beg / Pray take more care dont show your leg / Thro your monstrous crinoline.' Inscribed *Dean & Son / 103 Ludgate . . .* Mid-19th century. 7.6″ x 4.7″. Donor : Mrs. R. E. Edmund Jones. 30.607/3.

377. Valentine : hand-coloured engraving of two women in a garden. Sliding of tab moves part of the picture thus stimulating water flowing from a watering can. Embossed ' WOOD.' With verse : ' You say your hearts in a flame / And pining away every hour / The very best thing for your pain / is by cooling you well with a shower.' Embossed border. Mid 19th century. From Cardiff. 5.3″ x 3.5″. Donor : Miss Ruth E. St. Leger. 45.104/1. Duplicate 45.104/2.

378. Valentine : hand-coloured wood-cut of a woman holding a dog in her arms. The dog's tail moves when a tab is pulled. With the verse : ' You horrid looking dressed up old maid, / To pair with you I'd be afraid ! Altho you ape the young and fair, / Yourself and dog are a well matched pair / With your croaking voice and Tido's whine—/ You ne'er shall be my Valentine.' Paper lace border. Third quarter 19th century. From Cardiff. 6.9″ x 4.7″. Donor : Miss Ruth E. St. Leger. 45.104/3.

379. Valentine : hand-coloured wood-cut of woman with muff in hand. When a tab is pulled the hand holding the muff moves up and down. With verse : ' You little ugly stuck-up thing ! / With such eyes, nose, mouth and chin, / Your very looks and dress so gay— / Proclaim a Servants holiday !

/ All men of you have had enough ! / You've got your value, that's a 'muff.' Paper lace border. Third quarter 19th century. From Cardiff. 6.9″ x 4.7″. Donor : Miss Ruth E. St. Leger. 45.104/4.

380. Valentine : hand-coloured, showing old woman with shawl and umbrella. Inscription reads : ' Mrs SARREY GAMP, MONTHLY NURSE / NO CONNECTION WITH ANY OTHER SHOP. / *Begs to acquaint Ladies and Gents / has also young People about to be hunighted in oly Marriage that she / will be pleased to wate on them on / the hinteresting accasion has his her duty /. N.B. Please to observe that she his / the honely real Sairey G . . .*' With embossed border and scalloped edge. Mid 19th century. 7.5″ x 4.7″. 14.159/280. [Plate 13].

381. Valentine : paper lace with oblong centre on which paper cut-outs of boiling kettle, clouds of steam (with inscriptions) and tea-cloth have been pasted. Inscribed ' *Songs / Of a Bachelor's Tea Kettle.*' Bouquet of paper flowers conceals manuscript inscription. Embossed ' DOBBS.' c. 1853-73. From Chepstow, Monmouthshire. 7.8″ x 4.9″. Donor : Mrs. Amy Hartland. 33.77/2.

382. Valentine : paper lace with scalloped edge. In a large gap in the centre of the valentine are pasted cut-outs of tulips and birds and a loose cut-out of a butterfly secured by two long threads to the rest of the card. With inscriptions ' *When / is a / Butterfly like a / Kiss ? / When it alights on / Tulips.*' / ' *Ever dear / to me / Your / smiles are / sunshine.*' Embossed ' DOBBS KIDD / & CO.' and watermarked ' J. Whatman / 1860.' From Chepstow, Monmouthshire. 7.6″ x 5.2″. Donor : Mrs. Amy Hartland. 33.77/6.

383. Valentine : card lithograph of man in orator's pose with head enlarged and embossed. Black background with faint outline of table with top-hat, glass of water and posters advertising meetings. With verse : ' *Yes you can spout and you can preach, / But what does all your talking teach, / We know as much when you have done, / As when you that long speech begun.*' Third quarter of 19th century. 6.8″ x 5.3″. 14.159/254. Duplicate 14.159/263.

384. Valentine : card lithograph of monocled man, with head enlarged and embossed, nursing crying baby. Black background with faint outline of a room. With verse : ' *Every man should have his due, / So some kind person thought of you, / Then do not bluster, fume, or fret, / Nor waste your time in vain regret, / The likeness plainly shews you are, / The darling little creature's Pa.*' Third quarter of 19th century. 6.8t x 5.3t. 14.159/255. Duplicate 14.159/259.

385. Valentine : card lithograph of monocled man with head enlarged and embossed. Black background with faint outline of room. With verse : ' *You pompous self conceited man, / So mighty and so wise, / But, Sir, you are a thorough sham, / In decent peoples eyes, / So shut your mouth and learn to try, / A little self humility.*' Third quarter of 19th century. 6.8″ x 5.3″. 14.159/256.

386. Valentine : card lithograph of drunkard, with head embossed and enlarged, clinging to lamp-post. Black background with faint outline of street and approaching policeman. With verse : ' *What, at your tippling tricks again, / Once upon the spree, / Slink home, and hide yourself, for shame, / Such sights are sad to see, / Staggering, Reeling, through the Street, / The Scoff and Jeer of all you meet.*' Third quarter 19th century. 6.8″ x 5.3″. 14.159/258.

387. Valentine : card lithograph of cat with head enlarged and embossed wearing woman's clothes. Black background with faint outline of street pavement. With verse : ' *This is your style to a T | As much like a Cat as can be, | But Puss you will never catch me. | You offer a soft looking paw, | But who grasps it will find I am sure, | It can prove a most treacherous claw.*' Third quarter 19th century. 6.8″ x 5.3″. 14.159/253. Duplicate 14.159/260.

388. Valentine : card lithograph of a weeping widow with head enlarged and embossed. Black background with faint outline of gravestone and of man. With verse : ' *Tired of your lonely state, | Longing for another Mate, | But this fact pray understand, | Men don't like Women second-hand.*' Third quarter 19th century. 6.8″ x 5.3″. 14.159/261.

389. Valentine : card lithograph of woman with head enlarged and embossed. Black background with faint outline of a man and a rider on horseback. With verse : ' *Got up in killing style, | Some Booby to beguile, | But who would care to wed, | Such an empty head, | You are not fit to rule a home. | Since folly claims you for her own.*' Third quarter 19th century. 6.8″ x 5.3″. 14.159/262. Duplicate 14.159/264.

390. Valentine : card lithograph of dog with head enlarged and embossed, wearing man's clothes. Black background with faint outline of street and pedestrians. With verse : ' Well, Mr. Pup, are you loose for a stroll, / You certainly cut a figure most droll, / You are looking so fierce so pert and so funny, / But Puppies are never the men for my money.' Third quarter 19th century. 6.8″ x 5.3″. 14.159/257. Duplicate 19.23/2.

391. Valentine : card lithograph of woman smoking a cigarette. She has a dog by the lead with her right hand and has a riding whip under her left arm. Inscribed ' Such ideas of "Woman's rights" wont suit me / in the mean time.' Last quarter 19th century. 7.7″ x 5.0″. 14.159/265.

392. Valentine : card lithograph of top-hatted man with forked beard. Inscribed ' *Such a display, success is certain.*' Last quarter 19th century. 7.7″ x 5.0″. 14.159/266.

393. Valentine : woodcut showing a man at a bar drinking from a tankard. With verse : ' Beastly pursey, powdered flunkey, / Partly man, but more the monkey, / Here thy tinselled form we view, / A peacock vain, a magpie too, / Bloated beast, we pass thee by, / There are you, and here am I, / Laughing loud and laughing free, / At such a paltry knave as thee.' Manufactured by ' London Lace Paper & Valentine Co., 278 & 279, Strand.' Third quarter 19th century. 8.6″ x 5.3″. Donor : Martin Phillips. 45.150/10.

394. Valentine : woodcut by J. T. Wood, 278 & 279, Strand, London ; hand-coloured, showing pup in man's clothes. With verse : ' You are about as ugly a looking pup, / As e'er eat a cow or a donkey up, / Can you think wretch so stupid a swain, / Will e'er cause a maiden one moment of pain, / No, rather than marry so ugly a dog, / I'd walk to the altar with a lazy old hog.' Third quarter 19th century. 9.5″ x 7.1″. Donor : Martin Phillips. 45.150/11.

395. Valentine : hand-coloured woodcut showing bearded policeman holding a boy by his dress. With verse : ' Brave defender of the civil rule, / No one will think you show yourself a fool, / By letting those escape who can fight or make a noise, / And only grappling women, or little girls and boys.' Third quarter 19th century. 8.5″ x 6.5″. Donor : Martin Phillips. 45.150/12.

396. Valentine : woodcut showing woman on early bicycle and two other cyclists in the background. With verse : ' A pretty thing it is to see, / A lady riding so, / Thus making in the thoroughfare, / A very funny show. / I never thought you were so vain, / As ever to suppose, / That any one now seeing you, / Would for your hand propose.' Manufactured by the ' London Lace Paper & Valentine Co., 278 & 279, Strand.' Third quarter 19th century. Donor : Martin Phillips. 45.150/13.

397. Valentine : printed, showing husband with bit in mouth drawing a one-wheeled carriage in which his wife sits smoking a cigarette and with a whip in her hand. With verse entitled ' *Bicycles Superseded* ' : ' This is how I'll drive you love, / When you are wed to me. / In harness I will keep you tight, / Away from Company. / And I will smoke my cigarette, / While pony you will be.' Early 20th century. 17.5″ x 5.6″. 14.159/284.

398. Valentine : printed, showing woman in early twentieth-century dress. With inscription and verse : ' I love you fust class my own factory lass, / You're my own darling duck of a mate, / And the ring I will buy, and the wedding knot tie, / And give you a kiss on the pate.' ' Don't make a show of yersel ' / goin' home at night jeerin ' / and laughing at the folk.' Early 20th century. 17.4″ x 5.5″. 14.159/285.

399. Valentine : printed, showing smartly dressed man carrying ragged umbrella ; woman in background. With verse entitled ' *Not / To be Caught* ' : ' All your coaxing will not do, / And soothering talk, young fellah, / For I must have a chap that has / A better umbrellah. / And with a bloke like thee, I bet / I'll never get my ribands wet.' Early 20th century. 17.4″ x 5.6″. 14.159/286.

400. Valentine : printed showing caricature of man in bowler hat with tailor's bill in pocket, with verse : ' You really are a dog, you know, / In shoddy clothes and tie ; / But if you pay back all you owe, / The girls won't pass you by.' Early 20th century. 17.5″ x 5.7″. 14.159/287.

401. Valentine : printed, showing maidservant with finger in mouth and brush in hand. With verse : ' Instead of ogling every man / Do get about your work. / To serve your mistress is a plan / You try so hard to shirk.' Early 20th century. 17.7″ x 5.7″. 14.159/288.

402. Valentine : printed, showing butcher sharpening knife. With verse : ' Your chops and your steaks may be good, / it is true, / I'm sure that you'd brook no denial ; / I'd give better weight though if I were / but you ; / Then more folk would give you a trial.' Early 20th century. 17.5″ x 5.6″. 14.159/289.

403. Valentine : printed, showing cook rolling pastry. With verse : ' Did cookie lose her Bobby's heart ? / But cookie's tears must dry, / For Bobby finds young Cupid's dart / Stuck in a Rabbit Pie.' Early 20th century. 17.3″ x 5.6″. 14.159/290.

404. Valentine : showing milkman with yoke and pails. With caption ' FRESH / FROM / THE / PUMP / OO ! ' and verse : ' When going your rounds you really seem / To be gay as the man in the moon ; / I wish your milk were as rich in cream / As your voice is rich in tune.' Early 20th century. 17.3″ x 5.7″. 14.159/291.

405. Valentine : printed, showing dressmaker with dummy labelled ' WAS / 20/- / NOW / 40/- ' ; and hat labelled ' WAS 10/6 / REDUCED / TO / £1.1.0.' with verse : ' The things you make no doubt are nice / For those who buy and wear. / But why stick on a fancy price ? / Just try and be more fair.' Early 20th century. 17.4″ x 5.6″. 14.159/292.

406. Valentine : printed, showing grocer with egg in hand. With verse : ' I will not say your eggs are bad, / No doubt you try to sell 'em, / You sell the folk and make them sad, / For really you can tell 'em ! ' Early 20th century. 17.5″ x 5.6″. 14.159/294.

407. Valentine : printed, showing housewife with brush and pail in her hands. With verse : ' It's no good bewailing the fact, now you're wed, / I thought that your love was a sham, / I've heard people say that you wish you were / dead— / Poor hubby's not married a lamb ! ' Early 20th century. 17.5″ x 5.7″. 14.159/295.

408. Valentine : printed, showing policeman winking and holding his hand out for a tip. With verse : ' Tho' you close one eye to bribery, / It's just as well to know, / You keep the other wide to see / To earn a bob or so.' Early 20th century. 17.3″ x 5.7″. 14.159/296.

409. Valentine : printed, showing spinster, with verse : ' You're fifty years, if you're a / day, / I'd stake my life upon it. / The folk around all grin and say / You ought to wear a bonnet.' Early 20th century. 17.4″ x 5.6″. 14.159/297.

410. Valentine : printed, showing maidservant drinking out of a milk can. With verse : ' When neighbours say the mea- / sure's short, / The cat gets all the blame ; / I think it's time that you were / taught / To have a little shame.' Early 20th century. 17.5″ x 5.7″. 14.159/299.

411. Valentine : printed, showing spinster with cat and parrot. With verse : ' You cannot get a wedding ring, / You hate the men, you say. / But chance, you know, is a fine / thing ; / They will not come your way.' Early 20th century. 17.5″ x 5.7″. 14.159/300.

412. Valentine : printed, showing man with halo and wings. Half-smoked cigarette and broken glass at his feet. With verse : ' I think you are a hypocrite, / Your virtue's all pretence, / For I've heard tell you swear / a bit / When giving Peter's pence.' Early 20th century. 17.4″ x 5.7″. 14.159/302.

413. Valentine : printed, showing man with battered hat and baggy clothes. With verse : ' Your meanness is known to the whole / country round— / The barber I'm sure won't defend it ; / You've got a big store of small coin I'll / be bound. / Why don't you stop hoarding and / spend it ? ' Early 20th century. 17.4″ x 5.6″. 14.159/303. Duplicate 14.159/293.

414. Valentine : printed, showing soldier and woman arm-in-arm. With verse entitled ' SHE LOVED THE BOLD DRAGOON ' : ' There's a dear little girl, who is sobbing and sighing, / For a sweetheart—who perhaps— on the battle field dying, / She gave him her love, they hoped soon to wed, / But duty called for him, no more need be said ! / Well, dear friends, let us hope you and me, You and I, / It will be set right in the sweet by-and-by ! ' Early 20th century. 22.6″ x 8.7″. 14.159/305.

415. Valentine : printed, showing policeman with mug in hand. With inscriptions ' WHERE'S / THAT PIE / COOKIE ? ' ' I FEEL / LIKE / WORK / TO-DAY.' and verse : ' Oh Robert, leave poor cookie be, / She feeds you like a pig, / If you don't stop, I'm sure you'll / bust, / You're really far too big.' Early 20th century. 22.5″ x 8.8″. 14.159/306.

416. Valentine : printed, showing milkman filling his can at a pump. With inscriptions ' THIS IS THE COW.' ' NEW / MILK / DIRECT / FROM / THE COW', and verse : ' Oh ! you are an artful screw, / You clean the pails with water, / But customers don't know that you / Don't drain 'em as you oughter.' Early 20th century. 22.1″ x 8.7″. 14.159/307.

417. Valentine : printed, showing woman with parasol. With inscriptions ' CHARMING AND DIVINE CREATURE ' ; ' GOOD STYLE, I am your Slave / for ever,' ' xxx / Kisses,' and verse : ' To wed you soon I do intend, because you've a stylish / bend, / And dress in lovely style. / You know, I'm sure, I love you well, because you are a / charming belle, / And have a winning smile.' Early 20th century. 22.5″ x 8.8″. 14.159/308.

418. Valentine : printed, showing fishmonger holding his nose with one hand and a fish in the other. With the inscriptions ' WO ! / I'LL HAVE / TO GET / A / GAME / LICENCE.' ' FRESH FISH / ONCE / A YEAR ' / and verse : ' You diddle folks with ease, / And have them on the sly, / Your prices like your stock, / Are getting somewhat high.' Early 20th century. 22.5″ x 8.7″. 14.159/309.

419. Valentine : printed, showing two babies in perambulator. One has broken his feeding-bottle and is trying to take the other's. With inscription ' GURN / ITS MY / TURN,' and verse : ' Your screaming and howling / We wish you would stop it ; / If I were your father, / I swear I should "hop it".' Early 20th century. 22.5″ x 8.8″. 14.159/310.

420. Valentine : printed, showing man and woman standing in punt. With verse : ' To take a boat out on the stream, to you seems very well, / But what the end of it will be is not so hard to tell, / You cannot row a boat for nuts, and foul at ev'ry stroke, / And when you run yourself aground, it seems to you / a joke, / You'd better stop your boating now, before it is too late, / To save yourself and sweetheart from a very dreadful / fate.' Early 20th century. 22.5″ x 8.8″. 14.159/311.

421. Valentine : printed, showing woman on bicycle with large heart, shaded black, in the background. With inscriptions ' AN OUT AND OUT / HANDSOME / BYKIST'. ' NO RESISTING / YOUR CHARMS ' ' MY HEART WILL GET AS BLACK AS THIS IF YOU DO NOT SMILE UPON ME.' With verse : ' My sweet charming girl you're greatly admired, / For your elegant costume and beauty, / And to tell you as much this St. Valentine's / Day, I think most strictly my duty. / But as I am writing I must not forget, / To enclose you my heart, my own dearest pet.' Early 20th century. 22.4″ x 8.9″. 14.159/312.

422. Valentine : printed, showing nursemaid wheeling child in a perambulator. With soldier in background. Inscribed ' DRAT / THE / KID ' ' WHY DID MISSUS GET MARRIED ' ; with verse : ' You love the sweet kid when missus / is near, / Of course it's plain that's sham, / But when the missus has gone I fear, / You rave and curse and d-n.' Early 20th century. 22.7″ x 8.7″. 14.159/313.

423. Valentine : printed, showing honeymoon couple sitting hand-in-hand. In the background are a Bathing machine and a minstrel singing ' Do not / trust him / Gentle maiden /'. With verse : ' Your honeymoon may be a treat, / If no intruders you should meet / But on a newly married pair, / Some make a rule to rudely stare. / If you want comfort take my trip, / And far from all such people skip.' Early 20th century. 22.6″ x 8.8″. 14.159/314.

424. Valentine : printed, showing carpenter sawing wood and with hammer in the other hand. With verse : ' To be Jack of all trades and master of none, / May sometimes appear to be jolly good fun, / But those who employ you don't think it a joke, / When they find they've been sold by such a soft bloke, / You'd better start work on your hard wooden pate, / And sharpen your brain e'er you find it too late.' Early 20th century. 22.5″ x 8.8″. 14.159/315.

425. Valentine : printed showing cricketer being bowled out ; a duck and an umpire in the background. With verse : ' You think you are clever, my fine flannelled fellow, / I think you're a muff all the same, / Just before you go in for your innings you bellow, / That you will of course, save the game / Then you lift up the bat and down goes a peg, / We all know you're safe to make one fine duck's egg.' Early 20th century. 22.4″ x 8.7″. 14.159/316.

426. Valentine : printed, showing man with umbrella. With inscription ' *You're the / Show of the / Place you / 2 penny / halfpenny / beggar /*', and verse : ' You great silly ass, / Get some other young lass, / And should you propose, / You'll get one on the nose.' Early 20th century. 22.5″ x 8.8″. 14.159/317.

427. Valentine : printed, showing a parlour-maid with brush in hand. Inscribed ' Priscilla Prim, Parlour Maid ' With verse : ' Though by no means a coward, I confess I'd / not care / To make love to a girl who says " come if / you dare !" / To the men, one and all, it is "right about, / march !" / Is it true my sweet maid, that you live upon / starch ? ' Early 20th century. 22.4″ x 8.6″. 14.159/318.

428. Valentine : printed, showing man playing tennis and woman with angry expression on the other side of the net. With inscription ' SILLY GOAT ' and verse : ' When you tog yourself up in your cheap fal-de-rals, / And your trousers you brace up and sash 'em, / While you pose for a while, as a treat to your pals, / And the racket you smite and you smash 'em, / And you think that you smash all the hearts of the gals, / For you only play tennis to mash 'em.' Early 20th century. 22.3″ x 8.7″. 14.159/320.

429. Valentine : printed, showing mother nursing child and offering it her finger to suck. With inscriptions ' DIDDUMS / HAVE / A / TOOSEY-WOOSEY / PEG ' ' WASH YER HANDS ' and verse : ' I hope it won't grow up like / Mama or Dad, / Their faces, I'm sure, are / equally bad.' Early 20th century. 22.5″ x 8.6″. 14.159/321.

430. Valentine : printed, showing girl with monocle. With inscription ' *You're / awfully / Pretty* ' ' *None / can / touch your / style* ' ' *You / can play / this toone / on the pianner.*' With music and verses : ' You're a nice little lass, You're just in my / eye, Oh ! I like you first-class. And I'll wed you by'n / bye, So kindly get ready. You're dress a good / fit, To go on our wedding, My own dearest tit. / So ta ta my darling, / Your love I must win, / So I'll meet you to-night with a tip on the chin. / We'll walk in the moonshine, / We'll whisper and coo, / Oh ! yes my own darling, / I love none but you.' Early 20th century. 22.6″ x 8.8″. 14.159/322.

431. Valentine : printed, showing workman with mallet in hand, and machinery in the background. With inscriptions ' MECHANIC / AND ENGINEER' ' You should / practice to stand / straight at / your tinkering ' / and verse : ' Young man, I hope you'll not delay, / But pop the question right away, / Through thick and thin I've stuck to you, / And now you get a decent "screw", / So please pluck up and axe me soon, / To join you in the Honeymoon.' Early 20th century. 22.3″ x 8.7″. 14.159/323.

432. Valentine : printed, showing double-faced man. With verse : ' You're double faced as all can see, / And such as you, I'd scorn to be, / In both your smile or frown 'tis clear, / Danger is always lurking near. / The girl will lead a dreadful life, / Who's fool enough to be your wife.' Early 20th century. 22.5″ x 8.8″. 14.159/324.

433. Valentine : printed, showing man. With inscriptions ' Baboon ! ! ! ' ' I would not / kiss you for anything,' ' You'd like / to be a great / swell / Eh ? ' ' I know you / my dandy 10/6 a / week bloke ' and verse : ' I want a better looking coon, / So take your hook, / my gay baboon ; / You're not my style, you will not do, / So just clear off to your home in the Zoo.' Early 20th century. 22.4″ x 8.7″. 14.159/325.

[Non-Welsh]

434. Valentine : Home-made, consisting of manuscript verses on writing-paper decorated with crude flourishes, one or two small rough drawings of faces and two crudely drawn swastikas. Legend reads : ' Feby 14th 1832 / To . . . Jane /

1st verse
Join Dearest girl with me I pray
and crown my ever faithful love
Nee'r from thee I will ever stray
Each hour my constancy shall prove

2nd verse
Join heart and hand with me sweet maid
Unto my suit attend
Let little Cupid lend his aid
In making you my friend
And thus let all my fears at rest be laid

3rd verse
Ah dearest girl with love for you I pine
No other fair one ever shall be mine
None other have me for her Valentine.'

From Upton Sear, Gloucestershire. 9.5″ x 7.5″. Donor : Col. Lionel V. Evans. 56.25.

435. Valentine : paper lace with scalloped edge. An envelope with paper lace and gilt embossed paper decorations is gummed to the centre of the valentine. This opens to reveal central oval medallion with paper cut-outs of flowers and of Cupid. With inscription ' *I adore thee* ' and couplet : ' Thou gather a wreath from the garden Bowers / And tell the wish of thy heart in flowers.' Small envelope also encloses a sheet of paper lace with addressee's name in handwriting. In original envelope with Chatham address and postmarked ' Chatham / Fe 13 / 1857.' 7.5″ x 4.9″. Donor : Mrs. A. C. Fox. 34.225.

436. Valentine : embossed paper with scalloped edge. Central medallion consists of oval paper lace flap on which coloured paper figures of boy and girl are pasted. On the separately mounted paper lace frame is a coloured paper figure of a man on early bicycle. With inscription ' I DREAM / OF THEE.' In original embossed envelope bearing Jersey address and postmark dated 1874. 4.7" x 3.2". Donor : Mrs. E. Briard. 44.321/4.

437. Valentine : paper lace with cut-outs of cherubs in each corner. Central medallion consists of garland of flowers surrounding ' CUPID'S THERM-OMETER.' Medallion lifts to reveal paper cut-out of man and woman. Third quarter 19th century. 7.0" x 4.8". 17.197/1.

438. Valentine : paper lace with cut-outs of figures and animals ; central oval medallion with cut-out of a posy of flowers. With verse : ' *Love in my heart / Sits smiling, / Life's sweetest hours / Beguiling.*' Third quarter 19th century. 7.0" x 4.7". 17.197/2.

439. Valentine : paper lace with scalloped edge and cut-out flower decorations. Central medallion showing girl holding large flower has a frame of paper lace and narrow blue ribbon separately mounted on hinges. With inscription ' Remember / me.' Third quarter 19th century. 7.0" x 4.5". 17.197/3.

440. Valentine : paper lace with cut-out flowers decorations. Central medallion with separately mounted frame of paper lace shows church surrounded by garland of flowers. Third quarter 19th century. 6.8" x 4.7". 17.197/4.

441. Valentine : paper lace base overlaid by gilded and embossed cut-out of leaves and branches. Central medallion consists of bouquet of flowers with the inscription : ' Be my / guiding / star.' Third quarter 19th century. 7.0" x 4.5". 17.197/5.

442. Valentine : embossed paper. Central medallion showing bouquet of flowers has separately-mounted frame of silver paper lace. With inscription ' TO HOPE IS TO LIVE.' Third quarter 19th century. 7.0" x 4.6". 17.197/6.

443. Valentine : paper lace with central medallion showing thatched roof and window decorated with cut-outs of birds, flowers and leaves. With verse entitled ' HOW TO BUILD A HAPPY HOME ' : ' *Let Integrity be the Architect, / Tidiness the Upholsterer, / Let it be warmed by Affection and / Ventilated by Industry, then with / the blessing of Sunshine from above* / HOME WILL BE HAPPY.' Third quarter 19th century. 7.0" x 4.5". 17.197/7.

444. Valentine : paper lace, with central medallion consisting of cut-out of ferns and flowers. Encircling the medallion is a bouquet of roses in pink embossed paper with paper lace decoration. Third quarter 19th century. 7.0" x 4.6". 17.197/8.

445. Valentine : paper lace partly gilded and decorated with blue ribbon and cut-out flowers. Central medallion showing angel carrying flowers is set in a garland of flowers. The angel and the medallion are both separately mounted by means of paper hinges on a fine net. With inscription : ' Hear a Lover's Lay.' Third quarter 19th century. 6.9" x 4.5". 17.197/9.

446. Valentine : silver paper lace with scalloped edge with medallion consisting of a lithograph of a woman. At the base of the medallion is a bouquet of cut-out flowers on which is gummed a small envelope which opens to reveal the words ' Forget / me not.' Third quarter 19th century. 7.1″ x 4.6″. 17.197/10.

447. Valentine : embossed paper with scalloped edge, overlaid by paper lace frame, separately mounted on paper hinges, central medallion set in frame consists of cut-out showing girl reaping, with a sheaf of corn over one shoulder and sickle in her hand. With inscription ' YOURS / FOR EVER.' Third quarter 19th century. 6.7″ x 4.5″. 17.197/11.

448. Valentine : green paper lace. Central medallion consisting of bouquet set in a garland of flowers has frame of scalloped paper lace separately mounted on paper hinges. With inscription : ' AFFECTION'S OFFER-ING.' Third quarter 19th century. 6.8″ x 4.5″. 17.197/12.

449. Valentine : embossed paper with central medallion showing cherub carrying flowers and a rake. Over this is a frame the same size as the card of paper lace coloured gold and blue and decorated with paper cut-outs of flowers. With inscription : ' *Truth & Love*.' Third quarter 19th century. 5.7″ x 3.9″. 17.197/13.

450. Valentine : embossed paper decorated with gilt and cut-outs of flowers. A central bouquet has the inscription : ' TRUE LOVE CAN NEVER PASS AWAY.' Third quarter 19th century. 5.5″ x 3.6″. 17.197/14.

451. Valentine : embossed paper overlaid by a separately-mounted paper lace frame for the central medallion which depicts king-fisher against back-ground of flowers. With inscription : ' I ADORE / THEE.' Third quarter 19th century. 5.5″ x 3.7″. 17.197/15.

452. Valentine : plain paper lace overlaid by separately-mounted silver paper lace frame with cut-outs. Paper cut-out of bird and flowers separately mounted within the frame. With inscription : ' I love you.' Third quarter 19th century. 4.6″ x 3.5″. 17.197/16.

453. Valentine : embossed paper with scalloped edge. Central medallion consists of oval piece of glass mirror partly covered by paper lace. Card decorated with cut-outs and artificial leaves. With inscription : ' THE MESSAGE / OF LOVE ' and couplet : ' Believe in me dear Valentine, / My heart is ever only thine.' Third quarter 19th century. 5.0″ x 3.5″. 17.197/17.

454. Valentine : embossed paper decorated with paper cut-outs of flowers and with central medallion showing cupid's bow and sheath of arrows and same flowers. Separately-mounted frame of silver paper lace. With inscription : ' True Lover's / offering.' Third quarter 19th century. 3.6″ x 2.5″. 17.197/18.

455. Valentine : embossed paper lace mounted on a folded card ; with a litho-graph of Cupid as a medallion. The latter is encircled by a separately-mounted frame of gilded paper lace. With inscription ' Truth ' on a posy of cut-out flowers. Inside the card is the verse : ' To the Absent ' : ' Do you know that the air / Everywhere, / Is filled with prayer / For you today ? / Heaven is near, / And God can hear, / Though you are far away, / H.R.R.' On the back is written ' My darling Tatty.' Third quarter 19th century. 6.4″ x 4.3″. Donor : Miss G. Gordon-Lee. 20.219/1.

456. Valentine : blue and gold paper lace overlaid by garland of gauze leaves
which acts as frame for medallion consisting of paper cut-outs of cupid's
bow and arrow, cherub, and flowers, mounted on silk base. With inscription : ' I / LOVE THEE DEARLY,' and, on the sheet pasted in the
valentine, six manuscript verses entitled 'Well I love thee, O my child ! '
(' From "Pictorial Keepsake" '). Third quarter 19th century. 7.0″ x 4.6″.
Donor : Miss G. Gordon-Lee. 20.219/2.

457. Valentine : mounted in box. An oblong velvet pad with gilt paper decoration and invitation forget-me-nots has an oval medallion with verse
entitled ' LOVE.' 'That / saucy little / cupid—Hath / fired a shaft at me ; /
He did it through thy / eyes, love.—When last I / gaz'd on thee.—My
heart / is deeply wounded,— / On me you've laid a / spell,—Then pity /
take on me, love, / None else can / make me / well.' The pad which lies
in a narrow frame of braid opens to show verse entitled ' *Love's Fancy* ' :
' LINGERING in love's fancy bowers, / I form sweet wreaths with
memory's / flowers. / One spotless bud may whisper / well, / My hopes
for thee are "Immortelle", May joys so spring of lasting hue, / That life's
bright dreams shall be / e'en true.' Box edged with paper lace. Late
19th century. Bought in Commercial Road, London. 6.0″ x 4.8″ x 5″.
19.23/20.

458. Valentine : mounted in box. Fringed oblong folded card in centre of box
has on it artificial flower and leaves with gilt decoration and lettering ;
inscribed ' *A Tribute of Love* '. Card opens to show verse entitled ' LOVE '.
' O Lassie wilt thou not / consent / To be my own / So sweet a flower
was never / Meant / To bloom alone.' Box edged with paper lace. Late
19th century. Bought in Commercial Road, London, 1913. 6.0″ x 4.8″ x
5″. 19.23/21.

459. Valentine : mounted in box. Oblong folded card with triangular-shaped
velvet pad and frame of woollen cord. On the pad is a bouquet of artificial
flowers labelled ' *A tribute / of affection* '. Card opens to show verse entitled ' TOKEN ' : ' Send me some little token, / However small it be, /
A faded flower I'd treasure love, / If it but came from thee. / Do send
me quickly some love token, / Or my poor heart will soon be broken.'
Box edged with paper lace. Late 19th century. Bought in Commercial
Road, London, in 1913. 6.0″ x 4.8″ x .5″. 19.23-22.

460. Valentine : mounted in box. A fringed oblong folded card covered with
padded velvet is decorated by an artificial flower-bouquet, a strip of
gilded paper and a cut-out showing hand holding bouquet of flowers.
Inscribed ' *Yours / always* '. Card opens to show verse entitled ' LOVE '.
' O Lassie, wilt thou not / consent / to be my own / So sweet a flower was
never / meant / to bloom alone '. Box edged with paper lace. Late 19th
century. Bought in Commercial Road, London, in 1913. 6.0″ x 4.8″ x .5″.
19.23/24. *Duplicate* 19.23/23.

461. Valentine : mounted in box. Oblong folded card framed by cord is decorated with padded velvet and two artificial flowers ; it is inscribed ' *A
Tribute of Love* ' in gilt lettering. Card opens to show verse entitled
' To my dear one '. ' 'Tis but an old chord sounds / again, / The heart's
warm echoes sweet / refrain. / In earnest, truest tones that tell, / Incense
from friendship's deepest / well, / May perfumed zephyrs, light and /
free, / Cast love and gladness over thee.' Late 19th century. Bought in
Commercial Road, London, in 1913. 6.0″ x 4.8″ x .5″. 19.23/25.

462. Valentine : hand-painted picture of milliner's assistant sitting with dummy head on her knee. Man in top-hat stands at the window. Tab operates woman's head and right hand. With verse : ' A Milliner's must be a dreary trade, / Such a fate I should quite bemoan / For every day you are stitching away / On finery not your own, / For a very small pay you give all your time / To making the Noddles of others fine.' Scalloped and embossed border. Mid 19th century. 7.0″ x 4.4″. 19.23/7.

463. Valentine : hand-painted picture of man singing in his church pew. Tab slides to change expression of his eyes. With verses : ' The Saint like look you cunningly wear, / A look which is all propriety, / With sensible girls will never pass, / While your words are but mag-piety. / The horrible row you in Chapel make, / For your voice like your head is cracked / Is one, which the girls have all agreed, should be put down by "Bass's Act".' Scalloped and embossed border. Mid-19th century. 7.6″ x 4.8″. 19.23/8.

464. Valentine : card lithograph of woman with exaggerated nose peering in looking-glass. Black background. Inscribed ' HAMLET ' and ' LET HER PAINT AN INCH THICK TO THIS (FAVOUR) SHE MUST COME '. Third quarter 19th century. 7.0″ x 4.7″. 19.23/1.

465. Valentine : lithograph, hand-coloured, showing caricature of bearded man standing with stick in one hand and top-hat in the other. With verse : ' *Not all your powder, plush and gold, / Will make you—if the truth be told—/ Other than a vulgar flunkey, / One part man, and three parts monkey.*' Third quarter 19th century. 7.3″ x 4.6″. 19.23/3.

466. Valentine : lithograph, hand-coloured, showing snake in man's clothing with two women in the background. Part of snake's body is separately mounted on folded flaps. With verse : ' *I'm not attracted by your glitter. / For well I know how very bitter / My life would be, if I should take. / You for my spouse, a rattlesnake / Oh no, I'd not accept the ring, / Or evermore 'twould prove a sting.*' Last quarter 19th century. 7.6″ x 4.6″. 19.23/4.

467. Valentine : lithograph, hand-coloured, showing elephant in male clothing at a dance. Upper part of elephant's body is separately mounted on folded flaps. With verse : ' *As clumsy as an Elephant / When you aim at dancing / Enough to make one crack their sides / To see your awkward prancing. / I'm sure that animals like you / Are fitter inmates for the Zoo*'. Last quarter 19th century. 7.5″ x 4.6″. 19.23/5.

468. Valentine : lithograph, hand-coloured, showing dog in coachman's uniform. The upper part of his body is separately mounted on folded flaps. With verse : ' *Most noble Pug, arrayed in state, / Perched aloft so high and great, / You look just like, so I've heard said, / Some poor old dog that's over fed. / I hope you're sober, for if not, / You'll very soon upset the lot.*' Last quarter 19th century. 7.6″ x 4.6″. 19.23/6.

469. Valentine : woodcut by Mark & Sons, London, hand coloured ; showing butcher kneeling and offering a heart to maid behind railings of a house. With verse : ' My Butcher dont cast at me such sheeps Eyes, / Oh look at my blushes and hear my deep sighs, / Just look at the beauty in every feature, / Of your handsome face, you dear killing creature, / Oh have you the pluck to offer your heart, / I cant be a Liver, if we two must part, / So make a Joint of me so fine, / My greasy looking Valentine.' Third quarter 19th century. 9.7″ x 7.3″. 19.23/9.

470. Valentine : woodcut by Marks & Sons, London, hand-coloured, showing coachman with whip in hand. With verse : ' A bloated tartar thou dost seem ! / God help the maid that marries thee, / With horrid spur and bit I ween ; / Your wife would ever driven be, / Pray bridle those love thoughts of thine, / For I'll never be thy Valentine.' Third quarter 19th century. 9.7″ x 7.3″. 19.23/10.

471. Valentine : woodcut by Marks & Sons, London ; hand-coloured ; showing ploughman in smock sitting on fence with knife in one hand and bread in the other. With verse entitled ' PLOUGHMAN '. ' My Country Bumpkin in your smock, / You seem to me a jolly cock, / Your mouth is like a tunnel wide, / With rows of tombstones set inside, / Your hair is red as any fire, / Your spindle shanks I can't admire, / Ah, no my turnip-headed friend, / With you my days I'd never end.' Third quarter 19th century. 9.7″ x 7.3″. 19.23/11.

472. Valentine : woodcut by Marks & Sons, London, hand-coloured, showing groom leaning against fence. With verse : ' When your not riding out so gay, / And charming as you think, / Pray mind, sweet groom your oats and hay, / And give your horses drink. / But never dream of marriage joys, / With such a frightful face, / You ugliest of stableboys, / The stable is your place.' Third quarter 19th century. 9.7″ x 7.3″. 19.23/12.

473. Valentine : woodcut by Marks & Sons, London, hand-coloured, showing man with top-hat and monocle. With verse entitled ' SWELL '. ' Jumping dancing Barber's Clerk, / You think you are a gay young spark, / With little coat and trousers tight, / You are quite an ugly sight. / In fact you ugly little snob, / You on your back spend every bob, / Some other girl that is quite silly, / May have you, you stupid billy.' Third quarter of 19th century. 9.7″ x 7.3″. 19.23/13.

474. Valentine : woodcut by Marks & Sons, London, hand-coloured, showing man with antler's horns sprouting from his head raising his hands in surprise as he sees himself in the looking glass. With verses : ' Poor fool, you lead a life called gay, / But you don't know what's doing when your away ; / But now you well may look shame faced, / When a pair of horns your head has graced. / To have you would be no great catch, / The poorest woman you would not match, / But no ! don't think those horns of thine, / Could ever sprout on one of mine.' Third quarter 19th century. 9.7″ x 7.3″. 19.23/14.

475. Valentine : woodcut by Marks & Sons, London, hand-coloured, showing widow with inscription ' TO BE LET ' on bonnet. She exclaims ' *Dear soul ! I cannot forget him / although he has been Dead a month / come next Saturday a-week* ! ' With verse : ' Poor widow wooding for the loss, / Of one you'll ne'er forget / And yet the thought my minds will cross, / That you are to be Let, / But in you no charm I see, / And therefore frankly own / That all the chance you have with me, / Is to be let alone.' Third quarter 19th century. 9.7″ x 7.3″. 19.23/15.

476. Valentine : woodcut by Marks and Sons, London, hand-coloured, showing dairy maid using a plunger-churn. With verse entitled : ' DAIRY MAID '. ' O Dolly, Dearest Dairy Maid, / To wed you I would be afraid, / But there you're giving such a leer, / It almost churns my heart my dear. / To see you churning at that churn, / And legs with such a graceful turn, / I'm sure my dear, my heart you'd win, / But still you're rather short of tin.' Third quarter 19th century. 9.7″ x 7.3″. 19.23/16.

477. Valentine : woodcut by S. Marks & Sons, London, hand-coloured, showing charwoman with valentine depicting heart pierced by Cupid's arrow in one hand and mop in the other. With inscription ' *O Crikey aint I got one non and a* / *good un too* ' and verse : ' Lovely squeeze mop hear my sighs, / Think of the woes which I endure, / My heart before you bleeding lies, / 'Tis you alone the wound can cure, / Oh when I gaze upon thy face, / And think of all thy charms divine, / All other thoughts to thee give place, / Now wont you be my Valentine.' Third quarter 19th century. 9.7″ x 7.3″. 19.23/17.

478. Valentine : woodcut by Marks & Sons, London, hand-coloured, showing cook with ladle in one hand and saucepan lid in the other. With verse : ' My dear Miss Cook, you are a buxom dame, / Such a sweetmeat place for you is a shame ! / Though the big drops roll on your fat face, / I cannot at all your beauty trace ; / Your stout dumpy figure and full behind, / The men ought to win, if they were not blind- / To add to your grace just drink some more gin, / Some other Valentine to try to take in.' Third quarter 19th century. 9.7″ x 7.3″. 19.23/18.

479. Valentine : woodcut by Marks & Sons, London, hand-coloured, showing milkmaid with yoke carrying two pails labelled ' SHEEPS BRAINS ' and ' SIZE / 8 / CHALK'. With verse : ' New milk from the cow-w-w-w ! / In a shrilled tone you daily yell, / But many people loudly vow / It is not only milk you sell, / But sheep's brains, size, and nice white chalk / which form at least one half your milk. / No, water forms one half of that I vow, / Then cease to cry milk from the cow.' Third quarter 19th century. 9.7″ x 7.3″. 19.23/19.

MARRIAGE

480. Bidding Letter : inscribed ' *August 25, 1798.* / *Having lately entered the Matrimonial* / *State, we are encouraged by our Friends to make* / *a Bidding on the Occasion, on Thursday, the 13th* / *Day of September next, at the Dwelling-House* / *of Daniel Thomas, (the young Woman's Father)* / *called Iscoed-Mill, in the Parish of St. Ish-* / *mael, at which Place we humbly solicit the Favor* / *of your good om- / pany ; and whatever Donation you* / *may then be disposed to bestow on us, will be* / *grate- / fully received, and cheerfully repaid, whenever de- / manded on the like Occasion, by* / *Your most humble Servants,* / *Ebenezer Jones,* / *Mary Jones.* / The young Man's Grandmother, and young Woman's / Father and Mother, desire that all Gifts of the above Na- / ture, due to them, may be returned to the young Couple / on the said Day, and will be thankful for all Favors con- / ferred on them.—The young man's Uncle (*David Thomas* / of *Iscoed Ucha*') and young Woman's Sisters, who will also be / thankful for any Favors conferred on the young Couple.' Folded and addressed in handwriting ' R. M. Philipps Esq.' From St. Ishmael, Carmarthenshire. 7.3″ x 5.8″. Donor : L. C. Bickerton. 57.179. [Plate 14].

481. Bidding Letter : inscribed ' *February* 18*th* 1804 / *A*s we intend to enter the Matrimonial State on *Fri-* / *day* the 9th Day of *March* next, we purpose to make a BID- / DIGN (sic) on the Occasion the same day, for the young Man at his / Mother's House, called *Cwm-y-Gerwn* in the Parish of *Llan-* / *deilo-fawr*, and for the young Woman at her Father's House, / called *Plas Bach*, in the Parish of *Llanvihangel-Aberbythych*, when and where the favor of your good Company is humbly / solicited, and whatever Donation you'll be pleased to confer / on us then, will be gratefully received, and cheerfully repaid / on a similar Occasion, by / *Your humble Servants,* /

Thomas Lloyd, | Mary William. | The young Man's Mother, desires that all Gifts of the above Na- / ture due to her, may be returned to the young Man on the above / Day, and will be thankful with the young Man's Brother and / Sister-in-law (William and Mary Lloyd) and Brother-in-law and / Sister (Evan and Anne Harries) for any additional Favors bestow- / ed on him.—Also the young Woman's Father, Mother, Brother / John, and his Cousin (William Williams) and his wife, desire / that all Gifts of the above Nature due to them, may be returned / to the young Woman on the above Day, and will be thankful / with her Brother William and his wife for any additional Favors / bestowed on her /. J. Evans Printer, *Carmarthen.*' From Llandeilo, Carmarthenshire. 7.0″ x 6.0″. Donor : W. H. Ackland. 31.108/2.

482. Bidding Letter : inscribed ' October 9, 1820. / *A*s we have lately entered the *M*ATRIMONIAL / *S*TATE, we are encouraged by our friends to make a / BIDDING on the occasion, on *W*EDNESDAY, the 25th / Day of *O*CTOBER instant, at our Dwelling-House, called / *G*LANDUWLAS, near *L*AMPETER *P*ONT-*S*TEPHEN, in the / County of *C*ARDIGAN ; at which place the favor of your / good company is humbly solicited ; and whatever do- / nation you may be pleased to bestow on us then, / will be thankfully received, warmly acknowledged, / and cheerfully repaid, whenever called for on the like / occasion, by / Your obedient humble servants, / THOMAS THOMAS. / MARGARET THOMAS, / (Late Davies.) / *₊* The young man's father and mother (David and Rachel / Thomas, Pontfane, Kellan,) and brothers, (John and Evan Thomas) / desire that all gifts of the above nature, due to them, be re- / turned on / the above day, and will be thankful, together with his brothers and / sisters, for all favors granted.—Also, the young woman's father and mother, (David and Martha Davies, Lampeter Mill,) and her brothers / David and Joshua Davies,) desire that all gifts of the above nature, due / to them, be returned on the above day, and will be thankful for all fa- / vors granted. / J. EVANS, PRINTER, CARMARTHEN.' With decorative border. The letter was folded and addressed ' To / Miss Elizabeth Godsall, / Penegillivour / Near Newcastl.' From Lampeter, Cards. 7.8″ x 6.0″. Donor : P. E. Poel. 39.484.

483. Bidding Letter : inscribed ' *A*ugust 4, 1822. / *A*s we have lately entered the *M*ATRIMONIAL *S*TATE, / we are encouraged by our Friends to make a BIDDING / on the occasion, on *T*UESDAY, the 20th Day of *A*ugust in- / stant, at the *S*HEAF, in *B*RIDGE-*S*TREET, *C*ARMAR-THEN ; at / which time and place the Favour of your good and / agreeable company is most respectfully solicited, and / whatever Donation you may be pleased to confer on either / of us then, will be thankfully re-received, warmly acknow- / ledged, and cheerfully repaid, whenever called for on a / similar occasion, / By your obedient humble Servants, / DAVID WILLIAMS, / (*Mariner*) / CHARLOTTE WILLIAMS, / (*Late Robinson, at Capt. Vaughan's.*) / The Young Man's Brother and Sister-in-law (John and Margaret / Williams,) and his Aunt, (Mary Rees,) and Cousins, (Sarah Jones and Eliza- / beth Beynon,) desire that all Gifts of the above Nature due to them, be re- / turned to the Young Man on the above Day, and will be thankful for all ad- / ditional Favours conferred on him.—ALSO, the Young Woman's Mother, / (Mary Robinson) and Brother, (John Robinson,) and Sisters, (Mary Fran- / cis and Elizabeth Harries) and Brother-in-Law and Sister, (David and Rachel / Evans,) desire that all gifts of the above nature, due to them be returned to / the Young Woman on the above Day, and will be thankful for all Favors / granted. / J. EVANS, PRINTER, CARMARTHEN.' With decorative border. From Carmarthen. 7.5″ x 5.7″. Donor : Dorset Natural History & Archaeol. Soc. 47.370.

484. Lantern Slide of Bidding Letter : inscribed ' *Pembrokeshire, October 4th,* 1828. / *A*s we intend to enter the Matrimonial State on *T*UESDAY / the 21st day of *O*CTOBER instant, we purpose to make / a BIDDING on the occasion the same day, at our house, / called the Coach-and-Horses, at Tavernspite, in the Parish / of Lampeter-Velfrey, in the County of Pembroke, when and / where the favour of your good and agreeable company is / most respectfully solicited, and whatever donation you / may be pleased to confer on us then, will be thankfully / received, warmly acknowledged, and cheerfully repaid / whenever called for on a similar occasion. / By your humble servants, / HENRY THOMAS, / ELIZA-BETH PALMER, / *The Young Man's Father and Mother (Thomas and Jane Thomas of Seven-Acres), with Mr. William Thomas (of Tavernspite), and his / Daughter Jane Griffiths), desire that all gifts of the above nature due / to them, be returned to the Young Man on the above day, and will be thank- / ful for all favours granted.—Also the Young Woman's Father and / Mother, (Francis and Margaret Palmer, of Tycoch) her brothers / (William and Allen Palmer), and her Sister (Mary Palmer), request / that all gifts of the like nature due to them, be returned to the Young / Woman on the said day, and will be thankful for any additional favours / conferred on her. / The Young Woman's Father will repay all gifts con-ferred on the Young Couple on the above day.* / J. P. DAVIES, PRINTER, SPILMAN-STREET, CARMARTHEN.' With a decorative border. From Lampeter-Velfrey, Pembrokeshire. Donor : Arthur L. Leach, M.A., F.G.S. 49.192/1.

485. Bidding Letter : inscribed ' YNYS-Y-GWAELOD, GORPHENAF 1oed, 1829. / *G*AN ein bod yn ddiweddar gwedi myned i'r / Cyflwr Priodasol, annogir ni gan ein cyfeillion i / wneud Neithiawr, ar ddydd Gwener, y 7fed dydd / o Awst nesaf, yn nhy ein hunain, a elwir Blaenduen, / Gwynfe, plwyf, Llangadog ; lle y byddwn yn taer / erfyn am eich cyfeillach siriol ar yr amser, a pha / roddion a chyfraniadau bynag y weloch yn addas / a theilwng ein cynnysgaeddu, a dderbynir yn ddi- / olchgar, ac a delir yn ewyllysgar, bryd bynag y / gelwir, amdanynt ar achos cyffelyb, gan / Eich gweision gostyngedig, / JOHN JONES, / MARGARET JONES, / (Diweddar Rees.) / Dymuna y dyn ieuanc, ynghyd a'i dad a'i fam, John ac / Ann Jones, Onenlas, ar bawb ddychwelyd pob rhoddion o'r natur / uchod sy ddyledus iddynt hwy ar y diwrnod uchod, / a byddant yn ddiolchgar gyda'i frodyr a'i chwaer, William Lewis, a Mary Jones, am bob rhoddion chwanegol.—Hefyd, y wraig, ieu- / anc ynghyd a'i thad a'i mam, Evan ac Elizabeth Rees, Gwaunhên, / Gwynfe, a ddisgwyliant ar bawb ddych-welyd pob rhoddion o'r un- / rhyw natur sy ddyledus iddynt hwy, i'r wraig ieuanc ar y diwrnod / dywededig, a byddant yn ddiolchgar, gyda'i brodyr, Dafydd a / Gruffydd Rees, am bob rhoddion a gyfranir yn chwanegol. / Argraffwyd gan J. JONES, LLYFRWERTHWR, Llan-ymddyfri.' With decorative border. From Llangadog, Carmarthenshire. 6.5″ x 5.4″. Donor : E. Odwyn Jones. 55.121/1.

486. Bidding Letter : inscribed ' *October 14th,* 1834 / HAVING lately entered the Matrimonial State, we / are encouraged by our Friends to make a BIDDING / on the occasion, on Saturday, the 1st of November / next at our own House, called, Ynystredeg, Cwm- / twrch, in the Parish of Ystradgunlais, when and / where the favor of your good and agreeable com- / pany is most humbly solicited, and whatever do- / nation you may be pleased to bestow on us then, / will be thankfully received, warmly acknowledged, / most cheerfully and readily repaid, / whenever called / for on a similar occasion, by / Your most obedient Servants / THOMAS THOMAS, / JANE THOMAS. (Late Griffiths). The Young Man, with his Father and Mother, desire that all Gifts of the above nature, due to them, may be returned on the above / day, and will be thankful for all

favours granted /. Also the young woman, with her Father, desire that all Gifts of the / above nature, due to them, may be returned on the above day, and / will be thankful for all favors conferred. / D. R. AND W. REES, PRINTERS, LLANDOVERY.' With decorative border. From Ystradgynlais, Brecknockshire. 8.5″ x 6.75″. Donor : W. H. Ackland. 31.108/3.

487. Bidding Letter : inscribed ' JANUARY 30, 1836. / *WE* take the liberty of informing you, that we / intend to enter the Matrimonial State on Tuesday, / the 8th day of March next, and are encouraged by our friends to make a *BIDDING* on the occasion, / the same day,—the young man at his father's house / called *BRYNYRODIN*, in the parish of Llan-fihangel- / Aberbythych—and the young woman at her own house / called *PLACENEWYDD*, in the parish of Llanedy ; at / either of which places your company is humbly solicited, and whatever donation you may be pleased to bestow on us then, will be thankfully received, / and cheerfully repaid, whenever called for on a / similar occasion, by / Your most obedient servants, / DAVID CLEAVER, / MARY EVANS. / The young man, with his father and mother (William and Sarah Cleaver) desire that all debts of the above nature, / due to them, be returned to the young man on the said day, / And will be thankful together, with his brother (William Clea- / ver, Llandilo), for all favors granted. / The young woman, with her mother (Sarah Evans, Erw- / wastadfach, Llanedy), and her brothers and sisters (John Evans, Gellywrenisaf, Llangyfelach,—William Evans, Gellygeidrym,—David Evans, Place-newydd,—Evan, Sarah, & Margaret Evans, / Erw-wastadfach), desire that all debts of the above nature due / to them, be returned to the young woman on the said day, and / will be thankful together, for all favors granted. / No money will be received on the following Sunday. / Gold wedding Rings Sold by / T. AND H. WILLIAMS, PRINTERS, LLAN-DILO.' With decorative border,   From Llanfihangel-Aberbythych, Carmarthenshire. 7.3″ x 6.2″. 50.333/9.

488. Bidding Letter : inscribed ' JANUARY 2, 1837. / *WE* take the liberty of informing you, that we / intend to enter the Matrimonial State on Friday, / the 3rd day of February next, and are encouraged / by our friends to make a *BIDDING* on the occasion, / the same day, at our own house, near Capel-Gwinfe, / in the parish of Llangadock ; when and where / the favor of your good and agreeable company / is humbly solicited, and whatever donation you may / be pleased to bestow on us then, will be thankfully / received, and cheerfully repaid, whenever called for / on a similar occasion. / By your humble servants, / JONAH REES, / MARY COSLET. / The young man, with his father and mother (Evan and / Elizabeth Rees), desire that all debts of the above nature, due / to them, be returned to the young man on the said day, and / will be thankful together, with his brothers and sister (David, / Griffith, and Anne Rees), for all favours granted. / The young woman, with her sister (Sarah Coslet), desire / that all debts of the above nature, due to them, be returned to / the young woman on the said day, and will be thankful together, / for all favors granted. / Gold Wedding Rings sold by / T. & H. WILLIAMS, PRINTERS, LLANDILO.' With decorative border. From Llangadog, Carmarthenshire. 7.4″ x 6.1″. Donor : E. Odwyn Jones. 55.121/2.

489. Bidding letter : inscribed ' PENYBONT, APRIL 29, 1839. / BEING betrothed to each other, we design to ratify the / plighted vow by entering under the sanction of Wedlock ; and as a prevalent custom exists from time unmemorial amongst / *Plant y Cymry* of making a BIDDING on the

occurrence of a / homogeneal occasion, we have a tendency to the manners of the / *oulden tyme*, and incited by friends as well as relatives to do the / same, avail ourselves of this suitableness of circumstance of / humbly inviting your agreeable and pleasing presence on the / 20th day of May next, (being Whit-Monday), at the young / man's father's house, called PENYBONT, near the town of / Llangadock ; and whatever your propensities then feel to grant, / will meet with an acceptance of the most grateful, with an ac- / knowledgement of the most warmly, carefully registered, and / retaliated with promptitude and alacrity whenever an occurrence of a similar nature presents itself, by / your most obedient Servants. / DAVID JEFFREYS, / MARY JONES. / The young man, with his father and mother (Jeffrey and Mary / Jeffreys), in concert with his brother and sister (Owen and Sarah Jeffreys), make their claims in his favor, on all whom they have at any time befriended / in a similar circumstance and that the same may be returned to the young / man on the above day, and will express then gratitude for all additional / gifts. / Also, the young woman, with her mother (Margaret Jones, of Llansad- / wrn), make their claims in her behalf on all whom they have befriended in / a similar occasion and will be thankful together, with Mrs. Davies, of / Penybont, for the bestowment of all kindnesses conferred on the young / woman on the said day. / *Gold Wedding Rings Sold by* / T. AND E. WILLIAMS, PRINTERS, LLANDILO.' With decorative border. From Llangadog, Carmarthenshire. 8.25″ x 6.25″. Donor : Miss Clara Martin. 36.644.

490. Bidding Letter : inscribed ' CARMARTHEN, MAY 5TH, 1847. / As we intend to enter the *MATRIMONIAL STATE* on / *TUESDAY*, the 25th day of *MAY* inst., we are encouraged / by our Friends to make a BIDDING on the occasion / the same day, at the Young Woman's Father's House, / called *PENROSE COTTAGE*, when and where the favour / of your good and agreeable company is humbly solicited, / and whatever donation you may be pleased to confer on / us then will be thankfully received, warmly acknowledged, / and cheerfully repaid whenever called for on a similar / occasion, / By your most obedient servants, / PHILIP REYNOLDS LEWIS, / BUTCHER, / ELIZABETH DAVIES, / The young Man's Father (David Lewis), his Brother / and Sister-in-law (John and Anne Lewis), his Nephew / (John Lewis), his Brothers (David and Thomas Lewis,) / and his Brother-in-law and Sister (John and Jane Evans), desire that all gifts of the above nature, due to them, be / returned to the Young man on the above day, and will / be thankful for additional favours granted. / The Young Woman's Father and Mother (Thomas and / Anne Davies), her Brothers (John, David, and Henry / Davies), and her Brothers-in-law and Sisters (John and / Mary Harries, and David and Anne James), desire that / all gifts of the above nature due to them be returned to / the Young Woman on the above day, and will be thank- / ful for all favours conferred on her. / W. SPURRELL, PRINTER, CARMARTHEN.' With decorative border. Addressed on back to ' Mr. W. Warren, / King Street.' From Carmarthen. 7.2″ x 4.5″. Donor : The Museum & Art Gallery of the City and County of Bristol. 33.255/1.

491. Bidding Letter : inscribed ' CARMARTHENSHIRE, SEPTEMBER 8th, 1853. / As we intend to enter the Matrimonial State, on Monday, the / 12th day of September next, we are encouraged by our Friends / to make a Bidding on the occasion, the same day, at our own / House in Dame-Street ; at which time and place the favour of / your good and agreeable company is most humbly solicited, and / whatever donation you may be pleased to confer upon us on that / day will be thankfully received,

warmly acknowledged, and / cheerfully repaid whenever called for on a similar occasion. / By your most obedient Servants, / DAVID JONES, / MARIA THOMAS. / The Young Man, his Father and Mother (David and Jane / Jones), and his Sisters (Jane and Mary), desire that all gifts of the / above nature due to them be returned to the Young Man on the said day, and will be thankful, for all favours granted. / The Young Woman, her Father and Mother (William and / Martha Thomas), her Brothers (Henry, John, William and Griffith), and her Aunt (Anne Thomas), desire that all gifts of / the above nature due to them be returned to the Young Woman / on the said day and will be thankful, for all favours granted. / Printed by William SPURRELL, King-street, Carmarthen.' With decorative border ; from Carmarthen. 8.2″ x 5.5″. Donor : The Museum and Art Gallery of the City and County of Bristol. 33.255/2.

492. Bidding Letter : inscribed ' CARMARTHEN, May 30th, 1857. / As we intend to enter the Matrimonial State on / Tuesday, the 23rd day of June next, we are encouraged by our friends to make a BIDDING on / the occasion of the same day, at the Sign of the OLD / PLOUGH, situate in Lammass St., in the said Town ; / when and where the favours of your good company / is humbly solicited, and whatever Donation you may / be pleased to confer on us then, will be thankfully / received, warmly acknowledged, & cheerfully repaid / whenever called for on a similar occasion, / By your most obedient Servants, / JOHN JONES, / ELIZA MACKINTOSH, / The Young Man, with his Mother, Elizabeth Jones, his Sister, / Anne Jones, and his Brother -in-law and Sister, Anthony and / Elizabeth Fisher, desire that all Gifts of the above nature, due to / them, may be returned to the Young Man on the above day, and / will be thankful for all favors granted. / Also, the Young Woman, with her Father and Mother, Henry / Jones, Cabinet-Maker, Water Street, & wife, and her Sister, Mrs. / Adams, Old Plough, desire that all Gifts of the above nature, due / to them, may be returned to the Young Woman on the above day, / And will be thankful for all favors granted. / W. THOMAS, PRINTER, CARMARTHEN.' / With decorative border, From Carmarthen. 7.1″ x 4.5″. Donor : The Museum and Art Gallery of the City and County of Bristol. 33.255/3.

493. Bidding Letter : inscribed : ' Carmarthenshire, February, 1885. / DEAR FRIENDS,— / AS we entered the MATRIMONIAL / STATE, on Wednesday, February 4th, 1885, we are / encouraged by our friends to make a BIDDING on / Friday, 13th February, 1885, at the young man's / house, in the Village of Dryslwyn, when and where / the favour of your good and agreeable company is / most humbly solicited, and whatever donation you / may be pleased to bestow upon us then, will be / thankfully received, warmly acknowledged, and cheerfully repaid, whenever called for on a similar / cocasion, / By your most obedient Servants, / HENRY JONES, / THIRSA DAVIES / The Young Man, together with his Brothers, John and Thomas, and his Sister, Ann Davies, desire that all Bidding / Debts due to them, be returned to him on the above day, and / will be thankful for all additional fabours conferred. / Also the young woman desires that all Bidding Debts due / to her be returned on the above day, and will be thankful for / all additional favours granted. / J. LOCKYER, PRINTER AND STATIONER, LLANDILO.' With decorative border. From Dryslwyn. Carmarthenshire. 7.1″ x 4.9″. Donor : J. R. Gabriel, M.A., 31.347.

494. Bidding Letter : inscribed ' LOWLAND, LLANARTHNEY, / MAWRTH
Y 15FED, 1888. / Gan ein bod yn bwriadu myned i'r ystad briodasol
dydd / Sadwrn, y 7fed o Ebrill, 1888, anogir ni gan ein cyfeillion i wneud /
NEITHIOR ar y cyfryw amgylchiad : y mab ieuanc yn nhy ei fam, a /
elwir Gelliglyd, yn Mhlwyf Llanon, Sir Gaerfyrddin, a'r ferch ieuanc /
yn nhy ei thad a'i mam, a elwir Lowland, Plwyf Llanarthney, Sir / Gaerfyrddin ; a pha roddion bynag a weloch fod yn dda i roddi y / pryd hwnw,
a dderbynir yn llawen, pa bryd bynag y gelwir am danynt, ar am- /
gylchiad cyffelyb, gan / yr eiddoch yn ffyddlawn, / JACOB EVANS, /
MARY REES. / Dymuna y mab ieuanc, yng nghyd a'i fam, Mary
Evans, a'i / frodyr, Daniel a Robert Evans, ar i bob rhoddion o'r natur
uchod, / dyledus iddynt hwy, gael eu talu i'r mab ieuanc ar y dydd
crybwyll- / edig ; a pha roddion bynag a roddir yn ychwanegol a dder-
bynnir yn / ddiolchgar, ac a ad-delir yn sicr, mewn dyledus barch, pa
bryd bynnag / y gelwir am danynt mewn amgylchiadau cyffelyb. /
Dymuna y ferch ieuanc hefyd, yng nhyd a'i thad a'i mam, / William a
Maria Rees, a'i brodyr, David a Russell Rees, ar i bob / rhoddion o'r
natur uchod, dyledus iddynt hwythau, gael eu talu i'r / ferch ieuanc ar y
dydd crybwylledig ; a pha roddion bynag a roddir / yn ychwanegol, y
pryd hwnw, a dderbynir yn ddiolchgar, ac a ad- / delir yn sicr mewn
dyledus barch, pa bryd bynag y gelwir am danynt / mewn amgylchiad
cyffelyb.' Framed. From Llanarthni, Carmarthenshire. 8″ x 5″. Donor :
Arthur Mee. 94.151.

495. Bidding Letter : inscribed ' Priodas Gwahodded-igion. / Cymaint a'n
bod yn bwriadu myned i'r / Stâd Priodasol ar Ddydd Sadwrn, Tach.
9fed, / 1901, gwahoddir Pwythion, y rhai a at-delir yn / ddiolchgar
ar y cyfryw amgylchiad. / TOM WILLIAMS, Llandebie. / ELIZABETH
THOMAS, Red Cow. / Bydd Te &c yn y Red Cow ar y dydd nodedig. /
Disgwylir y telir Pwythion dyledus iddynt, / a'u rhieni, a'u brodyr, ar
ddydd y briodas. / *Gwilym Vaughan, Argraffydd, Ammanford.*' From Llandybïe, Carmarthenshire. 8.2″ x 5.2″. Donor : G. O. Williams,B.A. 29.536.

496. Wedding Card : a small oblong glossed card with silver margin and bearing
the name ' Mr. Robert Phillips ' is attached by means of a tinselled wire
decoration to a similar but larger card bearing the name ' Mrs. Robert
Phillips.' Four copies, with two envelopes inscribed ' Edith Thomas '
inside the flap. From Monmouth. Donor : Sir Leonard Twiston Davies.
LL.D., K.B.E., F.S.A. 43.91/2-8.

497. Wedding Card : decorated with embossed ivy leaf design, MW and BR
monograms and dated ' December 29th 1896,' on cover flaps. These lift
up to either side to reveal the inscription ' With / Mr. & Mrs. James
Bertram Russell's / Compliments. / 183 Manchester Road, / Burnley ' in
silver lettering. An arrow is superimposed diagonally over the bride's
surname. In an envelope addressed to ' E. Davies Esq.' (of Rumney,
Monmouthshire). Card 3.25″ x 2.25″, Envelope 4.0″ x 2.5″. Donor : Miss
Mavis Cooke. 55.236/25.

498. Wedding Card : glossed card with monograms ' H.L.E.' and ' J.D.D.' on
the cover flaps. These lift up to either side to reveal the inscription
' With / Mr. & Mrs. John D. Davies' / Kind Regards' in gold lettering.
An arrow is superimposed diagonally over the bride's surname. In
envelope. From Rumney, Monmouthshire. Card 3.3″ x 2.5″, Envelope
3.8″ x 2.6″. Donor : Miss Mavis Cooke. 55.236/26.

DEATH

499. Stockings : pair of white woollen stockings with inscription ' ELIZA
LEWIS ' and decorations worked in scarlet wool. Knitted by donor's
aunt of that name to be worn on her body after death. c. 1850. Knitted
at Esgaironnen, Llanarth, Cardiganshire, with handspun wool from
sheep kept on that farm. Length 24″. Donor : Miss S. Lewis. 41.51/1-2.

500. Memorial Card : in ink, with partly inked drawing of an angel blowing a
trumpet ; with inscription ' In Memory / of / David Thomas / who died
Sept. 18th 1849, / Aged 66 years. / Leaving a wife and child- / ren to
deplore his loss." Mi a ymdrechais ymdrech / dêg, mi a orphenais fy
ngyr- / fa, mi a gedwais y ffydd. Tim / . W. Edwards Lammas St. Carmarthen.' Mounted in frame. Donor : T. H. Thomas, R.C.A. 12.24.
[Plate 15].

501. Memorial Card : with black border. Inscribed ' In Memory of /
THOMAS JOHN KING, ESQ., C.E. / OF KENSINGTON PLACE,
MAINDEE, / NEAR NEWPORT, / Who Died 29th October, 1864, / Aged
38 years. /'. At the bottom of the card is added ' RICHARD B. EVANS,
UNDERTAKER.' 4.5″ x 3.0″. Donors : The Misses Isambard Owen.
51.438/51.

502. Memorial Card : with thick black line framing the following inscription :
' In Affectionate Remembrance / of / MARY ANN TOOGOOD / THE
BELOVED WIFE OF GEORGE WAUGH TOOGOOD, HAYDEN
KNOLL, / Boddington, Gloucester, / AND ELDEST DAUGHTER OF /
THOMAS AND ELDEST DAUGHTER OF / THOMAS AND SARAH
DAVIES, Batslays, Lantwitt Major, Glamorganshire. / Born November
30th, 1813—Died November 25th, 1867, / And was this day interred at
Staverton, Gloucestershire. / Nov. 29th, 1867.' 4.5″ x 3.0″. Donor : Miss
M. E. D. Thomas. 12.211/20.

503. Memorial Card : with black border and embossed outline of urn mounted
on a pedestal on which is inscribed ' In Memory of / WM. H. C. PER-
KINS, ESQ., J.P., / WHO DIED / April 19, 1870. / INTERRED AT
LANTRYDDYD, GLAM.' On the base of the pedestal is embossed
' THY WILL BE DONE ' and, in one corner, ' MANSELL '. From
Peterston-super-Ely, Glamorgan. 4.5″ x 3.0″. Donor : Miss M. E. D.
Thomas. 12.211/6.

504. Memorial Card : with black border and coat-of-arms in colour. Inscribed
' In Affectionate Remembrance of / the Rt. Honble Gertrude Baroness
Dinorben, / Widow of William Lewis Hughes 1st Baron Dinorben, /
Died January 3rd. 1871. Aged 62 years. / BLESSED ARE THE DEAD
WHICH DIE IN THE LORD.' In envelope with black border, and
insignia on back. 8.2″ x 5.4″. Donor : Miss Sydney F. Lloyd. 37.212.

505. Memorial Card : with black border. Inscribed ' In Affectionate Remembrance of / HENRIETTA MARIA PERKINS, / Who died Dec. 28th,
1872, / AGED 93 YEARS. / INTERRED AT LLANTRYTHYD, JAN.
3rd. 1873. " HER END WAS PEACE." From Peterston-super-Ely,
Glamorgan. 4.5″ x 3.0″. Donor : Miss M. E. D. Thomas. 12,211/7.

506. Memorial Card : with black border. Inscribed ' In Affectionate Remem-
brance of / JOHN DAVIES, of Eglwysbrewis, / DEPARTED THIS
LIFE AT PENDOYLON HOUSE, / March the 3rd, 1874, Aged 77 years. /
Interred at Eglwysbrewis, on Monday, March 9th. / ' The Lord gave :

and the Lord hath taken away ; blessed / be the name of the Lord —
Job. i, 21' With hand-written note added : ' Born Jan 23rd.' From
Pendoylan, Glamorgan. 4.5" x 3.1". Donor : Miss M. E. D. Thomas.
12.211/17.

507. Memorial Card : with black border. Inscribed ' In Affectionate Remembrance / OF / *CHARLES GEORGE KING*, / *who departed this life at New-*
port, Mon., / On the 8th October, 1874, / *AGED* 20.' From Newport,
Monmouthshire. 4.5" x 3.0". Donors : The Misses Isambard Owen.
51.438/52.

508. Memorial Card : with black border. Inscribed ' In Affectionate Remembrance / OF / *CATHERINE KING*, / who departed this life at Pwllheli,
On the 22nd October, 1874.' From Pwllheli, Caernarvonshire. 4.5" x
3.0". Donors : The Misses Isambard Owen. 51.438/50.

509. Memorial Card : Welsh, with black border, of the Rev. Robert Ellis,
(Cynddelw). ' Er Cof Hiraethlawn am / (photograph of deceased) /
"*G*WERTHFAWR YN NGOLWG YR *A*RGLWYDD YW / MAR-
WOLAETH EI SAINT."

> "*W*EDI y loes caf dawel hedd,—wedi'r
> "Cyfnewidiad rhyfedd ;
> "Os holir, dyma'r sylwedd,—
> "CYNDDELW'n farw'n ei fedd."

Ganwyd Chwefror 3ydd, 1812. / Bu farw Awst 19eg, 1875. / *Gorphwysa*
yn Mynwent Glyn Ceiriog.' From Glyn Ceiriog, Denbighshire. 4.5" x 3.1".
Donor : Oliver A. Bown. 47.287/2. [Plate 15].

510. Memorial Card : with black border. Inscribed ' In sad Remembrance /OF /
264 MEN AND BOYS / WHO WERE KILLED / *In the Prince of Wales Pit*,
Abercarne, / BY AN EXPLOSION. / ON WEDNESDAY, SEPTEMBER
11th, 1878.' With biblical text and a note of the number of married and
single men and boys and the number of their dependants. From Aber-
carn, Monmouthshire. 4.5" x 2.9". Donor : Miss Helen Barlow. 42.37/1.

511. Memorial Card : with black border. Inscribed ' In Sad Remembrance of /
63 MEN AND BOYS / WHO WERE / KILLED IN THE MIDDLE
PIT, / DINAS COLLIERY, RHONDDA VALLEY, / BY AN EX-
PLOSION, / *On Monday Night, January 13th, 1879*.' followed by a note of
the number of married and signle men and boys and the number of their
dependants. From Dinas, Rhondda, Glamorgan. 4.5" x 2.9". Donor :
Miss Helen Barlow. 42.37/2.

512. Memorial Card : folded card, Welsh, with black border, of the Rev. William
Thomas, (Islwyn), ' Er Cof am / Y Parch. WILLIAM THOMAS,
"Islwyn" / GLYN, YNYSDDU, / YR HWN A FU FARW TACHWEDD
20FED, 1878, / YN 46 MLWYDD OED. / *Claddwyd ef yn mynwent y*
Babell, Tachwedd, 27ain. / Myfi a'i hadgyfodaf ef yn y dydd diweddaf.
— CRIST.' From Ynys-ddu, Sirhowy Valley, Monmouthshire. 4.5" x
3.0". (folded). Donor : Miss E. Ellis Roberts. 50.166/2.

513. Memorial Card : folded card, Welsh, with black border, of the Rev. Daniel
Jenkyns. ' *E*R *C*OF AM Y / Parch. DANIEL JENKYNS, / BABELL, /
Yn (sic) hwn a fu farw Medi 16eg, 1884, / YN 69 MLWYDD OED /
Claddwyd ef yn Mynwent y Babell, Medi 22ain. Ffyddlawn weinidog i
Grist.' From Y Babell, Monmouthshire. 4.5" x 3.0". Donor : Miss E.
Ellis Roberts. 50.166/3.

514. Memorial Card : folded, with silver and black border on each side. Cover has lithographed flowers with scroll inscribed ' In Memoriam '. Inside the cover a text from Revelations xxi, is quoted. Inside back is inscribed ' *IN LOVING MEMORY* / OF SAMUEL FRANKLYN HARRIS, / OF GWENFFRWD, LLANOVER, / WHO DIED ON AUGUST THE 9TH, 1889, / AGED 73 YEARS. / INTERRED AT HANOVER (sic), AUGUST 14th.' On the back is a text from Psalm xc. From Llanover, Monmouthshire. 4.5″ x 3.0″. Donor : Miss Mavis Cooke. 55.236/27.

515. Memorial Card : folded card with black and silver border on outside and silver border inside. Inscribed ' *THY KINGDOM COME.* / In Loving Memory / OF *JOHN H. DAVIES*, / THE OAKS, / Born, November 10th, 1839. Entered his rest, Nov. 11th, 1895. / INTERRED AT NEWLAND CHURCH, GLOS. / *THY WILL BE DONE.*' With Biblical text and quotation from the hymn ' Lead Kindly Light '. In black bordered envelope. From Caerleon, Monmouthshire. Donors : The Family of the late Mrs. F. M. Edmunds. 4.7″ x 2.5″ (folded). 37.37/67.

516. Memorial Card : grey cardboard folder with silver border on each side. Cover inscribed ' In Memoriam '. Inside cover : ' In life beloved, / In death lamented '. Inside back : ' In Affectionate Remembrance of / Thomas Alexander, / *Late of Monkton and Croescade, Glamorganshire, who died / at Glan-yr-afon, Holt, Wilts, March 25th, 1891,* / Aged 67 years. / His end was peace. / INTERRED IN HOLT CHURCHYARD. ' 4.5″ x 2.75″. Donor : Miss M. E. D. Thomas. 12.211/23.

517. Memorial Card : a folded card with black borders. Inscribed ' In LOVING MEMORY OF ELIZABETH, / Widow of the late RICHARD MORRIS, Cwm, Llandinam / who Died on Monday, August 8th, 1904, / AGED 80 YEARS, / Interred in Llandinam Churchyard, August 12th. On the cover is the inscription ' In / Loving / Memory '. Inside the cover is a biblical text. 4.5″ x 3.0″ (folded). Donor : Dr. T. Alwyn Lloyd, F.R.I.B.A. 51.162/4.

518. Memorial Card : folded, with black border on each side. Cover inscribed ' In Memoriam '. Inside the cover is the following verse : ' Then let us stretch our hands in darkness, / And call our loved ones o'er and o'er ; / Some day their arms will close about us, / And the old voices speak once more.' Inside back is inscribed ' In Affectionate Remembrance of / *MARY*, / the beloved wife of Henry Davies, / OF PLASMARL (LATE OF ABERDARE), / WHO DIED DECEMBER 24th, 1906, / AGED 78 YEARS. / Interred at Mynyddbach Chapel, on Saturday, Dec. 29th.' 4.5″ x 3.0″. Donor : Miss Mavis Cooke. 55.236/28.

519. Memorial Card : a folded card with black borders. Inscribed ' In Memory of / MARGARET EVANS / Angel Hotel, Pontneathvaughan. / *Who died Thursday, July 12th, 1906* / Aged 102 years.' With a photograph of the deceased and a biblical text in Welsh. In original black-bordered envelope. From Pontneddfechan, Glamorgan. 4.5″ x 3.0″. (folded). Donor : Mrs. Edmund Jones. 15.84/5.

520. Memorial Card : with black back and a black border decorated with perforations and scalloped edge. Inscribed ' In Affectionate Remembrance of / THOMAS MORRIS / Beloved Husband of Ann Morris, Maldwyn House, Gelli Pentre, / Rhondda-Valley. / *who departed this life, October 21st, 1907,* / AGED 61 YEARS. / *Interred at Llandinam Church ground*, Oct. 25th.' With the following verses :

' A father dear, a friend sincere,
A Kind and tender partner dear,
But now he's gone, left us behind,
The world to try and friends to find.

Farewell my wife and children dear,
For you I have toiled for many a year ;
I have always strove to do my best
And now I have gone to take my rest.'

The name of the undertakers, H. Williams & Son, Ystrad, is also printed. The card folds in three and is embossed in gold on a black background ' In / Loving Memory / With the Family's / Kind Regards.' With a black cord and tassel. 4.4″ x 3.3″ (folded). Donor : Dr. T. Alwyn Lloyd, F.R.I.B.A. 51.162/1.

521. Memorial Card : similar to No. 520 except for the inscription inside which reads :
' When a mother breathes her last farewell,
The stroke means more than words can tell ;
This home seems quite another place,
Without the smile of mother's face.

In Affectionate Remembrance of / Ann Morris, / The beloved wife of the late Thomas Morris, / Dinam House, Bronllwyn, Gelli Pentre / *Who departed this life July 11th, 1920, / Aged 78 years, / And was interred at Llandinam / Church Ground, July 15th.*

A loving mother, true and kind,
She was to us in heart and mind,
A careful one, who loved us well,
When she on earth with us did dwell.'

4.4″ x 3.3″ (folded). Donor : Dr. T. Alwyn Lloyd, F.R.I.B.A. 51.162/2. Duplicate 51.162/3.

522. Handwritten memorial verses, framed. With small ink sketch of angel blowing trumpet. 'Deigryn / ar Farwolaeth / David Griffiths / Myfyriwr yng Ngholeg Athrawol Caerfyrddin, Mab Rees a Mary Griffiths, / Treforis, diweddar o Dafen, ger Llanelli, yr hwn a fu farw Gorphenaf y 3ydd, / 1860 o'r darfodedigaeth, yn 20 mlwydd oed, a chladdwyd ei ran farwol yn mynwent Eglwys Cwmavon / Gorphenaf y 6ed. /

Angau ! angau ! nid oes derfyn
Ar dy weithrediadau di ;
Eto cwympaist hardd blanhigyn
Lawr i'r beddrod tywyll dû . . .

. . . Ninau'n fuan a'i dilynwn,
Ni cheir aros yma'n hir ;
Iesu'n Geidwad oll 'mofynwn,
Uchel alw mae yn wir.

W. Edwards.   1863.   Caerfyrddin.'
From Carmarthen. 19″ x 13½″. Donors : The Misses A. Gower & Olive Jones. 48.118./8.

523. Bidding to a funeral : black-bordered notepaper with the following inscription : ' 95, *Bridgend Road, / Aberkenfig, / June 9th, 1913. / Dear Mr. Thomas / It is with extreme sorrow that we / have to announce the death of my*

loving husband, who passed away on Monday, the | 9th inst., at the above address | The Funeral is to be public for gentlemen, | and will take place on Thursday, June 12th | at 3 p.m., for Llansantffraid Parish Church. | Yours in deep sorrow. | S. A. Jones | and Family.' 7.0″ x 3.5″. Donor : Alderman Sir Illtyd Thomas. 13.171.

524. Mourning Acknowledgement Card : with black border. Inscribed ' Miss Nicholas | Return thanks | to Miss Thomas | for kind enquiries.' The names of the sender and recipient are in hand-writing. Late 19th century; from Monmouth. 4.4″ x 2.9″. Donor : Sir Leonard Twiston Davies, LL.D., K.B.E., F.S.A. 43.91/9.

525. Mourning Acknowledgement Card : with border. With manuscript inscription : ' Mr & Mrs Price / return thanks for | Mr & Mrs Thomas' / kind enquiries.' Late 19th century ; from Rockfield Park, Monmouth. 4.5″ x 2.9″. Donor : Sir Leonard Twiston Davies, LL.D., K.B.E., F.S.A. 43.91/10.

526. Mourning Stationery : two envelopes of similar design. A black band passes diagonally over the top left hand corner of the envelope and is continued both on the back and on the flap where it partly hides a silhouette of a bamboo cane and twigs. Also on the back of the envelope is a representation of a flower in black and white. Late 19th century. 4.7″ x 3.8″. Donor : J. B. Garsed Price (Bequest). 47.81/14-15.

527. Mourning Stationery : two envelopes of similar design. A bamboo cane with twigs is depicted in silhouette on the front of the envelope continuing over the left edge to the back. A small circular medallion with black and white petal decoration is found on the back of the envelope and on the flap a bamboo twig with leaves. Late 19th century. 4.7″ x 3.8″. Donor : J. B. Garsed Price (Bequest). 47.81/11 ; 47.81/16.

528. Mourning Stationery : two sheets of folding notepaper of similar design ; on the front cover is a circular centre medallion, with a silhouette of a branch of a tree. A diagonally-arranged geometrical design in black and white begins near the top right-hand corner of the cover, occupying the lower part of the page, and is continued in the bottom right-hand corner of the back. Late 19th century. 6.9″ x 4.4″ (folded). Donor : J. B. Garsed Price (Bequest). 47.81/19-20.

529. Mourning Stationery : two sheets of folding notepaper with two envelopes to match. Along the fold of the notepaper on the outside and the left edge of the envelope is a black border with a circular medallion having a representation of twigs and leaves in black. The edge of the envelope and of the notepaper (when folded) divides the border and medallion in two. On the flap of the envelopes and in the bottom left-hand corner of the back of the notepaper is another motif consisting of a section of a circle with twig and flower decoration. Late 19th century. Notepaper (folded) 6.9″ x 4.4″. Envelopes 4.7″ x 3.8″. Donor : J. B. Garsed Price (Bequest). 47.81/12-13, 17-18.

530. Mourning Envelope : with black border. With postmark dated 1897 and addressed to Mrs. J. H. Davies, The Willows, Caerleon, Mon. 4.7″ x 3.7″. Donors : The Family of the late Mrs. F. M. Edmunds. 37.37/66.

531. Memorial Shell, with topmost layer removed to reveal the irridescence ; decorated with an engraving of a horn which follows the spiral shape of the shell. There is an engraved representation of a church monument on

which the following is inscribed ' Hic Jacet / Thomas Roberts / quit-nortuus (= qui mortuus ?) Est / Novr 23rd A.S. 1827 / Annos Natus / 44.' There is also a verse : ' A loving husband, and Father dear / Freed from his earthly cares lies slumbering here / A sincere friend, devoid of worldly pride / He liv'd respected, and regretted died.' From Conway, Caernarvonshire. Donor : W. J. Hemp, M.A., F.S.A. 16.39/1.

532. Memorial Shell, similar to No. 531 with inscription ' Hic et Jacet / Catherine Quellyn / Thomas Roberts / uxor / quae orbet Nov. 17th / A.S. 1833 / dictatus suae / 52 ' ; with verse ' A tender Wife a Mother dear / A faithful friend lies burried here / In love she liv'd, in peace she died / Her life was crav'd but God deni'd.' From Conway, Caernarvonshire. Donor : W. J. Hemp, M.A., F.S.A. 16.39/2.

533. Mourning Ring : gold, the outer side of the hoop is divided into five panels (plus bezel) separated from each other by groups of four vertical incisions. With inscription reserved in letters in the metal upon ground of white enamel in the panels : ' [REES] [POWELL] [OB] [17 NOV] [1738].' Formerly in possession of the Lewis family, Greenmeadow, Tongwynlais, Glamorgan. Diam. (outside) .8″. Donor : W. D. Clark. 49.509.

534. Mourning Ring : gold, slender hoop expanding at shoulders ; marquise bezel with an angel appearing to a figure seated by an urn mounted on a pedestal. Inscribed ' HEAVEN / HAS IN / STORE / WHAT / THOU / HAST / LOST.' The following inscription is reserved in letters in the metal on ground of black enamel and forms an oval border in the bezel : ' MARY EDWARDS OB : 29 FEB : 1776. AE 46.' The bezel is covered by glass. On the inner side of the ring are plaited strands of hair covered by glass. The ring is mounted in its original case. From Llansanffraid, Montgomeryshire. Diam. .9″ (outside). Donor : John D. Evans. 51.319/1-2.

535. Mourning Ring : gold, slender hoop expanding at shoulders ; marquise bezel with a figure standing by an urn on a pedestal, and inscription ' NOT LOST BUT GONE BEFORE ', all on a white ground covered by glass and bordered by pearls. Inscription engraved on inner side : ' Sarah / Davies / Ob. 10 Sep. / 1783 / aet 21.' Originally from the family of Davies of Montgomery town, later of Rhydwhiman, Montgomery. Diam. (outside) .85″. Loan : J. D. K. Lloyd, O.B.E., M.A., F.S.A. 36.2/1. Duplicate 36.2/2.

536. Mourning Ring : gold, plain hoop, with inscription on the outer side reserved in letters in the metal upon ground of black enamel. ' IAS HOTCHKIS OB : 4 DECR 1786 AET : 68.' From Cardiff. Diam. (outside) .8″. Donor : J. A. Daniell, A.M.A., 39.411/3.

537. Mourning Ring : gold, plain hoop, with inscription on the outer side reserved in letters in the metal upon ground of black enamel. ' H. BRIGHT. OB : 21. OCT : 1789. AE : 50.' Originally from the family of Davies of Montgomery town, later of Rhydwhiman, Montgomery. Diam. (outside). .75″. Loan : J. D. K. Lloyd, O.B.E., M.A., F.S.A. 36.2/3.

538. Mourning Ring : gold, hoop expanding at the shoulders ; bezel contains entwined human hair covered by glass and bordered by brilliants. The hair is that of Benjamin Franklin (1706-90), the American statesman, and of Dr. Richard Price (1723-91), the Welsh political philosopher.

Inscription engraved on inside : ' Benjamin / Franklin, / died 17 April,
1790. / Aged 84.' On the outside is engraved : ' Richd Price D.D. died
19 April 1791 Aged 68.' In original box. Inherited by the depositor, a
descendant of Dr. Price's sister. Diam. (outside) .75". Deposit : E.
Crawshay Williams. 51.91.

539. Mourning ring : slender hoop expanding at shoulders ; marquise bezel
with plaited strands of hair and monogram ' D ' covered by glass. Inscription engraved on inner side : ' *Mary / Davis, / Ob. 9 Dec. / 1790. /
aet. 64.*' Originally from the family of Davies of Montgomery town, later
of Rhydwhiman, Montgomery, Diam. (outside) .75". Loan : J. D. K.
Lloyd, O.B.E., M.A., F.S.A. 36.2/4.

540. Mourning Ring : hoop expanding at shoulders ; circular bezel with strands
of hair and monogram ' D ' covered by glass and bordered by pearls.
Inscription engraved on inner side : ' *William Davies / died / 6 May 1800 /
Aged 79.*' Originally from the family of Davies of Montgomery town,
later of Rhydwhiman, Montgomery. Diam. (outside) .75". Loan : J. D.
K. Lloyd, O.B.E., M.A., F.S.A. 36.2/5.

541. Mourning Ring : gold, hoop formed of three wires united at the back, but
diverging at the shoulders. Oval bezel with plaited strands of human
hair covered by glass and bordered by pearls. Monogram ' MO ' engraved on inner side. Of late eighteenth- or early nineteenth-century
date. Originally from the family of Davies of Montgomery town, later
of Rhydwhiman, Montgomery. Diam. (outside) .85". Loan : J. D. K.
Lloyd, O.B.E., M.A, F.S.A. 36.2/6.

542. Mourning Ring : gold, with raised border ; the inscription ' IN MEMORY
OF ' on the outer side is reserved in letters in the metal upon ground of
black enamel. On the inside is engraved ' John Jones Esq., died 21 June
1817 Aged 68.' Commemorating John Jones, Derry Ormond, Betws
Bledrws, Cardiganshire. In original box. Belonged to the Reverend
Ebenezer Richards (1781—1837), Tregaron, his distant relative. Diam.
(outside) .85". Donor : Rev. H. R. Evans, M.A., M.C. 55.401.

543. Mourning Ring : gold, the hoop is formed of four wires united at the back,
but diverging at the shoulders, the two inner wires being twisted to give
a circular design. The bezel is set with pearls and contains some strands
of hair mounted under glass with a gold frame. Early 19th century.
From Nantceirio, Llanbadarn-fawr, Cardiganshire. Diam. (outside)
.8". Donors : The Misses G. F. & H. B. Morgan. 51.453/20.

544. Mourning Ring : gold, the hoop is channelled at the back expanding
towards the shoulder in the form of three loops. Rectangular swivel bezel
on one side of which are strands of hair enclosed within chalcedonic
agate ; on the other side the inscription ' NOT / LOST / BUT / GONE /
BEFORE ' is reserved in letters in the metal upon ground of black
enamel, within a narrow border of white enamel. c. 1860-70. From
Nantceirio, Llanbadarn-fawr, Cardiganshire. Diam. .75". Donors : The
Misses G. F. & H. B. Morgan. 51.453/19.

545. Mourning Ring : gold, slender hoop expanding at shoulders where there
is some decoration reserved in the metal upon ground of black enamel.
Bezel is set with one pearl and six diamonds and decorated with black
enamel. Hall-marked Birmingham 1871. From the family of the Rev.
R. J. Jones, M.A., Hen Dŷ Cwrdd, Aberdare, Glamorgan. Diam.
(outside) .75". Donor : Miss E. J. O. Jones,. 54.198/4.

546. Mourning Ring : gold, hoop with inscription on the outer side reserved in letters in the metal upon ground of black enamel. ' IN MEMORY OF '. The hoop expands towards the shoulders where there is a hinged bezel with geometrical decorations reserved in gold on ground of black enamel. Bezel opens to reveal glass which probably enclosed strands of hair : it is now empty. Hall-marked Birmingham 1875. From Aberdare, Glamorgan. Diam. .7″ (outside). Donor : Miss E. J. O. Jones. 54.198/5.

VARIOUS

547. Bottle, once containing toothache specific, and pins from St. Baruch's Well, Barry Island, Glamorgan. Excavated by J. Storrie in 1895. L. 2¼″. Donor : Barry Urban District Council. 37.88/1-4.

548. Rag-offerings : consisting of pieces of rag tied to twigs and commonly suspended from trees overhanging holy wells. They were used to bathe a diseased part of the body with water from the well before being tied to the twigs. From Llancarfan, Glamorgan. Donor : T. H. Thomas, R.C.A. Pro. 93.

549. Rag offering : similar to No. 548. From a well near Cardiff. Donor : T. H. Thomas, R.C.A. Pro. 94.

550. Rag Offerings : tied, in this case, to a hawthorn branch. Similar to No. 548. From a wishing well at Tremains, near Bridgend, Glamorgan, 1904. Donor : T. H. Thomas, R.C.A. 10.3.

551. Elder-tree cross : consisting of small elder branch with the twigs cut to give a cruciform effect. Crosses of this type were thought to be potent against witches and other malevolent influences. Formerly in use in a Monmouthshire farm-house. L. 4½″. Donor : T. H. Thomas, R.C.A. 98.325.

552. Elder-tree cross : similar to No. 551 but somewhat thicker and larger. Cut, by the farmer who used No. 551, at the request of the donor. L. 7″. Donor : T. H. Thomas, R.C.A. 98.324.

553. Charm : to cure erysipelas and ' for a thorn '. ' Flee tantine (? St. Anthony) flee / here I follow the we three maidens / and we three shall this tantine we will / quell sheep shear a Maiden hat (?) god and / Saint telpins Bought send this man whole / hand and foot in the name Father son Holy / gost Amen. // for a thorn / Dain Drush a drain / drain Esquel drain erine / drain persee bod short a drain / awer Saviour was nailed to the cross and / nails and spikes drove through he / never mattered nor Putrified / in the Name of the Father son and / Holy Goste Amen.' From Saundersfoot, Pembrokeshire. Donor : D. H. Pennant, M.D., D.S.O. 34.199. [Plate 16].

554. Amulets or charms : consisting of pins and buttons recovered from the Wishing Well near Mamhilad, Monmouthshire. Donor : T. H. Thomas, R.C.A. Pro. 95.

555. Charm : a written charm against witchcraft. ' In the name of the father and of the son and of the Holy gost amen xxx and in the name of the Lord Jesus Christ his redeemer and saviour he will Relieve Thomas Ellis Pen y garnedd the cows calves milk butter catll of all ages and his wife and all of the children to relieve from all witchcraft and all evil diseases amen xxx gospel . . . (illegible) . . . amen xxx . . . Jesus Christ . . . Ellis

pen y garnedd his cows calves milk butter catll of all ages and all of his children and his wife and to relieve them from all witchcraft and all evil wizards . . . amen xxx and this I trust in Jesus Christ thy . . . and saviour he will Relieve . . . Thomas Ellis pen y garnedd his cows calves milk butter cattl of all ages and to Relieve his wife and children from all witchcraft by the same charms as he did . . . Jehovah amen xxx . . . pater pater pater noster noster noster one one one . . .' At the foot of the charm the triangular abracadabra appears, together with crosses, hieroglyphics, a wheel-figure and signs of the Zodiac. Given by a sorcerer to Thomas Ellis, Pen-y-garnedd, near Llanfyllin, Montgomeryshire, c. 1916. Donor : Rev. O. T. Davies. 17.7.

556. Charm : a holed flint stone of a type formerly hung outside houses and barns to bring good luck. Formerly used at Tythegstone, Glamorgan in 1890. Donor : T. H. Thomas, R.C.A. o8.79.

557. Charm : ' lucky ash ' consisting of mountain-ash leaves with two terminal leaflets instead of one. Believed to bring good luck to the finder. Donor : T. H. Thomas, R.C.A. 10.4.

558. ' Adder's stone ' or ' glain y nadroedd ' : a Romano-British ribbed bead of earthenware, covered with blue cuprous glaze ; found at Twyn-y-tila, Caerleon, Monmouthshire in 1875. These beads were used in Wales as a cure for cataract. diam. 1″. Donor : T. H. Thomas, R.C.A. 16.68/66.

559. ' Adder's stone ' : similar to No. 558 but with a diameter of ¾″. From Llangynwyd, Glamorgan. oo.111.

560. Hydrophobia stone : known locally as *carreg cynddaredd* (hydrophobia stone) or *llaethfaen* (milk stone) ; a small nodule of pink alabaster, such as occurs in the Triassic Marls of Penarth (Glamorgan) and elsewhere. From Henllan, Cardiganshire. Donor : J. Evans. 29.102.

561. Hydrophobia stones etc. : two pieces of white alabaster, balance, weight, and powdered alabaster. Formerly owned by Mr. William Jones, Blaen-wyre, Lledrod, Cardiganshire and last used in the 1860's. The alabaster is of the type that occurs in Derbyshire or Nottingham. Donor : J. R. Morgan. 44.242/1-5.

562. Horn-core : portion of *Bos primogenius* known as ' Mabcorn yr Ych Bannog '. Preserved for centuries in the church of Llanddewi Brefi, Cardiganshire ; from 1823 onwards in the keeping of the family of Hughes of Glan Rheidol, and later in possession of donor : Donor : G. W. R. Marriott Parry. 53.289/1.

563. Water-diviner's rod : consisting of forked hazel twig. L. 22″. Made and used by donor : from St. Fagans, Glamorgan. Donor : T. W. Proger. 32.455.

564. Water-diviner's rod : of wire .1″ thick and looped at one end. L. 16½″. From Brecon. Donor : P. J. Mountney. 29.462.

[*Non-Welsh*]

565. Water-diviner's rods : four rods from Sussex. 19.46/1-4.

566. Pewter Plate : used in the 19th century to hold salt, and placed on the breast of a person after death. From Worcestershire ; a similar custom was known in several parts of Wales. Diam. 9.8″. Donor : Mrs. Fanny Ward. 19.189.

567. Rag-offerings : pieces of rag tied to bramble branch ; from a well near Fasaroe, Co. Dublin, Ireland, 1903. Donor : A. C. Haddon. 10.2.

SELECTED BIBLIOGRAPHY

Arensberg, C. : *The Irish Countryman.* 1937.
Ashton, Charles : ' Bywyd Gwledig yng Nghymru ' in *Transactions of the National Eisteddfod of Wales, Bangor, 1890.* pp. 36-92.
Banks, M. M. : *British Calendar Customs : Scotland,* 3 vols, 1937-4'.
Bateman, D. : ' The Churches of the Holy Cross, Mount and St. Pedrog, Verwig ' in *Ceredigion,* II, 1955. pp. 206-13.
Beale, Anne : *The Vale of Towey or Sketches in South Wales.* 1849.
Beirdd y Berwyn. 1902.
Bingley, W. : *A Tour round North Wales during the summer of 1798.* 1800.
Bourne, H. : *Antiquitates Vulgares.* 1725.
Brand, John : *Observations on Popular Antiquities.* 1841.
Buday, George : *The History of the Christmas Card.* 1954.
Burne, C. S. : *Shropshire Folk-Lore.* 1883.
Bye-gones relating to Wales and the Border Counties. 1871—.
Chitty, L. F. : 'A Harvest Figure from Yockleton, Shropshire', in *Shropshire Archaeological Transactions,* XLVIII, 1935. pp. 61-3.
Curtis, Mary : *The Antiquities of Laugharne, Pendine, and their Neighbourhoods.* 1880.
Davies, D. R. and Z. S. Cledlyn : *Hanes Plwyf Llanwenog.* 1939.
Davies, J. Ceredig : *Folk-Lore of West and Mid-Wales.* 1911.
Davies, J. D. : *A History of West Gower.* 4 vols. 1877-94.
Davies, J. H. : *The Letters of Lewis, Richard, William and John Morris, ' Morrisiaid Môn.'* 1728—1765, 2 vols. 1907 and 1909.
Davies, William : ' Llên gwerin Meirion ' in *Transactions of the National Eisteddfod of Wales, Blaenau Ffestiniog, 1898,* pp. 84-269.
Davies, W. J. : *Hanes Plwyf Llandyssul.* 1896.
Dodd, A. H. : *Studies in Stuart Wales.* 1952.
Eskeröd, Albert : *Årets Åring, etnologiska studier i skördens och julens tro och sed.* 1947.
Evans, D. Silvan : *Ystên Sioned,* 1882.
Evans, G. : ' Carmarthenshire Gleanings (Kidwelly) ' in *Y Cymmrodor,* XXV, 1915, pp. 92-160.
Evans, G. Nesta : *Religion and Politics in Mid-Eighteenth Century Anglesey.* 1953.
Fisher, John : ' The Welsh Calendar ' in *Transactions of the Honourable Society of Cymmrodorion,* 1894-5. pp. 99-145.
Fisher, John : ' Two Welsh-Manx Christmas Customs ', in *Archaeologia Cambrensis,* LXXXIV, 1929, pp. 308-16.
Frazer, James : *The Golden Bough.* 1929 (abridged edition).
Frimannslund, Rigmor : ' Skikk og tro ved friing og Bryllyp '. in Wikman, K. Rob. V. : *Livets Högtider.* 1949.
Funk and Wagnall : *Standard Dictionary of Folk Lore.* 1949.
Gruffydd, W. J. : *Owen Morgan Edwards.* 1937.
Hamer, E. : ' Parochial Account of Llangurig,' in *Montgomeryshire Collections,* III, 1870. pp. 262-272.
Hodgen, M. : *The Doctrine of Survivals.* 1936.
Homans, G. C. : *The Human Group.* 1951.
Hone, W. : *The Every-Day Book.* Vol. I. 1825.
Hone, W. : *Year Book.* 1832.
Howells, W. : *Cambrian Superstitions.* 1831.
Howse, W. H. : *Radnorshire.* 1949.
Hughes, H. : *Barddoniaeth Edward Morris, Perthi-llwydion.* 1902.
Hughes, H. : *Yr Hynafion Cymreig.* 1823.
Huizinga, J. : *Homo Ludens : A Study of the Play Element in Culture.* 1949.
Isaac, Evan : *Coelion Cymru.* 1938.
Jenkins, D. : 'Carolau Haf a Nadolig' in *Llên Cymru* II, 1952-3, pp. 46-54.
Jenkins, Emlyn G. : *Cofiant Elfed.* 1957.

Jenkins, R. T. : *Bardd a'i Gefndir*. 1948.
Jones, David : ' The Mari Lwyd : a Twelfth Night Custom ' in *Archaeologia Cambrensis*, 1888, pp. 389-94.
Jones, D. Parry : *Welsh Country Upbringing*. 1948.
Jones, Edward : *The Musical and Poetic Relicks of the Welsh Bards*. 1784.
Jones, Edward : *The Bardic Museum*. 1802.
Jones, Francis : *The Holy Wells of Wales*. 1954.
Jones, F. P. : ' Danfon Offrwm ' in *Gwerin*, I, 1956. pp. 91-2.
Jones, John : *Llên Gwerin Sir Gaernarfon*. [1909.]
Jones, L. D. : ' Hunting the Wren ' in *Journal of the Welsh Folk Song Society*, I, 1909—1912. pp. 99-113.
Jones, Owen : *Cymru : yn hanesyddol, parthedegol, a bywgraphyddol*. 2 vols. 1875.
Jones, O. Gethin : *Gweithiau Barddonol a Llenyddol*. 1884.
Jones, Robert : *Drych yr Amseroedd*. 1898 edition.
Jones, T. G. : ' A History of the Parish of Llansantffraid-yn-Mechain ' in *Montgomeryshire Collections*, IV, 1871, pp. 75-141.
Jones, T. Gwynn : *Welsh Folklore and Folk Custom*. 1930.
Kroeber, A. : *Anthropology*. 1948.
[Lane], Amy : *Sketches of Wales and the Welsh*. 1847.
Laws, Edward : *The History of Little England beyond Wales*. 1888.
Lee, Ruth Webb : *A History of Valentines*. 1953.
Lewis, D. Craionog : *Hanes Plwyf Defynog*. 1911.
Lewis, H. (edit.) : *Llanwynno Glanffrwd*. 1949.
Lewis, Henry, Roberts, Thomas, and Williams, Ifor : *Iolo Goch ac Eraill*. 1937.
Marrett, R. R. : ' Folklore and Psychology ', in *Folk-Lore*, XXV, 1914. pp. 12-33.
Mellor, H. : *Welsh Folk Dances : An Inquiry*. 1935.
Meyrick, S. R. : *History and Antiquities of Cardiganshire*. 1810.
Mostyn, Lord, and Glenn, T.A. : *History of the Family of Mostyn of Mostyn*. 1925.
Owen, Elias : ' On some customs still remaining in Wales ' in *Y Cymmrodor*, II, 1878. pp. 133-137.
Owen, Hugh : *The Life and Works of Lewis Morris (1701—1765)*. 1951.
Owen, Trefor M. : ' Chapel and Community in Glan-llyn ' in Hughes, T. J., Jenkins, D., Jones, E., Owen, T.M. : *Welsh Rural Communities*. 1959.
Parry, Thomas : *Baledi'r Ddeunawfed Ganrif*. 1935.
Parry, Thomas : *Gwaith Dafydd ap Gwilym*. 1952.
Parry-Williams, T. H. : *Llawysgrif Richard Morris o Gerddi*. 1931.
Peate, Iorwerth C. : ' Corn-customs in Wales ' in *Man* 30, 1930, pp. 151-5.
Peate, Iorwerth C. : ' The Wren in Welsh Folklore ', in *Man* 36, 1936. pp. 1-3.
Peate, Iorwerth C. : ' Mari Lwyd : A suggested explanation ' in *Man* 43, 1943. pp. 53-8.
Peate, Iorwerth C. : ' A People's Court ' in *Folk-Lore*, LVI. 1945, pp. 273-4.
Pembrokeshire Antiquities, 1897.
Pennant, Thomas : *Tours in Wales*. 3 vols. 1810.
Phillips, D. R. : *History of the Vale of Neath*. 1925.
Plomer, William (editor) : *Kilvert's Diary*. I. 1938.
Powell, E. : *History of Tredegar*. 1902.
Pratt, S. J. : *Gleanings through Wales, Holland and Westphalia*. I. 1797.
Price, F. S. : *History of Llansawel*. 1898.
Puckle, Bertram S. : *Funeral Customs, their origin and development*. 1926.
Redfield, R. : *The Primitive World and Its Transformations*. 1953.
Redwood, Charles : *The Vale of Glamorgan : Scenes and Tales among the Welsh*. 1839.
Rees, Alwyn D. : *Life in a Welsh Countryside, A social study of Llanfihangel-yng-Ngwynfa*. 1950.
Rhys, M. : ' Unpublished Traditions of Glamorganshire.' in *The Cambrian Journal*, II, 1855. pp. 68-72, 115-124.
Richards, Gwynfryn : ' Y Plygain ' in *Journal of the Historical Society of the Church in Wales*, I, 1947, pp. 53-72.
Roberts, Gomer : *Atgofion Amaethwr*. n.d.

Roberts, Gomer M. : *Hanes Plwyf Llandybie*. 1939.

Roberts, Peter : *The Cambrian Popular Antiquities*. 1815.

Roberts, W. : *Crefydd yr Oesoedd Tywyll neu Hynafiaethau Defodol, Chwareuol a choelgrefydd* . . . 1852.

Royal Commission on Land in Wales, Report. 1896.

Royal Commission on Labour : The Agricultural Labourer, Vol. II., *Wales*, 1893.

Sayce, R. U. : ' The Old Summer Pastures, I ' in *Montgomeryshire Collections*, LIV, 1956, pp. 117-145.

Scott, G. R. : *The History of Cock-fighting*. n.d. [1957].

Sikes, Wirt: *British Goblins : Welsh Folk-lore, Fairy Mythology, Legends and Tradtions*. 1880.

Spalding, K. : ' A German Account of Life in Wales in 1856 ' in *Gwerin* II, 1958, pp. 38-43.

Tales and Traditions of Tenby. 1858.

Trevelyan, Marie : *Folk-Lore and Folk Customs of Wales*. 1909.

Vallee, F. G. : ' Burial and Mourning Customs in a Hebridean Community ' in *The Journal of the Royal Anthropological Institute*, LXXXV, pp. 119-30.

Van Gennep, A. : *Les Rites de Passages*. 1909.

Whistler, Laurence : *The English Festivals*. 1947.

Williams, David : *The Rebecca Riots, A Study in Agrarian Discontent*. 1955.

Williams, D. G. : ' Casgliad o Lên Gwerin Sir Gaerfyrddin ' in *Transactions of National Eisteddfod of Wales, Llanelly, 1895*. pp. 277-397. 1898.

Williams, E. A. : *Hanes Mon yn y bedwaredd ganrif ar bymtheg*. 1927.

Williams, G. J. : ' Wiliam Robert o'r Ydwal ' in *Llên Cymru* III, 1954-5. pp. 47-52.

Williams, G. J. : *Iolo Morganwg*. 1956.

Williams, G. J. : ' Dyddiadur William Thomas o Llanfihangel-ar-Elai ' in *Morgannwg*, I, 1957, pp. 13-30.

Williams, G. J. : ' Glamorgan Customs in the 18th century ' in *Gwerin*, I, 1957, pp. 99-108.

Williams, Ifor, and Roberts, Thomas : *Dafydd ap Gwilym a'i Gyfoeswyr*. 1935.

Williams, Iolo A. : *English Folk-Song and Dance*. 1935.

Williams, Maria J. : *Ancient National Airs of Gwent and Morganwg*. 1844.

Williams, Richard : ' History of the Parish of Llanbrynmair ' in *Montgomeryshire Collections* XXI—II, 1887 & 1888.

Williams, Robert : *History and Antiquities of the Town of Aberconwy*. 1835.

Williams, W. : *Hynafiaethau a Thraddodiadau Plwyf Llanberis a'r Amgylchoedd*. n.d. [1892].

Williams, William : *Observations on the Snowdon Mountains*. 1802.

Williams, W. Maddock : ' A slight Historical and Topographical Sketch of the Parish of Llanfechain.' *Montgomeryshire Collections*. V, 203-84. 1872.

Williams, W. S. Gwynn : *Welsh National Music and Dance*. n.d. [1933].

Wright, A. R., and Lones, T. E., : *British Calendar Customs, England*. 3 vols. 1936-40.

PLATE I

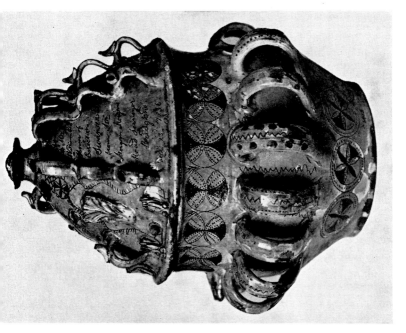

Wassail bowls, Ewenny pottery (left, No. 40 ; right, No. 41)

PLATE 2

Mari Lwyd from Pen-tyrch, Glam. (No. 36)

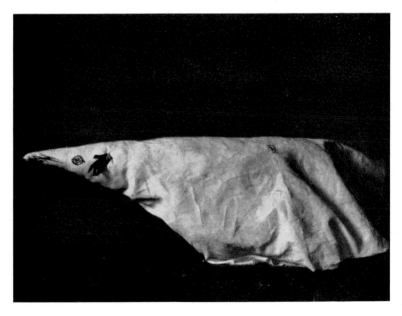

Model of Pembrokeshire *Mari Lwyd* (No. 37)

PLATE 3

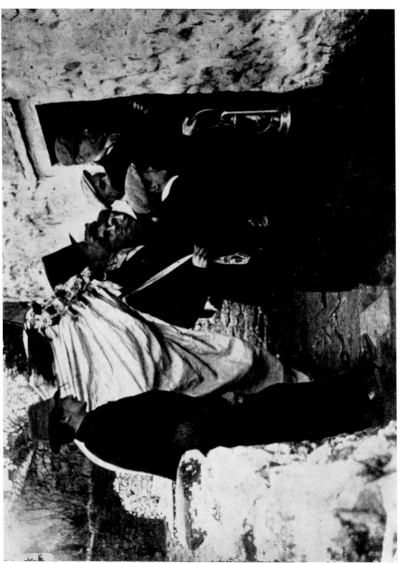

Mari Lwyd procession at Llangynwyd, Glam., about 1908

PLATE 4

Christmas Card (No. 14)

Christmas Greeting Notepaper (No. 3)

PLATE 5

Wren-house, from Marloes, Pembrokeshire (No. 47)

PLATE 6

Calennig (cf. Nos. 25 & 26)

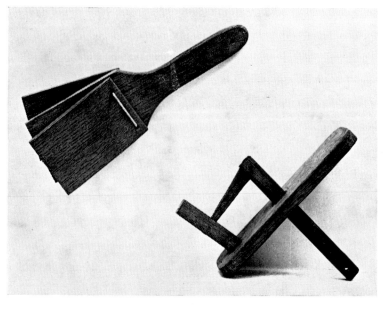

Egg-clappers (Nos. 49 & 50)

PLATE 7

Corn maidens, from Llangynllo, Radnorshire
(l. to r. Nos. 55, 57, 56)

PLATE 8

Corn maidens (l. to r. : No. 58, Ciliau Aeron, Cards., No. 61, Llan-non, Cards., No. 62, Yockleton, Salop.)

PLATE 9

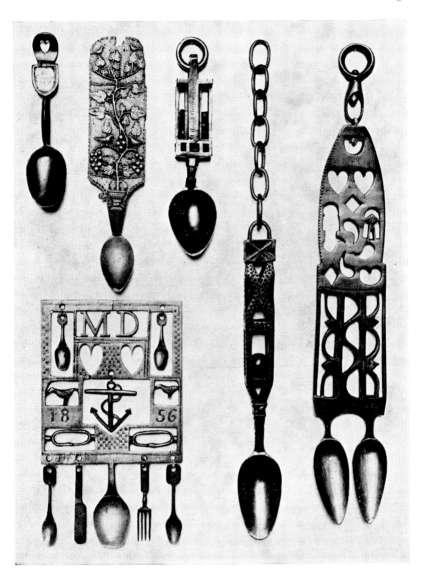

Love-Spoons
(l. to r. Nos. 80, 142, 101, 100, 218, bottom left No. 193)

PLATE 10

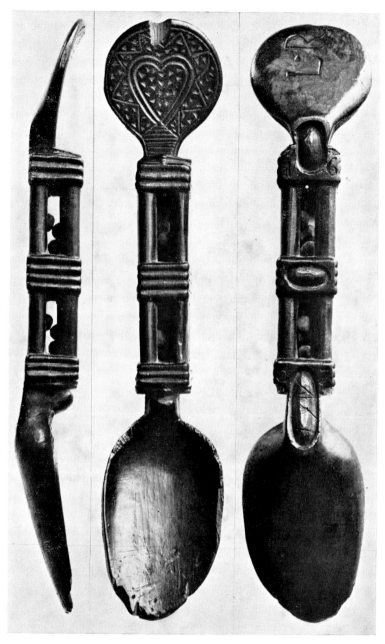

Detail of Love-Spoon dated 1667 (No. 99)

PLATE 11

Hand-made Valentine from Narberth, Pembrokeshire (No. 251)

PLATE 12

Hand-made Valentine from Llanbryn-Mair, Montgomeryshire (No. 252)

PLATE 13

Lithographed and hand-coloured Valentine (No. 253)   Comic Valentine (No. 380)

PLATE 14

August 25, 1798.

Having lately entered the Matrimonial State, we are encouraged by our Friends to make a Bidding on the Occasion, on Thursday the 13th Day of September next, at the Dwelling-House of Daniel Thomas, (the young Woman's Father) called Ifcoed-Mill, *in the Parish of St. Ishmael, at which Place we humbly folicit the Favor of your good Company; and whatever Donation you may then be difpofed to beftow on us, will be gratefully received, and cheerfully repaid, whenever demanded on the like Occafion, by*

Your moft obliged humble Servants,

Ebenezer Jones,
Mary Jones.

☞ The young Man's Grandmother, and young Woman's Father and Mother, defire that all Gifts of the above Nature. due to them. may be returned to the young Couple on the faid Day. and will be thankful for all Favors conferred on them.—The young Man's Uncle (*David Thomas* of *Ifcoed Ucha'*) and young Woman's Sifters, will alfo be thankful for any Favors conferred on the young Couple.

Bidding Letter from St. Ishmael, Carmarthenshire (No. 480)

PLATE 15

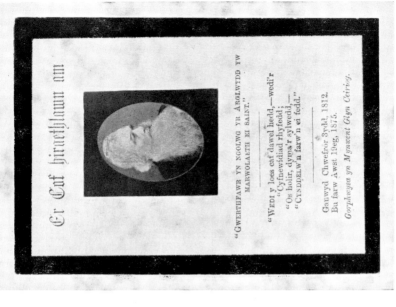

Memorial Cards (left, No. 500 ; right, No. 509)

PLATE 16

Flee tantine flee
here I follow the we three Maidens
and we three shall this tantine we will
quell sheep shear a maiden trot god and
Saint telpins Baught send this man intals
hand and foot in the name Father son Holy
goost Amen

for a thorn
dain Brush a drain
drain Esquel drain erine
drain kersee bod shoot a drain
auer Saviour was hailed to the cross and
nails and spikes drove through he
never mattered nor Putrified
in the name of the Father son and
holy Goste Amen

Charm from Saundersfoot, Pembrokeshire (No. 553)